THE GREATNESS AND DECLINE
OF THE CELTS

THE GREATNESS AND DECLINE OF THE CELTS

HENRI HUBERT

Constable · London

Published in Great Britain 1987
by Constable and Company Limited
10 Orange Street London WC2H 7EG
First published in Great Britain 1934
by Kegan Paul, Trench, Trubner and Co. Limited
Printed in Great Britain by
St Edmundsbury Press Limited
Bury St Edmunds, Suffolk

British Library Cataloguing in Publication Data
Hubert, Henri
The greatness and decline of the Celts.
1. Civilization, Celtic
I. Title   II. Mauss, Marcel   III. Lantier,
Raymond   IV. Marx, Jean   V. Les Celtes
depuis l'époque de la Tène. *English*
936.4′Q04916   CB206

ISBN 0-09-467800-6

Edited and brought up to date in 1934 by
Marcel Mauss, Raymond Lantier and Jean Marx

Translated from the French by
M. R. Dobie

New Introduction for this edition by
Professor Gearoid Mac Eoin, University of Ireland

CONTENTS

v

CONTENTS
PART TWO
THE END OF THE CELTIC WORLD

PART THREE
THE CIVILIZATION OF THE CELTS

MAPS

INTRODUCTION

The early years of the twentieth century, when Henri Hubert planned this book, must have seemed to him an opportune time to undertake a synoptic history of the Celtic peoples. During the previous 150 years the Celts had come to be known to the literate public in a way that was completely new. This was due, in the first instance, to the popularity of the writings of James MacPherson which, whatever one may say about their legitimacy or merit as literature, succeeded in drawing Europe's attention to the existence of a people and a tradition which was neither Germanic nor Latin but which represented an early phase in the growth of European civilization. Ernest Renan's *Essai sur la poésie des races celtiques* (1854) and Matthew Arnold's lectures *On the Study of Celtic Literature* (1867) served in some measure to correct the exaggerated impression of wild romanticism given by MacPherson's poems and pointed to the existence of a literature in the Celtic languages which bore little resemblance to MacPherson's compositions. The work of German and French philologists in elucidating the descent and history of the Celtic languages within the Indo-European family gave a scientific basis and an international linguistic dimension to the work being done on medieval texts, contemporary languages and folk traditions in Britain and Ireland by native writers who traced their scholastic ancestry to seventeenth-century scholars like Archbishop Ussher, Sir James Ware, and Edward Lhuyd, and even beyond them to the last remnants of the schools of native learning which survived the collapse of the indigenous social institutions in the Celtic regions of Britain and Ireland in the sixteenth and seventeenth centuries. Celtic literature began for the first time to appear in reliable translations in English, French, and German. Publications like Lady Guest's *Mabinogion*, de la Villemarqué's *Barzaz Breiz*, and Windisch's *Táin Bó Cuailnge* made original documents available to modern Europeans, and allowed a glimpse

viii

of the true form of that literature which proved in many respects more exciting than the romancings of James MacPherson. In the second half of the nineteenth century archaeologists laid bare in the soil of Europe the material evidence for the early Celtic culture which Greek and Roman authors had tantalizingly alluded to and even partly described, and which medieval Celtic literature described in an imaginative and fictional form. The intellectual climate of France in the Second Empire was particularly receptive to a sympathetic view of the Gauls whose martial qualities the French always liked to imagine as foreshadowing their own. So we find Hubert repeatedly claiming that the French are the heirs and descendants of the Celtic Gauls and that 'the civilization of the Celts lies at the bottom of French civilization' (I. 14).

By background and experience Hubert was perhaps not the most likely likely author of a history of the Celts. His education at the École Normale led to an *agrégé* in History in 1895, and his subsequent interest was in the history of religions, particularly those of the Near East. But he found employment in the Musée de Saint Germain in Paris, where he came under the influence of the great archaeologist and art-historian, Salomon Reinach, and at the École des Hautes Études, where he became acquainted with Joseph Vendryes, the greatest of French Celtic linguists, so that Hubert's interests turned to Celtic archaeology and history. However he had not yet published anything on Celtic matters when Henri Berr invited him to write the Celtic volume for his series 'L'Évolution de l'Humanité'. That was some time before the First World War, and Hubert accepted. In 1927 Hubert died at the age of fifty-five without having quite finished his task. The work was brought to a conclusion and seen through the press by a group of friends who included an archaeologist (Lantier), a linguist (Vendryes), and a social historian (Marx).

In the sixty years since the death of Hubert our knowledge of the Celts, their language, and their civilization has increased considerably and become more discriminating. The picture of wandering hordes of richly caparisoned warriors which Hubert gives us, while it has not been altogether abandoned, is now seen to be only part of the reality of Celtic civilization in the 500 or so years in which it flourished on the continent of Europe. Today one would probably say that the Celts were first and foremost farmers tilling their fields and raising their stock on the good lands of Germany and France. Their wealth derived in the first instance from food-production, and the proclivity of its owners to flaunt it by acquiring prestige goods led to the manufacture of high-quality, artistically decorated weapons, horse-trappings, household goods, and particularly ornaments for personal wear. The second source of their wealth was in mining the natural resources of the land, gold, silver, tin, lead, iron, and, by no means the least important, salt. These products provided the purchasing-power which enabled the Celts to buy the luxury goods, above all wine, which the Mediterranean climate of Greece and Italy produced more easily than the cooler air of the North European plains. The valleys of the great rivers running on a north-south axis, the Rhône/Saône, the Loire, the Seine, and the Rhine/Mosel, provided the routes along which trade developed in the sixth century BC between the Mediterranean coasts and Europe north and west of the Alps. Round the eastern flanks of the Alps another trade-route linked the valley of the Danube to the plain of the Po. This trade had the effect of making the rich Celts richer and the less rich avaricious. Thereby began the first expansion of Celts outside their own traditional territories in the first years of the fourth century. Hubert's (II. 10, n. 8) idea of connecting the 300,000-strong mob which then descended into Italy with the inheritance-customs of the Celts as exemplified in Early Irish Law seems to be a particularly valid insight. Similar mobs of fighting men, camp-followers, and cattle are known from Ireland in the later Middle Ages (in contemporary English called *creaght* from Irish *caoraigheacht*) and it has been suggested that the nucleus of these bands was formed by landless men who were forced to move about, driving their cattle before them, in search of unoccupied or unguarded land where they could let their stock out to pasture. They were men of low legal status and tended to become outlaws and the scourge of the countryside. Similar economic and social pressures may have been the reason why so many Celtic warriors left their homes at the turn of the fourth century BC and set in motion one of the great migrations of European history.

In the swirl of peoples which resulted from this movement we try to identify the Celts in the dim twilight between historical linguistics and archaeology. The definition of 'Celt' varies with the background and terms of reference of the definer. The Celts never called themselves 'Celts' in any source known to us before modern times. The name is first found in Greek sources and may be a variant of the name given to the Anatolian branch of the family, Galatae, which must itself be a variant of Galli, the name by which the Romans knew the Celts who occupied Gaul and Northern Italy. Medieval British and Irish sources, though they sometimes recognized the relationship between their languages, never expressed that relationship in ethnic terms and were probably unaware that their languages were any closer to one another than they were to Latin or Scandinavian. The concept of a Celtic race originated among the Greeks and Romans who applied it only to the nations known to them on the continent of Europe. The extension of the definition to the natives of Britain and Ireland is due to modern historians, linguists and archaeologists, beginning with the Scottish historian, George Buchanan, in the sixteenth century. In our own time the linguists would define 'Celt' historically as a person who spoke a Celtic language, but the weakness of this definition for any period becomes clear when one considers that many of today's native Irish speakers are shown by their surnames to be of Scandinavian or English descent. Archaeologists, on the other hand, would define 'Celt' as a person belonging to a particular culture, namely that which they label 'Hallstatt' and 'La Tène', though they might differ among themselves as to where they would draw the line in a chronological or geographical sense. In the case of most Celts known to us in prehistory or protohistory, their language and material culture would qualify them under either definition. But the two definitions are not co-extensive. There were speakers of Celtic languages whose material culture was not in the Hallstatt-La Tène tradition – the Irish are perhaps the best example of this. There were people whose culture was of the Hallstatt-La Tène type but whose language was not Celtic, like the Belgae or the Suevi. We have no means of discovering the limits of the area in which Celtic was spoken before the emergence of these material cultures which define the Celtic world in early historic times. But it has to be accepted that the language existed somewhere in Central Europe between its formation as an Indo-European dialect and our earliest written testimony on North Italian inscriptions.

The emergence of the Celts is seen by Hubert in terms of an incursion from an area such as the Indo-European homeland or from some intermediate staging-point. Modern writers tend rather to see the Celts as an indigenous population who, under some impetus from outside, developed a particular culture in the area which they had inhabited for many generations. The impetus came mainly through trade with the Mediterranean countries but also through contacts with other barbarian peoples who were their neighbours in northern and central Europe, the Scythians, the Thracians, and the Germans. One is tempted to think that the Celtic language may have come into being in a similar process of merging and separation among the closely related languages or dialects spoken by a number of neighbouring peoples somewhere in Central Europe in the second or early first millennium BC. However, the good Indo-European ancestry of so much of Celtic grammar and vocabulary would seem to indicate a direct descent from the ancestral language.

In his account of the spread of the Celts throughout Europe, Hubert, in company with many older writers, exaggerates the importance of the dialect divisions perceptible among them, and turns dialect groups into nations and tribes. Thus he speaks of 'Brythons' and 'Goidels' traversing the Continent and settling in Britain and Ireland respectively. Contrast this with the axiom enunciated by the late David Greene at the Sixth International Congress of Celtic Studies in 1979, that 'the only useful meaning of the terms "Brythonic" and "Goidelic" is as labels for the forms of Celtic attested from the islands of Britain and Ireland respectively'. No scholar would today write of Brythons and Goidels on the Continent or see in the allophonic variants of their dialects the distinguishing marks of rival nations. Today these terms are applied only to the languages of Britain and Ireland and, by extension, to the speakers of these languages. The fact that some of the typical differences between the Celtic languages of the two islands are also found between some of the Celtic languages of the Continent does not entitle us to assign the names of the insular peoples to any on the Continent.

Since Hubert's day our knowledge of the continental Celtic languages has increased considerably, though not to the extent that it is possible to construct anything like a complete grammar for any of them. The fragmentary state of the languages means that research must proceed by piecing the fragments painstakingly together before attempting an interpretation of the result through comparison with other languages. The state of the art has been described authoritatively by D. Ellis Evans: *The Labyrinth of Continental Celtic* (Rhys Memorial Lecture, British Academy, 1977) and by Karl Horst Schmidt: 'The Celtic Languages of Continental Europe', *Bulletin of the Board of Celtic Studies*, xxviii, Pt. ii, May 1979. On the early history of the insular Celtic languages Kenneth Jackson's *Language and History in Early Britain* (Edinburgh 1956) is unsurpassed.

In archaeology progress has been no less impressive than in linguistics. In all the countries of continental Europe which were at one time inhabited by Celtic peoples, noteworthy excavations and finds have brought the material culture of the Celts to light and established immediate contact with the reality of Celtic civilization. The most spectacular excavations have been those of the 'princely' graves of Germany and France; the most informative possibly that of the Dürrnberg near Salzburg in Austria, where for the last twenty years the excavation has been going on of a prehistoric salt-mining settlement consisting of a village, a cemetery containing 2,000 graves, and a salt-mine which is still in use. To bridge the gap between Hubert and the present time the reader may find the following books in English useful: Jan Filip, *Celtic Civilization and its Heritage* (2nd ed., Prague 1977); Jean-Jacques Hatt, *Celts and Gallo-Romans* (London 1970); J. V. S. Megaw, *The Art of the European Iron Age* (Bath 1970); Anne Ross, *The Pagan Celts* (2nd ed., London 1986); and in French the magnificent volume of Paul-Marie Duval, *Les Celtes* (Paris 1977).

On the religion and mythology of the Celts the main works of this century have been: Jan de Vries, *Keltische Religion* (Stuttgart 1961, also in French translation); Thomas F. O'Rahilly, *Early Irish History and Mythology* (Dublin 1946); Marie-Louise Sjoestedt, *Gods and Heroes of the Celts* (London 1949); Proinsias Mac Cana, *Celtic Mythology* (London 1970); and Alwyn Rees and Brinley Rees, *Celtic Heritage* (London 1961).

Since no documentary evidence survives which relates immediately to the social insitutions of the Celts on the continent of Europe, our sources of information about them are references in the writings of Greek and Roman authors, deduction from archaeological evidence, and comparison with the relatively well documented social structures of early medieval Ireland and Wales. The greatest achievement in this field has been D. A. Binchy's *Corpus Juris Hibernici* (6 vols., Dublin 1979) which provides an authoritative text for the early Irish laws. It contains no translation and very little commentary. This work is being done for individual texts in periodical publications and in monographs. No general account of Celtic law and institutions yet exists but Eoin Mac Neill's *Early Irish Laws and Institutions* (Dublin 1935) and D. A. Binchy's 'Irish History and Irish Law' in *Studia Hibernica* 15 (1975) 7–36, 16 (1976) 7–45, go some way towards filling that gap. On Welsh law there have been many important publications during this century but it may be sufficient to mention Dafydd Jenkins's *Hywel Dda and the Law of Medieval Wales* (Cardiff 1985).

The time which has elapsed since the first publication of Hubert's book, in French in 1932 and in English in 1934, provides us with the distance from which to judge it. As a summary statement of what was known about Celtic history in the early years of this century it is excellent. Inevitably it champions some ideas and attitudes which have since fallen out of favour, such as the theory of Italo-Celtic unity (I. 57–62). The progress which has been made in Celtic scholarship during the past half-century requires that a new summary of current knowledge and thought should be compiled. But increased specialization has brought about the fragmentation of the discipline, so that it would be difficult today to find an author with the competence in archaeology, history, and linguistics, not to speak of the familiarity with Latin and Greek, which Hubert possessed. The future history of the Celts will probably be the cooperative effort of many scholars and will clearly be the work of many years. Until such a book appears Hubert's two volumes may stand us in good stead, as they have done in the past.

Gearóid Mac Eoin
Department of Old and Middle Irish and Celtic Philology,
University College,
Galway

FOREWORD

THE CELTIC GENIUS

I HAVE already explained and justified the division of Hubert's work on the Celts into two volumes.

With the present volume we find ourselves in the La Tène period. It begins by describing a new expansion, then a retreat, the florescence and decline of the Celtic world.

It is about 500 B.C. that the La Tène civilization appears with an increase of the population, which descends from the heights into the plains, an advance in technical processes, and a growth of prosperity which give rise to the great historical expeditions. The movements which now take place are different from those described in the previous volume, about which we have little direct information. From definite evidence it can be seen that operations now assume a " co-ordinated, concerted, and, one might say, political character " (p. 18), and that is a great novelty among the Celts. All round the circumference of the Celtic world this activity manifests itself—first in Italy, the Danube Valley, and Britain, and then in Eastern Europe and Asia Minor, the south-west of France, and even in Spain. They found settlements, or rather the previous inhabitants mingle with them, and they contribute and receive in varying proportions. But what the advanced bodies receive— for example, the idea of a political life in Italy, and intellectual and moral culture in Greece—will benefit the whole Celtic world, doubtless in different degrees. The Celts " enter the history of the world " (p. 32). " Unsettled and unruly elements," bands of barbarians, " great companies," will still break in ; the energy, courage, and " roving spirit " of the Celts will make some of them mercenaries in great demand, free-lances scattered among many peoples. " Mercenary service was a regular Celtic industry, and a well paid one " (pp. 64, 66, 90). But the mass of the race is settled, and the Celts are involved in the politics and economics of the whole world. Being both inventive and receptive, they are agents for the unification and progress of mankind. There are, it is true, Gallic Celts and British Celts, Celts of the Danube and

Germany and Italy ; but a Celtic civilization has grown up which is comparatively homogeneous and comparatively native in its character.

From the end of the third century onwards the Celts are in conflict with Rome on every side. Their civilization stands face to face with a different, and in some respects higher, civilization, while from behind they are pressed by a people of lower culture, the Germans, with whom, as we know, they have a real " intimacy " (p. 93). The more active the civilizing and political influence of the Celts is in Germany, the harder they will be pressed by their neighbours, to be finally driven back. There was a twofold process— " a process of assimilation of the German world on the one hand, but on the other, as a result of that very assimilation, a process of penetration by the Germans into the Celtic world " (p. 103). The Cimbri, Teutones, Suevi were Celticized Germans, mixed with Celts to a various extent.

Gradually the Celts are driven back on themselves. The Rhine becomes the frontier of the western Celts. In the course of their disturbed history main peoples and subordinate groups have parted, reunited, mixed, and passed one another. Now they are in what are almost their final positions. The Celtic world has assumed what Hubert strikingly describes as " the face under which it was last known to antiquity, and it was a face of death ". At this moment " its features appear in broad daylight and that thanks to its conqueror " (p. 119). The Romans, and Cæsar above all, help us greatly to picture them.

Hubert, in the part of his work describing the civilization of the Celts, begins by studying their social structure. As a sociologist, he compares one Celtic society with another, he compares them with other Indo-European societies and points out their common characteristics, and he looks in them for survivals of primitive organizations, earlier than the Indo-European societies, traces of clan life (pp. 190, 198, 201). For this task he gets valuable information from Irish and Welsh sources, his use of which he justifies. In short, he is concerned with the evolution of society as such, and, if he draws upon his general sociological knowledge for the study of the Celts, he makes repayment in bringing interesting data and confirmations to sociology.

In doing this Hubert followed his natural inclination ; he was applying and reinforcing the knowledge born of his wide interest. But he was also adhering to the programme of this series. One feature of this synthesis, l'Évolution de l'Humanité, is that it presents sociology and history in intimate association. Not only do we, in the case of each human group, pay due attention to the study of institutions, but we endeavour to determine the role of society as society, to make plain the relations of the social and the individual. Our readers know this ; and they also know that, on account either of the subject or of the bent of the author, some volumes more than others enable us to set the social in its place in history and to reflect on problems of a theoretical nature.

Hubert's work, in its contribution to the study of the Celtic societies and of society in general, raises some most interesting problems.

Although he speaks here and there of Celtic " nations " and seems in one passage to credit the Celts with a national conscious-ness,[1] he points out clearly in several places the distinction between society and nation. There was no more a Celtic nation than a Greek.[2] The Celts are no more a nation than they are a race [3] ; they are " a group of peoples, or, to speak more accurately, a group of societies " (Rise of the Celts, p. 33). As the greater Celtic world missed the opportunity to become a kind of great confederation, so the smaller Celtic world of Gaul " missed, in Vercingetorix, the opportunity of becoming, side by side with the Roman Republic, the prototype of the modern great nation " (pp. 147–8). Now—and this is the important point—that was because Gaul " had not at that time acquired the rudiments of a state structure without which a nation cannot be made " (ibid.).[4] A society may have every kind of aptitude for forming a nation but fail to be a nation if it is not strongly rooted in a soil and definitely organized as a state. And, however wide a society, or a collection of societies having the same civilization, may be, one cannot speak of empire (as I have said) [5] when no central power has asserted itself, when there is no unifying state.

---

[1] " But if a nation already existed, it was because that which makes the deep-seated unity of a nation existed—a common ideal, the same ways of thinking and feeling, in short, everything that nations express by symbols and all the most intimate part of their civilization " (Rise of the Celts, p. 13).

[2] See Jardé, Formation of the Greek People, in this series, pt. iv. Cf. Jullian, Histoire de la Gaule, i, ch. ix.

[3] See Rise of the Celts, Foreword, p. xiii.

[4] In a Celtic society, the state usually remains rudimentary and almost undifferentiated. . . . The Celtic societies are at the tribal stage, and have only a private law " (p. 196).

[5] Rise of the Celts, Foreword, p. xx.

Of Celtic civilization, on the other hand, we can speak, for the various branches of the Celts had a real sense of oneness, a family likeness, a common language, and we know that language is among the most typical phenomena of a culture (p. 187 ; Rise of the Celts, p. 33). *But among all these phenomena a distinction must be made, and this is important. And, although the study of civilization and that of society seem to coincide, all that constitutes a civilization* (*and goes on* in *a society*) *is not properly and essentially social.*

With the conception of sociology now in vogue (which is ethnographic) and the present conception of history (which is in a certain sense synthetic), the word " civilization " is used more and more in a broad and sometimes rather vague way. No doubt there is no reason why one should not, in describing racial groups and in order to define them, make use of political and economic institutions, arts, crafts, and religion, all together and as of equal relevance. There is no reason why one should not, under the word " civilization ", include the most diverse manifestations of human activity. From any point of view other than that of scientific causality, of synthesis of the second degree, there is no need for a closer discussion of the valuable information which Hubert presents in the third part of this volume, entitled " Civilization " under the headings " Structure of Society ", " Setting of Social Life ", and " Social Activities ". But for a fundamental explanation *it is possible and legitimate to consider matters in more detail.*

Hubert himself would not deny it ; and we found in his work, here and there, statements which enable us to press our explanation deeper. When, for instance, he says : " Every group of men living together forms a physical, social, and moral unit " (Rise, p. 21), *he makes an interesting distinction. And when he says elsewhere that the love of the Celts for* general ideas *helped to make the lofty, mellow civilizations of antiquity into the civilization of the world* (Rise, p. 15), *he quite clearly shows the part played by the* logical *factor, as distinct from the social.*

What strikes one in the Celts is just the fact that the part which they played in history was logical, and civilizing in the limited sense of that term, rather than social in the proper and strict sense of the word.[1] *If they do not seem to have excelled as citizens, if they failed politically, " through having no sense of the state or an insufficient sense of discipline," they take their revenge and are*

[1] *See* Rise of the Celts, *p.* 15.

important in history by the value of the individual and the develop-
ment of personality (pp. 9–10, 271, 276). The tribal system lasted a
long time among them ; gradually, through contact with the land, it
became aristocratic, feudal ; then, in town life, an urban class
grew up. As always happens where the social organization is not
heavy, oppressive, centralizing, and levelling, the conscience was
able to waken and the mind to exert activity.[1] *The Celts were at*
once inventors (p. 260) and ready assimilators.

"Eager for everything that was not Celtic" (p. 140),
"with their curiosity about civilization" (p. 10), they fell
surprisingly quickly into the ways of the more civilized peoples
with which they mingled or had dealings of any kind (p. 55).[2]
"The stranger from the Mediterranean always had a special
charm for them" (p. 140). So, with their physical mobility
and mental elasticity, they acted as middlemen of civilization ;
they were "torch-bearers" in Europe (p. 62 ; Rise, p. 15).

But, receptive though they were, they had their own native
character, a common ideal, a "soul of the people", one might
say, of course, without giving the words a metaphysical meaning.
Camille Jullian has said that Celtic unity was "in the domain
of poets rather than of statesmen"[3] *; it was, indeed, a work of*
the mind, the work of the poets—and of the Druids. Druidism
was the chief uniting factor, the "cement" of Celtic society
(p. 227). There was nothing of the priest-king in the Druids ;
their part was more specifically spiritual. They were men of
God, depositories of wisdom and science, directors of consciences,
and teachers of the young and of their whole people.[4] *Their*
doctrine turned towards nature, in agrarian festivals, but still
more towards man, in its concern for morals. With a high,
manly ideal of life, they at once despised death and aspired to
the immortality of the soul. "To worship the gods, to do nothing
base, and to practise manhood"—this Druidical axiom, which
Hubert takes from Diogenes Laërtios, is admirable.[5] *Certain*
elements of Druidism come from the Indo-European foundation
and are related to the teaching of the Brahmins, of the Magi,
of the Orphicists[6] *; but the accent of their religion is*

---

[1] Cf. Formation of the Greek People, *Foreword*, p. *xii* ; Israel, *Foreword ;*
both in this series.
[2] Cf. Primitive Italy *and* Ancient Persia, *both in this series, Forewords.*
[3] *Jullian,* Hist. de la Gaule, *i, p.* 381.
[4] Cf. *Albert Bayet,* La Morale des Gaulois, *pp.* 163–4.
[5] Rise of the Celts, *p.* 14 ; *cf. below, p.* 271.
[6] *See the volumes in this series on Greek religion, ancient Persia, and India.*

thoroughly Celtic, deeply human, as it is in its haunting sense of death and its worship of heroes.

Hubert follows Celticism, after its collapse, in its various survivals. He shows it holding out with its language in the extreme west of Europe, cherishing and writing down its legends, and long afterwards, in the twentieth century, making an independent nation in Ireland.

But the essential survival of Celticism he finds and shows us in Romanized Gaul, in the France of all ages. We cannot conceal the fact that this historian, with all his devotion to objective science, seems to have a sort of tenderness for the Celtic genius. I do not think that it leads him astray, but it infuses emotion into many pages of his work, particularly those which tell of the effects of Celticism on the history of the French nation.

The Celts made the France of to-day. They are responsible for the appropriation of the soil, the judicious choice of dwelling-places and roads. Above all, into this setting they introduced their " soul of the people ". For Gaul to acquire a true national consciousness, only a strongly organized state was needed. We have, too, seen a wonderful agent of unification, social discipline, and energetic but elastic government come into being and grow up in Rome.[1] With a dim sense of what they lacked the Celts welcomed Roman rule with astonishing readiness. For, in the penetrating words of Renouvier, " what they liked was not so much independence as to be dependent only on what they liked." [2] In their evident superiors the Celts were willing to see friends and guides.[3] They yielded, and at the same time they resisted. They accepted the authority and culture of Rome, but they kept their Celtic soul, or the essential part of it. " The Gallo-Romans mostly continued to be disguised Celts (Rise, *p. 14).*

---

[1] Primitive Italy *and* Roman Political Institutions ; *cf. below*, pp. 69, 154.

[2] Introduction à la philosophie analytique de l'Histoire, *p. 390 ; " Their devotion to Julius Cæsar, who defeated them for ten years, followed on their devotion to Vercingetorix, who defended their liberty. . . . From the Druids they accepted a kind of Papacy. . . . Of Rome, lastly, that is, of the Empire, they at once appreciated the scientific administrative methods and the admirably formulated law, so much so, that they set themselves up as the successors and, when necessary, the substitutes of the last Romans. That, in fact, is what they became, and among modern peoples the principle of the strong state for a long time had them for its champions."*

[1] *For the relations of the Celts and Rome, see* pp. 86, 97, 148. *See also* Bayet, *op. cit., p. xi.*

Like Chapot in his account of Roman Gaul in The Roman World, *Hubert here in his account of the Gallic Celts finds the intellectual and moral foundations of France. It is true that the Romans, for all their tolerance, seem to have persecuted the Druids, but Romanization, which was accepted partly willingly and partly perforce, allowed certain mental qualities of Celticism to survive, and, indeed, developed them in Gallo-Roman civilization, and those qualities are an essential part of the spirit of France—observation, justice, measure, elasticity.*

Plastic art rose to no great heights in Gaul, but decorative art adorned everything with that delicate sense of the beautiful which is called taste.

The Latin language, adopted by the Gauls, not only retained certain Celtic ingredients, but was intimately transformed, becoming analytical. We see the men who gave it a new character as " great talkers " ; they had talents for eloquence and poetry, for an eloquence which aimed at action and for a poetry which readily turned to the dramatic or gnomic.

Of the literature of the Celts, which for a long time was popular, oral, a somewhat untrue idea was at first formed, as a result of Renan's famous article on the poetry of the Celtic races.[1] It was supposed to be elegiac and very feminine in character. This conception was only justified by the state of Celtic studies at the time. Since then, the labours of such men as Gaidoz, d'Arbois de Jubainville, Loth, Ernault, Le Braz, and Dottin have revealed a poetry " bursting with heroic sap ", the expression of " vehement, passionate, almost brutal natures, eager for action and intoxicated with movement and noise ".[2] No doubt the Celts gave a very large place to woman, both in life and in lyric poetry. But the romantic and marvellous, the workings of love and fate, those themes which surround the adventures of the British heroes—Arthur, Tristram, Parsifal—must not blind us to a whole side of masculine poetry, nor to one of humorous observation.

When the Celts of Gaul had thrown over their epic tradition, " attracted by the more refined civilization which the Romans brought," they kept its spirit, and it is this spirit, according to

---

[1] *In* Rev. des Deux Mondes, 1st *February,* 1854.

[2] *Anatole Le Braz, " Le Drame dans l'épopée celtique," in* Rev. des Deux Mondes, 1st *July,* 1904 : " *A people at once violent and sensitive, imaginative, and pugnacious, greedy for ideals and for action.*" *Dottin, " La littérature gaëlique de l'Irlande," in* Rev. de Synth. hist., iii, *p.* 63.

Hubert, that animates the work of the French chroniclers and gives them a dramatic character. From Gregory of Tours and the monks of Saint-Denis they made the history of France " the finest historical narrative in the world ". And the actual story of France, like its written history, " the history of that undestroyable people of peasants, warriors, and artists, with its glories and tumults, its hopes and enthusiasms, its discords and rebirths, is surely the story of a nation whose blood and bones are mainly composed of Celtic elements " (Rise, pp. 14–15 ; below, pp. 269, 276).

One cannot lay too great emphasis on the range of the work done by Hubert in this study of the Celts, which will be completed by that of the Germans. It helps one to understand France. It is rich in teaching, without ever revealing a desire to generalize. It makes one see how men, beyond societies, create nations, how they arrive at the feeling and then at the idea of a fatherland. Patria nostra *will soon become* France dulce. *Perhaps the misfortunes of the third century, " by the suffering of the country," contributed to the national education of the people of Gaul. " They gave it those venerable wrinkles which men have always loved to see on the face of their motherland "* (p. 155)— *an exquisite phrase which is the expression of the whole Hubert, historian, thinker, and writer.*

HENRI BERR.

PART ONE

CELTIC EXPANSION IN THE LA TÈNE PERIOD

CHAPTER I

THE CELTS IN ITALY

I

THE CIVILIZATION OF LA TÈNE. EXTENSION OF GALLIC SETTLE-
MENTS IN GAUL

THE new movements of expansion mentioned in the last chapters of the previous volume, *The Rise of the Celts*, are the effects in general history of something that had been going on inside Gaul and the Celtic regions of Germany since the time of the first Celtic settlements in Aquitaine and in Spain and first Celtic inroads into Italy, that is, since 550 B.C. These events are marked in archæology by the change from the civilization called after Hallstatt to that called after La Tène.[1] All over the region situated west of the Alps and the Central Plateau, the change took place in less than a hundred years. From Provence [2] to Thuringia [3] the civilization of the first La Tène period is represented. It begins about 500. The spread of the new styles strikes one less by its rapidity than by its universality. Everywhere the Celts fell into line with those who had started the fashion. This is interesting evidence of the unity and continuity of the Celtic world. But the fashion did not change merely in dress, arms, pottery, or art ; funeral rites also changed, and equally universally. Moreover, the area covered by the La Tène civilization almost everywhere extends beyond that of the Hallstatt culture. Inhabited sites are found closer together ; vacant spaces are filled up. The Celtic population is at once more numerous and, in general, denser. Certainly

---

[1] See *Rise* (i.e. Hubert, *The Rise of the Celts*, in this series), ch. iv, § i.
[2] Déchelette, **CCCXVIII**, ii, 3, p. 999 ; cf. p. 1055, fig. 435, 6 (Gard).
[3] Schumacher, **CCCCIX**, i, p. 120.

colonization went on inside the Celtic world, and there were shiftings of the population, perhaps conflicts and disorders. But on the whole there was an increase of power which had for consequence the colonizing expeditions into Britain and Italy and, later, into the Danube valley and, lastly, into Spain.

In craftsmanship [1] the civilization of La Tène is the direct continuation of that of the last period of Hallstatt. It develops the legacy of Hallstatt; at least, it implies it as an immediate predecessor. We have seen this already: the La Tène sword is a dagger with antennæ, elongated; the La Tène brooch is a Certosa brooch, with an upturned foot, the end of which curls back towards the bow; the bracelets and torques are very much alike; and the pottery carries on the Hallstatt types with provincial peculiarities. The chief difference comes from the imitation of Greek objects and decoration, due to relations established either on the Marseilles side or by way of the Danube valley. The problem raised by these changes is entirely one of the simple problems connected with the history of the progress of civilizations. It is not so, in my opinion, with the funeral rites. Here the changes come about in quite a peculiar way.

At the end of the Hallstatt period, the practice of cremation was almost universal among the Celts. Moreover, the ashes of the dead were laid in tumuli of the same type as those containing the previous burials. On the other hand, we may say that for a period of over two hundred years, beginning about 500 B.C., the practice of cremation was almost abandoned, and that fairly abruptly, as it would appear. The change was not absolutely instantaneous, nor quite universal. Cremation-tombs of La Tène I have been found in the Haute-Marne and Haute-Saône and, above all, in the valley of the Rhine. But they are exceptional, and we may take it that the exception confirms the rule. It shows that the disappearance of the earlier rite was due to its being dropped by the same people as had formerly practised it, and that, since the new rule did not prevail all at once, it was not adopted as a matter of course.

Furthermore, the use of tumuli was given up in the Celtic world as a whole. The typical tomb of the La Tène period

[1] For changes introduced in material civilization, see *Rise*, ch. v.

is an oblong grave, in which the body is laid with or without
a coffin.[1] This change, too, was abrupt in certain parts,
but it was not universal.

In the old Hallstatt settlements, the Celts continued
to build tumuli in the La Tène period. In Germany [2] all
the tombs which can be dated between 500 and 400 B.C.
are tumuli, and so are some of those dating from 400 to 300.
In Switzerland,[3] this practice continued for about a hundred
years, till about 100. In Alsace,[4] Lorraine,[5] Haute-Marne,[6]
Burgundy, and Franche-Comté,[7] the vast majority of La
Tène tombs were found under tumuli.

But we must make a distinction. For one thing, the
Celts of the tumulus countries utilized the old tumuli and
dug new tombs in them ; for another, we know a certain
number of tumuli which were deliberately erected to cover
several burials. So each tumulus might become a little
cemetery. But it is none the less true that tumuli were built
in the La Tène period in these regions to cover at least one
principal tomb. On the whole, tumulus-building lasted in
certain parts of the Celtic area until the third period of
La Tène, that is, till the first century B.C.

Where Hallstatt tumuli were rare, the La Tène tombs
are always flat-graves. This is so in the Department of the
Marne, where there are so many La Tène cemeteries.[8]

But here again there is a point to consider. In the
cemeteries of the Marne and Aisne, mounds have been noted,
which are tumuli, apparently empty. The cemetery of
Nanteuil, in the Aisne, consisted in part of a vast tumulus,
like the Burgundian tumuli which contain many graves.
Lastly, such place-names as Les Buttes, La Motte, La Motelle,
La Tomelle, coinciding with Gallic cemeteries, suggest
tumuli which have disappeared. What is more, single tombs
(like the chariot-burial at Berru) [9] and groups of tombs are

---

[1] Déchelette, ii, 3, pp. 1030 ff.
[2] Ibid., pp. 1063 ff.
[3] Ibid., pp. 1082 ff. ; Gruaz and Viollier in **XVII**, 1914 pp. 257 ff. ; 1915
pp. 1 ff. (Gallic cemetery at St. Sulpice, Vaud).
[4] Déchelette, ii, 3, pp. 1069–1070.
[5] Ibid., p. 1042.
[6] Ibid., pp. 1041–2.
[7] Ibid., pp. 1043 ff.
[8] For maps of cemeteries of the La Tène period in the Dept. of the Marne
see ibid., p. 1018, fig. 423.
[9] Ibid., p. 1026, fig. 426.

surrounded by a circular ditch. Circular enclosure and tumulus are found simultaneously in yet other regions, in England for example, and stand for the same culture. It should be noted that in two places the tumulus won the day —in England [1] and in the lower valley of the Rhone,[2] where there were new Celtic settlements dating from La Tène. In both cases, we may suppose that the settlement took place before the time when the flat-grave was beginning to gain the upper hand. In England, moreover, the La Tène tumuli are probably just continuations of the round barrows of the previous inhabitants. So there was, at least, a period of varying practice, which continued longer, or even indefinitely, where there were many tumuli.

We have already seen one group of Celts giving up its tumuli for cemeteries of flat-graves. This was the branch which occupied Aquitaine and Spain.[3] This is a change similar to that which we have just noted all over the Celtic world, and it may have come about in the same way. I am inclined to think that the flat-graves are tombs reduced to their simplest expression by communities which were denser than those of the Hallstatt age, and, therefore, more anxious to save space and not to spread out their cemeteries. These are considerations which matter in the history of funeral rites.[4]

But we are still left with some novelties—the oblong grave, the coffin, and, above all, the orientation. In the flat-grave cemeteries, the dead are laid east and west, with the head to the west, and the older the cemetery is the more regular is this rule.

New practices imply new ideas. There can be no question of a cataclysm, with new peoples taking the place of old peoples wholesale. The spread of the new ideas may have been due to propaganda. More than once, one has to resort

---

[1] Ibid., pp. 1102 ff.
[2] Ibid., p. 1056.
[3] See *Rise*, pp. 283 ff.
[4] Déchelette (ii, 3, p. 1015) ascribes the abolition of the tumulus to a desire to hide the grave, for protection, from the eyes of the foreigners in the midst of whom the Celts were advancing. But it must not be forgotten that the La Tène flat-graves are grouped in cemeteries. If they had been completely hidden, these tombs would have been dug one above another or would have cut one into another. This does occur, but rarely. We must conclude that the graves had outward marks, a monument perhaps or a small mound, a wooden post, or something of the sort.

to this hypothesis to explain some general phenomenon revealing the moral life of prehistoric peoples. But how did the propaganda take place and who conducted it ? It seems to me that we must imagine imitation on the one side and authority or the preponderance of new elements on the other —in any case, new demographic and social conditions.

For every change in the appearance of the prehistoric civilizations there has been a movement of the population, greater or less. So it was at the beginning of the La Tène period. The arrival of new peoples can be seen clearly at certain points.

One of these is the Department of the Marne.[1] If we go by archæological finds alone, we find it with very few inhabitants in the Bronze Age and almost completely depopulated in the Hallstatt period. In the La Tène period, on the other hand, it was covered with a very dense population. No less than 191 Gallic cemeteries have been found there. Within about twenty years, over a hundred tombs have been explored. In the cemetery of Les Croncs, at Bergères-les-Vertus, over a thousand have been opened. This large number of cemeteries represents a numerous and entirely new population. For one cannot suppose that all Hallstatt tumuli have succeeded in escaping the eye of the antiquary in this department, where tomb-hunting is almost a sport.

Another region, which was, indeed, inhabited in Hallstatt times, but sparsely, received in the La Tène period a fairly large population, quite differently grouped, and that was Switzerland.[2] There the La Tène tombs are distributed in two groups. An eastern group extends from Basle to the lakes of Zurich and the Four Cantons. Near Basle there is a large cemetery, that of Muttenz. The valleys of the Glatt, the Limmatt, and the Reuss contain Celtic cemeteries. A region in which the Aar still receives a few small tributaries divides this group from the western, which extends from the neighbourhood of Berne to the Lake of Geneva. The centre of the first group is Zurich and that of the second is Berne. In the district of Berne alone, in the immediate environs of the city, eighteen cemeteries of the La Tène period are known.

[1] Ibid., p. 1020, and app. v.
[2] Viollier, **CCCCXCII**, pp. 59 ff.

The Hallstatt tumuli were in quite small groups, corre-
sponding to a population which changed its abode easily.
The cemeteries of La Tène are those of a fixed population. In
some of them over two hundred tombs have been opened.
Between these two settlements, the old groupings of the
Hallstatt population do not seem to have been touched.
We shall see later to what extent we must suppose them to
have been penetrated by new elements.

We may picture bodies forcing their way across older
settlements. In Haute-Saône [1] a small Marne cemetery has
been found, which probably represents the settlement of a
small colony of new-comers. Further south, in Dauphiné
and the Alps,[2] cemeteries or single tombs of the Marne type
stand for recent settlements, the density of which we have
no means of estimating. In Provence [3] there are no burials
of the new type, but objects of the first La Tène period found
in the fortified enclosures, particularly brooches, announce the
arrival of Celts in a new domain.

In the west, except in Normandy [4] and certain places in
Brittany [5] and Berry,[6] the chance which guides archæological
discoveries has been very unfavourable to the Gauls. The
archæological map of the cemeteries is almost blank.[7] The
few swords found in the dragging of rivers would not fill it.
And yet we must suppose that at this time there were Celts
settled everywhere between the Seine and the Garonne.
This blank space in the map leaves room for all kinds of
conjecture. In any case, we may suppose that the settlements developed gradually and that those which reached
furthest forward do not belong to the early phase of the
La Tène civilization.

No normal increase of the old Celtic occupants of Lorraine
and Alsace, of Burgundy and Franche-Comté, would have
sufficed for the foundation of the new settlements in

---

[1] Déchelette, ii 3, p. 1046 (cemetery at Mercey).
[2] E. Chantre, in *Bull. Anthr. et biolog. de Lyon*, 1913–17, pp. 17 ff. (cemetery
at Genas, Isère) ; H. Muller, in **CXLVI**, 1920, pp. 16 ff. (cemetery at Pariset,
near La Tour-sans-Venin, Isère).
[3] Vasseur, in **XI**, xiii, 3, 1903 (Le Baou-Roux) ; cf. Déchelette, ii, 3, p. 1001.
The fortified enclosures of Provence were occupied from 600 B.C. onwards
and abandoned about 125 B.C. Cf. Justin, 43, 4.
[4] Déchelette, ii, 3, p. 1060.
[5] Ibid., pp. 945–6, 1060.
[6] Ibid., pp. 1049–1050.
[7] Ibid., map iii (La Tène tombs and cemeteries in France).

Champagne, Switzerland, Dauphiné, and Provence, to say nothing of the others. We are therefore compelled to imagine something similar to what I have suggested as an explanation of the Hallstatt occupation, a sort of drift of the Celtic tribes from the Rhine valley and beyond, or possibly definite invasions. It is, moreover, hard to believe that the evolution of the Hallstatt types of object from which the types characteristic of the La Tène culture sprang occurred anywhere but in the German domain of the Celts. Indeed, transitional forms abound in Germany whereas they are rare in France. It is in Germany that the civilization of La Tène makes its first appearance and first becomes really rich. I think, therefore, that on the whole it originated in Germany, and that it was from Germany that, between 500 and 400 B.C., the bodies set out which peopled Switzerland on the one side, Champagne on the other, and all the other districts which we can suppose to have been covered by this colonization. From where exactly did they start ? Probably from more than one point in Celtic Germany.[1] The question will arise later.

Lastly, although the funeral rites of the Gauls of this epoch are those of a military people which sends its men into the next world in fighting-gear, or at least in parade-dress, I cannot help noting the peaceful character of the new Celtic settlements.

We must picture the population of Champagne as dispersed in large open villages, which must necessarily have been agricultural villages. Champagne had not attracted the Hallstatt stock-breeders. I am inclined to think that, among the progress made by Celtic civilization in the La Tène period, there was some in agriculture, and that the men who stayed in Champagne knew how to make use of the dry slopes of its hills and, still more, of the richer uplands of the Aisne, with their heavy soil, where we also find them established. It is probable that the plough,[2] a good plough, the Gallic name of which survived in Roman Gaul (*carruca*), with a coulter and probably wheels, was the invention which made it possible to till this ground. I imagine the landscape

---

[1] Rademacher, in Ebert, **CCCXXIV**, s.v. " Kelten ", vi, pp. 285–6.

[2] Déchelette, ii 3, pp. 1378 ff. ; Dottin **CCCXXII**, pp. 192 ff. ; Reinecke, in **LXVII**, 1919, pp. 17 ff.

which they created in Champagne and the Aisne as something
like that part of the country which has not been given over
to vineyards, with ploughed fields running down the sides of
the hills.[1] Their settlements in Switzerland were of the same
character, and presented the same appearance.   They
still do ; the contrast between the ploughed hillsides and
the upland pasture-ground about Berne and the Lake of
Thun is very remarkable and strange. It is a spectacle which
implies peoples of different economic habits living side by
side. But in my opinion it is a prehistoric spectacle.

I have called attention to the great number of Gallic
names in -*magus* and in -*ialum* in Gaul properly so called.
They designate settlements in the plains, agricultural markets
or centres of activity.[2]

But there is something more. Except in Germany and
Provence, where special circumstances and the presence of
unruly neighbours compelled the Gauls to stand on their
guard, there are no fortified places belonging to the earlier
periods of La Tène. The Hallstatt forts had been abandoned
and the Gallic *oppida* were not yet built. For instance, in
Franche-Comté, the occupation of the camp of Château-
sur-Salins,[3] which was an admirable site for a fortress, seems
to have been interrupted in La Tène I.

It is surprising to come upon a peaceful Gaul just before
the invasions of Italy and Greece, but we have to accept it.
That all went smoothly always, it would be rash to imagine.
That there were no shiftings of population, no fluctuations
of frontiers, is very unlikely ; that there were no small wars
is impossible ; and we should find evidence of them if we
examined these very cemeteries of the Marne. But the Gauls
of France did not live in a world of constant violence and
strife. Therefore their communities developed and multiplied
in peace.   Their nations and tribes generally lived on terms
of international justice and policy which made it possible
for social life to become organized.   Indeed, that is why
they had the surplus man-power and the inter-tribal concord
which allowed them to make the great expeditions to which
we now come.

[1] H. Muller-Brauel, in **LXXXV**, 1926, pp. 184 ff.
[2] Jullian, **CCCXLVII**, i, pp. 238 ff.
[3] Piroutet, in **CXXXIX,**, 1928, 2, pp. 266 ff.

II

The civilization of La Tène spread in France between 500 and 400 B.C. It is just about this latter date that we must place the Celtic invasion of Italy which was the first of the great historical expeditions of the Celts.

All the ancient historians agree in describing the descent of the Celts into Italy as a mass invasion on the part of a people which was a huge army, speedily ending in the extermination of the former occupants of the country and the foundation of a very large colony. At the bottom of all their accounts there is doubtless a version written for the occasion which probably comes from Timagenes.[1] But, apart from the fact that Timagenes generally had fairly good information, in the account of the earliest Gallic wars there are probably good traditional elements, for which the Celts themselves were partly responsible. Gallic historians like Cornelius Nepos, who was an Insubrian, and Trogus Pompeius, who was a Vocontian, may have had a part in handing them on. This history, in which both sides have collaborated, is assuredly epic and heroic rather than purely historical.

But after all, the accuracy of the anecdotal details does not matter much. The history of the first Gallic wars appears to have been built up on a fairly sure chronological foundation with materials which are rather fabulous, but nevertheless of very great value, much like all that part of ancient history which has not been written by contemporaries. On the whole, it has survived criticism remarkably well. Archæology adds to it without correcting it.

It is of capital interest to us, in that it gives us the earliest information that we have of at all a detailed kind about the making of a Celtic settlement, and this information seems to be trustworthy. There is an artificial confederation of tribes from different districts, some newly formed, others old, among which foreign bodies may find a place. They go forward. Some settle down at once. Others hesitate and take longer to find their resting-place. They go about the country,

---

[1] Niese, in Pauly and Wissowa, **CCCLXVIII**, vii, col. 613 ; Hirschfeld, in **CLXVIII**, 1894, p. 331 ; d'Arbois, **CCXLVIII**, xii, p. 51 ; Müllenhoff, **CCCLXII**, ii, p. 613 ; Jullian, **CCCXLVII**, i, p. 281.

fighting, treating, employing policy. Others follow them, summoned by them or tempted by their example. At last they are so many that they form a huge mass. Corners and outlines are rubbed away. The Gauls, with their curiosity about civilization, become assimilated to their new surroundings. They prosper in peace, but their political formations disintegrate and finally collapse.

All the historians except Livy [1] run events together, placing them between 396 and 386 B.C.[2] But Livy's account is not substantially different from the rest. Of the first invasion he only gives the date, and on the whole he passes it over. A certain number of chronological concordances have been established—the first year of the ninety-eighth Olympiad and the Archonship of Pyrgion in Athens (388–387 B.C.),[3] the Archonship of Theodotos, the Peace of Antalcidas, the siege of Rhegion, and the second year of the ninety-eighth Olympiad (387–386 B.C.).[4] Cornelius Nepos [5] places the entrance of the Gauls into Italy at the same time as the capture of Veii by Camillus, in 396. In Roman chronology, the uncertainty of the particular date is due to the way in which dictators may have upset the reckoning of Consulships.[6] At all events, we may agree to place the capture of Rome in the year 387–386.

The most interesting thing which Livy adds to the accounts of his fellow-historians is the idea of a kind of political plan, which he supposes to have lain behind the expedition. The *Celticum* formed a confederation, at the head of which was the King of the Bituriges, whose name at that time was Ambicatus.[7] The population exceeded the normal size of agricultural tribes attached to the land.[8] Ambicatus

---

[1] See *Rise* pp. 263–4.

[2] Homo, **CCCXLI**, English, pp. 165 ff. ; Grenier, **DXXIX**, pp. 64 ff. ; Meyer, **CCCLIV**, v, pp. 151 ff.

[3] Dion., i 74 ; App., *Celtica*, 2, 1.

[4] Polyb., i, 6 ; Diod., xiv, 113, 1 ; Just., vi, 6, 5.

[5] Pliny, *N.H.*, iii, 125 ; Unger, *Römisch-griechische Synchronismen vor Pyrrhos*, repr. from **XXI**,, 1876, 1.

[6] O. Leuze, **CCCLI**, *passim*.

[7] Livy, v, 34. The Gaul of Ambicatus, with its High King, provided by one of the confederate nations, is constituted like the Ireland of St. Patrick's day.

[8] The development of the Celtic family, as we know it in Ireland and Wales, results in the exclusion of a certain number of individuals from the original property of the family, and this necessitates periodical divisions of property between families or emigrations.

resolved to send out two colonies under the command of
his nephews on the distaff side,[1] his heirs, Sigovesus and
Bellovesus.   He made them strong enough to break all
resistance.[2] Trogus Pompeius compares the Gallic expedition
to a *ver sacrum*,[3] that is to one of the religious emigrations
practised by the Italic peoples.

Apart from this difference, the facts are set forth by
most historians in much the same fashion.[4] The Insubres,
Boii, and Senones destroy a large Etruscan town, Melpum,
perhaps Melzo, west of Milan. They found Milan and a
certain number of other towns. Following up their successes
against the Etruscans, they attack Clusium (Chiusi). The
Romans grow disturbed, negotiate, and send a relief army
which is defeated on the Allia. Rome is taken, and then
saved by the geese of the Capitol and Camillus.

According to some, the Gauls are wiped out. According
to others, they retire fairly quietly to their settlements in
Romagna, being recalled by an inroad of Veneti.[5] The Gauls
are said to have had guides. Some accounts speak of a noble
of Clusium named Aruns,[6] seeking vengeance on his wife
and his Lucumo ward ; others, more significant, refer to
Elico, an Helvetian smith working in Rome.[7]

In every case, it is the riches of Italy, the fruit, the figs,
the wine, that draw the barbarians from their less kindly
regions. The men who summon them bring them samples
of these delights. What all historians have faithfully recorded,
is the terror sown among the peoples of Italy by the approach
of the Gauls.[8] These queer-looking barbarians, coming from
so far, were to the Italy of the fourth century before Christ
what the Scourge of God was to the Gaul of the fifth century
after Christ, an unavoidable, irresistible, God-sent calamity.
The army which came down into Italy is rated at 300,000
men, that which triumphed at the Allia at about 30,000.

[1] Livy, loc. cit. : *sororis filios.*
[2] Ibid. : *ne qua gens arcere advenientes posset.*
[3] Just., **XXIV**, 4.
[4] Plut., *Cam.*, 15 ; Dion., xiii, 14 ff. ; Polyb., ii, 17 ff. ; Pliny, ii, 125 ;
xii, 5 ; Cato, p. 36 ; Aul. Gell., xvii, 13, 4 ; App., *Celtica*, ii, 1 ; *Historia
Romana*, iv, 2 ; Diod., xiv, 113, 1 ; Just., xx, 5.
[5] Polyb., ii, 18, 3.
[6] Livy, v, 35 ; Plut., Dion., locc. citt.
[7] Pliny, xii, 5.
[8] Livy, v, 35, 4 ; 36, 2 ; 37, 2 ; 38, 6 ; 39. 1.

These were terrifying hosts for Etruria and Latium, which were only accustomed to wars between one city and another. The battle of the Allia, *Alliensis clades*, was a rout, for which the Romans blushed until the end of the Empire. The war-cry of the Gauls, rising on all sides before the troops made contact, seems to have provoked a wild stampede. As for the evacuation of Rome, of which Livy gives us a remarkably objective picture, it was creditable to a few only. In any case, the Gauls were no gentle foes. They were in the first frenzy of their onrush. They came forward ravaging the country and burning the towns.[1] No doubt, they had a law covering foreign relations and were accustomed to negotiating ; indeed, we are told that they did negotiate.[2] But one can easily believe that these parleys gave rise to hopeless misunderstandings. The Gauls, being strong, and not properly understood, were touchy, and they seem to have been lacking in patience.

The deliverance of Rome did not put an end to their attacks. They returned into the valley of the Tiber and to Rome itself in 367,[3] in 361–360,[4] and in 350–349.[5] They descended into Campania in 360 and in 349. In 367 and in 349 they went as far as Apulia.[6] The dates of these expeditions are uncertain, and so is their relative size, but we have one piece of archæological evidence in the shape of a small cemetery at Canossa di Puglia.[7] At the same time they went much further, into Greece, whither Dionysios I of Syracuse sent a body of them which he had taken into his service.[8]

South of the Apennines, these Gallic expeditions were merely raids, which began to turn into expeditions of mercenaries. They had not the rapid successes of the campaigns in the plain of the Po. The fact is, that north of the Apennines the Gauls had had only Etruscans before them,

---

[1] e.g. Mazarbotto (Montelius, **DXXXIV**, p. 410 ; Grenier, **DXXIX**, p. 99). Herr von Duhn (in Ebert, **CCCXXIV**, s.v. " Kelten ", vi, p. 207) seems to deny that the city was destroyed ; but I think he is mistaken. Doubtless it was partially reoccupied by the Gauls.

[2] Livy, v, 35.

[3] Livy, iv, 42, 8 ; vii, 1, 3 ; Polyb., ii, 18, 6–7.

[4] Livy, vii, 11, 1 ; 12, 8.

[5] Ibid., vii, 26, 9 ; cf. Homo, **CCCXLI**, English, p. 175.

[6] Livy, loc. cit. ; Diod., xiv, 117, 7.

[7] *Prähist. Blätt.*, 1898, pp. 49–56.

[8] E. Cavaignac, in **CXL**, 1924, pp. 359 ff. The first relations of Dionysios with the Gauls seem to have been in 379, at the time of the siege of Croton.

who really formed nothing but a fairly recent colony there,
and fortified places were rare. South of the Apennines, both
in Etruria and in Latium and Umbria, the Gauls found themselves in the midst of a quantity of very ancient little cities,
all fortified and perched in good situations. But the strength
of their walls was only the instrument of their resistance.
The cause of that resistance and its success was that they
were political bodies, which refused to yield in a war under-
taken *pro aris et focis*, and would not die. The greatest disaster
seems to have been that of Rome, and Rome had at once
formed again with its army outside its ravaged soil.

Livy, in the chapters of Book V in which he describes the
Gallic invasion, makes it plain, with the understanding,
lucidity, and descriptive power of a great historian, that
the Gauls were not then capable of subduing the determination to live and to conquer embodied in political units which
were far superior to their own. Moreover, they did as all
conquering armies do in warm and fertile countries. At first
they let themselves go, taking what they pleased. Livy shows
them to us, gorged with eating and drinking, even rasher
and more careless than usual after their too easy victories,
and falling into drunken slumber wherever the night happened
to overtake them. Then comes the plague, which we may
take to have been dysentery. They are encamped among the
ruins of Rome, in the dust and ash of the burning city.
It is summer, and the weather is hot for these men of the
north. Disease spreads among them like cattle-plague,
vulgatis velut in pecua morbis. Dead bodies accumulate,
and have to be burned in heaps (usually they buried their
dead). With the plague comes famine. The Gauls are no
better organized for conducting large armies than the Italic
peoples, but the latter at least know how to conduct small
ones. They have no commissariat, and they have laid the
country waste. Lastly, they know nothing about field
fortification or intelligence, and they allow themselves to
be surprised.

None the less, the effects of the terror died hard. Until
349 the Romans remained on the defensive. From that
date onwards, it seems, they took courage, and turned upon
their enemies. The Gauls were so surprised at the first
encounter, Polybios tells us, that they stopped short and

scattered.[1] Indeed, peace seems to have been concluded about 335.[2]

The general outcome was that, while Gallic inroads penetrated as far as the end of Italy, the Gallic conquest stopped at the Apennines. But in what manner did it take place ? Is it true that the Gauls came in like a whirlwind, and where did they make their entry ? That is the first question which we shall discuss. After that, we shall inquire how the Gauls conducted themselves in Italy, what were their general relations with their neighbours, and what became of their civilization in that country.

III

HOW THE GAULS ENTERED ITALY

The Gauls came in, according to Livy,[3] in several bands, crossing the Alps in succession or by different routes.

Bellovesus, who, according to the same author, directed the whole venture, had with him only the Insubres.[4] They arrived first. When their movement had been accomplished, a force of the Cenomani under a leader named Elitovius [5] followed them by the same pass, and Bellovesus assisted them on the way down. Livy then mentions, in vague terms, an advance on the part of the Libui and the Salluvii,[6] but it is doubtful whether they arrived so early. The Boii and Lingones came over together by the Pennine Alps, that is by the Simplon or the St. Gothard, and, passing the first two bodies hustled the Etruscans and Umbrians on the other side of the Po. The Senones arrived last and, passing the leading bodies in the same manner, provided the army of about thirty thousand men which crossed the Apennines and took Rome. Livy does not assert this positively ; he says that he believes it.[7]

To transport over the Alps, without any scientific dis-

[1] Polyb., ii, 18, 7.
[2] Ibid., xix, 1 (the Thirty Years' Peace).
[3] Livy, v, 34–5. Cf. Homo, **CCCXLI,**, English, pp. 165 ff. ; Jullian, **CCCXLVII**, i, pp. 289 ff.
[4] Livy, v, 34, 9.
[5] Livy, v, 35, 1.
[6] Livy, v, 35, 2.
[7] Livy, v, 35, 2–3.

position of supply-posts, a mass of men large enough to form
a whole nation, with women and children, flocks and herds,
a great number of chariots, and an indefinitely large train
of very primitive little waggons and pack-animals, was an
extremely difficult undertaking. It required at least some
organization if it was, as history relates, a concerted movement. What was done was to divide the host into separate
bodies, and it was most natural to form these according to
tribes. So Livy's account seems quite credible. Recon-
naissances, too, had to be made, guides to be found, extra
provisions to be obtained, and help of all kinds to be secured,
and there must have been negotiations or battles with the
local natives, all combining to delay and slow down the
advance ; and, even if we exclude the suggestion that they
made temporary settlements, it must have been necessary
to clear and till the land which they occupied for the time
being. The passage of the Gallic columns needed a fairly
long time, and we must suppose that there were big intervals
between one body and the next.

But how big were these intervals ? The largest is that
separating the invasion of the fifth and sixth centuries from
that of the fourth.

It is very remarkable that the fourth century Gallic
cemeteries in the Cisalpine country are all south of the Po,
the oldest being round Bologna.[1] Those north of the Po,
which are in two main groups, one west of the Ticino [2] in
the province of Novara, and the other about Como, date from
the last three centuries before Christ.[3] The dead in them
were burned, and their tombs are like contemporary tombs
in the Alpine valleys, but also resemble those of Golasecca.
This looks as if the Gauls of the fourth century had rapidly
advanced on Bologna, leaving Lombardy in the possession
of their predecessors, who had arrived a century or two earlier
and are said to have opened the gates of Italy to them. As
a matter of fact, the earlier settlement no longer existed.
The first Gallic cemeteries north of the Po were broken up
by the construction of towns or by cultivation (*grandiaque*

---

[1] Déchelette, ii, 3, p. 1087.
[2] Ulrich, **DXLI.**
[3] Déchelette, ii, 3, pp. 1093 ff., 1097 ; von Duhn, in Ebert, **CCCXXIV,**
s.v. " Kelten ", vi, p. 286 ; s.v. " Bologna ", ii, p. 112.

effossis mirabitur ossa sepulcris). A few isolated objects [1] are sufficient evidence that this district was taken by the Gauls at the same time as the Cispadane region, or even before it. The columns of Bellovesus must, therefore, have followed one on another at intervals of a few years or a few months. At the very most we may suppose, if we cannot accept this blank in the archæological map, that the Insubres and Cenomani arrived after the Boii and Senones with reinforcements which continued to descend from the Celtic interior for a long time yet.

But this, too, is hard to believe, and the order of march of the five Gallic nations (apart from the Libui and Salluvii) is quite as probable. It follows from their position. The first-comers doubtless stopped as soon as they could. The way down into the great valleys which spread out towards the Po is very attractive, and must have been so then. The country had been brought under cultivation by the people of the *terremare* and the pile-villages, and here the first invaders stopped. Those who followed had to go further. Those who are found at the end of the line are evidently the last-comers. Thus the Insubres, after their first collision with the Etruscans, settled south of the Lake of Como, between the Ticino and the Adda, occupying the provinces of Como and Milan. The Cenomani, coming next, settle between the Adda and the Adige, south of the lakes of Iseo and Garda, around Brescia and as far as Verona. On this side the Celts were stopped by the Veneti, whom they could not oust and had to take into consideration. The Boii occupied the region of Lodi, north of the Po, between the Ticino and the Adda. There they are said to have founded the city which is now Lodi (Laus Pompeia). But, finding themselves cramped, they crossed the Po with the Lingones and filled the plain under the Apennines between Parma and Bologna, while the Lingones occupied the whole of Lower Emilia. The Senones, prolonging the chain of Cisalpine Gauls, occupied the coast of the Romagna from the Utens (Montone) to the Alsis (Esino) on the outskirts of Ancona, according to Livy ; but they advanced a little further, to the valley of the Chienti.[2]

---

[1] Montelius, **DXXXV**, i, pp. 63-4.
[2] Livy, v, 35, 2-3. Regarding the Senones, Livy is not absolutely

We must suppose that they did not settle down all at once. The *Periplus* of Scylax,[1] written about 350, which enumerates all the peoples of the coasts of the Mediterranean one by one, does indeed speak of the Gauls on the Adriatic seaboard, or, more exactly, of the remnants of the expedition against Rome (ἀπολειφθέντες τῆς στρατείας), but only as covering a small area (ἐπὶ στενῶν). They cannot have occupied more than the mouths of the Po, their territory being bounded on the south by that of the Etruscans, which extended to Spina, an old Greek colony on the southern mouth of the Po, and on the north by that of the Veneti, which extended to Adria, another Greek colony a few miles north of the northern mouth. The mouths of the Po seem to have been in the domain of the Lingones. A too literal interpretation of the text would lead us to look for the Senones here, since it seems to have been they who made the expedition against Rome. But according to the author of the *Periplus* the Adriatic coast between Ancona and Spina still belonged to the Etruscans about 350, not to the Senones. The continuous succession of campaigns between 390 and 350 makes one think that the Senones were not permanently established before 350. One may suppose, too, that they did not occupy the coast but the terraces of the Apennines ; for it is here that Gallic settlements have been found, and not on the coast. In that case the *Periplus* of Scylax, which is really a " Pilot " for the use of navigators, might have ignored them, if we suppose that Ancona and Spina were still in Etruscan hands.

It is about this same date of 350 that the series of Greek vases found in the Etruscan cemetery of Bologna (La Certosa) comes to an end.[2] This means that the Etruscans had maintained themselves in the city, keeping up constant intercourse with the Greek colonies on the mouths of the Po, under the eyes of the Gauls established all round them. In general, the cities in this neighbourhood also seem to have

correct, but he only needs the slightest amendment. The domain of these peoples extended south of Ancona. In recent years, Gallic tombs have been found in the region of Filottrano and Osimo, e.g. that at San Genesto, near Tolentino. See von Duhn, in Ebert, s.v. " Kelten ", vi, p. 292. This observation enables one to judge how much trust one can place in the information supplied by the ancient historians.

[1] Scylax, 18.
[2] Grenier, **DXXIX**, pp. 160 ff., 320 ff. ; id. **CCCLXXVIII**, p. 72.

held out. Como, which has been assigned to the Insubres, and Bergamo, which has been assigned to the Cenomani, did not come under their power until later. Mantua continued to be an Etruscan enclave to the end.

So, from Como to Ancona and from Milan to Verona the five great peoples of which we are speaking made themselves one continuous territory. They had found it there, ready made for them, for the greater part of it coincides with the Etruscan territory on the Po. When the Etruscans were defeated, the political organization of their province had broken down. The five nations which succeeded them sooner or later assumed their position. This fact should be borne in mind, for it explains the cohesion of the group which they formed and the co-ordinated, concerted, and, one might say, political character which the historians ascribe to their first operations.

But there were other Gallic peoples south of the Alps —the Libui and Salluvii, mentioned by Livy.[1] Polybios [2] adds the Libici and Laevi north of the Po and the Ananes, Anares, or Anamari,[3] south of it, west of the Boii. These last two are perhaps not Gauls. But the others certainly are.

The Libui and Libici are probably identical and had Vercellae for their centre ; in their territory was a Rigomagus (Trino). From a somewhat obscure passage in Pliny,[4] the source of which is the *Origines* of Cato, it appears that they were a sub-tribe of the Salluvii. The Salluvii, who are also called the Salassi,[5] must have spoken a Celtic language, for their capital was Eporedia, the name of which is undoubtedly Gallic. They were probably a section of the Salyes of Provence, whom the ancient ethnographers label Celto-Ligurian. Between the Libici and the Insubres were the Vertamocori of Novara, who are described as Ligurians by Cato and as Gauls by Pliny.[6] The latter says that they were a *pagus*, that is a sub-tribe of the Vocontii of Dauphiné. North of the Vertamocori, the Lepontii, established in the

---

[1] Livy, v, 35, 2.
[2] Polyb., ii, 17, 4.
[3] Müllenhoff, **CCCLXII**, ii, p. 267.
[4] Pliny, iii, 134 ; Cato, fr. 27 ; Strabo, iv, 6, 8, on the Rhaetians. Cf. Meyer, **CCCLIV**, iv, p. 150.
[5] Holder, **CCVII**, s.v.
[6] Pliny, iii, 124 ; cf. d'Arbois, in **CXL**, xi, p. 154.

Val d' Ossola and the Val Leventina, were Gauls.[1] At the mouth of each of these two valleys we have a large cemetery, corresponding to their two main settlements, at Ornavasso [2] and Giubiasco.[3] These are La Tène cemeteries. At Ornavasso a certain number of vases have been found bearing *graffiti* which seem to be Celtic so far as they can be read at all.

The Lepontii must probably be attached to the people of the Valais. The Vertamocori and Salluvii are related to the Gauls of Dauphiné and Provence. The two sections were linked up by a series of Gallic peoples occupying the Alpine valleys—the Centrones on the upper Isère, the Medulli in the Maurienne, and the Caturiges on the upper Durance. These last had been settled for a short time in Italy.

The Gallic tribes of Piedmont seem to form a distinct group from the five large nations in Lombardy and Emilia, more recent and less solidly welded together. They are the advanced posts in Italy of the Alpine tribes or of those which had come as far as the foot of the Alps in the Rhone valley and had remained there. Immediately after the fall of Rome, Polybios [4] mentions frequent raids by men from across the Alps as causing agitation among the Cisalpine Gauls, whose successes had tempted them. The arrival of the Piedmontese tribes may correspond to those expeditions.

The Insubres, Cenomani, Boii, Lingones, and Senones came direct from much further away—from the banks of the Rhine, Appian says, and in any case from the interior of the Celtic world.[5]

Livy [6] gives us a list of the peoples among which Bellovesus raised his army, namely the Bituriges, Arverni, Senones, Ædui, Ambarri, Carnutes, and Aulerci, which appear for the first time in history. Over-critical scholars have attacked this list, but unjustly.[7] It is a document of the greatest importance, for it represents a fundamental grouping of the Gallic peoples. It shows what section of them took

[1] Pliny, iii, 134.
[2] Binachetti, in **XXVIII**, vi, 1895 ; v. Duhn, in Ebert, **CCCXXIV**, vi, pp. 292 ff.
[3] Viollier, in **CLXXX**, pp. 229 ff.
[4] Polyb., ii, 18–19.
[5] App., *Celt.*, i, 2, 390 ; cf. Prop., x, 10, 19.
[6] Livy, v, 34.
[7] D'Arbois (**CCXCIX**, pp. 139 ff.) and Bertrand (**CCCIII**, p. 20) regard the Celts of Italy as a colony of the Danubian Celts.

part in the great movement of expansion which was then taking place towards Britain and to the south-east.

The Insubres are Ædui; the Cenomani are Aulerci; the Senones of Italy are doubtless the same as the Senones of Gaul. In the Italian settlement the Bituriges, Arverni, Ambarri, and Carnutes do not appear, but we find the Lingones, who were afterwards neighbours of the Senones and Ædui in Gaul, and the Boii, who were one of the most widely scattered of all the Celtic peoples, but seem to have kept their main body in what I regard as the original home of the Celts, east of the Volcae. So the two lists do not agree absolutely, but there is nothing very disturbing in that.

Later on, we shall inquire where the peoples of the first list can have been at that time. We should note that neither list includes the two nearest neighbours of Italy—the Helvetii and Sequani. They must have had their hands full in their old or new possessions in Switzerland and Franche-Comté. Perhaps they stand in the same relation to the invaders of Italy as the Insubres to the Senones; settling in the country first, they were passed by those who followed them.

By what road had the invaders come ? There are two views, both based on the text of Livy, which is in such imperfect condition that both sides quote the same sentence as their authority.[1] The Gauls are said to have come through the country of the Ligurians of Turin (Taurini) and by the Julian Alps (*saltusque Juliae Alpis*). There is no doubt about what Livy thinks, for in the preceding sentence he mentions the Gauls as being in contact with the people of Marseilles. It is hardly credible that they crossed the Julian Alps, for the way was blocked by the Veneti, whom the Gauls did not touch. A happy conjecture has replaced the name of the Julian Alps by that of the River Duria.[2] But the geographical position of the Gauls solves the problem. The Insubres established south of Lake Maggiore and the Lake of Como had not come over by the Mont Cenis and the Val d'Aosta. They had crossed the Alps either by the St. Gothard, coming down on to Lake Maggiore, or by the Maloja, descending on to the Lake of Como. They stopped at the

---

[1] v. Duhn, in Ebert, **CCCXIV**, vi, pp. 285, 292.
[2] Jullian, **CCCXLVII**, i, p. 289, n. 5 ; p. 291, n. 4.

mouths of the Alpine valleys between the Ticino and the
Oglio. Those who came after gathered round them there,
and went on from there; those who crossed the Pennine
Alps doubtless came by the Simplon, which brought them
to the same point by the Val d'Ossola. The Celts might come
from Bavaria; the valley of the Rhine and the Engadine,
leading to the St. Gothard and the Maloja respectively,
were the natural routes up to the crest of the Alps for a people
coming from South Germany. The Boii and Lingones, who
crossed the Pennine Alps, came from the same region, working
round the Bernese Oberland.

It was only later, as I have suggested, that they passed
through the Ligurians who lay between their Lombard
settlements and the French Alps. It does not seem that they
ever went through the peoples that lay to the north-east
of their settlements.

IV

CHARACTER OF THE GALLIC SETTLEMENT IN THE VALLEY OF THE PO

So the Gallic peoples of the Cisalpine country were
portions of certain great Gallic tribes settled in various
other parts of the Celtic world. The invasion had not been
carried out by complete nations or tribes, nor yet by
temporary formations of a purely military kind, having no
political ties. These fractions of tribes had become tribes.
But the various elements in the political organization of
the Celts were perfectly homogeneous and only differed in
size.[1] They had combined to some extent for their venture,
but when their object was attained they at once went back
to their old freedom of action. Thus it is that we find the
Senones operating alone against Etruria and Rome.

How were those bodies made up? It is an interesting
question, but we cannot answer it completely. Were they
merely composed of the men that each happened to get
together? Were they sub-tribes or clans? They were
probably groups which already existed. The Insubres and
the Cenomani, indeed, were either sub-tribes or fractions of

---

[1] On the divisions of the tribe, see Czarnowski, **CCCCXXIII**, pp. 231 ff.

sub-tribes of the Ædui and Aulerci. The Cenomani were
in the same group as the contingents of a people which seems
to have formed part of their confederacy, the Andecavi;
this must be the explanation of the presence of the village
of Andes [1] on their territory, close to Mantua.

Another question is the size of the bodies. We can form
an approximate idea of it. It may be remembered that the
ancient historians reckon the victors of the Allia at 30,000
men. It is quite a credible figure. It was required, and it
was sufficient, to produce the effect of irresistible mass of
which I have tried to give a notion. We must multiply it
by at least seven to allow for the women, children, old men,
sick, cripples, and slaves. This would bring the number of
the Senones up to about 200,000 in all. The Boii must have
been about as many. Pliny, still quoting Cato's *Origins*,
tells us that they had 112 tribes,[2] no doubt at the time when
their country came under Roman sway. By this he must mean
112 clans, 112 groups of a social and territorial nature, each
of which must have been of some size. Indeed, the object
of the statement is to suggest that the Boii were a very
considerable people. Populations of this size were capable
of occupying the country effectively, and we must take the
historians almost literally when they tell us that they drove
out the Etruscans and Umbrians. That a few settlers, a
large number of slaves, and perhaps a few subject and
associated groups survived [3] is very probable, but it is even
more evident that a Celtic occupation took the place of the
Etruscan and Umbrian occupation, that it formed a whole
new Gallic colony.

Another very remarkable thing is that the Italian colony
of the Celts was on the plains. Nothing could show better
that something had changed in the civilization of the Celts
since the Hallstatt period. The Hallstatt men made for the
hills. The Gauls of the La Tène period made for uplands and
plains suited for agriculture. The Senones got the worst share,[4]

---

[1] Moreover, the Cenomani seem to have preserved in both their homes
the same habits or rules of place-naming. The name of Tridentum (Trent)
is to be compared with that of Tridentus (Trans in Mayenne). D'Arbois,
CCCI, 2, p. 324.

[2] Dottin, **CCCXXII**, p. 306.

[3] e.g. the Comenses (Como), Ausuciates (Osuccio), Gallianates (Galliano),
etc. Cf. Niessen, **DXXXVII**, ii, 1, pp. 185, 188–9.

[4] Diod., xiv, 113, 3. Cf. Jullian, **CCCXLVI**, i, p. 247.

for nothing was left for them but the slopes of the Apennines, though these were far from barren. Perhaps that is what drove them over the crests which barred their way to look for better land. Having failed, they contented themselves with what they had and throve on it. Therefore we cannot picture the Gallic settlers of the Cisalpine country as the nomads and stock-raisers described by Polybios; these characteristics belong to another branch of the Celts. They remained settled on the soil which they had conquered. They really colonized it, and as agriculturists.[1]

It is said that they founded cities—Milan, Brescia (Brixia), Bergamo (Bergomum), Como, Vicenza, Modena (Mutina),[2] and probably Lodi and Sinigaglia (Sena Gallica). Some of these towns no doubt existed before their coming, as was the case with Como, Brescia, Bergamo, and Bologna. To this last they gave a Gallic name, Bononia. Others kept their old names, which came from the Ligurians.[3]

If they did not Celticize the country sufficiently to give Gallic names to the towns, it was still more natural for them to keep the old names of the rivers.[4] The name of the Reno, however, is Celtic. Some have maintained that Benacus, the name of the Lake of Garda, is Celtic, meaning the Lake of the Points (Irish *benn*, " point "),[5] but the derivation is doubtful. Lastly, among the place-names of the country there are to this day many ending in *-asco* and *-usco*, which are Ligurian. Some of these date from before the Gallic occupation; others were doubtless given afterwards, but they were still formed on the same principles.[6]

The Cisalpine Gauls have left behind them funerary inscriptions, *graffiti* on pottery, and manufacturers' marks in surprisingly large numbers for a people which had had no knowledge of writing at the time when it arrived.[7] By a

---

[1] Diod., v, 40, 4–5 ; Dion., xiii, 11.

[2] Just., xx, 5, 8 ; Livy, xxxiv, 9 (Milan) ; Pliny, *N.H.*, iii, 124–5 (Como, Bergamo). Verona is supposed to have been founded by Brescia (Catull., 67, 32) ; its name may be Celtic. Cf. Niessen, i, p. 204. Against this view, see Philipon, **CCCLXIX**, p. 138. For Parma, see Mart., v, 13, 7 (*Gallica Parma*).

[3] Pliny, iii, 17.

[4] Philipon, op. cit., p. 189 ; cf. 139 (Ticinus).

[5] Pokorny, **CCCXIV**, v, in Ebert, p. 297, s.v. " Kelten ".

[6] D'Arbois, **CCCI**, ii, pp. 46, 63.

[7] J. Rhys, **VI**, pp. 59–75 ; Stokes, **CCXXXVIII**, xi, pp. 112–18. Of the inscriptions published as Celtic, many have nothing Celtic in them but a few proper names. Others are thoroughly Celtic—notably those from

curious chance, far the greatest number have been found north of the Po and on the fringes of the Gallic country. They seem to be later than the best days of Cisalpine Gaul.

The archæological remains, the known amount of which increases constantly, are distributed equally irregularly. Nothing remains of the towns, which were destroyed when Roman towns were built on their sites. The cemeteries represent wealthy but scattered settlements.[1] They confirm history, which fills up the gaps in their evidence.

On the whole, the Gauls formed a compact and lasting settlement in the central part of the Po valley. They took root there firmly enough to change the face of the countryside for ever.

According to historical tradition, the beaten Etruscans retired into the Euganean Hills overlooking Verona, and became the Raetians, so-called after their leader Raetus.[2] The Cenomani had advanced on this side. Justin attributes to them the foundation of Trent, and indeed Tridentum is a Gallic name.[3] North of Trent, in the Val di Non or Nonsberg, the little village of Cavareno has a Gallic name,[4] and the name of the district recalls that of the Anauni, a small people belonging to the group whose centre was Trent; their name certainly seems to be Gallic.[5] Near by, in the valley, a Gallic cemetery has been explored at Mechel-in-Nonsberg.[6] But the slopes of the Alps north of Cisalpine Gaul on this side remained in the hands of the Raeti and Euganeans.[7] Whoever these last may have been, there were undoubted Ligurians among them. There were, for example, the Trumpilini, who have left their name to the Val Trompia. They naturally recall the Trumpilini of the Maritime Alps,

Briona, near Novara, and Brescia. The former contains some Latin names (Legatus, Quintus), and the latter is half-Latin, half-Celtic.

[1] See above, p. 15.
[2] Just., xx, 5, 9.
[3] See above, p. 22, n. 1.
[4] *Cauaros*, hero ; Irish *caur*, giant.
[5] Ptol., ii, 1, 32 ; I, v, p. 537. **anavo-*, cf. Welsh *anau*, harmony. D'Arbois, **CCCI,**, ii, p. 159.
[6] Much, **CCCLXI,** lxv, 149 ; further east, is another cemetery in the Val Sugana (v. Duhn, in Ebert, s.v. " Kelten ", i, p. 295). The last Gallic cemetery on the Venetian side is that of Pavigliano Vennese (**CXII,** 1880, pp. 236 ff.).
[7] D'Arbois, **CCXCIX,** p. 143. Cf. Trumpilini, in an inscription from La Turbie (**I,** v, 7817), and Stoeni, in Pliny, iii, 134 ; **I,** i, p. 460 (117 B.C.) ; cf. Holder, **CCVII,** s.v. " Stoeni ".

whose existence and defeat are recorded by the monument at La Turbie. There were also the Ligures Stoeni, who have left their name to the village of Stenico, in the upper valley of the Sarca.

The western edge of the Gallic domain in Italy presents a similar spectacle. The ethnography of the region must have been so entangled as to involve the ancient writers in mistakes without end. Cato seems to have made a serious effort in his *Origins* to establish the identity of the peoples in those parts on the strength of the information at his disposal. The result is that he describes the Vertamocori and the Salluvii, whom we have good reason to call Celtic, as Ligurians.[1] The Gallic peoples of the north of Piedmont were evidently not to be compared to the consolidated peoples of Lombardy and Emilia. We must imagine them as mixed up with Ligurians, Gallic villages standing next to Ligurian villages and inter-marriage going on between the two sides. The races of the mountain districts must have been equally intermixed. Switzerland is the proof of it, and, still better, Upper Piedmont, with its history, its dialect, and its French villages on the Italian slopes of the Matterhorn separated from French-speaking Switzerland by a wide belt of German Swiss.

So we can see how it was that people like the Bagicuni in the neighbourhood of Cueno, whom all the historians agree in calling Ligurian, could be regarded as descendants of the Caturiges,[2] who were Gauls. Associations of all kinds grew up, for which we can lay down no rules. But on the whole the Ligurian was on top, or rather he was all round. Later on the Gallic peoples of the mountains—Centrones, Medulli, Caturiges—were comprised in the Ligurian kingdom of Cottius.[3] But, though politically incorporated by the Ligurians, the Celtic colonies of Piedmont faithfully preserved their language, as is shown by inscriptions,[4] of which some at least are not very ancient, and by certain features of their civilization, long after the Romans had destroyed the Gallic organization of the Milanese and Emilia. They even made their neighbours accept them. In short, it does not seem

[1] Pliny, iii, 124.
[2] Pliny, iii, 47, 135 ; Ptol., iii, 1, 31. Cf. d'Arbois, in **CXL,** xi, p. 154.
[3] Müllenhoff, **CCCLXII,** ii, p. 249.
[4] Inscriptions from Briona and Ornavasso (Rhys, **VI,** p. 47).

that there was any conquest or attempt at conquest on the
part of the Ligurians. There was certainly association, whatever the causes may have been.

North of the Insubres, in the Como district, similar
formations were organized, whose sway extended up to
the Ligurians of the Euganean country. In this region,
cemeteries and single tombs have been excavated at Introbbio,
Civiglio, Soldo, Legnano, Esino, and Pianezzo.[1] These the
archæologists generally describe as Gallo-Ligurian, perhaps
because most of the tombs contain cremations. Funerary
stelæ have also been found here, at Rondineto, Algate,
Civiglio, and Cernusco Asinario, and *graffiti* containing
Celtic names on the bottoms of vases, for instance at
Ornavasso and Giubiasco. But as a whole, those so-called
Lepontian inscriptions are probably not Celtic ; they belong
to a dialect which has a touch of Italic in it, and may be
Ligurian, or perhaps stands in the same relation to Italic
as Macedonian to Greek.[2]

South of the Po the Ligurians extended to Etruria.
There is nothing after the great invasion like the little colony
which left the cippi of the Vara behind it. But the boundary
may have been vague. Among the Ananes there was a
town named Comillomagus, now Broni.[3] This is certainly
a Gallic name. But the westernmost of the cemeteries
representing Gallic civilization which is yet known was found
at Saliceto di San Giuliano, about five miles from Modena.[4]

V

CIVILIZATION OF THE CISALPINE GAULS

In the valley of the Tiber, at Todi, south of Perugia,
a funerary inscription has been found, in Latin and Celtic,
in honour of one Ategnatos, son of Druteos.[5] It is the

---

[1] Montelius, **DXXXIV**, pls. 63–5 ; Castelfranco, in **LIII**, 1886, p. 184;
A. Magni, in *Rev. archeol. della prov.-di Como*, 1907, pp. 3 ff. (Liguro-Gallic
cemetery at Pianezzo).

[2] H. Pedersen, in **CXVI**, 1921, pp. 38–54 ; cf. Vendryès, in **CXL**, 1923,
491 ; v. Duhn, in Ebert, **CCCXXIII**, s.v. " Kelten ", vi, p. 287. On the
other hand, Pokorny declares that these inscriptions are Celtic (ibid., 136–8).
Cf. Philipon, **CCCLXIX**, pp. 136–8.

[3] Nissen, **DXXXVII**, ii, 1, p. 271.

[4] **LIII**, 1876, p. 30 ; 1886, p. 159 ; 1888, p. 40.

[5] Dottin, **CXCVI**, p. 153, No. 17 *bis* ; cf. *Rise*, p. 38, n. 9.

southernmost of the Celtic inscriptions and it stood well inside Umbria, far north of the Latin territory. The Celtic domain certainly did not reach so far as that.[1] It may be a relic of a Celtic expedition like the tombs of Canossa, or it may merely record the fact that a Gallic family came and settled here at an early date, before Rome encroached on the conquests of the Gauls in her work of uniting Italy. But why is the inscription in two languages, and why is one of them Latin ? It gives us a glimpse of the kind of society formed by the invaders together with the aborigines. Each side stood its ground and kept its language, but they did not ignore one another, or keep themselves to themselves. This is not the grim picture of the Gallic wars which Livy gives us. Besides, even in that picture we can see some features of policy and social life which correct it.

The same story is told by the tombs of the Senones [2] found at Montefortino, Filottrano, Ripa Bianca, and elsewhere. They are surprisingly wealthy. They are full of gold in two forms—purely Gallic ornaments and Etruscan ornaments. The Gallic ornaments are rings and buffer-torques, recalling those of the Rhine valley. The Etruscan ornaments are crowns of gold foliage, collars with pendants shaped like eggs or amphoræ, of a well-known type, and bracelets ending in snakes' heads. It has been said that, if the Senones took home the thousand pounds of gold which formed the ransom of the Capitol, the wives and daughters of their chieftains must have been richly arrayed. But there are not only articles of adornment to speak of their wealth. There are ivory boxes, bronze vases with richly decorated handles and feet, and painted Attic pottery. The whole points to a taste no less refined than that of the contemporary peoples of Campania and Etruria. Moreover, the Senones copied from the latter the practice of laying in their tombs kitchen utensils, lamps, spits, and lamp-stands, which were unknown to the great majority of Gauls. The men took with them to their graves strigils, which prove that they had adopted the fashion of rubbing themselves with oil. They kept their own swords and spears ; but the helmets were Italic, and, it seems, they were beginning, under the influence

---

[1] Cf. d'Arbois, **CCXCIX**, p. 4.
[2] See above, p. 15 ; Déchelette, pp. 1088, 1181.

of their neighbours, to give up the war-chariot with which they had descended upon Italy. In short, they had fallen, or were falling, into line with the peoples all round them, they had adopted their manners, because they had dealings with them, and in less than fifty years they had ceased to appear, in their new colony, as wild and terrifying savages. The first generation of Gauls born in Italy was doubtless quite as much Italian as Gallic.

The Gallic cemeteries round about Bologna likewise testify to such extensive borrowing from the civilization of the conquered that one may ask whether the Gauls were there as besiegers or as neighbours and allies.[1]

Besides, they had, in the course of the long succession of wars which we usually have in our minds, long periods of peace. Polybios mentions a period of thirty years between 329 and 299, and one of twelve between 347 and 335.[2] The archæologists of Ancona were led to seek for Gallic tombs by the discovery of open settlements situated on the terraces of the Marche.[3]

We find the same kind of relations with the Veneti of Este. The Gauls were not far from the town ; no doubt they came into it, but without hostile intent. They took service as mercenaries, they came as visitors, perhaps they worshipped in the temples ; in any case, they were known in the place and attention was paid to them. In the ruins of the temple of the goddess Rehtra, among the votive statuettes, there is one representing a Gallic warrior with a belt and a La Tène sword slung on his right. Another statuette represents a Gaul with a dagger or short sword stuck in his belt on the right. These are votive offerings which may have been dedicated by Gallic visitors. A fragment of a stamped plaque shows a horseman with a La Tène shield. Lastly, in the same area brooches of La Tène Ic have been found.[4]

There were individuals with Celtic names at Este. One of those names is recognizable in its Venetian transcription Verconzarna.[5] If we suppose that the Etruscan z is equivalent

---

[1] See above, p. 15. Cf. v. Duhn, in Ebert, **CCCXXIV**, s.v. " Kelten ".
[2] Polyb., ii, 19.
[3] Déchelette, ii, 3, p. 1091, n. 2.
[4] Montelius, **DXXXIV**, pls. 61, 4 ; 60, 5.
[5] Rhys, **CCXXX**, 38.

to the Gallic d,[1] we get Vercondarna, which falls into the class of Celtic names which includes Vercondaridubnus, Tarcondarius, etc. It is composed of the preposition *ver-* (= ὑπέρ) and an adjective [2] related to the Welsh substantive *cyndared* " rage ", and the adjective *cynddeiriawg* " enraged ". Vercondarna is a feminine name, for all its warlike meaning. It probably tells us of mixed marriages between Venetian men and Gallic women, and there must also have been marriages between Venetian women and Gallic men, and that just about the date at which we have halted.[3]

The cultural exchanges to which this intercourse led were chiefly to the advantage of the Gauls, but not entirely so.

In the common vocabulary of the Italic and Celtic languages, there is not only the residue of an old undivided stock ; there are words borrowed by one side or the other. Some of those borrowings are ancient, and seem to date from the time when the Italic peoples, and the Latins in particular, found themselves face to face with the Celts. What is more, it was the Latins who borrowed from the Gauls.

It is generally accepted to-day that the Latin word *gladius* " sword " is of Celtic origin.[4] The Latin grammarians knew that it had once had the form *cladius*, and accordingly they derived it from *clades*.[5] It comes from a word which must in Gaulish have been **kladios*, which is represented by Welsh *cleddyf*, from which comes Irish *claideb*. The ancient historians tell us that the Romans subsequently adopted the sword of the Celtiberians, which had the advantage of being equally useful for cutting and thrusting. But it is hard to make the adoption of the word *gladius* as late as the time when the Roman armies were operating in Spain. Besides, the hypothetical word **kladios* does not seem very appropriate for a thrusting weapon. It has the same root as κλάδος,

---

[1] See *Rise*, p. 265.

[2] For the suffix *n*, see Dottin, **CXCVI**, iii ; cf. Marstrander, in **CLXXI**, 1910, p. 378.

[3] Gallic names survived in Venetia ; e.g. (**I**, v, 8740), at Concordia, near Portoginaro, north-east of Venice, ILATEUTA, with which compare Welsh Elltud. Rhys, **CCXXX**, p. 15.

[4] Vendryès, in **CLXXXIII**, p. 309. The *kl* of the Celtic word became *gl* in Latin. There are other examples of this mutation, such as the word *gloria*, which comes from a form *klouesia* and is related to Greek κλέος (κλέϜος). Cf. κυβερνᾶν, *gubernare*. The transformation had taken place in the second century (cf. *Miles Gloriosus*).

[5] Varro.

meaning " stick ", Old Slavonic *kladivo*, which means
" hammer ", and perhaps κόλαφος, meaning " blow ". The
root *kela* or *kla* seems to have meant striking so as to split,
and not so as to pierce. The word well fits the weapon into
which the La Tène sword was tending to develop. Derived
from the dagger, it was becoming a weapon intended for
delivering great cutting blows. In spite of the poor opinion
which Livy and Polybios had of the weapons of the Gauls,[1]
it is probable that the Roman troops, though better organized
and better led than the Gallic, had not really good arms
and readily changed them.[2]

The Gauls also had a better shield than the Italic troops,
and one which covered them better. It is probable that the
Latins adopted it, and with it the word *scutum*.[3] Attempts
have been made to explain this word by *obscurus*, or by
cūtis ; it covers and hides, or it is made of skin. Welsh and
Irish have the words *ysgwyd* and *sciath* respectively, meaning
both " shield " and " shoulder ". The semantic derivation
of the meaning is quite clear in Celtic, but is absent in Latin.
It is to be noted that *scutum* is specially used for a large tall
shield. Livy contrasts the Celtic *scutum* of the heavy infantry
of the Celtiberians with the Iberian *caitra*, the round target
of their light infantry.[4] This contrast is repeated. The
Celtic origin of the word *scutum* is therefore probable. The
large shield of the Roman infantry is not unlike the La Tène
shield. What is more, the innovation is ascribed to Camillus.[5]

Another borrowed word, of a different kind, is *vates*.[6]
This word stands alone in Latin. Its close similarity to
Irish *faith*,[7] which has exactly the same meaning, Cæsar's
use of it to designate the men who in Gaul had exactly the
position of the *faith* in Ireland, and Strabo's transcription
οὐάτεις with the same meaning, all show that the word was

[1] Polyb., ii, 33 ; Livy, xxii, 46 ; S. Reinach, in **XV**, 1906, p. 344.
[2] The word *lancea* was admittedly borrowed, apparently from Spain
(Diod., v, 30 ; Aul. Gell., xv, 31, following Varro). Cf. Déchelette, ii, 3,
p. 1150. Middle Irish *do-lecim*, I throw, has been compared to Irish *laigen*,
Welsh *llain*. Walde, **CCXLIII**, s.v. The word fits the all-iron javelin found
in tombs in the Pyrenees and at Hallstatt. Cf. A. J. Reinach, in **CXXXVIII**,
1907, i, pp. 243, 426 ; ii, pp. 125, 225–6.
[3] Walde, **CCXLIII**, s.v.
[4] Livy, viii, 8.
[5] Plut., *Cam.*, 40. Cf. Dion. Hal., xiv, 9 ; Polyb., vii, 7, 2. See Reinecke,
CCCCVI, p. 10.
[6] Walde, **CCXLIII**, s.v. ; Strabo, iv, 4, 4.
[7] Dottin, **CXCVI**, p. 115.

borrowed and that it kept its special sense. When we read the story of the Gallic wars in Livy or Justin, we find that the barbarians appeared to the Latins, who themselves were pious folk and much given to divination, as superstitious in the extreme. If we suppose that the Cisalpine Gauls had the two castes or colleges of the Druids and the *vates*, and that these latter had the same function, social, political, and religious, as they have in the Irish epics, having a finger in every pie, and being always ready to produce a poem to meet the occasion—satire, war-song, or prophecy—or to interpret in inspired verse all the circumstances which were perturbing their audiences, the presence of the inspired bard in the ranks of their adversaries must certainly have appeared a novelty to the Romans. If the name *vates* really comes from Celtic, it is because there were such bards in Cisalpine Gaul. It is interesting evidence on the history of Druidism, for the word must have been borrowed fairly soon to have passed into common use. It can only have been learned in Italy or Spain, and Italy is the more likely. The Celts have been and still are great versifiers, great lovers of songs and poetry. They certainly were so at that time.

That the Romans benefited by the imagination of the Gallic poets is very possible. The story of the Gallic wars, out of which Livy, a historian of genius gifted with the spirit of divination, has made a very remarkable historical work, is something quite by itself, rather fabulous and very epic. Monsieur Jullian has suggested that the tradition was probably made up of Celtic epics.[1] The well-known story of Valerius Corvus,[2] who was rescued in single combat with a Gallic chief by a crow which pecked the Celt's face and hid the Roman from him with its wings, is an example. The episode is unlike anything else in Roman history and literature. But it is like a famous episode in the great Irish epic of Ulster, the *Táin Bó Chuailgné*,[3] in which the goddess Morrigu attacks Cuchulainn, who has scorned her love, in the form of a crow. The crow is not a mere flight of fancy ;

[1] Jullian, **CCCXLVII**, i, p. 294.

[2] Livy, vii, 26 (the campaign of 345) ; Dio Cass., fr. 34. The interpretation suggested above was put forward in my lecture at the École des Hautes-Études.

[3] A similar episode is represented on one of the decorated faces of an Etruscan alabaster vase in the Florence Museum, among scenes of the Trojan War, although it is foreign to that tradition. Milani, **DXXXIII**, ii.

it is the creature which stands for battle and the gods and goddesses of war. The story of Valerius Corvus came down from the family tradition of the Gens Valeria to Fabius Pictor, from whom Livy got it ; but how did it come in ? Some Valerius must have .had dealings with the Gauls, or at any rate a kind of international tradition of those heroic wars must have tended to accumulate.

These separate facts suggest a picture of the little world in which the Gauls of Italy played their part, and give an idea of what they had brought to it and what they had got from it. But the chief novelty which then appeared in the Celtic communities of Italy was of another kind. The small Italian cities of Etruria, Umbria, Samnium, Latium, and Campania were highly developed societies. They had their internal politics, which were party politics, with constitutional problems, of the queerest kind but quite definitely envisaged. The problems were the same as in the Greek cities, but they had been raised and studied, particularly in the Greek colonies of the south of Italy, by Pythagoras and his school. The Italian cities also had a foreign policy with a programme, far-sighted plans, systems of alliance, and even conflicting systems. In all this the Gauls suddenly found themselves involved. When we pass from the story of Ambicatus to the chapter in which Polybios (ii, 19) sums up the events which occurred from 299 onwards, we are in another world. We pass from the world of the tribe to that of the state. In 390 the Gauls attack Etruscans and Latins without distinction. They rush blindly forward and cause their enemies to unite to meet the common danger. A hundred years later most of them have selected their opponent. It is Rome. They enter into alliance with her enemies. They are probably led more then they lead ; but they use diplomatic methods, they have a policy.

In coming into relations with the Italian cities, the Gauls entered the history of the world, and they never fell out of it. We shall see them again once or twice acting in their old character of barbarous hordes rushing to the conquest of fertile lands. But they had learnt to play their game in the manner of the Mediterranean cities, and little by little they all took to it.

The settlement of a large colony of Gauls in Italy had

more effect on the Celtic world as a whole than to attract
new bands of invaders at intervals. In material civilization
there is every evidence that between the beginning of the
La Tène period and its last phase new crafts were acquired,
such as glass-working, the stock of tools was increased,
and habits of life, methods of construction, domestic arrangements, and ideas of comfort were transformed. In all this,
imitation of the Italic peoples and the Greeks was certainly
the chief factor. The civilization of La Tène was affected
by the economic progress of the world in general. But in
the present state of our archæological knowledge we cannot
follow the order of these facts in detail.

VI

THE EARLIEST GALLIC SETTLEMENTS IN THE EASTERN ALPS
AND ON THE MIDDLE DANUBE

The Celts expanded in the same period in other directions
as well as into Italy. If the Gauls did not enter that country
by the Danube valley, it does not follow that they made
no advance on that side. They had come there as early as
the beginning of the fifth century. When the Romans found
it necessary to pay attention to what was going on beyond
the Alps, they found Celts in Noricum (Austria) and Pannonia
(Western Hungary).[1] The Carni, who were in the Alps
between the Drave, Istria, the Adriatic, and the Tagliamento,
were Celts.[2] Behind them, a whole new Celtic world reached
as far as the Black Sea. But when did those settlements
begin ?

The tradition used by Livy tells of an expedition, the
counterpart of that of Bellovesus, led by his cousin Sigovesus
into the Hercynian Forest, which had long been occupied
by the Celts but was certainly not the limit of their advance.
Justin's summary is more detailed.[3] According to him, one
part of the Gallic *ver sacrum* made for Illyria *ducibus avibus*,
guided by birds, " for the Gauls are pre-eminent in the augur's
art." The adventurers settled in Pannonia, " had various

---

[1] See *Rise*, pp. 272 ff.
[2] I, i, p. 460 ; Holder, CCVII, s.v.
[3] Justin, xxiv, 4.

wars with their neighbours which lasted long, and at last reached Greece and Macedonia, overthrowing everything before them." It is an excellent summary of the facts, except that it mentions no interval between the Illyrian wars of the Gauls and their descent on Delphi.

But for a long time yet the Raeti on the one hand and the Veneti on the other remained in the Central Alps and the north-eastern corner of Italy, forming a broad, continuous belt between the Cisalpine Celts and those of the valley of the Danube ; on the Italian side the enclave of the Trentino bit into it but did not pierce it. In 350 there is no question yet of the Carni between the Veneti and Istria. The Veneti march with the Istri, and these latter extend to the Danube.[1]

But about the same time, the Gauls had already come into collision with the Illyrian people of the Ardiaei or Vardaei, which touched the Dalmatian coast opposite the islands of Pharos and Corcyra Nigra (Lesina and Curzola) somewhere near the mouth of the Naron (Narenta). This incident was related by Theopompos, who died in 306.[2]

More serious and more fruitful in results was their encounter with the Antariatae.[3] These seem to have been at that time the predominant people among the Illyrians. At the time of the *Periplus* of Scylax, the Antariatae reached down to the Dalmatian coast at the mouth of the Narenta.[4] They were at constant war with the Vardaei for the possession of the salt-deposits of the upper valley of that river. Inland, they extended to Bulgaria, for they had evicted the Triballi from the valley of the Morava. How far north they went at this date it is hard to say. Their eponymous hero, Antaricos, son of Illyrios, was the father of Pannonios.[5] In any case, they were a very large people and seem to have been then at the height of their military power. They had used it

---

[1] Ps.-Scylax, p. 20.

[2] Theompomp., fr. 41 ; Athen., x, 60 ; d'Arbois, **CCCI**, i, p. 305 ; id., **CCXCIX**, p. 118 ; Schulten, **DXIX**, p. 93.

[3] Or Autariatæ. Antariatae seems to be more correct. The particle *an* is a formative of racial names in Albanian, and there seems to be little doubt that the Albanians are the direct descendants of the ancient Illyrians. The Antariatae are the men of the Tara, a tributary of the Drina, which separates Montenegro from the former Sanjak of Novi-Bazar. Their capital was Tariona (Pliny, iii, 26). Cf. Fischer, in **CLXIX**, 1911, p. 3 ; Baron Nopsca, ibid., p. 913 ; d'Arbois, **CCXCIX**, p. 118 ; Strabo, viii, 5, 11.

[4] Ps.-Scylax, 25.

[5] D'Arbois, **CCCI**, i, p. 303 ; Dottin, p. 152.

against the Macedonians.   In 393 the Illyrians, that is to
say the Antariatae, had driven Amyntas II, the father of
Philip, from the throne and had then made him pay them
tribute.   In 359, Bardulis, King of the Illyrians, utterly
defeated the army of Perdiccas III, Philip's brother, who
lost his life in the battle.   Philip, becoming king, made a
vigorous effort, drove the Illyrian garrisons out of the towns
of Macedonia, and defeated the Antariatae.

It is probable that the Celts came into his political
schemes,[1] but not without payment ;   this would explain
the abundance of coins of Philip found among the Celts of
the Danube.   The defeated Illyrians became disturbed again
in 335, after the accession of Alexander the Great. We may
suppose that the Celts, whose ambassadors appeared at his
court when he was on his Danubian campaign, kept the
Antariatae occupied while he tackled the Thracians.   The
historian of these events, Arrian, who used the " memoirs "
of an eye-witness, Ptolemy, son of Lagos, tells us that these
Celts lived on the Ionic Gulf.[2] Were they the Celts of Italy ?
These have left no Macedonian coins. Did they come on to
the Adriatic north of the Veneti ? Arrian's language is vague,
and doubtless only testifies to the great place that the Celts
of Italy had in the world of that day. Celtic envoys crossed
Asia in 324 to pay their court to Alexander in Babylon.[3] When
the Antariatae caused the Macedonians anxiety, the Celts
kept the former quiet, to their own advantage.

Now, all of a sudden, in 310, the Antariatae were seized
with panic and began to flee in masses.[4] The event appeared
so extraordinary· that historians had recourse to absurd
prodigies to explain it. What had happened was an invasion
of large numbers of Celts, led by a chief named Molistomos.
The flying Antariatae ran into the Macedonians. Cassander
planted some 20,000 on his frontier as military settlers.[5]
Others established themselves among the Veneti and among
the other peoples of the Dalmatian coast.

This fact suggests that the Celtic attack on the Antariatae
at a certain moment assumed the character of a sudden

---

[1] D'Arbois, **CCCI**, ii, p. 314.
[2] See *Rise*, p. 5.
[3] Diod., xvii, 113, 2 ; Arr., *Anab.*, vii, 15, 4.
[4] App. *Illyr.*, 4.   Tomascek, in Pauly and Wissowa, s.v. " Autariatai ".
[5] Diod., xx, 19.

cataclysm, and that the original positions of the two peoples
had not been perceptibly altered before then. The Italian
settlement of the Celts had for a long time lain very much
in front of the Celtic frontiers, being flanked right and left
by Ligurians and Illyrians. North of the Illyrians, other Celts
had advanced by the Danube, filtering in among the Illyrian
inhabitants. But they do not appear in large and irresistible
numbers until the end of the fourth century. That, if one is
to trust the historians, is the position in the south-eastern
part of the Celtic world during the fourth century.

Examination of the archæological finds does not contradict
this view.

It is impossible that the Celts should have arrived in
the middle valley of the Danube in the Hallstatt period.[1]
The Negau helmets are isolated, or rather, apart from the
inscription, they only appear in association with objects
which are not Celtic.[2] Celtic civilization, and the Celts with
it, gained ground in the first period of La Tène, but more
probably at the end of that phase than at the beginning.[3]

La Tène finds in Upper and Lower Austria are
unfortunately scanty, and do not furnish the answer to our
question.[4] On the other hand, the cemetery of Hallstatt
itself has yielded an object which, though only one, is of
very great importance. It is a La Tène sword with a scabbard
of engraved bronze.[5] The chape is of the type of La Tène I
in appearance but without open-work, and the manner in
which the decorated surface is divided into compartments
recalls the transverse bars with which the scabbards of
La Tène II are strengthened. On the central part of the
scabbard [6] three foot-soldiers are engraved, carrying a spear
on the shoulder, wearing no helmet, and holding a large
oval shield with a central ridge of the Gallic type. Behind
the foot-soldiers are four horsemen, advancing with spear
couched, wearing a cap to protect the head and, apparently,
body-armour. The second seems to have struck with his
spear a foot-soldier, who is lying on his back. On each side

[1] Cf. Hoernes, in **CXXX**, 1888, p. 333.
[2] See *Rise*, pp. 272 ff. Cf. Reinecke, **CCCCVI**, pp. 5–6.
[3] Reinecke, op. cit., p. 9. The La Tène civilization extended into
Transylvania, perhaps from the La Tène period itself (ibid., n. 27).
[4] Déchelette, ii, 3, p. 1081 ; Lindenschmit, **CCCXCIX**, v, p. 284, n. 1.
[5] Ibid., iv, pl. 32 ; Déchelette, ii, 2, p. 770.
[6] See *Rise*, fig. 19.

of these figures is the same scene, of two persons clad in a long-skirted coat and tight striped hose, holding a wheel in their hands. On the chape is a partially serpentine creature struggling with a fallen man. This object is unique, and the art which it represents is very different from the art of La Tène. The costumes are without parallel. On the other hand, the procession of warriors recalls those on the Italic and Venetian buckets. The wheel, doubtless solar, with its two supporters, recalls a motive familiar to the art of Villanova. In fact, this sword from Hallstatt stands not so much for a replacement of Illyrian civilization by Celtic civilization as for the mixed culture which may have been the result of the contact of the two peoples.

There are a certain number of cemeteries in Carinthia and the valley of the Isonzo containing Celtic objects,[1] at Watsch, at Sankt-Michael near Adelsberg, at Nassenfus, at Vital near Prozoz in Croatia, at Idria near Bača in the province of Gorizia. The Celtic objects are isolated, as at Watsch, or late, belonging to La Tène II, as at Sankt-Michael. They are found mixed with Certosa brooches and even with Villanovan brooches which have survived so long.

The cemetery of Idria might have been the successor to the neighbouring cemetery of Santa Lucia.[2] The latter suddenly ceases to be used when the former becomes important. The native town to which the cemetery of Santa Lucia belonged was doubtless destroyed. The population fled. Strangers came and took up their abode elsewhere. But were these Celts ? Inscriptions have been found in the cemetery of Idria, and they are not Celtic. We cannot argue from these facts that the Celts began to advance in Friuli at the time when they were making that concentration in the north of Bosnia which caused the Antariatae to leave their homes.

There was the same activity at that time all round the skirts of the Celtic world. The Celtic colonization of Britain was approaching completion. Fresh tribes of Gauls were making their way to the Garonne, where the Iberians held them. Later we shall examine, as a whole, for a longer period, what was going on on the Germanic side.

---

[1] Déchelette, ii, 3, p. 1098.
[2] Szombathy, in **CIV**, i, p. 318 ; G. Cumin, 1915, p. 219.

CHAPTER II

THE CELTS IN THE EAST

I

THE GAULS IN THE BALKAN PENINSULA

WE have come to the neighbourhood of the year 300 B.C. At this date, the development of the civilization of La Tène takes a turn which has long been noted by archæologists, who have marked it by a new period, La Tène II. We shall again see, all round the fringes of the Celtic world, movements similar to those which in the sixth century took the Celts to the British Isles, Spain, and Italy, and at the end of the fifth took them to Provence, Italy, the Danube valley, and again to Britain. We shall see them spreading and wandering about in the East, establishing themselves strongly in the valley of the Danube ; new bands descending on Italy and Spain, and others reaching Britain and Ireland. A new group of Celtic tribes takes part in those expeditions or directs them.

When the power of the Antariatae was destroyed, the conquerors camped in their place, probably in the valley of the Morava, whence they threatened Thrace, Macedon, and Greece at once, for they did not settle down at first ; they remained on the move and no doubt received new contingents, perhaps summoning them.[1] These great movements of tribes never stop all at once. Besides, if the Gauls were looking for a settled abode, they could do better than in the present Serbia.

In 298 a body of them advanced as far as Bulgaria. They came up against the Macedonians, and were defeated by Cassander on the slopes of Haemos.[2] A little later a second body, led by one Cambaules, seems to have reached Thrace.[3] In 281, the death of Lysimachos and Seleucos and

---

[1] For Brennus's propaganda for the expedition of 279, see Paus., x, 19 ; Polyaen., *Strat.*, vii, 35 ; Thierry, **CCCLXXXVIII**, i, p. 226.
[2] Jouguet, **DXLIV**, English, p. 176.
[3] Paus., x, 19.

the ensuing prolongation of the dynastic war and the dis-
organization of the Macedonian kingdom weakened the
obstacle which still held the Gauls in check. They saw this,
and seized their opportunity.

We are told that they resumed their advance in 260,
in three armies.[1] The eastern army, commanded by
Cerethrios, attacked the Triballi on the Bulgarian side.
The western army, crossing Illyria, must have entered
Macedonia somewhere near Monastir; it was preceded by
envoys.[2] Ptolemy Ceraunos, who, after betraying and killing
Seleucos, was at the time King of Macedon, refused to listen
to them. He was utterly defeated and slain. This army was
led by a chieftain called Bolgios, whose name we must bear
in mind.[3] Historical tradition, which dates from the time of
the actual events, records that he crowned his victory by
sacrificing prisoners.[4] The Macedonian army was scattered
and the state, lacking its head, appeared to be destroyed.
The Gauls ranged over the country, looting. Little by little,
the Macedonians rallied [5] and by well-conducted warfare on
a small scale compelled them to retire behind the mountains.

The central army, commanded by Brennus and
Acichorius,[6] had advanced on Paeonia and had to fight
throughout the year with the hillmen of Haemos. It did not
descend on Macedon until the following year, after it had
received large reinforcements, including Illyrian contingents.[7]
It was a large host, reckoned by the historians at 150,000
foot and 15,000 or 20,000 horse. Each horseman was accompanied by two mounted servants, the body of three being
called a *trimarkisia*. We should note this appearance of
cavalry in the Gallic forces. The army seems to have been
fairly well organized and skilfully led.[8] In the eighty years

---

[1] Jouguet, **DXLIV**, English, p. 178. Thierry, op. cit., i, pp. 221 ff. ;
Stähelin, **DLIV**, p. 2 ; Jullian, **CCCXLVII**, i, p. 300 ; Dottin, **CCCXXII**, p. 316 ;
Justin, xxiv, 5–8 ; Paus., i, 4 ; x, 19 ; Diod., xxii, 9. These writers' accounts
are derived from common sources, among which we must reckon the history
of Hieronymos of Cardia, who lived at the time of the events ; cf. d'Arbois,
CCXLVIII, xii, pp. 81 ff. ; Jullian, op. cit., i, p. 301, n. 5. Was there a Gallic
tradition in this ? See ibid., and F. P. Garofalo, in **CXXXV**, xiii, p. 456.

[2] Just., xxiv, 5, 1.

[3] See below, p. 67.

[4] Diod., xxxi, 13.

[5] Under Sosthenes ; Just., xxiv, 5, 12–13.

[6] Diodoros calls him Cichorios.

[7] Particularly the Antariatae ; App., *Illyr.*, 4.

[8] Especially in the crossing of the Spercheios ; Paus., loc. cit.

or so that the Gauls had been serving as mercenaries by the side of Greek troops,[1] they had learned something and gained experience. Old trained mercenaries may have rallied to the army of Brennus. At all events, it left a name for resource-fulness and alarming ingenuity.[2] Brennus crushed the re-organized Macedonian army, and then descended into Greece by way of Thessaly. At Thermopylae he was met by a force composed mainly of Athenians.[3] While one body, detached on Ætolia, sacked the town of Callion with appalling savagery,[4] the main force managed to turn the position and came by the gorges of Parnassos to Delphi. The Ætolians and Phocians came to the rescue of the god, and the Gauls had to retire to Thessaly.

The Phocians owed something to Apollo, for they had looted Delphi some seventy years before in the course of the second Sacred War, and had come away with consider-able sums. They had not, therefore, left much for the Gauls to take, except the statues. Nevertheless, the gold of Delphi has passed into legend.[5] In the great Gallic army there was a body of Tectosages, and the report went about that this treasure had been taken to Toulouse, to other Tectosages, who had migrated there from the same original home. A dark story grew up about this act of pillage and the problematical and accursed gold. The legend-mongers seized upon the sacrilege and gave Brennus a lasting reputation for impiety [6] which placed him on a level with the other Brennus, him of Rome and the Capitol.

Art did its share. This campaign of Brennus was commemorated in monuments. The battle of Thermopylae was depicted on a wall-painting in the council-chamber of Athens.[7] But there were also representations of the sack of Delphi, which were to be seen in various temples of Apollo in Greece and Italy, at Delos, and even in Rome, where, according to Propertius,[8] one of the ivory-plated doors of

---

[1] Jullian, op. cit., i, pp. 324 ff.
[2] Polyaen., *Strat.*, iv, 8 ; vi, 35, 42.
[3] Paus., i, 3, 4 ; x, 19. For the shield of young Cydias, cf. d'Arbois, **CCCI**, ii, p. 398.
[4] The Oatrians came to the assistance of Callion, and were completely defeated ; Paus., x, 22, 6 ; Cavaignac, **CCCX**, iii, p. 44.
[5] Just., xxxii, 3.
[6] Diod., xxii, 10.
[7] Paus., i, 3, 4 ; A. J. Reinach, in **CVII**, 21, p. 192.
[8] Prop., ii, 31, 3.

the temple of the Palatine showed *dejectos Parnassi vertice Gallos*, "the Gauls thrown down from the height of Parnassos," forming a pendant to the story of the Children of Niobe. The whole affair was one of the triumphs of Apollo. One or more of these commemorative monuments furnished motives to the minor arts of Greece or Alexandria. One portrayed a Gaul setting his foot on the cut-off head of the Pythia,[1] another showed Gauls gesticulating against a background of colonnades.[2]

It is certain that the Greeks thought of the Gauls as beautiful. The figure of Brennus in particular has benefited by their æsthetic indulgence. The story ran that Brennus had received three wounds from Apollo's own hand. He gave the order to retreat, and had the strength to lead his men through the gorges of Parnassos to join up with the rearguard of Acichorius, who had remained at Heracleia. He might have recovered, but he felt that he was condemned and determined to die. He got drunk and killed himself. A marvellous little bronze in the Naples museum (a replica) apparently represents the suicide of Brennus.[3]

Although the attack on Delphi did not last long, Central Greece was sufficiently disturbed for the celebration of the Panathenaea to be suspended in 278.[4] The Gallic army retired more or less in good order.[5] We find one section of it in Thrace, in the neighbourhood of Byzantion; it surprised Lysimacheia [6] at the root of the Gallipoli peninsula. Antigonos Gonatas drove the Gauls out of the place in a battle in which he surprised them while pillaging his camp, which he had abandoned to them.[7] This affair took place in 277.

After this victory, Antigonos seems to have taken into his service the force of Ciderios, and perhaps the remnants

[1] e.g. on a medallion from Capua; **CXXXVIII**, 1889, i, p. 198.
[2] On the bottom of a *poculum* from the factory of Cales; ibid.
[3] A. J. Reinach, op. cit., pl. xviii (= Bienkowski, **CCCIX**, fig. 117).
[4] Ibid., p. 187.
[5] According to Justin, xxiv, 8, nothing of it remained. But enough must have remained to take the gold of Delphi to Toulouse.
[6] Livy, xxxviii, 16; Just., xxv, 2; Stähelin, **DLIV**, 5. According to Livy, this was the force of Leonnorios and Lutarios; see below, p. 45. According to Justin, they were troops remaining to guard the country. Polyb., iv, 46.
[7] A. J. Reinach, op. cit., p. 37; Just., xxv, 2; Livy, xxviii, 16. For a painted Galatomachia in Athens, see Reinach, op. cit., p. 187.

of the vanquished, who helped him to take possession of
Macedonia. He still had some of them in 274 when he was
defeated by Pyrrhos, who gloried in the fact that he had
triumphed over them.[1] In 265 a body of Gauls, being ill-
paid, mutinied at Megara, and he put them all to the sword.[2]
But Pyrrhos likewise employed Gauls, whom he allowed to
violate the tombs of the ancient kings of Macedon at Ægae [3] ;
he had them in the attack on Sparta ; he had them again at
Argos when he was killed. Down to the very end of these
Macedonian wars of succession, bands of Gauls left their
dead scattered about Greece [4] in the cause of every party.
No tomb of them has survived. We shall return later to the
amazing story of the mercenaries.

A large part of Brennus's army returned to its starting-
point, under the lead of a chief whose name has come down
to us under the distorted form of Bathanattos,[5] and settled
permanently north of Macedonia between the Shar-Dagh
(Mons Scordus) and the Danube.[6] It doubtless consisted of
bodies of mixed origin. They took a name for themselves
from the country, and became the Scordisci. On the banks
of the Danube they founded or took over a capital,
Singidunum, which is now Belgrade.[7]

Among the Illyrian peoples of the coast of Epeiros,
opposite Corcyra, the ancient geographers mention the
Hylli, who are described in the *Etymologicum Magnum*
as a Celtic people.[8] They may, at least, have been Celticized
by their neighbours the Scordisci. The eastern part of the
new domain of the Scordisci was taken from the Triballi
who were driven out, at least to some extent.[9]

Excavation in Bosnia and Herzegovina has revealed
traces, still too rare, of the passage of the Celts and of Celtic
settlements in these new provinces of the Jugo-Slav
kingdom.[10] We know nothing of Serbia itself.

[1] Plut., *In Pyrrhum*, 26 ; Paus., i, 13 ; Just., xxv, 3.
[2] Trog. Pomp., *Prol.*, xxvi.
[3] Plut., loc. cit. ; Diod., xxii, 12.
[4] Just., xxvi, 2.
[5] Ath., vi, 234 *b*.   The name Bathanattos is supposed to have become
a family-name.
[6] Just., xxxii, pp. 3, 7.   It cannot have been that the Tectosages of
Toulouse returned to their own country.
[7] Ptol., iii, pp. 9, 3.
[8] *Etym. Magn.*, 776, 39 ; Scylax, 23 ; Scymnos of Chios, 404.
[9] App., *Illyr.*, 3 ; Niese, **CCCLXVIII**, p. 618 ; Jullian, op. cit., p. 303.
[10] Patsch, in **CV**, ix, 1904, p. 241.

Another body, which had likewise belonged to Brennus's army, retired on to the slopes of Haemos under a leader named Comantorios.[1] Little by little it gained the upper hand over the Thracian tribes of the vicinity and founded a Celtic kingdom in Thrace, which lasted until 193 B.C. Its capital was Tyle or Tylis, the site of which is difficult to establish. This people expanded south of Haemos to the basin of Adrianople and north of it, no doubt, to the Danube.

At first the proximity of the Gauls of Haemos perturbed the Byzantines.[2] But they showed themselves such good neighbours that they soon dispelled their alarm. They became Hellenized, and struck coins—very fine ones, with the type of Alexander. Some of these coins bear the name of one of their kings, Cauaros.[3] In short, they lived after the manner of the Hellenistic states of the time, and became so civilized that they finally succumbed to the attacks of the Thracians in 193.[4] Of their Celtic civilization, nothing has survived.

So the invaders of the Balkans who had found no room in the over-populated lands of Greece Proper, covered with cities, had carved themselves kingdoms in the north of the peninsula, among people who were less attached to the soil and did not occupy it so completely, in the wider plains of the Morava, Maritza, and Danube. At intervals along the Danube below the Iron Gates were towns with Gallic names —Bononia (Vidin), Ratiaria (Artcher), Durostorum (Silistria), and Noviodunum (? Isakcha) in the Dobrudja—which were outposts of the state of the Scordisci or of the Celtic kingdom of Thrace.

The forces which had formed the nucleus of these tribes had been very much reduced. We may suppose that they received additions, which cannot have increased the Celtic element in them very much, but there remained all round them Illyrians and Thracians, and even Illyrian and Thracian states,[5] and the states which they formed were composed

---

[1] Polyb., iv, 46 ; Trog. Pomp., *Prol.*, 25 ; d'Arbois, **CCXCIX**, p. 5 ; Jullian, op. cit., p. 303, n. 2 ; Just., xxxii, 3, 6.

[2] A heavy tribute was laid on them by Comantorios, and it continued, in a reduced form, into the time of Cauaros ; Pol., loc. cit.

[3] Blanchet, **CCCVI**, p. 466 ; Forrer, **DXLIII** ; Polyb., iv, 52 (219), for Cauaros.

[4] Ibid., viii, 24.

[5] For a Celtic name among those of the Thracian kings, see Forrer, **DXLIII**, p. 203.

of Celto-Illyrians and Celto-Thracians.[1]   I cannot picture
the Scordisci very clearly. But I imagine the State of Haemos
as something like the first Turkish states which were carved
out of the Arabian Empire round a small band of janizaries.
Those states were as good as their chiefs ; they depended
on the prestige of the chief. The kingdom of Thrace, at least,
seems to have had an admirable head—the King Cauaros
mentioned above.

But there is a region of Celtic names and sites, still more
thinly sown, running northwards along the Black Sea.
North of the Danube, in the angle formed by that river and
the Sereth, Ptolemy [2] mentions the Britolagae, whose name
looks Celtic. So does that of the town of Aliobrix. Further
north, on the Dniester (Tyras), there was a Camodunum
(Zaleszczyki in Galicia). Pausanias [3] speaks of a Gallic people,
the Cabari, remarkable for its great stature, which lived
in the far north on the edge of the frozen desert. If his
information is worth considering, it is hereabouts that we
must place them.

Evidence of the activity of the Celts of this region is
given by an inscription from Olbia on the Bug [4] dating from
the third century, when the city was purely Hellenic,
in honour of a citizen named Protogenes, who had distinguished himself when the place was threatened by the
Galatians. These latter had come and attacked it in mid-
winter, with the assistance of the Sciri, a Germanic people
which lived on the Lower Vistula in the first century of the
Roman Empire.

In addition, Gallic objects of La Tène have been found
in Southern Russia, for example in the cemetery of Jarubinetz
on the Dnieper (Government of Kiev).[5] These are, it is true,
quite recent and they may have been brought in by Germans
who had Gallic objects with them. All these facts are
evidence of the advance either of the Celtic kingdom of
Thrace and the groups which had gone about its territory
in search of settlements, or else of the Boii of Bohemia, of

[1] Jullian, op. cit., p. 249, n. 3 ; Strabo, vii, 1, 1. The Ister forms the
northern boundary of the Illyrian and Thracian population, with a certain
number of foreign tribes, some of them Celtic.
[2] Ptol., 3, 10, 7.
[3] i, 35, 5.
[4] Dittemberger, **IV**, 226, 103 ff.
[5] Déchelette, ii, 3, p. 1082.

whose roving spirit we have already seen something. Which-
ever it was, the Celts went as far as the Sea of Azov (Maeotis).
Here the ancient geographers fix the furthest limit of the
Celtic world.[1]

II

THE GALATIANS IN ASIA MINOR

In 278 Nicomedes, King of Bithynia, probably through
the agency of Antigonos Gonatas, summoned into Asia Minor
a body of Celts which may have included some of the men
defeated at Lysimacheia.[2] This body was commanded by
a chief named Leonnorios. It usually operated with another
body, led by one Lutarios. Both seem to have been detached
from the army of Brennus before its descent into Greece,
to repeat in Thrace the pillaging of Acichorius. Lutarios
seized vessels and joined his comrade on the other side of
the Hellespont.[3] A treaty was struck,[4] and for some time
the Galatians, for thus we must henceforward call them,
did good service, duly appreciated, to Nicomedes, or to the
Greek cities allied to him, from which they drove off Antiochos
the Seleucid who was threatening them from a distance.[5]

The two bodies amounted together to about 20,000
persons, 10,000 of whom were men under arms. They were
a difficult host for a petty king of Asia to keep under control.
They left Nicomedes and started working on their own
account, threatening, ravaging, and negotiating to raise
tribute from the terror-stricken cities.[6] We find them at
Troy,[7] at Ephesos, at Miletos. In St. Jerome's day people
still told of the Milesian Virgins, who had killed themselves
to escape outrage and mourned their lot in one of the most
beautiful epigrams in the Palatine Anthology.[8] Here again
the gods had manifested themselves; the River Marsyas

---

[1] Plut., *Mar.*, xi.
[2] Stähelin, " Galatia," in **CCCLXVIII** ; Thierry, **CCCLXXXVII**, i, pp. 255 ff.,
379 ff. ; Jouguet, **DXLIV**, p. 182 ; Jullian, op. cit., i, p. 303 ; d'Arbois,
CCXCIX, p. 195.
[3] Livy, xxxviii, 16. Cf. Just., xxv, 2.
[4] Memnon, 20 ff.
[5] Ibid., 11. Cf. Thierry, op. cit., i, p. 260.
[6] See also Ps.-Plut., *Parall. Min.*, 15, 3096 (following the *Galatika* of
Cleitophon) ; Strabo, xii, 5, 1 ; xiii, 1, 27 ; Durrbach, **V**, 31.
[7] Callim., *Hymn to Artemis*, v, 257.
[8] *Pal. Anthol.*, vii, 492 ; Paus., x, 22, 4 ; St. Jerome, *Agst. Jovinian*, i, 41.

had defended Celaenae with his waters,[1] and Heracles, Hermes, and Apollo had shown the people of Themisonion a cavern where they could take refuge.[2]

There as elsewhere the Gauls looked for a place in which to settle down. When and how they succeeded it is very hard to say. Livy says that they divided Asia between them.[3] One tribe took the Hellespont ; another, Æolis and Ionia ; a third, the south of Asia Minor to the Taurus ; finally, they had established themselves on the River Halys in the centre of the peninsula, to threaten Syria and exact tribute from it. In writing this part of the history of Asia, Livy and the rest of them lacked objectivity, sense of proportion, and, above all, a good map of Asia Minor. Their judgment was led astray by the terror of those who had lived through the invasions and naturally exaggerated the number and power of the destroyers. However prolific they may have been,[4] the 20,000 Gauls, male and female, of Leonnorios and Lutarios were still, a few years after the invasion, only a very small army, which could not hold a country of that size and was lost when it spread itself.

Antiochos Soter defeated them badly about 270.[5] The Gallic cavalry is said to have been crushed by the elephants of the Syrian army. This battle of the elephants was suitably glorified in after years. The memorial was a painting,[6] which must have been exhibited at Pergamon beside the other " Galatomachies ".

It was probably Antiochos Soter who established the Galatians astride of the Halys and on the Phrygian plateau, for he was the lawful ruler of those regions. This was the most sparsely populated part of Asia Minor, the poorest and least desirable, and it is more likely that the Galatians made the best of what they got than that they chose it for themselves. Their settlement on the plateau of Asia Minor has been compared, with some justice, with their settlement on the plateau of Spain.

---

[1] Paus., x, 30, 9.
[2] Paus., x, 32, 4–5.
[3] Livy, loc. cit. ; cf. Just., loc. cit.
[4] Just., loc. cit. : *tantæ fecunditatis inventus fuit.*
[5] Celebrated in verse by Simonides of Magnesia (Suidas, s.v.). There is a paraphrase in Lucian, *Zeuxis or Antiochos*, 9–12.
[6] A. J. Reinach, in **CVII**, xxi, p. 195. Small terra-cotta figures of war elephants are probably derived from this monument.

It was some time before they gave up their wild ways, and the Greek cities had to pay the tax known as *Galatika* (Gaul-Geld) for many years. Moreover, their real military value caused their services to be greatly sought after by one and another of their neighbours. They played a part in the game of Asiatic politics. Their history becomes intermingled with that of the Hellenistic states, and ceases to belong to the general history of the Celts. They took sides in the question of the Bithynian succession ; they warred against the Kings of Pontus and the people of Heracleia ; they fought for the pretender Antiochos Hierax against Seleucos II Callinicos. This last war brought them up against the enemy who worsted them, the little kingdom of Pergamon. Having defeated Seleucos at Ancyra, they were beaten in 241 near the sources of the Caïcos by Attalos of Pergamon, who was backing Seleucos. This victory finally established the power of Attalos, who gained the title of King by it. Between 240 and 230, he again defeated one of the Gallic tribes—the westernmost, the Tolistoagii—four times. These defeats were decisive. The Gauls of Asia were confined to their own country, and hardly came out of it again ; even there they were not always independent, but they remained there.

These victories were gloriously commemorated. In any case, the acropolis of the new capital had to be adorned. Attalos and his successor Eumenes set up monuments which must have formed a single scheme.[1] In the excavation of Pergamon bronze statue-bases have been found on which the name of the sculptor Epigonos appears several times. Pliny mentions three other artists—Phyromachos, Stratonicos, and Antigonos. These men did a piece of work, the remnants of which are magnificent. They treated the Gauls admirably, idealizing them just enough. Of these Pergamene statues there are two certain copies in marble—the Dying Gaul of the Capitol and the Ludovisi group of a Gaul stabbing himself with his own sword after having killed his female

[1] S. Reinach, **CCCLXXV**, pp. 6 ff. ; A. J. Reinach, loc. cit. ; Pliny, 34, 84. The Thusnelda at Florence has sometimes been regarded as coming from the former monument. Cf. Kossinna, **CCCXLV**, 217, pl. xlv, 1. A statue since discovered in Asia Minor, in the walls of Halicarnassos, seems to be an independent work ; it represents a squatting figure, dressed in thick wool, with tight trousers, a belt, apparently of metal, and a cap (G. Karo, in **CII**, 1920, 160, pl. iv).

companion. These are Gauls sure enough, recognizable by
some detail of costume, their ornament, their weapons,
and their type, with the prominent eyebrows, deep-set base
of the nose, and stiff, rebellious hair. But they are also
very noble works of art. These sculptures did not lack
emotion or sympathy; the masterpiece of Epigonos,
according to Pliny, was a dead mother caressed by her
child. The monuments of the victor certainly contributed
to the glory of the vanquished.

On the Acropolis of Athens, Attalos I dedicated another
monument composed of groups representing four subjects—
a battle of Giants, a battle of Amazons, the battle of
Marathon, and the defeat of the Gauls in Mysia. Six statues
of half life-size from the battle of Giants are known, dispersed
between the Louvre and the Venice and Naples museums.[1]
There were also paintings in Pergamon,[2] and some of the
small objects representing Gauls are derived from those
famous works of art.

What we know of the Galatian state gives us our first
example of the organization of a Celtic state.

When they started on their migration, there were two
main bodies and seventeen leaders of bands.[3] Very soon
we find ourselves in the presence of three peoples formed
into twelve groups, four groups to a people—the Tectosages,
the Tolistoagii (or Tolistobogii or Tolistoboii),[4] and the
Trocmi or Trogmi. The Tectosages are probably Volcae;
it is very doubtful that the Tolistoagii or Tolistoboii are
Boii; the Trocmi are not found elsewhere and their name
cannot be explained. The twelve subdivisions are sub-
tribes, similar to the *pagi* which we shall find in Gaul. The
names of a few of them are known—the Teutobodiaci among
the Tectosages and the Voturi, Ambituti, and Tosiopes
among the Tolistoboii.[5] Historians have been misled by
the title of Tetrarch, borne by chiefs of tribes or sub-tribes.
Each of the three peoples, with its four sub-divisions, formed

---

[1] The Vigna Ammendola sarcophagus gives an idea of what this monument
may have been like. S. Reinach, **CCCLXXIII**, i, p. 36 (= Bienkowsky, **CCCV**,
pl. iv).
[2] Cf. **CXXXV**, 1913, p. 392 ; S. Reinach, **CCCLXXVI**, p. 149, n. 4. Attalos
and Nike before a trophy of Gallic arms, on a fresco at Naples.
[3] Memnon, 19 ; Livy, xxxviii, 16.
[4] Stähelin, **DLIV**, p. 42, n. 3.
[5] Pliny, v, 146.

a tetrarchy with proto-tetrarchs.[1] It is an organization,
a typical example of which is furnished by Ireland. Each
sub-tribe was the quarter of a tetrarchy. At its head was
a king (*regulus* or βασιλεύς), assisted by a council of nobles,
who were sometimes also called *reguli*. Ireland presents
just the same arrangement of royalties of different ranks.
For each sub-tribe there was, in addition, a judge (δικαστής)
and a military leader (στρατοφύλαξ) with two lieutenants.
The Celtic constitutions will give us instances of the same
distinction between the judicial, royal, and military
functions.

How was the tribe, the *gens*, *populus*, or *civitas* governed ?
We do not know, but the absence of information seems to
indicate that its rulers were only temporary and chosen by
common agreement among the sub-divisions. But the three
peoples formed a federation, which was exactly translated
under the Roman Empire by the expression κοῖνον Γαλατῶν,
the Commonwealth of the Galatians. It was governed by
a senate composed of the twelve tetrarchs and by an assembly
of three hundred representatives, that is twenty-five representatives to a sub-tribe, who met at the common shrine of
the Galatians, in a place called Drynemeton.[2] The powers
of this assembly seem to have been chiefly judicial. The
general policy of the confederate peoples apparently remained
independent. We always see them developing separately.

There is something artificial in the regularity of this
structure and its numerical symmetry, and indeed it is
probable that the Gauls who were collected together from
the remnants of military bands, sorely tried by the adventure
of Brennus and a succession of wars, bore no resemblance to
organized nations when they arrived in Asia Minor. They
must then have rearranged themselves, like the Scordisci,
on the ideal plan of the Gallic tribe, and we have the good
fortune to know how they did it. The plan was not modified
for the simple reason that the Galatians remained a closed
community. We have proof of this. Another band of Gauls,
the Ægosages, were summoned from Thrace in 218 by Attalos
of Pergamon, who afterwards tried to get rid of them.
They revolted and settled on the Hellespont, where

---

[1] Stähelin, op. cit., p. 43 ; id., " Galatia," in **CCCLXVIII**, p. 527.
[2] D'Arbois, **CCXCIX**, 203 ; Stähelin, **DLIV**, p. 43, n. 8.

Prusias I of Bithynia defeated them in 217. They did not attempt to unite with the Galatians of Phrygia.[1]

The three peoples lay one behind the other, from west to east. In the west, the Tolistoboii occupied the upper valley of the Sangarios ; Pessinus was their capital and Gordion was probably in their territory. Next came the Tectosages, with Tavium as capital. The Trocmi stood astride of the Halys, reaching westward as far as Ancyra ; they had the largest and least populous district.

The Galatians apparently settled down side by side with the Phrygian population without driving it out, by some process of endosmosis which we cannot follow.[2] The association of the new population and the old was probably peaceful. There was nothing to show that it was not, and certain facts suggest that it was,[3] although they do not justify us in supposing that relations were always cordial and that the domination of the Gauls was always endured with patience. They were a foreign minority encamped in the midst of a dense population of Greeks and Phrygians, who kept their own independence.[4] The great centres were not touched, and few new ones were created. Only three or four towns have names which are certainly new and at least partly Gaulish—Tolistothora in the south of the country of the Tolistoboii, Pitobriga in the north of the country of the Tectosages, and Eccobriga among the Trocmi.[5] What were these towns ? Were they like the camps of refuge in which, according to the historians, the Gauls shut up their women and children ? Where did the Galatians live ?[6] Being semi-mobilized and often at war, they remained an army for a very long time. The position of the Galatians in

---

[1] Polyb., v, 111. Cf. Rhigosages, who served in the army of Antiochos III in 220 B.C. against Molon, Satrap of Media (ibid., v, 53, 3).

[2] It has been supposed that they were in cantonments, like Ariovistus among the Sequani (Ramsay, in **LVII**, xxii, p. 341).

[3] Thierry, **CCCLXXXVII**, p. 983 ; Stähelin, **DLIV**, p. 47.

[4] Pliny, v, 22 ; 175 settlements in all. For intermarriage, see Livy, xxxviii, 9 ; O.G.I.S., 545.

[5] We should probably add Trocnades (= Tricomia ; cf. **I**, iii, suppl. 1, 6997), which was probably taken from the Galatians, Peion (cf. Welsh *pau*, " inhabited country "), Blucion (Welsh *blwgh* " box ", γαζφυλάκιον, Strabo, xii, 567), and perhaps also Tavium (Welsh *taw* " rest ").

[6] The mass of the Galatian population lived in villages (Livy, xxxviii, 18), and the chiefs in the φρούρια, some of which were the old cities (Stähelin, **DLIV**, 46).

Galatia must have been like that of the Franks in Gaul and the Mongols in China.

III

GALLIC MERCENARIES IN EGYPT. THE CIVILIZATION OF THE GALATIANS

Antigonos Gonatas, who had placed Gallic mercenaries at the disposal of Nicomedes of Bithynia, also lent a body of them to Ptolemy II Philadelphos in 277–6.[1] Ptolemy was at war with his brother Magas. He defeated him, but the mutiny of a corps of four thousand Gauls prevented him from following up his victory. Pausanias speaks of a conspiracy to take possession of Egypt.[2] What an adventure as a sequel to the sack of Delphi ! But, however disorganized we may imagine the great kingdoms of the Successors to have been, they were too big for a small band of janizaries, and however mad the Gauls may have been, perhaps they did not go to such lengths as this. More mildly and credibly, the scholiast of Callimachos, who celebrated their defeat,[3] speaks of an attempt to plunder the treasures of Ptolemy. The Egyptians shut up the Gauls on an island in the Sebennytic arm of the Nile. There they all perished, either by starvation or by a kind of ritual suicide of which we shall see other instances. In memory of this affair Ptolemy had a Gallic shield on his coins. The victory was considered of sufficient importance to deserve a monument. A superb fragment of it survives, and possibly three. The first is the head of a Gaul, with an intense expression of anguish, now in the Cairo Museum.[4] The others, which were found at Delos,[5] are a younger head, also expressing pain, and a wonderful headless body of a fallen warrior.[6] The whole monument must have represented the scene of the suicide and must have been a magnificent illustration of the epic of the Gallic mercenaries.[7]

[1] A. J. Reinach, in **CVII**, xviii, p. 37 ; id., in **CXXXIV**, 1910, p. 33.
[2] Paus., i, 7, 2.
[3] Callim., *Hymn to Delos*, 185–8.
[4] A. J. Reinach, ii, pl. vii.
[5] Ibid., pp. 99–101.
[6] S. Reinach, **CCCLXXVII**, ii, p. 199 ; **CXXXIX**, 1909, p. 2, 465. For smaller monuments derived from these great works and small Alexandrian monuments representing Gauls of Egypt, see A. J. Reinach, in **CVII**, xviii, pp. 102 ff.
[7] For collective suicide on the part of the Gauls, see Just., xxvi, 2.

Ptolemy II at the end of his reign, and Ptolemy III after him, enrolled more mercenaries. Under Ptolemy IV, we find some settled in Egypt ; those were the κάτοικοι, whose descendants were ἐπίγονοι.[1] Some of their graves, with painted tombstones, have been found in the cemetery of Hadra,[2] south-east of Alexandria. From these men a body of four thousand was raised, which appeared at the battle of Raphia in the Coele-Syrian campaign with ten thousand Gauls from Thrace.

There were likewise Gauls in the army of the Seleucids. Some took part in the campaign against the Maccabees. There was no prince in the East who could do without his corps of Gauls.[3]

Gauls appeared in the army of the Lagids which besieged Abydos in 186–185 in the repression of the revolt in Upper Egypt. Here is an inscription which they left on the walls of the temple of Seti I, in the small chapel of Horus [4] :

Τῶν Γαλατῶν	Of the Galatians,
Θόας Καλλίστρατος	we, Thoas, Callistratos,
Ἀκάννων	Acannon,
Ἀπολλώνιος	Apollonios,
ἤλθομεν	came,
καὶ ἀλώπεκα	and a fox
ἐλάβομεν ὧδε	caught we here.

It is a thrilling monument in its extreme simplicity, scribbled on the walls of the deserted, sanded-up old chapel one evening by men who had wandered there out of idle curiosity and had come on a jackal, which they took for a fox. It brings before one the glorious adventure of those simple-minded men, whose fathers had come from the banks of the Rhine to overthrow the order of sacred things in Greece, and who, since then, had been dragging their heavy hobnailed soles over every battlefield in the East.

But this inscription suggests yet other reflections. Those Galatians could write, and that by itself is interesting enough.

[1] Polyb., v, 65.
[2] A. J. Reinach, loc. cit., pp. 41 ff.
[3] Thierry, **CCCLXXXVII**, i, p. 219. There must have been Senones among these mercenaries, perhaps Senones of Italy. Cf. Steph. Byz., and also Domaszevski, p. 214.
[4] A. J. Reinach, in **CXXXIV**, 1910, pp. 55 ff. ; Dittenberger, **IV**, 757.

But they did not think of writing in Gaulish; they wrote
in Greek. Their Greek is very straightforward and shows
no subtlety, but Greek it is, and the spelling is so correct as
to shame our troops who record the simple distractions of
a soldier's life on the walls of monuments in distant lands.
Greek was the language of the Gallic troops. I do not know
that they ever had Greek officers [1]; so it is not a military
question, but a question of civilization. Greek was likewise
the official language of the Gauls of Asia Minor. They have
not left a single inscription in Celtic. All their inscriptions
are in Greek.

But we must add that they had not, at least in general,
forgotten their own tongue. Strabo vouches for it.[2] In the
second century after Christ, Lucian [3] tells us of a sorcerer
from Paphlagonia who could give answers in Celtic to people
who asked him for consultations. Still later, in the fourth
century, St. Jerome,[4] while saying that the Galatians used
Greek, admits that they had kept a Celtic dialect. Moreover,
the Galatians of Asia Minor have left a few Celtic words in
Greek, such as $\lambda\epsilon\iota o\acute{v}\sigma\mu\alpha\tau\alpha$ or $\lambda\epsilon\lambda o\acute{v}\sigma\mu\alpha\tau\alpha$, a kind of body-
armour; $\emph{\epsilon}\mu\beta\rho\epsilon\kappa\tau o\nu$, a kind of soup or porridge; $\emph{o}s$, the
kermes-oak; $\tau\alpha\sigma\kappa\acute{o}s$, a stake; $\kappa\acute{\alpha}\rho\nu os$, a trumpet.[5]

Another point to note is that none of the Gauls at Abydos
has a Celtic name, and many of those buried in the cemetery
of Hadra have Greek names. This would be easy to explain
if the corps of Galatians were recruited as the auxiliary corps
of the Roman army were afterwards recruited, being originally
formed of men of one race, the name of which was given to
the unit, but being filled up by men of all nationalities. But
we have no reason to suppose that this was so. The Gauls in
Greek lands assumed or gave to their children additional
names, Greek names, as a result of intermarriage, or simply
because they liked them.[6] In Galatia itself, such names

---

[1] On the other hand, there were Gallic leaders in command of troops of
other races (Polyb., v, 79, 11 ; 82, 11). The Galatian Lysimachos commanded
the Cardaces at the battle of Raphia.

[2] Strabo, xii, 567.

[3] Lucian, *Alexander*, 37.

[4] St. Jerome, *Prol.*, ii, *in Ep. ad Galatas* (Migne, *Patrologie latine*, xxvi, 382).

[5] And all the words which passed directly into Greek—*gaison, kartamera,
drouggos, karnyx*. A. J. Reinach, **CXL**, 1909, p. 65 ; Dottin, **CCCXVII**, p. 25.

[6] But even in Egypt the Gallic mercenaries had with them Gallic women
with Gallic names (Boudoris).

as Apaturios and Lysimachos appear as early as the events of 223–218.[1]

The Gauls of Asia and the mercenaries kept their own weapons,[2] at least the chief of them, certain peculiarities of armament, and certain military traditions. These were the marks of their units. They had the great sword with a central rib (this is what they kept most faithfully), the helmet, with or without horns, copied from the Italic helmet and derived by them from Cisalpine Gaul, the sword, worn on the right, the long sword of La Tène II,[3] besides Greek or Asiatic swords, and, finally, various types of javelin. Although they had body-armour, which is represented on the trophies, the historians describe them as fighting naked for choice. Some of the horsemen painted on the tombstones in the cemetery of Hadra are accompanied by their squires, so the system of the *trimarkisia* survived in the mercenary cavalry. The troops were always followed by women and children, who went with the baggage,[4] as with the Senegalese troops of France.

We have seen that those Gauls who formed political units adhered in a curious way to their national organization. If we are to believe the ancient anecdote-mongers, they remained true to their racial character and even to their manner of living. Plutarch depicts them in the bath with their children, emptying pots of porridge.[5] The one year's feast given to the Galatians by a noble called Ariamnes[6] (here is a man with a non-Gaulish name already) reminds one of the feasts of Luernius, King of the Arverni, or, in Celtic literature, of that prepared by Briccriu for the chief men of Ulster. It was a *potlatch*, as it would have been called in the north-west of America ; it was not a banquet of satraps. Among the settled populations of Asia with their urban civilization, the Gauls seem on the whole to have been not very strongly

---

[1] Polyb., v, 79. But Celtic names survived—Gaulotus, Cambolomarus, Epossognatus, Toredorix, Adiatorix, Bogodiatarus, Deijotarus. See the list in Stähelin, **DLIV**, p. 109 ; Bitorix, **CXXXIV**, 1912, 2, 290.

[2] P. Couissin, in **CXXXIX**, 1927, i, p. 138.

[3] Statuette found at Caere (in Berlin Museum), see ibid., pp. 148–157 ; statuette from Panticapaeon (in British Museum), see A. J. Reinach, in **CVII**, xviii, p. 97 ; Diod., xvi, 94, 9 (the Gallic sword used by the murderer of Philip).

[4] Just., xxvi, 2 ; Polyb., v, 78.

[5] Plut., *Symp.*, viii ; *Quæst.*, 9.

[6] Ath., iv, 34.

attached to one spot ; their chief wealth is pastoral.[1] But
excavation in Galatia has yielded nothing more than the
hope of finding a few portable objects of Gaulish origin—
a blue glass bracelet in a tumulas, a little pottery at Gordion,
and that is all.[2] In crafts and gear, as in language and the
habits of daily life, the Gauls borrowed largely from the
people among whom they lived, and indeed became merged
with them astonishingly quickly. They adopted their religion.
Plutarch twice tells us a story of a beautiful Gallic woman
named Camma who was priestess of Phrygian Artemis.[3] The
priest-kings of Pessinus were Celts ; the first of them is
mentioned in inscriptions of 153 and 139.[4]

In addition to the arts and crafts of material life, Greece or
the Hellenistic world had something to teach ·its guests
which was new to them, and that was, if not its moral culture,
at least its culture of the soul. For nearly three centuries
all Greece had been educated by the school of the rhetors
or the philosophers, who taught them to use their reason
and to use it about themselves, to analyse the motives of
human actions and to interpret the rules which govern
them. They were not more moral or more just than other
men—far from it—but there were in Greece men with more
lively and enlightened consciences than elsewhere. Greek
culture, grafted on the good instincts and solid morality of
the Gauls, produced excellent fruit. Plutarch tells us of
noble ladies who were not only beautiful but models of virtue.
Among the men, in the long list of chiefs of whom we do not
know much, two figures stand out—those of Cauaros, King
of Thrace, and Ortiagon, one of the four kings of the Tolistoagii who came into contact with the Romans a few years
after the date at which I stopped. Unfortunately, we only
see them in the summaries of the lost books of Polybios. But
the summaries tell us enough. Polybios had known Ortiagon.
He had conversed at Sardis with his wife Chiomara, who had
had, in the course of the war, an adventure which had certainly
lost nothing of its tragic character through her ; she was

---

[1] Strabo, xii, 6, 1 (the three hundred flocks of Amyntas in Lycaonia).
[2] A. J. Reinach, in **CXL**, 1909, p. 66 ; R. Zahn, in **XXX**, 1907, p. 87 ;
XX, 1907, p. 500 ; Stähelin, " Galatia," in **CCCLXVIII**, p. 534 ; Ebert,
CCCXXIV, iv, p. 284.
[3] Plut., *Amat.*, 22, p. 768 ; *De Mul. Virtut.*, 20, p. 257 ; Polyaen., *Strat.*,
viii, 39.
[4] Dittenberger, **IV**, No. 315 (i, p. 484).

a heroine by birth and by education.[1] Ortiagon doubtless inspired Polybios with equal enthusiasm. He aspired, the summary tells us, to the kingship of all Galatia. " He was well prepared for it by nature and by upbringing, for he was liberal and magnificent, full of charm in his personal dealings, and highly intelligent. Moreover, what the Galatians always hold in esteem, he was brave, and, in war, efficient (δυναμικός)." So, then, he was a fine man, able and well educated, with distinguished manners and lively intelligence. He shows these qualities in history. As for Cauaros, Polybios depicts him acting successfully as arbiter between Byzantion and the king of Bithynia. He was, then, both a diplomatist and a just man. The summary tells us that he had a kingly nature, greatness of soul.[2] He had displayed his phil-Hellenism in assisting the Greek traders of the Black Sea. It follows from this that he had an economic policy and that he kept good order in his dominions, which extended to the Black Sea.

The Hellenization of the Galatians does not seem to have greatly benefited the Celtic world as a whole, not so much because they were cut off from it by the states of Western Asia Minor as because they looked in another direction. We have a conclusive proof of this.

One result of the Hellenization of the Gauls was that they entered into a world which had long made use of coinage. It is true that the Celts of the West might have known (though not for long) of coinage through Marseilles and its colonies. But these cities were on the fringe of the Celtic world and the coins of Marseilles do not seem to have spread there in the form of imitations so very quickly. The Gauls of Italy had likewise seen coins. The Roman *as* has been found in Celtic surroundings. But Italy was ill-provided with coins at that date. The Gauls in the East suddenly found themselves with fairly large masses of coin in their hands—the tribute of the cities and the payment of their services. Byzantion, for example, paid a tribute of eighty talents a year, for which it obtained a loan of four thousand gold pieces from Heracleia. The Gallic tribes taken on by Antigonos Gonatas received a gold piece per man.[3] So the

---

[1] Plut., *De Mul. Virtut.*, 22, p. 258 ; Polyb., xxi, 38 ; Livy, xxxviii, 24.
[2] Polyb., iv, 52 ; viii, 24.   [3] Cf. Polyaenos, iv, 6.

Gauls had coins, and they made coins themselves, copying those which came their way. These were Macedonian coinages and those of certain cities such as Thasos [1] and Larissa.

Now, the coins of the Galatians are not Macedonian; they are imitated from the coins of Tarsos.[2] The coins of Tarcanos of Tarsos, bearing a woman's head on the obverse and a helmeted warrior on the reverse, were copied in Galatia. Other Galatian coins are imitated from those of Euthydemos of Bactriana, with a portrait on the obverse and a seated Heracles on the reverse. The diffusion of the former is perhaps explained by the commercial relations of Galatia. The choice of the models may have been imposed by the mercenaries.

It seems to me that, while the colonization of Northern Italy had a great and beneficial influence on Celtic culture as a whole, the colonization of Asia Minor had no effect on it whatever. That colony was lost to the Celtic world. It was not so on the Danube.

IV

THE CELTS ON THE DANUBE

To the ancient historians, the Celtic Danube was still an unknown world at the time at which we have taken our stand in order to view it. A few proper names, a few archæological data, scanty but valuable, may help us to picture that ancient world, not without having resort to conjecture.

Behind the armies and the roving bands whose expansion we have followed, the middle valley of the Danube was becoming peopled and organized as a Celtic country. Northwest of the Scordisci, two main groups had formed. The Taurisci [3] had carved a domain out of the territories of the Veneti in Upper Austria, Carinthia, and Styria. They had taken their name, as the Scordisci had done, from the mountain on whose slopes they had settled, the Taurus, now the Tauern. Later the country was called Noricum, from its capital Noreia. This group comprised the Ambidravi,[4] who lived in Styria and Carinthia on both sides of the Upper

---

[1] Forrer, **DXLIII,** pp. 226 ff.   [2] Ibid., pp. 238–9.
[3] D'Arbois, **CCXCIX,** 129.   [4] Ibid.

Drave, and the Ambisontes,[1] who were settled north of the Tauern, astride of the Isonta (Saltzach).

The other group was that of the Pannonians, who had settled in the northern domain of the Antariatae [2] in Lower Austria, Western Hungary, and Croatia. Attached to this group were the Osi [3] on the left bank of the Danube and the Aravisci [4] on the other side, extending from the station of Carpi (Κάρπις),[5] at the point where the river turns south, to the border of the Scordisci, whose country lay between Mount Scordus and the Danube.

Apart from the Aravisci, about whose origin there is doubt,[6] and who may have come with the Boii when the latter invaded Noricum, these are certainly Celtic peoples, or at least bands in which the Celtic element predominated. Thirty years before Cæsar wrote his *Gallic War*, a Latin historian, Sempronius Asellio, observed that Noreia was in Gaul.[7] Indeed, a great Danubian Celtic domain had come into being between the Celts of Germany and those of Italy. The map is dotted with a great number of Celtic names of towns and villages, some old, some formed later, even in the time of the Roman Empire, according to habits of name-making which outlive languages.[8] Noreia is a Celtic name, formed on a stem *noro* which appears in the proper names Noromertus (in Britain) and Norus (the name of a potter). In Carinthia [9] Matucaium (Treibach) is also Celtic (*math* "pig", *caion* "enclosure"), and so are Gabromagus, "the plain of goats" (Windisch-Garstein) and Lauriacum (Lorsch) in Upper Austria, Graviacae (*villa* understood) (Tamsweg) in the province of Salzburg, Cucullae, "the city of cowls" (Kuchl), and Masciacum, east of Innsbruck. In Pannonia [10] we have Vindobona (Vienna), Carnuntum (Petronell), Brigetio (Ószöny), Cornacum (Šotin); among the Scordisci there

---

[1] Pliny, iii, 137 ; cf. **I**, v, 7877 ; Ptol., ii, 13, 2.
[2] See above, p. 34.
[3] Or Onsi, *Ptol.*, ii, 2, 10 ; Ritterling, in **LXVII**, 1917, p. 132.
[4] *Ptol.*, xi, 15, 2 ; Tac., *Germ.*, 28 ; Pliny, iii, 148 (Eravisci). Cf. Tomaschek, in **CCCXXIV**, ii, p. 200.
[5] Kauffmann, **CCCXLVIII**, p. 221.
[6] Their coins are all Roman coins of the first century ; this suggests that they came later (Forrer, **DXLIII**, p. 120).
[7] Schol. on Virg., *Georg.*, iii, 47. Cf. d'Arbois, **CCXCIX**, p. 140.
[8] See d'Arbois, op. cit., pp. 121 ff. ; Kauffmann, op. cit., p. 219.
[9] D'Arbois, op. cit., p. 131 ; von Grimberger, in **LXXXI**, xl, pp. 135–9.
[10] Von Duhn, in Ebert, **CCCXXIV**, vi, p. 289.

are Singidunum (Belgrade), Capedunum (? Banostor), and Viminacium (Kostolatz). The Latin inscriptions of the country, especially in Pannonia,[1] present a great number of Celtic proper names—Enigenus " son of the Inn " ; Broccus " badger " (Irish *brocc*,Welsh *broch*) in Carniola ; Assedomarus, Excingomarus, Nertomarus, Ategnatus, and Devognata in Styria ; Iantumara in the province of Salzburg ; Ritumara and Ateboduus in Carinthia ; Atepomarus and Drogimarus in Austria ; Retimarus in Hungary. The inscriptions also speak of Teutates at Seckau in Styria and a Belinus at Klagenfurt in Carinthia.

We may reasonably imagine this great Celtic population of the Danube as a kind of hotch-potch in which the Celtic element predominated. What Strabo tells us of the country of the Iapodes [2] is very significant in this respect. They lived south of Pannonia, near the Adriatic ; the names of their towns, Metulum, Avendone, Monetium, are perhaps Celtic ; their weapons were those of the Celts and they tattooed themselves in the fashion of the other Illyrians and the Thracians. It is a mixed civilization and a mixed people. We may say the same of the Taurisci and the Pannonians, among whom the Venetian and Illyrian elements survived. The actual name of the Pannonians is an Illyrian racial name and, if we are to believe Tacitus,[3] the mixed people which they formed spoke a language which was not Celtic.

Given what we already know of the habits of the Celts at this time, we may suppose that the greater part of the country newly conquered by them was not of a kind to tempt them. They probably occupied the valley-bottoms and the lower slopes, which could be tilled ; they made for the bank of the Danube, where they had many settlements down to Pest. But these settlements were towns, crossing-points, between which the banks, being too low, were no doubt left unoccupied. Let us look at the map : Austria and what were until recently its southern provinces, with their mountains and their many valleys, offered the Gauls a very broken-up domain ; Hungary, too, was unsuitable, for other reasons, which are revealed in the fact that the river along

---

[1] Scholer, in **CLI,** x, 1923, p. 10.
[2] Strabo, vii, 5, 4.
[3] *Germ.*, 43.

its whole length in that country was occupied by the Aravisci, who may not have been Celts. Between the places held by the Celts the aborigines remained.

Everything, to the very names borne by these Gallic populations, shows that they were formed on the spot out of unrelated elements. We must imagine, with the ancient historians, a reflux of the great expeditions into Greece and a steady influx from early times of immigrants from Bavaria or Bohemia ; in short, a series of complicated happenings, very different from a systematic conquest made by one organized people. Even more clearly, the Gallic peoples scattered about from the Adriatic to the Black Sea and from the Ægean to the Sea of Azov were unconnected groups in the midst of the Illyrians, the Thracians, and the Scythians.

Archæological finds add something to this picture. A certain number of cemeteries of the second La Tène period have been found in what was once the Austrian Empire.[1] The civilization of the same period is very well represented in the Budapest Museum by objects discovered in the western part of Hungary. But this culture extended a long way beyond the Danube. A cemetery of La Tène II has been excavated at Apahida in the old county of Kolozs.[2] In the Kluj Museum (Kolozsvár) there is a chariot-burial with brooches of La Tène II, found at Balsa, near Szabolcs.[3] Celtic remains have been discovered between the Danube and Theiss.[4] Were these left by isolated Gauls who had strayed far from their own territory, or by the Dacians imitating Celtic culture ? The tombs at Apahida are indistinguishable from other Celtic tombs. It is quite conceivable that there was here a small body of Celts, lost in the midst of the Dacians and forgotten by history.

One thing is certain, and that is that the culture of the Danubian Celts came to be accepted by the Dacians, as it was by the Illyrians and Raetians. It would be extraordinary if the relics of the Celts alone had survived and those of their neighbours had disappeared, or the survival of native

---

[1] For La Tène civilization in Austria, see R. Pittioni, *La Tène in Nieder-österreich*, fasc. v of *Materialen zur Urgeschichte Œsterreichs*, Vienna, 1930.

[2] K. Itsvan, in **CLV**, ii, 1911, pp. 35 ff.

[3] Déchelette, ii, 3, p. 1082.

[4] L. Rödiger, in **XXI**, 1904, p. 351 (tomb at Hodsagh). For the archæology of La Tène in Hungary, see F. de Pulszky, in **CXXXIX**, 1879, pp. 158–172, 211–222, 265–275 ; Reinecke, in **LXXXIV**, ii, 1907, p. 45.

habits were represented only by objects of early date; indeed it is quite impossible. In any case, the Dacians, who had been under the influence of the Scythian civilization before the Celts descended the valley of the Danube, came under that of the Celtic civilization when it reached them. This is what one gathers from the series of archæological finds made in Dacia.[1]

The little that we know of these settlements points to a sedentary people, which, at least for a time, had given up adventurous undertakings. But we still have to record a few expeditions on the part of the Danubian Celts. At the end of the second century, they seem to have invaded Macedon and Thessaly again[2]; in 110 the Scordisci and Thracians menaced Delphi. The Balkan campaigns of the Romans Republic evidently woke up all the unsettled and unruly elements among them. But these were accidental episodes, and it would be wrong to regard these peoples, among which brigands were certainly to be found,[3] as a collection of freebooters. A passage in Livy[4] enables us to pass a fairer judgment on them. In the neighbourhood of Pella in Macedonia, the historian mentions Celts and Illyrians as being " indefatigable tillers of the soil ". These few words (which show, incidentally, that there were Gallic settlers outside the Gallic political formations) pick out of all the characteristics of the Celt one which distinguished him and won him the esteem of the Greeks and Latins ; he was a hard-working and efficient farmer. As we have already found him, so we find him here, more particularly in his own country —in Noricum, for example. It was a rich and peaceful country, anxious to have good relations with its neighbours, given up to its agriculture and its trade,[5] and, what is more, a mining country which produced an iron ore of some reputation.[6]

The Scordisci had the name of being rougher folk, more

---

[1] For the Celts in the Danube valley and their civilization, cf. Parvan, **DXLVIII**, pp. 459 ff. ; **DXLVII**, *passim*.

[2] Forrer, **DXLIII**, p. 142.

[3] Oros., v, 23, 17–18.

[4] Livy, xlv, 30, 5 ; *Permultos Gallos et Illyrios, impigros cultores.*

[5] Strabo, iv, 6, 10, 12 ; vi, 2, 2, ; 5, 2 ; 9, 21 ; Pliny, xxxix, 5, 1–4 xliii, 5, 2–9.

[6] Mines at Noreia, near Hallstatt. Rice Holmes, **CCCCXXXIII**, p. 231.

attached to the old ways of the Celts,[1] and readier to take up arms. What has been related of their partiality for silver seems to indicate that they worked the mines of the Drena.[2] Here they extracted the metal, which was beginning to spread among the Celts [3] and is still found in the region in the form of various objects. Political history shows them sometimes allied to Mithradates, sometimes combining with the Dacians,[4] in the capacity in which they must have constantly appeared, that of middlemen of civilization.

The archæological evidence of these exchanges is scanty— three small plaques of repoussé silver. One, which is said to have been discovered at Roermond in Dutch Limburg,[5] represents a human figure strangling a lion, crudely modelled in the style of the Gundestrup cauldron. All round are galloping animals, and above the man are two lions attacking a lamb, above which again are two confronted dogs with a bull's head between.

The two other plaques, which come from Asia Minor,[6] have the same arrangement : in the centre a wolf or a lion attacks a kid ; above it, the same beast is attacked by two winged monsters ; below is an ox's head flanked by two griffins ; the field is adorned with spirals and dotted lines representing foliage. They bear an inscription which was doubtless the same on both but is completely preserved on only one : *ΝΑΟΣ ΑΡΤΕΜΙΔ ΕΧ ΤΩΝ ΤΟΥ ΒΑ ΜΙΘΡΑΤ* . . . . . "Temple of Artemis, from the gifts of King Mithradates." We may suppose that this Artemis is she of Comana, and it is quite possible that the king is Mithradates Eupator, the ally of the Scordisci.[7] In any case, these two plaques are in quite a different style from that of Roermond ; they are more skilful, better drawn, and in higher relief. But the Dutch specimen was copied from a similar model. It is an imitation which might have been produced among a silver-producing people which had dealings with Pontus where its warriors took service, and exchanged gifts with

---

[1] Human sacrifices. Amm., xxvii, 4. D'Arbois, **CCXCIX**, p. 166.
[2] Reinecke, **CCCCVI**, p. 18 (silver treasures) ; Parvan, **DXLVIII**, 559 (list of finds of silver ware).
[3] Drexel, in **LXXII**, 1915, p. 24.
[4] Ibid., p. 23.
[5] Ibid. ; S. Reinach, **CCCLXXVII**, ii, p. 433.
[6] A. Odobesco, **DXLVI**, i, p. 513 ; in S. Reinach, op. cit., v, p. 239.
[7] App., *Mithr.*, iii, p. 107.

the kings of Pontus or traded with the Scythians, but was capable of getting models from them.[1] This description applies to the Scordisci.

The art of the Pontic medal-maker,[2] which recalls the very ancient art of the Hittites, is more truly like that of the Scythians. The kingdom of Pontus and Southern Russia were closely bound in civilization as in politics. Pontus was one of the stages through which the Scythian style would pass on its way to Celtic lands. At any rate, the Celts of the Danube must have passed it on. Déchelette[3] thought that the practice of wearing the torque as a sign of chieftainship had come to the Gauls from Scythia. But, while the torques of Southern France may be derived from the same region,[4] it is not at all likely that the Gauls waited until they were settled in the valley of the Danube, in contact with the Scythians, before they started wearing trousers.[5]

To a certain extent, the Gauls played the same part in the Danube valley as the Greeks round the Ægean Sea and in Asia Minor. Their racial origins were very mixed, and their cultures varied greatly in origin and in depth. The Greeks made one single world out of their motley world ; the Celts did the same, except for the language, in the valley of the Danube. In the culture of these kingdoms there was a special element, which, however, only appears in a very few monuments. To their relations with Asia Minor and Scythia they owed certain new forms of art, and they handed on a certain number of these acquisitions to the rest of the Celts.

They owed to the Greeks, and they left for us, something

---

[1] Relations with Scythia, Parvan, **DXCVII**, pp. 606–629. Græco-Iranian influences, ibid., pp. 550–561.

[2] Rostovtsev, in **CLXXXVII**, i, p. 257.

[3] **CCCXVIII**, ii, 3, p. 1310.

[4] The torques discovered at Lasgraïsses (Tarn) and Aurillac (Cantal) (ibid., pp. 1342–4) are to be compared (O. Costa de Beauregard, Autun, in **LX**, 1907, p. 824) with similar objects found in Hungary, Bohemia, and the neighbouring regions (e.g. at Herczeg-Marok, in the county of Baranya). Messrs. Read and Smith likewise ascribe an Eastern origin to a bronze torque adorned with animals' heads found at Vieille-Toulouse, **CCCLXXXIV**, p. 55).

[5] This costume was common to the Northern peoples, who had had it since the Bronze Age. But one cannot help comparing it to that of the Scythian archers at Athens (cf. the soldier of Rhesos on a Lower Italian vase in the Naples Museum) and that of the warriors on the Hallstatt scabbard (Déchelette, ii, 2, p. 770).

more important—coins.[1]   The gold and silver coins which
they received are chiefly of Macedonian origin ; they are
dated by the reigns of the rulers who issued them, and so they
constitute a new source of information for the history of
the Danubian Celts.

The oldest coins are gold staters and tetradrachms of
Philip II of Macedon (359–336),[2] silver coins of Alexander
(336–332),[3] Philip Anthidios,[4] and Lysimachos (d. 281),[5]
and, lastly, coins of the kings of Paeonia, Patraos (340–335)[6]
and Audoleon (315–306),[7] which were of the same type as the
Macedonian pieces.

It is evident that the Danubian Celts got the coins of
Philip at the very beginning of his reign, about 350,[8] and that
they copied them before they had any very large supply
of other current models ; that is, in the reign of Alexander
at the latest. They had, therefore, dealings with the
Macedonians which brought a quantity of money into their
hands long before they settled in the country of the Antariatae,
either because the services which they rendered to Macedonian
policy with regard to the Illyrians were not given for nothing,
or because they exported goods into Macedonia. These
models continued to be popular in the Danube region,
perhaps in consequence of the release of depreciated coins,
and the Celts remained faithful to them until the Roman
province was erected.

All these coins are of silver. The gold staters of Philip
and Alexander and those of Lysimachos were imported
direct into the Danubian country, but they also travelled
in other directions and seem to have gone to Raetia direct.[9]
The reason was that in ancient Greek times gold coins were
a kind of international coinage, and it was as such that
they entered Celtic lands by other sides.

The Celts of the Danube faithfully maintained the types,

[1] See Parvan, **DXLVIII,** pp. 598 ff. ; Forrer, **DLIII** ; Déchelette, ii, 3,
p. 1569.
[2] Coins with a bearded, laureate Zeus on the obverse and a horseman
on the reverse. Forrer, **DXLIII,** p. 143.
[3] Head of Heracles and Zeus with an eagle. Ibid., p. 157.
[4] Ibid., p. 174.
[5] Ibid., pp. 200, 205.
[6] Ibid., pp. 153 ff.
[7] Ibid., p. 163.
[8] Ibid., p. 143.
[9] Ibid., p. 192

alloys, and weights of the Macedonian coins. They had the same standard. Beyond Vienna, large coins are found at greater intervals, the size decreases as one goes westwards,[1] the type, while remaining the same, degenerates, and the influence of another coinage and another standard makes itself felt. Noricum was definitely the boundary of the Danubian Celts, who were more closely attached to the Hellenistic world than their neighbours and acted as middlemen between that world and the other countries subject to them. The Illyrian groups [2] copied the local coinages of Damastium and Pelepia Illyriae, while those of the Lower Danube and Black Sea copied the money of Thasos exclusively.[3] This special coinage corresponds to the commercial relations which the lower valley of the river and the shores of the Black Sea must have had normally with the region of the Bosphorus and Dardanelles. It also shows that in these eastern regions the Celts of the Black Sea formed a distinct province, looking in other directions than their kinsmen of the Danube.

On the two sides of the Julian Alps, with the Celts of the Po and those living north of the Danube, the Gallic peoples were in political communication.[4] Coins of the Aravisci, which have been found in considerable quantities in the district of Mortara, point to a commercial intercourse which had doubtless been going on for some time.[5] On the Upper Danube, the Boii of Bohemia, who had furnished so many men for the Celtic expeditions, were still sufficiently powerful to extend their sway to the Theiss.[6] In their rage for conquest they disturbed the peace of the peoples of Noricum [7] and Pannonia,[8] a large part of which they occupied. This was, indeed, the only important event in the history of these peoples, which is brief, before the arrival of the Romans. The area over which their coins are discovered—concave

---

[1] Ibid., p. 189 ; Blanchet in **CXLII**, 1902, pp. 160 ff.

[2] Forrer, op. cit., p. 237.

[3] Ibid., pp. 211, 226.

[4] Livy, xxxix, 45, 6 ; 55, 1–3 ; xliv, 5 ; xlv, 1–2.

[5] Forrer, op. cit., p. 120.

[6] Strabo, vii, 313 ; cf. **CLXVIII**, xlii, 1898, pp. 153 ff. ; Reinecke, **CCCXCIX**, v, ix, pl. l, and p. 287 ; cf. **XV**, 1907, p. 397.

[7] Cæsar (Gall. War, i, 5) relates that the Boii invaded Noricum and besieged Noreia. Cf. Jullian, **CCCXLVII**, i, p. 299 ; Blanchet, **CCCVI**, pp. 458–463.

[8] Pliny, iv, 146.

pieces known as *Regenbogenschüsselchen*, or "rainbow saucers", the most distant and barbarous derivatives of the stater of Alexander—is evidence of their roving disposition.[1]

V

COMPOSITION OF THE CELTIC ARMIES

Unlike the great army which invaded Italy,[2] the warriors who fell on Macedon and Greece were not, for the most part, grouped in tribes. They were a collection of bands, recruited no one knows how from groups which were politically unassociated.[3] It is possible that some of them came from a great distance.[4] The Gallic bands contained more than one adventurer who was attracted by the prospect of loot and a mercenary's pay.

But you cannot make a great army out of rovers alone, and the great companies of Gallic mercenaries never numbered more than a few thousand men. To form the army of Brennus, recruiting of a more regular kind was needed, drawing largely on groups of neighbouring tribes. Men to train them were needed, and leading tribes to direct the others.

This time the lead was taken by the Belgæ. Historians who lay stress on the different names of Celt, Galatian, and Gaul have not failed to point out that the name of Galatian prevailed from this time onwards.[5] But this is merely a question of pronunciation; the word which was written

---

[1] Forrer, **DXLIII**, pp. 214–17 ; Déchelette, ii, 3, p. 1569.

[2] See above, pp. 9 ff.

[3] We have a piece of evidence about the way in which these bodies were recruited in a little romance by Aristodemos of Nysa, preserved in a collection of love stories compiled by Parthenios of Nicæa (d'Arbois, **CCXCIX**, p. 199). It tells of the misadventures of a Milesian named Xanthos, whose wife had been carried off by a Gaul. The Gaul was named Cauara, and he came from the neighbourhood of Marseilles. Cauara was doubtless not a personal name, but a racial name—the men belonged to the country of the Cauari, who were settled later about Avignon and Orange.

[4] Justin (xxxii, 3, 8–9) assigns a double origin to these Danubian and Gallic bands, but perhaps he confuses the Tectosages of Toulouse with those of Bavaria. The same information is found in Strabo, iv, 1, 13, following Timagenes. For peoples or tribes from the Danube, Πραυσοι (Strabo, iv 1, 13) and Tolistoboii (Pliny, v, 141 ; Strabo, xii, 5, 1), cf. Jullian, **CCCXLVII**, i, p. 299, n. 1. These latter nations are unknown otherwise, and this information, even it it is correct, tells us nothing.

[5] Paus., i, 3, 6 ; d'Arbois, **CCCI**, i, p. 14.

down as Keltos (Κελτός) in Spain and the neighbourhood of Marseilles sounded differently in the ears of the Greeks of the Balkan Peninsula, who wrote it down Galates (Γαλάτης). But it was the same name ; the Gallic mercenaries buried in the cemetery of Hadra [1] were described on their tombstones as Keltos or Galates without distinction. " Galatian," therefore, does not mean Belgic ; but there are certain facts which indicate that there were Belgæ in the bands of Galatians and that they were at the head of them.

First, there is the name of the leader of the expedition of 281, Bolgios.[2] If Bolgios is a proper name, that in itself is significant ; and it would be still more so if the Greek historians had called the leader after the body which he led. In Pannonia, Pliny mentions a town called Belgites.[3] So the name of the Belgæ remained attached to these Danubian expeditions and to the settlements left by the invaders.

The archæological remains, too, preserve the memory of the descent of the Belgæ into the East. The statuette at Naples representing the suicide of Brennus,[4] the statue of a Gaul in the New York Museum,[5] and many other similar works show the Gauls of the Danubian armies dressed in wide, flapping trousers. Even the women wore them, and are depicted in that costume ; there is a statuette in the British Museum of a Gallic woman lying down, wearing trousers and cloak.[6]

Other representations of Gauls, of a semi-realistic character, namely the paintings on the tombstones at Hadra, show Gallic mercenaries wearing trousers which are not the wide *bracca*.[7] It is clear that this latter garment was not, and never was, worn by all Celts. It was peculiar to the northern Gauls, and more particularly to the Belgæ, who, as has been said before, owed their name to it.[8]

Lastly, St. Jerome states that in his time these Galatians still speak Gaulish, and he particularly compares their

[1] A. J. Reinach, in **CVII**, xviii, pp. 41 ff.
[2] D'Arbois, **CCXCIX**, p. 200.
[3] Pliny, iii, 148. There was a Belgida, a Celtiberian place whose site is unknown, in Hispania Tarraconensis.
[4] A. J. Reinach, op. cit., xxi, pl. xviii.
[5] Ibid., p. 182 and figs. 6–7.
[6] Ibid., p. 85 ; Lang, in *Œsterr. Jahr.*, 1919, pp. 207–280.
[7] Ibid., p. 64.
[8] See *Rise*, p. 227.

language to that of the Treviri, who were Belgæ.[1] That, too, is perhaps of significance.

That there were Belgæ among the Gauls who invaded the Balkans and Asia Minor, and also among those who settled in the Danube valley, is a fact beyond dispute, and we find them in the position of leaders. Their rank makes up for their lack of numbers.

[1] *Comm. on Galatians*, ii, 3 : *Galatas, excepto sermone Græco, quo omnis Oriens loquitur, propriam linguam eandem pene habere quam Treviros, nec referre si aliqua exinde corruperint.*

CHAPTER III

The Celts in the West. Italy and Spain

I

THE BELGÆ IN ITALY

FROM the end of the third century onwards, the Belgæ are to be found taking a part in every movement which occurs in the Celtic world. The other Gauls seek their help for special purposes, defend themselves against them, or follow them. While they are trying to carve out an empire for themselves on the Danube and in the East, new bodies descend on Italy and Spain. The political events of the second century bring the Celts into contact with a great organized state, a creator of order in its own fashion, the Roman Republic. The history of these peoples is henceforward the story of their struggle with Rome, in which, from the west of the Mediterranean to the east, they are vanquished, and it is through the ups and downs of that story that we catch glimpses of their internal life.

Yet another danger threatens them. To the north, over an area of the same extent, the Celtic world has at the same time to suffer encroachments and advances on the part of men of inferior civilization, speaking another language and forming another group, who have begun to move in the wake of the Belgæ, a hundred years after them. These are the Germans, whose name has already turned up in the course of this history, in Ireland, then in Italy, and finally in Spain, though in this last country its meaning is uncertain.[1]

A century after the first invasion, the peace of the Gauls of the Po valley was disturbed by the arrival of a large body of men from over the Alps.[2] The Gauls treated with them, and succeeded in diverting their attention to Rome,

---

[1] Livy, x, 107 ; Polyb., ii, 19, 1.
[2] Homo, **CCCXLI**, English, pp. 191 ff.

which was then engaged in the fourth Samnite War.[1] The
Samnites had as allies the Etruscans, to whom the Gauls
offered their assistance and that of the newcomers, who
asked for land and a home in return.[2] The Gauls descended
into Etruria and slaughtered a legion at Clusium, on the usual
road taken by invaders.   In 295 they found themselves
faced by a larger Roman army at Sentinum on the eastern
slope of the Apennines, near the source of the Æsis.   In
spite of their valour and dash, they were crushed.[3]

Ten years later the Gauls appear again, this time alone.
They besieged Arretinum [4] on the Clusium road. A Roman
army came to the relief of the town, and lost many prisoners.
Envoys, sent to obtain an exchange of captives, were ill
received. In 283 the Romans took the offensive and invaded
the country of the Senones,[5] whom they utterly defeated.
According to a family tradition of the Livii, the Consul
M. Livius Drusus found among them the thousand pounds
of gold which had been paid in ransom of the Capitol. In any
case, he was able to collect enough booty without that.
The Etruscans had meanwhile taken up arms again, and
while the Senones were getting beaten an army of Boii had
come down into Etruria.   It passed Clusium and Volsinii
and was defeated on the shores of the small lake of Vadimo
(Bassano), close to the Tiber between Volsinii and Falerii.[6]
The Boii made peace, and it lasted for forty-five years,
giving the Romans time to finish the Samnite War, to
dispose of Pyrrhos, and to conduct the first Punic War without
having anything to fear from the Gauls.

They had considered it wise to keep a foothold in the
country. The colony of Sena Gallica [7] was probably founded
in 283. The circumstances which led to the establishment
of a colony at Ariminum [8] in the north of the Senonian
territory in 268 are unknown to us. This was the terminus
of the Via Flaminia, which was not finished until 221. Possibly

[1] Livy, x, 10, 10 ; Jullian, **CCCXLVII**, i, p. 285.
[2] Cf. d'Arbois, **CCCI**, ii, p. 389.
[3] Polyb., ii, 19, 7–8.
[4] Livy, xxi, 20, 6.
[5] Suet., *Tib.*, 8.
[6] Polyb., ii, 20, 1–5.
[7] Vell. Paterc., i, 14, 7.
[8] App., *Celt.*, ii ; Polyb., ii, 19, 12.

it was already planned. Meanwhile, the Senones did not recover anything like their former power in the district and the Romans were consolidating their positions. It was not until 232 that the Lex Flaminia ordered that this territory should be divided up.[1] This was a serious matter. The Gallic settlements might be able to suffer small losses of ground and the foundation of colonies in towns which were hardly Gallic, but the dividing-up of the country meant eviction, and evicted they were.

This incident produced the greatest indignation, if not among all the Gauls, at least among the Boii and the Insubres, who had already, in 238 or 236, begun to call upon the Transalpine peoples [2] whom they had received with mixed feelings in 299. An army had at that time entered the country, and had advanced as far as Ariminum. They do not seem to have been received with open arms by the greater part of the population, for there was a rising against the Boian kings Atis and Galatos,[3] who came with them. The two kings were slain and the expedition came to nothing. No doubt there was some question of a division of land, and the Gauls were not fond of such methods. But in 232 the alarm occasioned by another division of land was general. Once more appeal was made to the men beyond the Alps.

These latter took their time to prepare for their invasion. But they seem to have managed things well, and it was a large and well-armed force which was sent into the plain of the Po in 225, led by the kings Concolitanus, Aneroestus,[4] and Britomarus.[5] The report of this new Gallic incursion was not without influence on the negotiations which brought the first Punic War to an end.

One of the Consuls of that year, L. Æmilius Papus, awaited the Gauls at Ariminum.[6] The other, C. Attilius Regulus, was engaged in Sardinia. In Etruria there was a small army under the command of a Praetor. The Gauls, with a force of 50,000 foot and 20,000 horse and chariots, having struck right across the Apennines, once again came

---

[1] Id., ii, 21–2.
[2] Id., ii, 21, 5.
[3] Id., ii, 23, 1.
[4] Id., i, 10 = ii, 4–3.
[5] Id., ii, 21, 4–6 ; Cf. Homo, op. cit., English, pp. 281 ff.
[6] Polyb., ii, 25, 2.

down the central road of Etruria, again appeared before
Clusium, and surprised the small army of the Praetor in
a fashion which proves that their leader was not without
military skill.[1]   The return of L. Æmilius caused them to
change their route.   They turned towards the coast, which
they reached at Telamon, north of Orbetello.[2]   There they
were met by all the Roman forces and with them those of
the whole of Italy.   This time the Gauls were not quite of
one mind.   The Cenomani had stood apart, and the Romans
had obtained from them not only neutrality but an auxiliary
corps,[3] which marched with a body of Veneti, forming with
it a unit of about 20,000 men.   This was one of the great
encounters between the Gauls and the peoples of Italy. The
Gauls were thoroughly worsted ; their army was destroyed.
Concolitanus was taken prisoner and Aneroestus killed
himself.[4]   In memory of this battle a magnificent temple
was built at Telamon, containing a symbolic arsenal and
relics from the battlefield.[5] Excavation has yielded a bronze
statuette of a fallen Gallic chief and terra-cotta fragments
of pediments.   One of these latter represented the two leaders
of the Transalpine tribes in the guise of Adrastos and
Amphiaraos, two of the Seven against Thebes, Adrastos
falling into an abyss made by a thunderbolt, and Amphiaraos
dragged away on his chariot by a Fury.

Next year the Roman army ravaged the country of the
Boii,[6] who begged for peace and submitted, as did the
Lingones.   In 223 the Romans, supported by the Anamari,
attempted to cross the Po near the mouth of the Addua, but
they were beaten and secured their escape by negotiation.
They returned to the attack with the support of the Cenomani,
and drove the Insubres as far as Milan.   The Insubres raised
50,000 men and brought out of the temple of their goddess
certain gold standards, which must have been the symbol
of their possession of the place. The Romans were victorious,
we are told, but they retired.

The Insubres took advantage of this to bring in, next

---

[1] Id., ii, 27–31 ; Cf. Homo, op. cit., English, pp. 282–3 and fig. 10.
[2] Polyb., ii, 22, 7–8 ; Dion, xii, 43. Cf. Jullian, CCCXLVII, i, p. 326.
[3] A. J. Reinach, in CVII, 19, p. 174.
[4] Milani, DXXXIII, i, pp. 125–143.
[5] Polyb., ii, 31, 8 ; 35, 2.
[6] Homo, op. cit., Eng., p. 284 ; Jullian. op. cit., i, pp. 449–450.

year, an army of 30,000 Transalpine warriors, led by a chief named Viridomar, who called himself a son of the Rhine. The collision took place on the right bank of the Po, at Clastidium, south-west of Comillomagus. The Consul M. Claudius Marcellus is said to have slain Viridomar with his own hand in single combat. The Gauls, flying with the Romans close at their heels, crossed the Po near the mouth of the Addua, abandoned Acerrae, and retreated to Milan, which was in its turn taken by the Consul. Peace was made, the Insubres surrendering part of their territory and giving hostages.

As they had done among the Senones, the Romans founded two colonies, one at Placentia on the right bank of the Po, among the Boii, and the other at Cremona on the left bank, among the Insubres. Mutina was held by a garrison, which commanded the road from Placentia to Ariminum, later the Via Æmilia.

In spite of the succession of reinforcements from across the Alps which they received during more than a hundred years, the Cisalpine Gauls did not succeed in extending their territory, and still less did they get the better of the Romans. On the contrary, they lost considerable ground to them, and above all lost their independence.[1] They were either allies or subjects of Rome. What independence they retained was precarious. They were to make a timid attempt to renew the struggle on the advent of Hannibal, only to fall still lower.

The newcomers who took part in the struggle of the Cisalpine Gauls against the Roman Republic are represented as Gauls of the Alps, the Rhone, or the region between them.[2] The contingents of 232 are said to have come from the remotest part of Gaul and from the Rhine district.[3] So they must have passed the Rhone and the Alps on their way, and their predecessors may have done so too.

According to the ancient historians, the Cisalpines regarded them as kinsmen of their own, being like them

---

[1] Polyb., ii, 15, 22.
[2] Id., ii, 34, 2. Cf. Jullian, op. cit., i, p. 450, n. 2.
[3] Polyb., ii, 22 ; Bertrand (**CCCIII**, p. 453) observes that Polybios seems to have used the name of Galatians to designate them, for choice, but not exclusively.

descended from the Gauls who took Rome.[1] They are described as a *Gaisatai*. This was a name which was known to
have a meaning. Polybios [2] suggests an etymology : " They
are called *Gaisatai* because they are mercenaries, for that
is what the word means." We have no confirmation or
explanation of this etymology. There is another interpretation of the term—that the *Gaisatai* are Germans armed with
a spear or javelin, the *gaesum*. [3] It is perfectly true that the
word *gaesum* is a transcription of a Gallic name, but the
Latins used it with a wrong meaning. They confused the
new weapon with other javelins, which had long been used
by the Etruscans [4] and the Roman light infantry.[5] But they
did not confuse it with the *pilum*—a mistake of which some
modern archæologists have been guilty.

Other documents, mainly inscriptions, mention *Germani*
and *Rheti Gaesati*.[6] These were probably bodies raised in the
Alps or in Germany. The population of the Roman Germanies
was for the greater part Belgic. The *Germani Gaesati* were
Belgæ. Of this we have proof. Just as they introduced the
name of *gaesum* into Italy, the Belgæ who went warring in
Ireland took into that country the weapon which has exactly
the same name.[7] They arrived with a better armament
than that of the natives, and the thought of those terrible
weapons (among which there was a special spear or javelin) [8]
is bound up with the memory of them. So the Gaesati or
Gaisatai were Belgæ, or at least there were a great many
Belgæ among them.[9] Perhaps this is why the ancient writers,
who so often confuse the Belgæ with the Germans, describe
the Gaesati as *Semigermani* or *Germani*.[10] Moreover, the
Gaesati had other characteristics of the Belgæ. Like them
they wore baggy trousers.[11] The historians who describe the

---

[1] Polyb., ii, 22, 1 ; Oros., iv, 15, 5. Cf. **CXC**, 38, p. 324.
[2] Polyb., loc. cit. ; Virg., *Æn.*, viii, 661 ff. ; Polyaen., vii, 33, 156
Eustath., ii, 774 ; Cæs., *Gall. War*, iii, 4, 1.
[3] Livy, ix, 36, 6 ; xxviii, 45.
[4] Id., viii, 8, 5.
[5] **CVIII**, vi, p. 188.
[6] **II**, vii, 1092 ; **I**, viii, 2786 ; vii, 1002 ; xiii, 1041.
[7] Irish *gai, gae* ; Corn. *gwaw*.
[8] Rhys, **CCCCL**, ii, pp. 205, 207.
[9] Jullian, **CCCXLVII**, i, p. 315, n. 6.
[10] See *Rise*, p. 13.
[11] Like the Gaul of Alesia and other representations of Gauls of the
Alexandrian age.

battle of Telamon describe them as fighting naked, that is to say, naked down to the waist but wearing trousers.[1]

But these were not the same Belgæ as those who invaded the Danube valley and the East. They were not confused with the Taurisci, who also figured in the army defeated at Telamon. Moreover, they still had the war-chariot, the *essedum*, which was no longer used by the army of Brennus or the Galatians of Asia. If there is one thing to remember in the battles in which the Gaesati engaged, it is the use of the large, heavy sword, made for cutting-strokes which were parried with the shield, and never bending save in the heat of funeral pyres, but less useful for hand-to-hand fighting than the *gladius* which the Romans had copied from their predecessors.

At all events, their expeditions in the south of the Celtic world contributed to the unification of Gallic civilization during the second La Tène period.

II

THE BELGÆ IN SPAIN. THE CELTIBERIANS

At the same time new bodies of Celts were entering Spain, which had for two centuries been separated from the rest of the Celtic world by the Iberian invasion of Languedoc and the valley of the Garonne.[2]

All through this period, the civilization of the Gallic settlements had developed on independent lines.[3] In the place of the La Tène I brooches, which are only found exceptionally, there are quantities of very curious types, transitional between Hallstatt and La Tène. The great sword of the first La Tène period is likewise absent. Down to the third century, its place is taken by small swords derived from the dagger with antennæ. All these objects can be dated fairly exactly by the Greek vases found with them in the same cemeteries.

This archaic civilization is succeeded immediately by that of La Tène II. The largest group of finds belongs to

[1] Polyb., ii, 28, 4.
[2] See *Rise*, pp. 298 ff.
[3] For post-Hallstatt civilization, see Bosch Gimpera, **DV** ; Pericot, **DXV**, pp. 51 ff. ; Schulten, **DXVII**, pp. 187–9 ; Siret, in **CXXXVI**, 1909.

the Castilian cemeteries of Aguilar de Anguita, Arcobriga, and Luzaga, some of the tombs in which contained brooches, swords, and shield-bosses of this period.[1] Some of the brooches and swords belong to earlier types. In Catalonia outside the old limit of Celtic settlements the cemetery of Cabrera de Mataro (Barcelona)[2] and in Andalusia that of Torre de Villaricos (Almeria)[3] have yielded many Campanian vases of the third century. But swords are still very rare. At that time the Celts used a kind of sabre with a hilt shaped like a horse's head, which archæologists call the Almedinilla sword.[4] This weapon is found in the graves, bent in the Celtic fashion, as are the small antenna-sword and that of La Tène II. It is shown on the Osuna relief[5] in the hands of a warrior who carries a great Celtic shield with a central rib. It has been suggested that this weapon is the κοπίς of the Thracians and Eastern peoples, imported into Spain by the Greeks. But it seems rather to have spread by the Celtic land-routes. The κοπίς is depicted in a caricature of a Galatian warrior on a crater of the third century found at Volterra[6] and in the Telamon statuette.[7] Sabres have been found in burials of La Tène II in Illyria and Germanic countries.[8] The κοπίς is the sister of the cutlass which takes the place of the sword in many Gallic tombs[9]; it is the result of an evolution of Hallstatt weapons parallel to that of the sword, and it came from Central Europe to Thrace, Greece, and Italy. Whether it originated in Celtic countries or was copied by the Celts on their Eastern expeditions, it was from the north that it entered Spain with the Celts of La Tène II.

In the Celtic place-names of Spain we can see a second stratum,[10] which appears to date from this second Celtic occupation. These are names of fortified towns ending in -dunum.[11] There are only four of these—Caladunum (Calahorra, near Monte Alegro in the Portuguese province of Tras-os-

[1] Déchelette, in LVIII, 1912, p. 433; Cerralbo, DVIII.
[2] Bosch, CCCCXCIX.
[3] L. Siret, in CXXXVI, Déchelette, DIX, p. 65.
[4] Paris, DXIV, ii, pp. 277 ff.
[5] Couissin, in CXXXIX, 1923, 2, p. 62.
[6] Déchelette, ii, 1, p. 435, fig. 178.
[7] See above, p. 72.
[8] Déchelette, ii, 2, 691.
[9] H. Hubert, in CXL, 1925, p. 259.
[10] D'Arbois, CCXCIX, p. 185.
[11] Ibid., pp. 111–112.

Montes) among the Callaici, who were Iberians ; Estledunum
(Estola, near Luque, province of Cordova) in the country
of the Turduli, who were not Gauls ; Sebeldunum (in
Catalonia, south of Gerona) among the Ausetani ; and
Arialdunum, the site of which is uncertain. We may also add
Berdum in the province of Huesca and Verdu in that of
Lerida, which were originally called Virodunum. The name
of Cogos, in the province of Gerona, recalls that of Cucullae.
There was a town of the Arevaci called Clunia. Lastly,
a Gallic leader slain by the Romans in 179 bore the name of
Moenicaptus, " Slave of the Main." [1]

There are names corresponding to this series at the other
ends of the Celtic world. Most of those ending in -*dunum*
have been discovered north of the Seine and east of the
Cevennes.[2] There is a whole string of places called Virodunum
from Tarn-et-Garonne to Germany. Kuchl in the province
of Salzburg and Cogolo in the Tyrol were once Cucullae.[3]

These analogies suggest that it is in the north and in the
east that we should seek the starting-point of the new body
of invaders, and many of them were certainly Belgæ. In
Hispania Tarraconensis there were a Belgida,[4] site unknown,
and a Belgica, which is also written Vellica. A third city,
Suessatium,[5] recalls the name of the Suessiones, who were
a Belgic people.

Lastly, we find in Spain people called Germani,[6] and that
among the Oretani, who were Celtiberians according to
a statement of Pliny the Elder.[7] These again are Belgæ,
whether they actually bore the name, which is clearly of
Celtic origin, or it was given to them by analogy.

We may try to imagine the order of events. Of the
portions of Celtic peoples which made for Italy in the fourth
century, some stopped or were stopped along the Garonne
towards the mouth—Bituriges Vivisci at Bordeaux [8] and
probably Senones at Cenon, opposite the town on the other
side of the river,[9] and Lingones at Langon, higher up.[10] At the

---

[1] Ibid., p. 16. [2] Ibid., p. 110. [3] Ibid., p. 123.
[4] Oros., v, 23, 2 ; Diod., xxxi, 39 ; App., *Hisp.*, 100 ; II, viii, 439.
[5] Schulten, **DXIX,** pp. 10, 106.
[6] Ibid., p. 124. [7] Pliny, iii, 25.
[8] Strabo, xiv, 2, 1 ; Cf. Jullian, **CCCXLVII,** i, p. 309.
[9] Jullian, op. cit., p. 305. Cenon is written Senon in the Chartulary of
St. Seurin (pp. 26, 93).
[10] Jullian, loc. cit. Langon is called Portus Alingonis in the *Letters* of

other end of the Pyrenees there were Volcae—Volcae Tectosages south of Narbonne and Volcae Arecomici (or Arecomii) between that town and the Rhone. These last, who took the place of the Iberians and Ligurians in Languedoc, came from the same regions as the first Celtic occupants of Aquitania. They did not enter Spain. But we may suppose that they were followed by Belgæ who managed to make their way to the Pass of Roncesvalles on the one side and into Catalonia on the other. These newcomers cannot have been very numerous.

All this doubtless happened between 350 and 250.[1] It may possibly have been some years before the irruption of the Gauls into the Balkan Peninsula and the later Italian expeditions.

In what condition did the arrival of the Belgæ leave the Celtic settlements in Spain ?

The Peninsula had been a Celtic land. Then it had become " Iberia ", and seems to have been given this name in Greek geography for the first time about 230 by Eratosthenes.[2] The peoples of the interior, roughly from the fourth century onwards, are called Celtiberians,[3] and this appellation probably goes back to Timaeos, about 260. It must have had a fairly precise meaning, for the Celtici of the south and west kept it, whereas the Berones are called simply Celts by Strabo.[4] What, then, were the Celtiberians ? A mere formation. But of what kind ? What proportion of Celtic elements did it contain ?

The most generally accepted notion, which is based on the sentiment of the ancient writers,[5] is that the Celtiberians were not very different from the Celts who were known to be in the Peninsula before the new name çame to prevail. They were Celts of Iberia, mixed in various degrees with Iberian elements. This is not the view of Herr Schulten.[6] He regards the Celtiberians as Iberians who had settled in the country

Sidonius Apollinaris (viii, 12, 3). This name may be derived from an ancient name ad Lingones.

[1] Ephoros (F.H.G., i, 245, fr. 43) includes the greater part of Spain in the Celtic world (341 B.C.).
[2] Schulten, DXIX, i, p. 97. Cf. Eph., fr. 38.
[3] Ibid.
[4] Ibid., p. 111.
[5] Pliny, xiv, 3, 13.
[6] Schulten, op. cit., i, p. 19.

of the Celts and had then moved towards the Pyrenees from 350 onwards under the pressure of the Ligurians and Celts ; these Iberians tried to extend their ground in Spain, and established themselves on the plateau, going up the valleys.[1] The new peoples whose names the historians then give— Oretani, Carpetani, Lusitani, Vettones, Arevaci, Vaccaei, Lusones, Belli, and Titti—are Iberian, not Celtic tribes.[2] Polybios, too, describes the Celtiberian Oretani, Carpetani, and Vaccaei as Iberians. The Celts, driven from their settlements on the central plateau, retreated westwards or were reduced to subjection or assimilated by the conquerors.[3]

But why, then, the name Celtiberians, which cannot in any way be taken as a national designation ? It is a Greek ethnographic term formed like the word " Libyphoenicians ", which obviously means Phoenicians settled on Libyan territory.[4] In fact, even if these terms are fundamentally ancient, their meaning is vague, and is intended to be so.

One thing at least is certain : the Iberian civilization reached the plateau.[5] In their states in the south, where they were in contact with the Greek colonies, the Iberians in the fifth and fourth centuries developed a culture some aspects of which are now well known—towns with stone ramparts and stone houses, large temples inhabited by a host of statues and statuettes, and painted pottery with geometric, animal, and vegetable ornament.[6] This culture, which had its birth in the south-eastern corner of the Peninsula, whence it spread in the fifth century along the east coast to the Rhone, makes its appearance in the fourth century in the upper valley of the Ebro, and then, gradually advancing, arrives a hundred years later in Castile, in the country which had once belonged to the Celts. There it spread in the southern part of the territory occupied by the Oretani, and further

---

[1] Id., **DXVII**, p. 80.

[2] Polybios (iii, 14) mentions only Celts in the south-west and north-west. In Hannibal's time, the centre is occupied by Iberians only.

[3] One should add, to understand Herr Schulten's argument, that the Celtic invaders of the fifth century had found the country in which they settled occupied, not by Iberians, but by Ligurians. The Iberians were strangers in Spain, colonists and conquerors from Africa.

[4] Schulten, **DXIX**, 19.

[5] Bosch, in **XIV**, vi, p. 671. For the excavation of Celtiberian sites on the plateau see B. Taracena Aguirre, " Excavaciones en las provincias de Soria y Logroño," in **XCIX**, No. 103 (1929).

[6] Paris, **DXIV** ; R. Lantier, **DXI** ; Bosch, **DI**.

north in that of the Carpetani. It also made its way into the northern parts of the domain of the Arevaci and into some of the groups established on the plateau. The scarcity of Iberian objects in the country of the Vaccaei, Vettones, and Lusitani seems to indicate that these peoples were less strongly Ibericized. The distinction made by the ancient historians between *Celtiberi citeriores* (closer to the coast) and *Celtiberi ulteriores* (further from the coast and wilder) may also have corresponded to a difference of race.[1]

Altogether, then, there is nothing against the supposition that the racial framework of the country was usually supplied by the Iberians. The Oretani and Carpetani have Iberian names similar to that of the Turdetani, for example, who are outside the Celtic area. The Lusitani are probably a branch of the Lusones which had advanced westwards, and we may by analogy suppose that the Arevaci and Vaccaei were likewise of Iberian origin,[2] But all these peoples allowed a considerable number of Celts to stay in the country and absorbed them. This is shown by the names which appear in the inscriptions of Celtiberian towns. Such Celtic names as Acco, Atto, Boutius, and Reburrus are frequent. They prove that Celtic elements lived on in the country and maintained their family organization.

But they did not live in a subordinate position. The leaders, the heroes in the Celtiberian war of independence are Celts—Rhetogenes (Rectugenos) Caraunios, Caros, Ambon (Ammo ?), Leukon, Megaravicus, and Auaros. Orosius[3] relates that after the fall of Numantia, Scipio asked a Celtic prince named Thyresius why the city had held out so long. Lastly, even if the Lusitani were Iberians, their chief Viriathus had a Celtic name.[4]

To explain this state of things, we may suppose that Celtic families which had been previously settled in the country entered the Iberian tribes or survived alongside of them. We may also suppose that the meeting of the Celts and the Belgæ who arrived on the Iberian plateau at the same time, moving in opposite directions, led to agreements by which the smaller body was incorporated in the larger.

The two hypotheses are equally reasonable and account

[1] Jullian, **CCCXLVII,** i, p. 307.   [2] Schulten, **DXIX,** i, pp. 247–8.
[3] v. 8, 1.   [4] Schulten, op. cit., i, p. 100.

for many features of Celtic civilization,[1] which are attested
by archæology and by the ancient writers, in the Celtiberian
tribes—the survival of cults such as that of Epona and that
of the Lugoves, the observation of Celtic funeral rites in the
cemeteries of Castile, the survival of Gallic armament, the
use of horse and foot together in tactical formation, the
use of standards and trumpets, the wearing of the *sagum*,
the drinking of beer.

But while something of Celtic civilization survived, there
were no vestiges of Celtic states (if they had ever existed)
in the centre of the Peninsula about the middle of the third
century. The coming of the Belgæ had neither revived
old political units nor created new ones.

III

THE CELTS IN THE PUNIC WARS

At the time when the Punic wars commenced, the races
of Spain were arranged as follows : in the centre on the
plateau there had grown up a group of peoples of great
military excellence which, though mainly Iberian, contained
a large number of Celts, who enjoyed a certain standing.
The collaboration of these two elements in Celtiberia was
not unlike that of the Arabs and the Berbers in Algeria and
Morocco before the European conquest.

In the first Punic War Carthage lost her Spanish colonies.
After the war, in 237, the first generation of the great generals
of the Barca family, Hamilcar and Hasdrubal, set out to
reconquer the country,[2] with the idea of extending the
Carthaginian domain and making it a base for the war which
they were preparing. The first operations among the Tar-
tessians brought them into conflict with bodies of Celts.[3]
They next crossed the Sierra Morena and attacked the
Celtiberians, whom Hannibal finally conquered in 221.[4] From
Cartagena to Burgos they had subdued the whole plateau.
It would doubtless be more correct to say that they had
concluded agreements with the Celtiberian tribes, which

---

[1] Ibid., pp. 246 ff.
[2] Polyb., ii, 1, 16.
[3] Diod., xxv, 10, 1.
[4] Schulten, op. cit., i, p. 99 ; Jullian, i, p. 460.

supplied them with mercenaries. In 218, the Lusitani are
mentioned for the first time as soldiers of Hannibal.[1]

The second Punic War began. Hannibal resumed or
started negotiations with the Volcae, who lived on the
northern slope of the Pyrenees. The envoys of the Roman
Senate, returning from Carthage, where war had been decided
on, landed on the coast of Languedoc, likewise with a view
to negotiation. Livy [2] describes them addressing the assembly
of armed Volcae. There they had to listen to all the complaints
of the Gauls of Italy, which were possibly a genuine expression
of public discontent but may have spread by the emissaries
of Hannibal preaching the cause of Celtic unity. The Volcae
remained undecided. They went through the form of opposing
the passage of the Carthaginian army at Ruscino, but they
came to terms before there was any fighting. Hannibal
passed without trouble through the land of the Volcae
Tectosages, and then through that of the Arecomici. At the
Rhone, the same undecidedness began again. An army of
Volcae or Salyes was disposed along the east bank. Hannibal
turned it and put it to flight, and then, instead of marching
up the Durance and crossing by Mont Genèvre—perhaps in
order to avoid observation by the army of Scipio, who had
landed a body of cavalry by the mouth of the Rhone—he
went up the east bank of the Rhone to the Isère, and passed
without fighting through the country of the Allobroges,
escorted by a king whose cause he had taken up. He probably
took advantage of his march through these peoples to repair
and renew the equipment of his force.[3] Leaving their territory,
he entered the Maurienne, where another Gallic people, the
Medulli, received him very ill. At Mont Cenis, yet another
tribe, the Centrones, disputed his passage. After that there
was Italy.

All this information about Hannibal's journey through
Gaul is of the greatest interest. For the first time, it shows
us Gallic peoples in Gaul, and places them. Although sometimes contradictory, it is all of good quality, and goes back to
the Greek historians who accompanied the expedition,
Silenos and others.[4] The Volcae occupied Languedoc [5] from
the Pyrenees to the Rhone. Between that river and the

[1] Ibid., p. 109.
[2] xxi, 20. Cf. Jullian, op. cit., i, p. 460.
[3] Ibid., 4, i, p. 475.
[4] Ibid., p. 455.   [5] Ibid., p. 459.

Durance, Livy [1] mentions the Tricastini and the Vocontii. The valley of the Isère belonged to the Allobroges up to the Maurienne.[2] North of the Rhone, Polybios [3] places the Ardyes, who are probably the Ædui. These positions are permanent, and we must conclude from them that, if there were large shiftings of peoples in Gaul, first before the earliest invasions of Italy and then at the time when the Belgæ made their appearance on the borders of the Celtic world, these movements were for the main part over by 218. Behind the Ædui must have been the Belgæ.

It is possible that the Celts missed their opportunity in Hannibal. He seems to have counted on a general Celtic invasion, but he did not succeed in bringing it about. The Gauls of Gaul were cool or hostile. Those of Italy, one nation of whom, the Boii, had summoned him, were hardly more enthusiastic. They made up their minds when the game was lost.

There was no general rising. All that Hannibal managed to do was to recruit Gallic mercenaries, whom he used skilfully to spare his Spanish troops.[4] But the Romans also had Gallic mercenaries.[5] They were able to maintain garrisons at Mutina and a small army of observation in Cisalpine Gaul, and to preserve their colonies at Placentia, Cremona, and Ariminum.[6] It is true that in 216, after Cannae, the Boii seem to have been tempted to do something. They cut down the little army of the Praetor L. Postumius in the Litana Forest.[7] But that victory led to nothing.

Hasdrubal, Hannibal's younger brother, came very near to succeeding where his elder brother had failed. Being placed in charge of operations in Spain, he managed to recruit troops north of the Pyrenees.[8] In 214, at the battle of Jean, two Gallic chiefs named Moenicaptus and Vismarus, who may have been Belgæ, are mentioned among the slain.[9] On his defeat in 208 Hasdrubal eluded the Romans who were waiting for him in the gorges of Roussillon by going round the west of the range [10] and travelled through Aquitaine and Languedoc, gathering a new army. Then he descended into

---

[1] Ibid., ii, p. 515.
[3] iii, 42, 8.
[5] Ibid.
[7] Ibid.
[9] Livy, xxiv, 42, 8.

[2] Ibid., i, p. 475.
[4] Jullian, op. cit., i, p. 492.
[6] D'Arbois, CCXCIX, 182.
[8] Jullian, op. cit., i, pp. 494 ff.
[10] Jullian, op. cit., i, p. 496.

Italy, where, after being better received than Hannibal, he was defeated with his Gauls on the banks of the Metaurus in 207.[1] Two years later, another brother, Mago, renewed the attempt. He landed at Genoa and held the district for two years. Then, being driven back into Savoy, he re-embarked, taking with him part of his European troops. Hannibal took back others, so that at Zama half of his army was composed of Celts and Ligurians.[2]

In Cisalpine Gaul, the Barcas had left a Carthaginian officer, Hamilcar, who succeeded in rousing the Cenomani, who had so long been allies of the Romans, and in taking Placentia. But he was defeated and killed before Cremona in 200.[3]

The war went on with hard fighting and much bloodshed, and the Gallic peoples submitted one after another, the Cenomani in 197,[4] the Insubres in 196.[5] The Romans gave them a *foedus* on good terms, and they became *civitates foederatae*. The Boii held out until 191 ; to them surrender brought the total destruction of their political organization. They had to give up half of their territory and three of their cities, Bononia (Bologna), which was made into a colony in 189, and Mutina and Parma in 183. Livy relates that only old men and children were left.[6] It is also said that a body of Boii went back over the Alps into their old home.[7] Of the Lingones nothing more is heard.

In 186 a new Gallic tribe appears in the north of Venetia. This was the Carni,[8] coming from Noricum, who settled in the country and vowed that their intentions were peaceful. A Roman army was sent against them in 183. They were defeated, but they remained. A Roman colony was established at Aquileia in 187.

A story went about that Philip of Macedon intended to bring the Celts down on Italy. In 178 yet another small body of 3,000 Gauls appeared, asking for land.[9] They had to go. This was the last Celtic invasion of Italy down to the campaign of the Cimbri. Henceforward the Roman

---

[1] Ibid., p. 498.
[2] App., *Lib.*, 40, 44 ; Jullian, op. cit., i, p. 500.
[3] Ibid., i, p. 501.   [4] D'Arbois **CCXCIX**, p. 182.
[5] Cic., *Pro Balbo*, 32.   [6] Livy, xxxvi, 40, 5.
[7] Strabo, v, 1, 6, 10 ; Polyb., ii, 35, 4.
[8] **I**, p. 460.   [9] Livy, xl, 53, 5–6.

people regarded the Alps as the boundary of the Celtic world, and did not allow the Gauls to cross it.[1]

It was not long after these events that Polybios [2] visited Cisalpine Gaul, of which he has left a very attractive picture : " Words fail," he says, " to describe the fertility of the country. Corn is so abundant that in our own time a Sicilian medimnus of wheat has more than once been seen to fetch only four obols, a medimnus of barley two obols, and a metretes of wine no more than a measure of barley. Millet and panic produce enormous crops. A single fact may give an idea of the quality of the acorns furnished by the oaks which grow at intervals on the plain [3] : many pigs are slaughtered in Italy both for daily life and for the supply of camps, and it is from this district that most of them come.[4] Lastly, here is conclusive proof of the cheapness and plenty prevailing there. Travellers stopping at the inns do not make terms over each item separately, but ask what the rate is per head ; as a rule the innkeeper undertakes to give them all they want for a quarter of an obol,[5] and this price is seldom exceeded. Need I speak of the enormous population of the country, of the stature and good looks of the people, and of their warlike spirit ? "

The Gauls had their share in the prosperity of this bountiful land. Everything, down to the system of inns, can be put down to them, for there were inns in Ireland too.[6]

They had suffered much in the recent wars. In 197 and 196 alone the Insubres are said to have lost 75,000 men. These were great losses. But there were still Gauls left in Italy. The excavations at Ornavasso [7] and the neighbourhood of Como show that the Lepontii and Insubres remained distinct, with their civilization, down to Imperial times. This does not mean that they had given up their unruly ways for good.

The misfortunes of the Gauls were not yet quite at an

---

[1] Id., xxxix, 54, 11 : proclamation of the Senate forbidding the Gauls to enter Italy.

[2] ii, 15.

[3] This is a feature of the landscape which has vanished.

[4] Pig-breeding is still important in Emilia.

[5] Something under a halfpenny.

[6] The six Bruidne of Ireland. For inns in the Transpadane country, cf. Jullian, op. cit., i, p. 377.

[7] **CXLV**, 1907, 101 ; 1908, 22.

end.   But the Gallic wars were over, for one cannot describe the revolt of the slaves, chiefly Gauls, which embarrassed the Romans at the end of the century as a Gallic war.

Not only in Italy did the Celts retire before the Roman Republic, which henceforward was mixed up in everything that happened in the Mediterranean world. In Spain and in the East the Celtiberians and Galatians presently lost their independence.

While Hannibal was carrying the war into Italy, a fleet commanded by Publius Scipio as Consul and his father Cneius was making for Spain. Publius Scipio returned to Italy, to get beaten on the Ticinus, and Cneius continued on his way and landed at Emporion.[1] At first he found allies among the Celtiberians. But in 212 they returned to their alliance with Carthage. The two Scipios, who had been in command since 217, were defeated separately and killed within a month of each other. Young Publius Scipio, Africanus that was to be, quickly restored the situation in 211 and, having driven out Hasdrubal, made ready in Spain for the African campaign which brought the war to an end.

The Spanish campaigns of the Scipios form a parallel to that of the Barcas, and what the Barcas had done for Carthage the Scipios did for Rome. But they went further.

In 197 they attacked the Celtiberian positions on the plateau[2] and commenced a stubborn war which went on until 133, with a few years of respite between 178 and 154. The fall of Numantia[3] brought the war to an end. The whole of Spain, except the Pyrenees and the free or federated cities of the coast, was organized as a Roman province.

From the rapid conquest of Gaul and the long resistance of the Celtiberians some have argued that there is no such thing as a Celtic character. The Gauls have left a name for quickly losing heart. Arguments of this kind, which do not take into account the circumstances on either side, are a fruitful source of error. Moreover, the Celts seem to have always had an idea of civilization which was quite opposed to their concern for their national independence, and led them to see a friend and guide where others saw an enemy.

---

[1] Jullian, op. cit., i, pp. 510 ff. ; Homo, **CCCXLI**, English, pp. 315 ff.
[2] Schulten, **DXVII**, p. 82.
[3] Id., **DXIX**.

But, for all their wavering, their resistance, even in Italy, lasted over a hundred years.

In the Eastern Mediterranean the Romans found it necessary to intervene in Macedon and Greece. They were constantly finding Gallic colonies on their way. They had to make terms with those in Noricum which were determined to be left in peace, to be wary with the Celts of Illyria, and to hold the balance between the Galatians and the Kings of Pergamon.

One of the first consequences of the Punic War was that the Romans came into contact with the Galatians. After Zama, Hannibal had taken refuge with Antiochos the Great, and finally with Prusias. Antiochos allowed himself to be won over. The Galatians took sides with him and shared his defeat at Magnesia on the Maeander. The Consul Manlius Vulso marched against them.[1] The first to be attacked, the Tolistoboii, retired to a fortified position on Mount Olympos, where the Romans blockaded them and took over 40,000 prisoners. The Tectosages and Trocmi were likewise compelled to take up their position in another stronghold on Mount Magaba. It was taken by storm. Manlius's campaign was memorable for disgraceful pillage,[2] but on the whole he dealt fairly generously with the vanquished, who were included in the general peace-treaty and allowed to keep their territory provided they did not come out of it. But the King of Pergamon seems to have now obtained a sort of protectorate, which had rather a disturbed history. The Galatians revolted several times. They were crushed in 166. But now the Romans intervened in their favour, and established their independence as a permanency. In 152 Attalos III of Pergamon bequeathed his kingdom to the Romans. The situation changed, though it is not possible to say exactly how, save that the Galatians were drawn into the wars against Mithradates [3] and that they thereby at first lost their independence. In 73 they succeeded in recovering it, and until the death of Mithradates they were faithful allies of Rome. At the end of the war, in 63, Pompey reorganized the Galatians in three principalities, one of which, reaching to the sea and including Trapezus, went to the famous Deiotarus. Deiotarus

---

[1] Jullian, op. cit., i, p. 514.   [2] Livy, 45, 7.
[3] T. Reinach, **DLI**, p. 74.

was not satisfied, and took advantage of the Civil War to intrigue between Pompey and Cæsar. He had to go to Rome to defend his conduct before Cæsar, and was defended by Cicero in 45 so successfully that he returned to Galatia as a king. By the favour of the Romans, the kingdom of his successors, Castor and Amyntas, was still further extended. But in 25 the whole kingdom was declared a Roman province.

The kingdom of Deiotarus had already ceased to be Celtic ; it was a kind of large satrapy, devoid of any racial or national character. The fact was that the Galatians had merged into the population of Anatolia, just as, at the other end of the world, the Celts of Spain had merged into the Iberian peoples. The most conspicuous trace of themselves which they seem to have left in Asia Minor was their blood. Travellers have noted in the country a considerable number of blond types, in which some of the physical characteristics of the Celts doubtless reappear.

In Thrace the little kingdom of Cauaros had disappeared in 193. In 171 the Romans entered Illyria to defend the colony of Aquileia, which was threatened by the Iapodes. An army marched through their country, and probably also that of the Scordisci, to attack Perseus in Macedonia. It seems to have behaved very badly there, for the Consul C. Cassius on his return found an embassy of Istrians and Iapodes who had come to complain to the Senate. From the middle of the second century onwards, the Scordisci were constantly at war with the Romans, and twelve expeditions were sent against them. In 135 they were severely beaten south of Haemos,[1] and they remained quiet for a time. In 110, in alliance with the Thracians, they threatened the Temple of Delphi, and they doubtless took part in the looting of 90. They were crushed by L. Scipio in 83 and planted on the other side of the Danube ; nevertheless, we find them again, about 78, in Macedonia, allied with Mithradates and supplying him with most of his Gallic mercenaries, and also plotting with the Dacians.

On the Adriatic the Illyro-Celtic pirates were driven back into the interior in 135. With 129 began a series of small expeditions against the Iapodes, ending in a treaty in 56. They started again in 52, and only ended with the

[1] Jullian, op. cit., i, p. 515.

subjection of the country. In A.D. 8 the whole Celtic region on the Danube, including the territory of the Scordisci, was made into a Roman province.

At the end of this stage in history, we have to note that the Belgic contingents had no real success save in the East. In Spain they established themselves, but did not last. In Italy their appearance was transitory. Their advance to the south of the Mediterranean was stopped in the first half of the third century, and after that the settlements founded or reinforced by them declined. Decisive defeats in the first half of the second century set the seal on those of the third. The Celts in Spain began by yielding ground to the Iberians, and those of the East to the Thracians and Pergamenes. All, one after another, were crushed, or wiped out, or subdued by the Romans. Those who suffered least were still the Galatians. But, as we have seen, Galatia was by that time no more than an island, lost to the Celtic world. The kingdom of Deiotarus and his successors was Galatian in name alone. The Celtic states and tribes lost all their dominions, one after another. But everywhere they left traces, stocks of men. Nor does it seem that these lands which they had conquered were in any great danger while they held them.

Moreover, the Gallic conquerors, old and new, do not seem to have declined in quality. During those two hundred years they were defeated often and thoroughly, and won the esteem of their opponents. Also, they fought more often for others than on their own account, like the bodies of mercenaries which they lent on every hand. This is especially true of the Belgæ.

This account would, therefore, not be complete if it did not once more mention the Gallic mercenaries, those roving bands which enormously extended the area covered by the Celts. As early as 307, Agathocles had taken Celts to Africa.[1] To the history of the Celts they added that of heroic, picturesque lands and they gained a great sum of individual experiences, which cannot all have been lost, in spite of the great slaughter of men involved.

Polybios [2] tells a story of 3,000 Gauls who were enlisted by the Carthaginians in Italy in 263 and transported to

[1] Diod., xx, 64, 2.
[2] ii, 7, 6 ; Jullian, op. cit., i, p. 327.

Sicily. They were a difficult body to keep in hand ; they looted Agrigentum and finally betrayed their employers. The Romans got rid of them as best they could. We find them later in Epeiros, about 800 in number, in the service of the city of Phoenice against the Illyrians, when they delivered up the city to the brigands. Thus we can follow them for thirty years.

Carthage had larger bodies of Gallic mercenaries in her service during the first Punic War, and it was one of their leaders, named Antarios (who, by the way, spoke Punic excellently, according to Polybios), who was responsible for the great mutiny of the mercenaries in 241–237.[1]

Mercenary service was a regular Celtic industry, and a well paid one.[2]   The 10,000 horse and 10,000 foot enlisted by Perseus was commanded by a *regulus* and had all the appearance of a tribal army.   It is, indeed, often very difficult in the Gallic wars to distinguish between large companies of mercenaries and belligerent armies.

[1] Ibid., i, p. 326.   [2] Ibid., p. 328.

CHAPTER IV

The Celts in the West. Germany and Gaul

I

CELTS AND GERMANS

IN the middle valley of the Danube the development of the Celtic settlements had been checked by the Getae and Dacians. The Boii advanced to the Theiss, but their sway extended no further. Beyond that there were doubtless Gauls in Transylvania, just as there were Saxons later. Celtic culture spread in this region, and the Dacians became Celticized.

On the Black Sea, an inscription from Olbia [1] records the appearance of the Sciri, who were probably Germans, in the company of the Galatians. But they were soon absorbed, In the same parts, at the same date, we find a much more important people, though of uncertain origin, the Bastarnae.[2] They are mentioned for the first time at the beginning of the second century, as newcomers on the Lower Danube. All these barbarians were employed as auxiliaries down to the time of the collision. In 182 Philip of Macedon sent them against the Dardanians.[3] In 179 there was a great drive of the Bastarnae, with which the Macedonians had great difficulty in dealing.

Some ancient writers, particularly Polybios,[4] who lived at the time of these events, regard the Bastarnae as Galatians.[5] Ptolemy,[6] on the other hand, makes them Germans, and in this he is justified by the names found among them.[7] It is possible that the Bastarnae were a confederation

---

[1] C.I.G., 2058. Cf. **LXX**, 3, pp. 441 ff. ; **CXLIX**, 34, pp. 56–61 ; Pliny, iv, 97 ; Müllenhoff, **CCCLXII**, ii, pp. 110 ff.

[2] A. Bauer, in **CXLIX**, clxxxv, 2, 1918.

[3] Livy, 40, 57.

[4] Polyb., 26, 9 ; 29 ff.

[5] Müllenhoff, op. cit., ii, p. 104.

[6] Ptol., i, 3, 5, 19.

[7] The leaders' names are Germanic : Clondicus, O. Sax. Indico ; Cotto, O. Sax. Goddo ; and indeed Alemannic names, Talto (Müllenhoff, op. cit.,

of Celtic and Germanic bands, like the army of the Cimbri and Teutones later.[1] However it may have been, whether they were associated with the Celts or not, the Germans broke through the Gallic barrier and joined them at the furthest limit of their expansion. Even more clearly than the example of the Sciri, the arrival of the Bastarnae tells of the vast Germanic drive which was beginning to bear down on the Celtic world. While the Celts were moving to the south of Europe, important things were about to happen on their north-eastern borders.

However far back we go, the original habitat of the Celts in Western Germany does not reach to the Elbe. On the west, the frontier, always fluctuating, takes in an increasing part of the future Gaul ; south and north, the boundary is marked by Switzerland and the North Sea.[2] The emigration of the Goidels[3] left the northern part of this region empty, but down to the first centuries of the La Tène period the Brythonic Celts kept their part of it. The expedition of Sigovesus,[4] forming a pendant to the great Celtic invasion of Italy, must represent an advance from the old positions in Bohemia to more northern or eastern ground and inroads from Thuringia into other parts of Germany, all somewhat different from the descents into Italy, Spain, and the East in character and in results.[5]

It is certain that in Bohemia the area of Celtic occupation increased from the first La Tène period onwards. This is attested in the centre and north of those regions by large cemeteries of that date. Further north, in Thuringia—where the crests of the Thüringerwald had in the Iron Age formed a frontier between two civilizations which must have been the racial frontier between Celts and Germans—the peoples of the southern slope moved forward at the end of the Hallstatt period.[6] At the beginning of La Tène, the Celts still extended

---

ii, 109). The name of the Qvenen, one of the Bastarnian peoples, reminds one of that of the Sitones, a nation of the Baltic coast (ibid.). Lastly, the suffix of *Bastarnae* or *Basternae* is found in the form -*erno*- in some Germanic derivatives, e.g. in Gothic *widuwairna,* " orphan."

   [1] See below, pp. 103 ff.   [2] See *Rise*, pp. 178 ff.

   [3] See *Rise*, p. 176.   [4] Livy, v, 34. See above, p. 33.

   [5] This is not the opinion of Herr Schumacher (in **LXVII**, 1918, pp. 98–9), who explains it by an advance of the Celts of the region of Metz on Thuringia.

   [6] This advance is revealed by a group of flat burial-graves discovered on the northern slope (Götze, **CCCXCII,** xxi).

beyond the Thuringian mountains eastwards in the upper valley of the Saale, in the Kreise of Saalfeld and Ziegenrück. Brooches of La Tène I are found in the Elbe valley, where it leaves Bohemia, and up to the river and beyond it at the level of the confluence of the Saale. They have been picked up, less frequently, all the way down to the mouth of the Elbe and in Mecklenburg, close to the Baltic coast.[1] But these do not come from recognizably Celtic tombs or cemeteries, and we must therefore conclude that outside the limits which we have already drawn there is no trace of a settlement of the Celts, permanent or otherwise.

But it is beyond doubt that the Celts had a very great political and military influence on the Germans at this date. This is shown by the words borrowed by Germanic from Celtic [2]—words connected with politics, law, warfare, and civilization in general. On the whole, the Celts seem to have been for hundreds of years, and in every matter, the educators of the Germanic peoples. But their influence was not due to their mere neighbourhood, and we may take it that it was enforced. There were in Germanic countries Celtic *kings*, or kings after the Celtic fashion, and where there was no king or kingdom we find Celtic *officials* or ambassadors. Celts and Germans strike treaties, exchange oaths and hostages, do business, and make contracts of marriage or friendship. In some instances the two races formed what may be regarded as a single society; they combined in political associations and their tribes formed a confederation or confederations in which the Celts were the larger and predominant element. These relations did not always develop in peace, for we must suppose that they engaged in wars, sometimes against each other and sometimes on the same side.

Another proof of the intimacy of the Celts and Germans at this time is afforded by certain names of Germanic peoples which are Celtic in form or are like Celtic names Germanized. The name of the Hessi, for instance, seems to be the same as that of the Cassi. The Burgondiones correspond to the Brigantes. The Nemetes, the Triboci, and the Marcomanni,

---

[1] Cf. Herr Beltz's map of the distribution of brooches in **CLXIX**, 1911 ; cf. id., in **LXXXV**, 1913, p. 117.

[2] See *Rise*, pp. 62 ff.

who lived next door to the Gauls, had Gallic names.[1] Yet
there is no doubt that these are Germanic peoples.

One should note that the borrowed words are found in
the eastern dialects of Germanic no less than in those of the
west and north. This diffusion enables us to judge how far
Celtic influence reached. It even went beyond German
regions and affected the Slavs and Finns.

To estimate how deep it went, we must turn to the
ancient authors. The association of the Celts and Germans
and its effects lasted long enough for these writers to bear
witness to it. If there was a difference between the languages
there was not much between the men. Cæsar [2] was the first
to make a great distinction between them. Poseidonios,[3]
before him, who was perhaps the first man to speak expressly
of the Germans, laid weight on their points of resemblance.
Strabo, who came after Cæsar, regarded the Germans as
Gauls in their original pure state ($\gamma\nu\eta\sigma\iota\sigma\upsilon\varsigma$ $\Gamma\alpha\lambda\acute{\alpha}\tau\alpha\varsigma$) and
suggests that this was what their name meant (" germane ").[4]
Their speech was different, but their institutions, manners,
costume, and arms were the same, and the Greek geographer
drew his picture of the early Celts from the Germans of his
own day.

But the Celtic domination of the Germans was a thing of
the past in Cæsar's time. The Germans now stood along the
Rhine from the Lake of Constance downwards, and about
sixty years before, the catastrophe of the expedition of the
Cimbri and Teutones had taken place. Can one determine
the stages of the retreat of the Celts and the date at which
it began ?

That retreat was long in coming, and was sudden when
it came. It was in the second La Tène period that Celtic
influence extended furthest. It is perfectly true that the
Germans followed close on the heels of the Celts. They
occupied every piece of country as it was left vacant, and
for every Celtic retreat there was a Germanic advance.

These movements began very early. About 400, and
probably long before, the Germans had reached the Rhine,[5]

---

[1] Dottin, **CCCXXII**, p. 452 ; Kluge, **CCXI**, i, p. 327 ; Müllenhoff, **CCCXLII**,
ii, p. 23, n. 7.
[2] Mommsen, **CCCLIX**, i, 47.   [3] Ibid.
[4] vii, i, 2.
[5] The Germanic name of the Rhine, Rinos, is not derived from the

but only on its lower course.[1] Moreover, the character of the Celtic sites in Western Germany suggests that the country between Thuringia and the Rhine was contested every foot of the way. The Thüringerwald was a first frontier, with its line of forts. The Rhön was a second, likewise with its fortresses, the redoubt being the Steinsburg near Römhild.[2] Further west, the Vogelsberg and beyond it the Westerwald and Taunus had their strongholds.[3] There were yet others south of the Main and in the valley of the Neckar.[4]

The great number of these forts is surprising, contrasted with the peaceful aspect which Gaul must have presented at that time. The Celts do not seem to have been fond of shutting themselves up in citadels. The fortified sites of Germany point to hard necessity.

One would like to be able to picture the resistance of the Celts on their different lines of defence. Unfortunately, their forts do not run in chronological order from Thuringia to the Rhine. Also, they are found on heights and in woods, like the Hallstatt defensive settlements in Gaul. Habitats changed with the population. Nor do the finds enable us to follow the steps of the Celtic retreat. At the beginning of the La Tène period we can define the limit of their settlements and those of the Germans in Thuringia and Saxony, and at the end of the period we can recognize the Germanic forts and villages of the Rhine valley, but we cannot trace the shifting frontiers intermediate between these two positions and dates.

Some have described the distant colonizing expeditions of the Celts as having been made at the expense of the peoples established in Germany. Instead of supposing an extension of their frontiers on this side as on the other borders of their domain, they have depicted the reservoir of men as emptying on this side and leaving vacancies, which were

---

Celtic name Renos but from Reinos. Otherwise the *e* would have survived. The change from *ei* to *e* occurred at the same time in Goidelic and Brythonic, and therefore cannot be much later than the separation of the dialects (d'Arbois, **CCCI**, ii, p. 326).

[1] Aristotle (*De Mirac. Auscult.*, clxxxii) says that the Rhine flows through the country of the Germans and is covered with ice in winter.

[2] A. Götze, " Die vorgeschichtlichen Burgen der Rhön und die Steinsburg auf dem kleinen Gleichberge bei Römhild," in **LXXXV**, ii ; id., **CCCXXXV**.

[3] **LXXXV**, 1912, pp. 115 ff. ; **LXVII**, 1919, p. 23 ff. ; 1923, p. 8 ; **CXVIII**, 1921-2, p. 212 ; 1916, pp. 145 ff.

[4] Schumacher, **CCCCIX**, pp. 138 ff.

soon filled up by neighbouring folk of an equally adventurous
spirit and equally greedy for land whereon to spread
themselves.

But that is not what happened. Among the Celtic peoples
of Germany there were two whose habitats are perfectly
well known, the Volcae and the Boii.[1]   They furnished
contingents to every Celtic expedition, no doubt to the very
earliest. Yet not only did they not vacate their old home,
but the Boii even advanced their frontier eastwards and
maintained it for a very long time. We may take it as certain
that, so long as the Celtic peoples did not emigrate *en masse*,
they kept their positions in Germany. It was the surplus
population, the marching forces, that emigrated ; the central
portion stayed where it was and spread out. The Turoni,
a section of whom (perhaps the majority) had settled on the
Loire, are mentioned in Ptolemy's time in the upper valley
of the Main, south of the Chatti.[2] They had become Germanized, like the Volcae later.

Two prejudices, one archæological and one historical,
keep alive the very widespread opinion that the Celts
abandoned a large part of Germany in the second La Tène
period, their decline beginning about 250.[3] The truth is
that, even if they had at that date lost ground in Italy, they
were still fighting there with considerable success, while
they were holding their own in the Celtiberian tribes in
Spain and were establishing themselves in Asia Minor. The
supporters of this view are obviously not thinking of the
general halt and retirement of the Celts which occurred soon
after, but of a decline in civilization which they see in the
second La Tène period, a decline which appears in a weaker
resistance to outside influences, and especially in Germany.

It is true that the archæological finds of this period are
not so brilliant as those of the first. The grave-goods are
not so rich. In Germany and in Gaul the beautiful Greek
objects, the earthenware vases and the bronze vessels, have
gone. From this, it has been concluded that communications
between the Mediterranean world and the Celtic interior
were interrupted. This view is incorrect. The culture of
La Tène III was indebted to the civilizations of the South

---

[1] See *Rise*, pp. 140–1.   [2] Ptol., ii, 11, 22.
[3] Déchelette, ii, 3, p. 918.

for many things—technical devices, domestic usages, methods of construction. These benefits were diffused in the course of the second period or as a result of relations commenced at that time. It was, too, at this date that coinage began to spread in the Celtic world,[1] and it cannot be said that the adoption of coinage and of copies of coins corresponds to a falling-off of relations with the peoples which supplied the models.

It is, moreover, very hazardous to try to show a decay in skill and taste in the Celtic craftsmen of this period. The fine swords with engraved scabbards, the most beautiful belts, and the richest bracelets date from La Tène II.

Besides, one would have to be very sure of being able to tell all the objects belonging to each of these two periods before speaking of a weakening of the Celtic societies and of depopulation. Archæology is often a deceptive mirror of the past, and usually it is a broken one.

Lastly, there is no constant relation between the civilization of a people and the extent of its political power. When the Celts finally bowed before Rome and her culture, they were by no means decadent. They were a strong, healthy social body, which benefited the Roman Empire by its healthiness and lived on in that Empire.

The second prejudice is that the Belgæ were Germans or semi-Germans. If so, the Germans encroached on the domain of the Celts a hundred or two hundred years before the date at which they appear in history under their own name.

In Cæsar's time [2] the Belgæ were all settled between the Seine and the Rhine. We have several lists of the peoples composing this nation, but they agree in the main.[3] They were: the Treviri, Mediomatrici, and Leuci in the east; the Remi and Suessiones in the west, with the Catuvellauni, Meldi, Parisii, and Silvanectes; and in the west again and north, the Veliocasses, Bellovaci, Caleti, Ambiani, Atrebates, and Morini, and after them the Aduatuci, Eburones, Nervii, and Menapii. Strabo included the Armorici and, although

---

[1] Livy (xxxvi, 40, 12 ; xxxiii, 3, 13), speaking of the triumph over the Boii in 196 and 191, says that among the booty there were 1,471 torques and 2,340 pounds *argenti infecti factique in Gallicis vasis.*

[2] Cf. for the Belgæ, Rademacher, in Ebert, **CCCXXIV,** s.v. " Belgen ".

[3] Cæs., ii, 3, 4, 11 ; iv, 19 ; viii, 6 ; Pliny, iv, 105 ; Ptol., ii, 9 ; Strabo, iv, 196, 15.

he is alone in doing so, his opinion is not to be despised. They formed a mass something like that of the Brythons of Gaul. The large scale of their movements suggests that their number was great. Like the Goidels and Brythons, the Belgæ were a family of kindred or associated peoples ; they were a group in which natural relationships were cemented by political ties. They were distinguished from other peoples by the affinities which they found between themselves and the strangers across the Rhine.

For part of the Belgic peoples, including some of the most important of them, called themselves Germans or were so called by the ethnographers.[1] First, there were the Aduatuci or Tungri.[2] But these had been left behind by the expedition of the Cimbri. Along the Meuse and the Sambre, the Eburones of Limburg, the Condrusi of Condroz, and the Paemani of the valley of the Lesse are classed together as Germans.[3] To them we must add the Segni [4] of the upper valley of the Ourthe. These peoples, which were grouped round the Treviri, called themselves their clients. Now, the Treviri and the Nervii, who surrounded them on the north, claimed to be of Germanic origin and were proud of it.[5] Lastly, the Menapii on the North Sea shore are placed by Cæsar with the Nervii under the description, " Germans from this side of the Rhine," *Cisrhenani*.[6] It is a term which is used by Cæsar several times, and always to designate the peoples of the Belgic group, and not the remnants of the expedition of Ariovistus.[7]

A good half of the Belgæ then, if we are to accept concordant evidence based on the traditions of the tribes themselves, should be regarded as Germans. Should one go further and do the same with the Remi, Suessiones, Bellovaci, and other Belgæ ? Or should one not go so far, but try to interpret the evidence ? Usually it is accepted literally.[8] It is agreed that there were among the Belgæ at least a great

[1] Cæs., ii, 4 ; Tac., *Germ.*, 2.
[2] Tac., loc. cit.
[3] Cæs., loc. cit. : *uno nomine Germani appellantur.*
[4] Id., vi, 32.
[5] Tac., *Germ.*, 28.
[6] Cæs., vi, 2, 3 ; ii, 3. Cf. Jullian, **CCCXLVII**, ii, p. 10.
[7] Cæs., v, 27, 8 ; vii, 63, 7 ; Jullian, op. cit., ii, p. 467.
[8] e.g. by Mr. MacNeill (**CCCCXLI**, p. 18), who regards the Belgæ as a product of this community formed by the C_lts and Germans on their boundary.

many Germans, and that in any case they all came from *Germania*, from beyond the Rhine, from the region bounded on the south by the Main. If we are to believe Pomponius Mela,[1] they came from still further, from the Cimbric Peninsula and the shores of the Baltic ; they were a branch of the Scythians or Celto-Scythians mentioned by Pytheas in that region, and their shores were opposite Thule, that is, Scandinavia. But Pomponius Mela may perhaps be confusing them with the Cimbri and Teutones, whom Pytheas had certainly met in Jutland.[2]

We may ask when these Belgic peoples, which we find on the edge of the Celtic world in the second La Tène period, crossed from the east to the west of the Rhine. Their preponderance explains the new development which appears at this time in the civilization of the Western barbarians. They are supposed to have acted during this period in the same way as the Brythonic Gauls at the beginning of La Tène, their settlements in Gaul, like that of the Celts of the Danube, being founded by their rear-guard. But at the same time there reappears in the Celtic world a practice which, during the first La Tène period, seems on the whole to have been confined within the probable frontier of the Germans—burning of the dead. Here is another reason for calling the Belgians Germanic. Cæsar,[3] too, says that their culture was different from that of Gaul and more like that of the peoples beyond the Rhine—municipal life less highly developed than in Gaul, merchants fewer and trade more rudimentary, a character wilder and more warlike.

As a matter of fact, the evidence of the historians is not so definite or so clear as it seems, for the name of *Germani* which they give to the Belgæ may not have the meaning which it is usually given. It is a late word,[4] perhaps a Belgic word like *Gaesati*,[5] used to designate different groups or elements of tribes, which, being applied by the Latins to

---

[1] iii, 36 and 57. Cf. Jullian, op. cit., i, p. 242.
[2] Strabo, i, 2, 27 ; xi, 6, 2 ; Plut., *Mar.*, ii.
[3] **I**, 1. Cf. Jullian, op. cit., ii, p. 469.
[4] Tac., *Germ.*, 2 : *vocabulum recens et nuper additum.* Various etymologies have for a long time been suggested for the word *Germani*—*garm, gairm* " place ", or *ger* " neighbour ", both Celtic. The latter is perhaps the better. It is supported by a gloss of Bede, v, 9 : *Garmani (a vicina gente Brittonum).*
[5] See above, p. 74.

the new family of strangers, took on a new meaning and was
used again by the historians to define the Belgæ.

While the Belgians claimed kinship with the peoples
beyond the Rhine, they also had public ties with the Celtic
peoples which were outside their confederation. The Remi
were the patrons of the Carnutes,[1] and the Bellovaci had
from time immemorial been friends of the Ædui.[2] Although
the peoples in question are only the Remi and Bellovaci, and
not the Treviri or Nervii, these facts are of no less account,
for the whole of Belgica or its various tribal bodies
several times combined with the rest of Gaul.

Besides, even if the Eburones, Nervii, and Treviri were
Germans, their chiefs had Gallic names. Doubtless this was
true of more than one Germanic king, but we should note
that there is never any word of the language of these
supposedly Germanic tribes of Belgica. This silence means
that they spoke Gaulish,[3] as might be inferred from the
names of places and men which they have left.[4]

A passage in Ausonius [5] enables us, to some extent, to
determine the place held by the Belgæ among the other Gallic
peoples. When he says that the Volcae Tectosages called
themselves *Belcae Tectosagi*, the poet seems to suggest that
the two names were closely related.[6] It is of no consequence
whether the word is spelt *Belcas* or *Belgas*.[7] Their identity
is undeniable, and recalls that of $K\epsilon\lambda\tau\acute{o}s$ and $\Gamma\alpha\lambda\acute{a}\tau\eta s$.[8]
From that identity, we may reasonably suppose that this
is one of those generic terms by which the Celts designated
themselves. A difference in pronunciation aggravated by
a false etymology would lead to the name of Belgæ being
given to the folk north of the Main.

So, though the Belgæ called themselves Germans, they

---

[1] Cæs., v, 4, 5.
[2] Id., ii, 14, 2. Cf. Jullian, op. cit., ii, p. 442.
[3] Strabo (iv, 176) says that the Gaulish of Belgica was not greatly different
from the Gaulish of the Ædui (Cic., *De Div.*, i, 41).
[4] We know an Æduan Diviciacus and a Diviciacus among the Suessiones
(Cæs., ii, 4).
[5] *Ordo Urbium Nobilium*, xiii, 7–10 :—
　　　Qua rapitur præceps Rhodanus genitore Lemanno,
　　　interiusque premunt Aquitanica rura Cebennæ,
　　　usque in Tectosagos paganaque nomine Belcas,
　　　totum Narbo fuit.
[6] Belcæ = Volcæ. Cf. Pauly, CCCLXVIII, iii, cols. 198–9.
[7] Pomp. Mela, 36, 57 : *Belcæ*.
[8] See *Rise*, pp. 21 ff.

were not Germans at all ; they were Gauls, who had come from the district north of the Main and other places as well.

The archæological evidence also tends to prove that no great movement of population can have occurred in Central Germany and Gaul during the second La Tène period.[1] In those Hallstatt sites in Western Germany which can, by the different types of the pottery,[2] be assigned to various tribes or groups of tribes, one finds a definite continuity of population. Two of these groups, the Helvetii in the south and the Treviri in the north, did not move in the La Tène period. In Cæsar's time, the Treviri were still in their old country on the west bank of the Rhine.[3]

There is yet another place where the settlements of the Belgæ were already fixed in the second La Tène period. In Champagne and Soissonnais there is no sign of the population changing at that time. The same cemeteries contain tombs of La Tène I and II, and in general the centres of population remained the same. Although few cremations of the third period happen to have been discovered, we may conclude that the Romans there found the Gauls in the places where they had settled in 400.[4] It would, moreover, be very hard to find a place on the map for the peoples which the Belgæ would have driven out of Champagne and Soissonnais about 300. Nor should we forget that in the time of Pytheas the Armorici, who may have been Belgæ, were already established in the west of Gaul.[5]

From their original home in the middle valley of the Rhine and on the right bank north of the Main, the Belgæ probably spread at the very beginning of this history over Belgium and Northern France, just as the Brythons or Volcae of the south of Germany spread over central and southern Gaul. It is true that they were not all established by 400,[6] but, since they were beginning to appear in Illyria,

---

[1] Herr Schumacher (**CCCCIX**, pp. 196 ff.) has very happily laid stress on the continuity of the population of the Rhine Valley from one age to another.

[2] The pottery of Salem, Koberstadt, and Mehren. Cf. Schumacher, in **CXVIII**, 1914, pp. 257 ff. ; H. Horning, in **LXVIII**, 1921, pp. 19 ff.

[3] Müllenhoff, **CCCXLII**, ii, pp. 201-2.

[4] In Cæsar, whenever the Remi and Suessiones come into question, these peoples appear as having been always established, and rather different from the peoples recently settled in the north of Belgica. Jullian, in **CXXXIV**, 1915, pp. 218 ff.

[5] Jullian, **CCCXLVII**, i, p. 323.

[6] The Menapii did not reach the neighbourhood of Tournai till 54. Before that, they were still on the two banks of the Rhine.

Italy, Spain, and probably Britain somewhere about 300, it is hard to believe that they were not permanently settled in the Gallic domain until some 150 years later. Since the point from which they started at the end of the fourth century was no longer the east bank of the Rhine, but the whole region between the Seine and the Harz, one must suppose that they had spread into the western part of that vast area while the earliest Gauls were wandering into Italy and the valley of the Danube. The settlements which they then founded must have been about a century later than the cemeteries of the first Gauls. Setting forth later, they expanded in the same manner all round their domain, including what is now Germany.

The distribution of the brooches of La Tène II, which have been found right up to the Oder and lower Vistula, the Magdeburg district, and the shores of the North Sea and Baltic,[1] points to the age when Celtic civilization in Germany spread widest and sank deepest, and the reciprocal penetration of Celts and Germans was most complete. It was also at this time that the German workers started to alter the types of objects, especially arms, furnished to them by their Gallic brother-craftsmen. The Germanic swords and spears are derived from those of La Tène II and III, not La Tène I.

The most important object in Celtic archæology, the silver vessel found at Gundestrup in Jutland, outside the true domain of the Celts, in the country of the Cimbri, comes from just about the end of the La Tène period. It is generally agreed that it was made about the beginning of the first century B.C. [2] among the Danubian Celts, in the country of the Scordisci, who were rich in silver.[3] It must have been used for religious purposes by the people who had charge of it among the Cimbri, for they left it in the brush, in a place which was probably forbidden ground, where no one set foot until the cauldron was completely covered over and the heath had become bog. It is of some importance that a sacred vessel, made by Celts and covered with Celtic mythological subjects, should have been used for religious ceremonies by a Cimbric tribe about a hundred years before Christ.

---

[1] Beltz, in **LXXXV**, 1913, pp. 117 ff.
[2] F. Drexel, in **LXXII**, 1915, pp. 1 ff.   [3] See above, p. 62.

So the civilizing and political influence of the Celts in Germany was in full swing during the third and second centuries.

But if we examine the facts more closely, looking not so much for signs of events as for evidence of the conditions which must have led to events which occurred later, we find two contrary processes taking place : a process of assimilation of the German world on the one hand, but on the other, as a result of that very assimilation, a process of penetration by the Germans into the Celtic world. Then there happened what would happen again to the Roman Empire. The Celts had auxiliaries, some of whom settled down among them, and, being the more occupied on the outer edge of their domains, they squandered the reserves of men which had fed their expeditions. The result was that one fine day a body of Germanic peoples grew restless, as the Belgæ had done, and led the Celtic tribes of the east bank of the Rhine off to new adventures which were to take them beyond the Celtic world. Then, and not till then, the Celts abandoned the east bank of the Rhine to the Germans. But the charm was not broken, for fifty years later, when Ariovistus appears in Gaul, it is not as a foreigner. He speaks Gaulish like a man who knows it and is used to speaking it.[1]

II

THE CIMBRI AND TEUTONES

Comparative calm had been restored for over a century in the region from which the chief expeditions of the Belgæ had started, when another mass of peoples began to move. These were the Cimbri and Teutones. They were probably Germans, but the story of their exodus is none the less linked with that of the Celtic migrations.

The expedition which Augustus afterwards sent along the coasts of Germany [2] came upon Cimbri, but these were only the tiny remnant of a great nation. They were then in Jutland, the Cimbric Peninsula.[3] We may suppose that

[1] Cæs., i, 47.
[2] Mon. Anc., 26.
[3] Strabo, vii, 2, 1–4 ; Pomp. Mela, iii, 32 ; Pliny, ii, 167 ; iv, 95–7, 99 ; Tac., Germ., 37 ; Ptol., ii, 11, 2, 7, 16. Cf. Müllenhoff, CCCLXII, ii, pp. 285 ff.

these had stayed at home when the rest went in search of adventure.

Pytheas had encountered the Teutones.[1] They held the trade in amber, which they got from the people of the island of Abalum (Œsel),[2] off the east coast of the Baltic, and sold to the merchants of the west. They doubtless lived on the Danish islands in what the ancient geographers called the Sinus Codanus.[3] It is very likely that they were neighbours of the Cimbri, since they combined with them, and it is certain that both extended to the seaboard between the Elbe and the Oder.[4]

Contemporaries regarded them as Celts.[5] But it was only after the Cimbric invasion, and probably as a result of the many prisoners left in the hands of the Romans, that the Romans and Greeks learned to distinguish between Celts and Germans. Their names do not help us to place them. That of the Teutones is Celtic in form. Germanic, Celtic, and Italic all have the root ; it is an old word meaning " tribe ", " town ", " people ".[6] The name of the Cimbri led Poseidonios to connect them with the Cimmerians,[7] and has led modern writers to connect them with the Cymry. The ancients had an etymology for the word which was Celtic, *Cimber* meaning " brigand ".[8]

The names of Teuton and Cimbric leaders given by the historians are Celtic or of Celtic form.[9] A Teuton chief is called Teutoboduus, and a Cimbrian Claodicus. Both of these names may have been Celticized ; but there are also a Boiorix, " King of the Boii," a Caesorix or Gaesorix, probably

---

[1] Pliny, xxxviii, 35. Cf. Müllenhoff, op. cit., ii, pp. 476, 479 ; d'Arbois, **CCCI**, i, p. 19.

[2] There is on it a village named Aboul. It is a town of apple-trees, and the island was an island of apples ; cf. the old Italic Abella—*Abella malifera.*

[3] Pomp. Mela, ii, 32, 54. After the Elbe comes the Sinus Codanus, full of islands ; *in ea sunt Cimbri et Teutoni.* Cf. Jullian, **CCCXLVII**, iii, p. 45.

[4] Pomp. Mela, iii, 32, 54 ; Pliny, iv, 99 ; xxxvii, 35.

[5] Cic., *De Orat.*, ii, 66 ; *De Prov. Cos.*, 266 ; Sall., *Jug.*, 114 ; App., *Celt.*, i, 2. Cf. Jullian, op. cit., i, p. 243, n. 3 ; Mommsen, **CCCLIX**, ii, p. 172 ; Holder, **CCVII**, s.v. " Cimbri ".

[6] Müllenhoff, op. cit., i, p. 113 ; d'Arbois **CCXIX**, p. 170.

[7] Müllenhoff, op. cit., ii, pp. 167 ff. ; Poseid., in Strabo, vii, 293 ; cf. Diod., v, 32 ; Plut., *Mar.*, ii.

[8] *Cimbri lingua Gallica latrones dicuntur.* Festus, *Epit.*, 43. Müllenhoff (ii, pp. 116 ff.) supposes that they got their Celtic name in Gaul. Old Irish has a word *cimb* " tribute ", " ransom ", and a word *cimbid* " prisoner ". D'Arbois (**CCXCIX**, pp. 205 ff.) supposes an active formation, *Cimb-r-os*, from the same root, meaning one who takes prisoner.

[9] Müllenhoff, op. cit., ii, p. 118 ; Jullian, op. cit., iii, p. 53.

" King of the Gaesati," and a Lugius, whose name, if it has
been correctly recorded, contains that of one of the great
Celtic deities, Lugh. All these names are Celtic, and they
cannot be anything else ; but that alone is not enough.

Most of the historians of the Empire speak of these
peoples as Germans,[1] and Tacitus,[2] who was an authority
on the subject, places them in the group of the Ingaevones,
one of the three great groups of Germanic tribes. So, too, the
archæology of Hanover, Holstein, and Schleswig [3] in the
Hallstatt and La Tène periods is utterly different from that
of regions where Celtic names are frequent. Cremation of
the dead was the usual practice, whereas further south burial
continued to prevail for a long time. The characteristic
objects of the southern culture, brooches and pottery, are
found there only sporadically.

So it was down to about 300. After that, the doors were
opened and Celtic influence and fashions gained ground
northwards, predominating more and more until the time
when Gallic industry became Roman industry. It was about
now that the Cimbri ordered from the Scordisci or perhaps
in Gaul the sacred vessels, of which the Gundestrup cauldron,
found in their country, may be regarded as the chief specimen.[4]
The Cimbri were Germans, Celticized by the trade or policy
of the Celts in the third and second centuries. Just as the
Galatians took Greek names, and the Scots and Welsh later
took Anglo-Saxon names, they took Celtic names, and spoke
Celtic, at least in their dealings with other peoples. Marius's
intelligence service, run by Sertorius, took the trouble to
learn Celtic, and found that language sufficient.[5] Needless to
say, these peoples were armed in the Celtic manner, and
indeed the throwing-axe of the Celts, the *cateia*, was called
the *teutonus*.[6]

It is possible that there were Celtic elements among
the Cimbri and Teutones. Names like Boiorix and Gaesorix,
which have a racial meaning, were perhaps not bestowed

[1] Dottin, **CCCXXI**, p. 21 ; Müllenhoff, op. cit., ii, p. 154.
[2] *Germ.*, 2. Cf. Jullian, op. cit., iii, p. 50.
[3] Schwantes, in **CXVIII**, 1909, pp. 140 ff.
[4] See above, p. 102.
[5] Mommsen, **CCCLIX**, ii, p. 172.
[6] Isid. Sev., *Orig.*, 18, 7, 7 ; Müllenhoff, op. cit., ii, p. 115. For helmets
and body-armour among the Cimbri, see Plut., *Mar.*, 25. Cf. Jullian, op. cit.,
iii, p. 55. For the white shield of the Cimbri, Plut., loc. cit.

lightly. Certainly they were followed by peoples, some of which were doubtless not Germans, while others were undoubtedly Celts.

The historians mention the Ambrones as being [1] a crack corps of the Teuton army. The origin of the name may perhaps be geographical.[2] Festus [3] calls them a *gens Gallica*. The Ligurians of the Genoese coast had the same name, and formed an auxiliary corps in the army of Marius.[4]

If there is any doubt about them, there is none about the Helvetii, who followed the Cimbri or were carried along by them. Tribes of this nation, the Tigurini and the Tugeni,[5] took part in these campaigns.

The history of the invasion of the Cimbri and Teutones [6] gives a fuller and more correct idea than does that of the expeditions of the fourth and third centuries of the great hordes which from time to time fell on the good lands of Europe—sometimes timid, sometimes furious, encumbered with baggage and spoil, inclined to straggle but also capable of a rapid, orderly march, sometimes led by extraordinarily clear-headed chiefs and sometimes apparently drifting under the guidance of chance and instinct alone.

In 113 the Cimbri started to move, possibly driven from their country by a tidal wave, like the Celts, and advanced to the south, where they came up against the Boii and were thrown back by them on to the Volcae. The Volcae drove them on to the Taurisci of Noricum. They went on into Pannonia, to the country of the Scordisci, but there they were compelled to turn in their tracks, and re-entered Noricum by the Save or Drave, till they reached Noreia (Neumarkt), the capital. The Romans were already interested in Noricum.[7] The Cimbri found in front of them the army of the Consul Cn. Papirius Carbo, which, after an attempt at negotiation, they routed. Nevertheless, they continued their retreat

---

[1] Plut., *Mar.*, 19 ; Müllenhoff, op. cit., ii, p. 114 ; Jullian, in **CXXXIV**, N. GR., lxxii.

[2] Several rivers in Celtic country were called Ambra. One is a tributary of the Weser in its upper course, the Emmer.

[3] *Epit.*, p. 17, 2 M.

[4] Plut., *Mar.*, 19.

[5] Jullian, op. cit., ii, p. 61.

[6] For the expedition of the Cimbri and Teutones, see Müllenhoff, ii, pp. 112–189. Jullian, **CCCXLVII**, iii, pp. 39 ff. ; Chapot, **CCCXI**, English, pp. 12 ff.

[7] See above, p. 65.

into Germany, where, in the region of the Main, they were joined by the Teutones.

There they remained from 113 to 109. They had wandered about for a whole year without stopping, living on the country—that is ravaging it. We must now picture them on the Main, founding colonies, sowing crops, and reaping them. In these four obscure years they probably achieved more than in their whole career. They occupied a country which had been Celtic and now ceased to be so. It was at this time, too, that they pushed forward the Helvetii, whose departure made a desert of the Gallic country south of the Main.

When the Cimbri and Teutones set off again in 109, they probably left rear-guards or colonies behind them.[1] Their name still survived in the Roman period in that region of the Limes which they occupied, and the memory of the great exodus, which had made a strong impression, had supplied a legend to the great fortified enclosures of the Taunus and Westerwald.[2]

In the same year the Teutones and Helvetii crossed the Rhine, and met the Consul Silanus and his army somewhere in Gaul. They must have remained facing each other for several weeks, for the Cimbri had time to send an embassy to Rome. They asked for lands, as they had already asked them of Carbo, but Rome had no land to give them. The conversations were broken off, and Silanus was defeated. But the barbarians did not advance. They changed their route, and for two years we lose track of them. In 107 the Tigurini, operating on their own account, descended into Provence and in the Roman province joined up with the Volcae Tectosages of Toulouse, who had revolted and were besieging the garrison. One of the Consuls of the year, L. Cassius Longinus, pursued them, but they escaped down the Garonne. Cassius made contact with them in the country of the Nitiobriges near Agen. He was defeated and killed, and his army had to capitulate. In this affair the Tigurini were commanded

---

[1] On the Greinberg, near Miltenberg, on the Main in Franconia, text regarding the boundaries of a Teutonic territory (I, xii, 6610) ; cf. J. Quilling, in LXXXV, 1914, p. 334).

[2] Dedications addressed *Mercurio Cimbriano*, on the Greinberg (I, xiii, 6604–5) ; *Mercurio Cimbrio* on the Heiligenberg near Heidelberg (ibid., 6402). Cf. Schumacher, CCCLIX, p. 159.

by a capable man named Divico, whom Cæsar knew. The other Consul, Servilius Cæpio, succeeded not only in saving the garrison of Toulouse, but in obtaining the surrender of the treasure of the Tectosages, estimated at 200,000 pounds of gold. It was sent to Marseilles but never arrived there, and the Consul was accused, not unreasonably, of being himself responsible for the theft. It was said that the gold of Toulouse was the gold of Delphi. It brought bad luck to Cæpio.

It seems very likely that the treasure of coins, ingots, and a torque found at Taillac-Libourne [1] in 1893 had something to do with this campaign of the Tigurini in southwestern Gaul. It may have been their war-chest. The coins can be divided into a few fairly large groups, which can be distributed on the map along the route taken by the Cimbri and Teutones. Sixty-five are gold staters of the Bellovaci, a hundred and ninety-five others belong to the Ambarri or the Arverni, and seventy-five are *Regenbogenschüsselchen*. These coins would, then, be shares or remains of tribute collected by the Tigurini on the road. After the battle of Agen the Tigurini would have reached the Atlantic coast, leaving a post to guard the treasure, which was buried in some emergency.[2]

In 105 Cimbri, Teutones, Ambrones, and Helvetii were reunited, and went down the Rhone. At Orange they came on the two Roman armies of Cæpio, now Proconsul, and Cn. Mallius Maximus, a Consul, and crushed them. Then once again Cimbri, Teutones, and allies went their different ways. The first reached Spain, where all trace of them is lost. The second went through Gaul from south to north, ravaging like wild beasts, and Cæsar more than once gives a picture of the terrible distress which they created. Only the Belgæ were able to stop them. Still, they left 6,000 men in Belgium, on the Sambre at Namur, to guard the baggage and protect their lines of communication. From this band was formed, fifty years later, the important, more than half Celtic tribe of the Aduatuci.

---

[1] Forrer, **DXLIII**, p. 316 ; Cartailhac, in **XV**, 1897.
[2] This hypothesis has not been accepted by M. Blanchet (in **CXXIV**, xii, pp. 21 ff.), who holds that the treasure of Taillac represents the movable property of a private individual. That would give us a high notion of Gallic capitalism. But I am much attracted by Herr Forrer's ingenious explanation.

Two years later, in 103, the Cimbri, sorely tried by the resistance of the Celtiberians, reappeared north of the Pyrenees, and were joined by the Teutones somewhere in Gaul. Their leaders agreed on an ambitious and well thought out plan, which was in part very well executed.

They had not found what they wanted in Gaul. They had not been allowed to settle down, or were incapable of doing so. The country was too full or too completely assigned to existing proprietors, except perhaps in the district of the Belgæ, who do not seem to have been inconvenienced by the colony of the Aduatuci. For ten years they had been hovering round Italy and beating Roman armies, but after each victory they had stopped. At last they decided to make a serious effort to force their way into the country ; they would attack it from two sides. The Teutones were to cross the Western Alps by the southern passes, following the Durance ; the Cimbri should move eastwards along the north of the Alps and then over the Brenner ; the Tigurini, on the left wing, should go yet further east, into Noricum, either as a reserve or to bring reinforcements from the direction of the Julian Alps.

Marius defeated the Teutones at Aquae Sextiae (Aix). The Cimbri crushed his colleague Catulus on the Adige, but once again they hesitated or dispersed in Venetia and Lombardy, and in the end lost time, which Marius gained. The two Consuls joined forces, and at Vercellae in Piedmont they put an end to the Cimbric danger. The Tigurini had remained in Noricum. Sulla was sent there and seems to have had no great difficulty in getting them to join the other Helvetii in Switzerland.

The battles of Aquae Sextiae and Vercellae were frightful slaughters. The dead and prisoners ran to thousands. Whole armies were wiped out, and with them all their following of women, children, old men, and the non-fighting people. After Aquae Sextiae, a small body of horse managed to escape and to reach the land of the Sequani, who gave them up. At Vercellae no one escaped.

What remained of the great hosts brought by the Cimbri and Teutones was in reality transplanted. The sequel to this destruction of peoples was that strange Servile War which broke out thirty years later. It was a class-war, no doubt, but it was also a national war, conducted by Gallic, German, and Thracian leaders, and for the Rome of Sulla it was as terrible a danger as the invasion of the Cimbri in the days of Marius.

The Servile War is interesting as guaranteeing the likelihood of the number of prisoners, and also of the generally different figures given by the historians. We hear of 300,000 Teutones at Aquae Sextiae and as many Cimbri. This is the fighting strength, not the whole people including women, children, and a great many other non-combatants. They were tribes, whole social units and probably groups of units or large political units. The expedition of the Cimbri and Teutones involved the peoples concerned almost in their entirety. The Cimbri left at home only the small remnant which was afterwards found there by the expedition of Augustus.[1] They sent an embassy to the Emperor, and presented him with a cauldron ; one thinks of that of Gundestrup. Shortly afterwards they disappeared.

Of the Teutones, there is no more question in their old home.[2] The Ambrones disappeared likewise. As for the Helvetii, the country which they had occupied is called " the Desert of the Helvetii " ; they left it empty and for a time nobody came to occupy it.

There are many interesting things about this half-Celtic half-Germanic adventure—the uncertain advance, the way in which peoples crossed each other's paths, without always fighting, the heterogeneous mass which followed it, and the anxiety for a permanent home which appears to have ruled these barbarians, although they seem to have had a notion that their settlement would send other peoples wandering off. But it left no settlement, save that of the Aduatuci and perhaps that of the Teutones of the Taunus. Gaul must have been populated to saturation point, and Rome was growing steadily. The depopulation and weakness of the Empire of five centuries later were needed before similar expeditions could lead to conquest and the creation of new states. The adventure of the Cimbri and Teutones was doubtless a perfect replica of the great earlier invasions, except in

---

[1] Tac., *Germ.*, 37.
[2] When geographers like Strabo and encyclopædists like Pliny speak of the Teutones on the coast of the Baltic and their share in the amber-trade, they are merely copying previous Greek historians.

that it failed. But we can judge of the alarm and the destruction which it created. The memory of it lasted long, for, although the Ambrones had vanished, the Latin grammarians of the Late Empire say that their name survived as a word of abuse.

III

RESULTS OF THE INVASION

The expedition of the Cimbri and Teutones had a great effect on the Celtic world and, indeed, turned it upside down. In 103 it was no longer what it had been in 113.

For nearly four hundred years the Gauls had lived as agriculturists, scattered in farms and open villages,[1] deserting the citadels in which the Hallstatt men and those of the Bronze and Neolithic Ages had shut themselves up, at least for long periods.[2] From the end of the second century onwards, Gaul bristled with fortresses, large and small,[3] and its people returned to the abandoned *oppida*, for example to Fort-Harrouard.[4] Except on the east bank of the Rhine and the Celto-Ligurian marches in the south of France, objects of La Tène III come directly after those of Hallstatt in the prehistoric forts.

Behind those ramparts the Gauls endured long and severe sieges, to which eloquent allusion is made in the speech which Cæsar places in the mouth of the Arvernian Cintognatus during the blockade of Alesia.[5] A process then took place in Gaul which was repeated four centuries later in the first Germanic invasions. The Gallo-Roman towns, sprawling wide over the plains, were in a very few years surrounded by walls hastily built with the materials of the demolished suburbs. In each case, a long period of peace and prosperity followed times of insecurity and distress. But Gaul had more vitality in the first century before Christ than in the third of our era.

To the same circumstances as these *oppida*, which are fortresses, not fortified cities, we may attribute the underground refuges which are usually some distance away from a

---

[1] See above, p. 7.   [2] See above, p. 8.
[3] Déchelette, in **CXXXIX**, 1912, i, pp. 101 ff.
[4] Philippe, **CCCCLXVII**.   [5] vii, 77.

group of dwellings and have two or more entrances, stairs, and passages barred by doors.[1]   They were used in several epochs, and are not all contemporary. But the Gauls certainly had them—witness the story of the Lingonian Sabinus, who lived in one with his wife Eponina after the failure of the revolt of A.D. 70.[2]

Another consequence of the Cimbro-Teutonic invasion was that the Celts retreated to the Rhine. In the middle valley of that river, north of the Main, the villages of La Tène III are Germanic settlements, whose culture, though reminding one that the Celts were near, is only an imitation of theirs.[3]   The Helvetii had cleared out completely, and it was to Switzerland that Divico returned to live. It was no doubt the same with the Celts north of the Main. The Germans advanced in their track between the Rhine and Bohemia. A fairly large Celtic population remained in and round Bohemia for some time yet, but it spread in the direction of the Danube and did not retreat to Gaul. The eastern frontier of the rest of the Celts, which had so long been fixed in Thuringia, was suddenly withdrawn to the Rhine.

It seems to have happened strangely easily, and in any case very quickly, between 113 and 109. The whole system of forts appears to have been abandoned without a blow. It was the result of causes which had long lain in the very nature of Celtic societies. This was the region from which all the thousands had set forth to settle or fight in Gaul, Spain, Italy, the Danube valley, and the East. However prolific these nations of the original Celtic country may have been, they were clearly much reduced in numbers. In that quarter, especially north of the Main and in Thuringia, there were now only the phantoms of peoples which had vanished, scattered, retired before the effective force of nations hitherto kept back by their prestige. These Gauls who lived north of the Main must have been very insignificant to have left no trace of themselves either among the Celts of the west bank who may have taken them in or among the Cimbri who may have absorbed them. There must have been some movements of peoples inside Gaul, and it has been

---

[1] Blanchet, **CCCLXV** ; **CXXIV**, 1910, ii, p. 265 ; **CXX**, 1924, p. 63.
[2] See below, p. 150.
[3] Schumacher, in **CXVIII**, 1914, pp. 277 ff.

suggested that one took place in the valley of the Garonne as a result of the expedition of the Tigurini. The name of Vevey in the canton of Vaud (*Viviscus*), may possibly indicate that a body of Bituriges *Vivisci*, whom we find established at the mouth of the Garonne, had followed the Helvetii in their wanderings. This is mere hypothesis, for the name may equally well record an earlier settlement of the same people. There is no archæological evidence to help us.

Still more important is the succession of great movements which were set going for over a century by the descent of the Cimbri and Teutones on Western Europe. When those peoples started, they must have gone up the valley of the Elbe, which the Boii blocked. The country was populous, and they probably did not create a void before them. They went through the tribes and came out on the other side.

These peoples of Central Germany, the Lombards, Hermunduri, and Semnones, whom the ancient authors [1] place in the group of the Herminones, were then united in a confederation whose members called themselves by the common name of Suevi.[2] To this adhered, but as a separate body, the Marcomanni,[3] the Marchmen, from the frontier strip which the Germans regarded as a kind of desert.[4] But the Marcomanni were not an old existing people ; they were probably a combination of the scattered bodies of Cimbri and Teutones which had remained in or returned to the old territory of the Helvetii. The Black Forest, which formed a backbone to their country, was called Abnoba in Celtic ; under the Empire, it was given the Germanic name of Silva Marciana, when the only inhabitants of the country were new settlers.

The Suevi were settled, since they remained. But perhaps they were not settled quite in the same way as the Celts.[5] The passage of the Cimbri and Teutones may have introduced

---

[1] Tac., *Germ.*, 38–9 ; Pliny, iv, 28 ; Strabo, vii, p. 290.

[2] Jullian, **CCCXLVII**, iii, p. 49.

[3] Müllenhoff, **CCCLXII**, ii, p. 300.

[4] Cæsar (iv, 3, 2) had heard say that the Suevi had on one side a desert march about 600 Roman miles wide.

[5] Speaking of the Suevi, Cæsar (i, 37, 3) mentions an annual redistribution of land. But we must not treat this information too seriously. Cæsar, even if his information is correct, does not always interpret correctly the social facts which he describes.

some disturbance into their social life. Indeed, they started moving in their turn, and forty years after the defeat of the Cimbri we find them on the Rhine and in Gaul.

They then formed a mass like that of the preceding invasion,[1] but, unlike their predecessors, they had a method. Their king, Ariovistus,[2] does not seem to have had any trouble at home. He co-ordinated all the unconnected operations of his people, and all the acts of the Suevi appear to be the result of a deliberate political purpose. They formed a state which methodically extended its frontiers and made settlements which lasted. Their leader, too, seems to have been an exceptional man. Cæsar, who defeated Ariovistus, gives him his due in ascribing to him acts and speeches, which look as if they were genuine, displaying clear-sightedness and great qualities as a leader of men. He was neither a barbarian nor a particularly simple soul.[3] He has rather the air of a statesman, and of one with large conceptions. His success tempted him to dreams of an overlordship of the whole of Gaul which, had it not been for Cæsar, might have become a Germanic state now instead of waiting till the sixth century.

If we suppose that the Suevi followed the lead of Ariovistus we must imagine them crossing from the valley of the Elbe to that of the Main about 75 B.C., and descending the Main unopposed to the great meeting of ways at Mainz.[4]   On coming into contact with Gaul, they were induced, between 72 and 62, to take sides in one of those squabbles for hegemony in which the Sequani and Ædui engaged.   The Sequani, being the weaker, looked for auxiliaries in Germany, and brought in Ariovistus with 15,000 Suevi.[5] But when their combined forces had won the day, Ariovistus began to talk as a master, demanding one-third of the territory of the Sequani, and taking it. We find, indeed, that from this date Alsace ceases to be part of Sequania, and further north

---

[1] One hundred *pagi* for the Suevi (Cæs., loc. cit. ; iv, 1, 4) and as many for the Semnones alone (Tac., *Germ.*, 39).

[2] Jullian, op. cit., iii, p. 153.

[3] Cæs., i, 44, 9 : *non se tam barbarum neque tam imperitum esse rerum.*

[4] Schumacher, in **CXVIII**, 1914, p. 273.

[5] Jullian, op. cit., iii, p. 154. Strabo (p. 192) says that the Romans bore a grudge against the Sequani because they had helped the Germans to invade Italy. This passage perhaps refers to the beginning of the expeditions of Ariovistus, if not to some unknown episode in the Cimbric war.

the Triboci, who are settled on the territory of the
Mediomatrici, are probably some of Ariovistus's Suevi.[1]
Further north still, the villages of the Nemetes round Spire
and those of the Vangiones round Worms made with those
mentioned a continuous chain of Germanic possessions on
both banks of the Rhine from Mainz to above Strasburg.[2]

Ariovistus' demands united the Gauls against him. He
defeated their great army at Admagetobriga and made them
give him hostages and pay tribute.

About the same time another people, the Dacians,[3]
repeated the Cimbric attack against another front of the
Celts, on the Danube. They were not Germans, but Getae
and perhaps Thracians too. Their origin and the extent of
their possessions are unknown. In the first century they
were in Hungary, east of the Theiss. Gradually they began
to assert themselves. Then, about 82, they, like the Suevi,
got a chief of wide vision in Boerebistas, who was a moral
as well as a political leader.[4] Their history is obscure. They
probably conquered the Bastarnae, for they took Olbia
about 63. With the Scordisci they had previously had
friendly relations,[5] and that people does not appear to have
resisted them. But further north they came into conflict
with the Boii and the people of Noricum.

The Boii had advanced their frontiers to the Theiss [6]
and now formed a kind of large composite state, governed
by a king named Critasirus. They went to war with the
Dacians over the question of the Theiss frontier. Critasirus
was defeated and the Boii were pursued to the south bank
of the Danube. They then vanished from the neighbourhood
of Bohemia, as the Helvetii had vanished from Wurtemberg,
leaving behind them the " Desert of the Boii ".[7]

According to Jordanes,[8] the Dacians carried the war
still further, to the country afterwards occupied by the
Franks. In any case, they did not join forces with the Suevi.[9]

[1] Strabo, iv, 3, 4 ; Pliny, iv, 106 ; Tac., *Germ.*, 27.
[2] Schumacher, in **CXVIII**, 1914, p. 269 ; Müllenhoff, op. cit., ii, p. 301.
[3] Brandis, in **CCCLXVII**, iv, col. 1948 ; Jullian, op. cit., iii, p. 144.
[4] **CCCCXVII**, vii, col. 626 ; Jullian, op. cit., iii, p. 152.
[5] See above, pp. 60–1.
[6] Ibid.
[7] Strabo, vii, 1, 5 ; v, 2 ; Pliny, iii, 146. Cf. Jullian, op. cit., iii, p. 145.
[8] xi, 67. Cf. Jullian, op. cit., iii, p. 154.
[9] Ariovistus had married the sister of a king of Noricum named Voccio
(Cæs., i, 53, 4).

The encroachments of the Suevi and Dacians on the frontiers, old or new, of the Celts, by creating a pressure in the border districts, caused the last migration of the Continental Celts, that of the Helvetii and Boii.

The Helvetii suffered from the inroads and forays of the Suevi quite as directly as the Sequani had done and the Ædui were now doing.[1] Moreover, some of their tribes had not yet taken root in Switzerland, and one can easily imagine that they were not satisfied with their new country. In Germany they had occupied a fertile region, hilly, certainly, but with rich belts of loess surrounding the hills, and their villages had been bound to the earth which fed them. Switzerland was less kindly.

Cæsar's account [2] presents a very vivid picture, and certainly gives an idea of the typical way in which great migrations were planned and carried out—the problems, the aims, the collective phantoms which arose, the powwows in which the programme was fixed and the exodus organized. A clan chieftain, Orgetorix, took the lead. He was a powerful man, who could bring 10,000 clients to the assembly of the Ædui. But the matter was not altogether simple. Orgetorix embarked on political intrigues for a condominium of three peoples, the Sequani, Ædui, and Helvetii, over the whole of Gaul, and aimed at the kingship for himself. He broke himself over these schemes, and finally committed suicide. The Helvetii returned to the original plan of simply emigrating.

They had laid it down as their object to reach the country of the Santones ; perhaps they knew it already.[3] They first entered into negotiations with their neighbours for reinforcements, and succeeded in winning over the Raurici of Basle, the Tulingi, and the Latovici or Latobrigi.[4] A large part of the Boii of Noricum, doubtless those driven out by the Dacians, also joined them. They treated with the Ædui and Sequani for the passage through their country and, after burning their own villages and what corn they did not

---

[1] Cæs., i, 40, 7.
[2] Cæs., i, 2 ff. ; Cic., *Ad Att.*, i, 19, 2. Cf. Jullian, op. cit., iii, p. 160.
[3] See *Rise*, pp. 153–4.
[4] These were fairly small peoples, which were not reckoned among the Helvetii and should doubtless be placed somewhere near the Raurici, along the Rhine. They may have been remnants of the Celtic population of Germany.

take with them, all the different bodies united on the 24th March, 58, to the number of 368,000 souls, of whom 263,000 were Helvetii, 36,000 Tulingi, 14,000 Latobrigi, 23,000 Raurici, and 32,000 Boii, or 92,000 combatants in all.[1] These figures are interesting, for they give one an idea of the relative forces of the various members of the combination. In the case of the Helvetii, however, they probably do not give a true ïdea of the size of the people.

There was no room in Gaul, where the various tribes, already crowded, had had to close in yet more to admit the Belgæ. Those most immediately exposed to attack grew disturbed and prepared to resist.

An unexpected event, the intervention of a foreign force to maintain the existing order and stability, wrecked the enterprise of the Helvetii. Cæsar marched against them. They were defeated in the country of the Ædui and driven home, being reduced to 110,000 in number.[2] The Ædui intervened on behalf of the Boii, with whom they were always on friendly terms.[3] They were allowed to settle on the triangle at the junction of the Allier and the Loire as a free part of the Æduan people.[4]

Cæsar, having decided to remain in Gaul, turned against Ariovistus, who had in 59 obtained from the Senate the recognition of his kingship and the title of Friend of the Roman people.[5] He summoned an assembly of Gaul at Bibracte, that it might ask him to intervene.[6] After some marching and counter-marching in the north of Sequania, he defeated Ariovistus in Upper Alsace and drove him with his forces across the Rhine, where they looked for a settlement, except the Triboci, Nemetes, and Vangiones, who remained on the west of the river.

North of Mainz some Germanic tribes, hard pressed by the Suevi, tried to cross the Rhine during the years in which Cæsar was campaigning in Gaul. At the level of Cologne the Ubii, who had long had relations with Gaul, were attacked

---

[1] From the census-tablets, written in Greek, which fell into Cæsar's hands (i, 29, 2–3).
[2] Jullian, op. cit., iii, p. 194.
[3] Coins from Gaul at Stradonitz. Cf. Déchelette, iii, 2, p. 1579.
[4] Cæs., i, 28, 5.
[5] Cæs., i, 35, 2. Cf. Jullian, op. cit., iii, p. 163.
[6] Cæs., i, 30 ff. Cf. Müllenhoff, op. cit., ii, p. 301 ; Jullian, op. cit., ii, p. 467.

by the Suevi, but they made terms and paid tribute. Further
south the Usipetes and Tencteri were compelled to give up
their country, and wandered away looking for land,[1] first
in Germany and then on the Rhine, which they crossed.
They were wiped out in 55.

So Cæsar introduced the Romans to the Rhine in that
character of policemen which they maintained for 500
years. He was the first to make this line the provisional
frontier of the Celts.

East of the river, the Boii still occupied Bohemia, but
not for long. They were in the centre of a group of peoples
which remained distinct until the times of Tacitus and
Ptolemy. There were Cotini in Silesia or Galicia,[2] who spoke
a Celtic dialect but were subordinate to the Quadi and
Sarmatians. To the south, along the Danube, the Carpi and
Rhacatae [3] were perhaps Celtic peoples,[4] remnants, with the
Tulingi and Latobrigi, of the Volcae, who are mentioned
by Cæsar for the last time,[5] and perhaps also of the Vindelici
of the Bavarian plateau. The Danube had stopped the
Germans and, as on the Rhine, the frontier was permanently
laid down by the Romans in the upper valley of the river.

All these expeditions and migrations have added little to
our picture of the Celtic world but losses. Apart from the
small settlement of the Boii on the Bec d'Allier and the
Germano-Celtic foundations of the Aduatuci, Triboci, Nemetes,
and Vangiones, these great movements of peoples left
no colonies. They failed, and these later movements were on
a far smaller scale than the earlier. Rome, too, was making
ready to conquer Gaul, and Britain shortly after.

IV

THE CHARACTER OF THE CELTIC EXPEDITIONS

The migrations of the end of the second century and the
beginning of the first take a great place in history because

---

[1] Cæs., iv, 1 ; 4 ; Müllenhoff, op. cit., iv, pp. 419 ff.

[2] Tac., *Germ.*, 43 ; Ptol., ii, 11, 12, 13, 14, 15 ; Jullian, op. cit., i, p. 198.

[3] Ptol., ii, 2, 11. Cf. Much, in Hoops, **CCCXLII**, iv, p. 424.

[4] The name of the Κάρποι may come from that of the Chamb, a
sub-tributary of the Regen, in which we may see Celtic *kambos* " curving,
winding ". The name of the 'Ρακάται reminds one of Welsh *rhagawd* (**racat*),
which expresses the idea of opposition, battle.

[5] vi, 24. Cf. Jullian, op. cit., iii, p. 297, n. 3 ; Much, in op. cit., iv, p. 425;
Müllenhoff, op. cit., ii, p. 300.

they are fairly well known, having been described by contemporaries. But they have a special interest for us, in that
they give a picture of what the earlier great invasions were
probably like.[1]

Except for the last move of the Boii, the migration of the
Atrebates from Gaul to Britain, the inroads and conquests of
the Goidels in these islands, and the settlement of the people of
Cornwall in Brittany, most of the Celtic peoples were now in
the last stage of their wanderings. The Celtic world now
assumed the face under which it was last known to antiquity,
and it was a face of death. What was to revive later would
be quite different, and much smaller. At this moment of
time, suddenly, just when it was about to be completely
conquered and absorbed, its features, hitherto obscure, appear
in broad daylight, and that thanks to its conqueror. We are
told the names of its peoples and the places where they lived.

However far we go back in the history of the Celts, we
find them distributed in great racial units or confederations
of neighbouring peoples, bound by alliance, kinship, and
every tie which makes for the stabilization and permanence
of a group of tribes. Goidels, Picts, Brythons, and Belgæ
all had their age of growth. Each race in succession spread
out from its original home. Each movement gave rise to
a series of expeditions, roughly contemporaneous and sometimes ensuing one from another.

These migrations have been explained by sudden
catastrophes,[2] by attacks.[3] The most likely reason is an
excess of power, resulting from the growth of the population
and a stronger political organization of its forces.[4]

When the great movements took place, the nations which
led them seem to have divided up and sent out swarms in
quite an organized fashion. The ancients compared this
regular dispersion to the *ver sacrum* of the Samnites,[5] the
great invasions of Italy. The Sacred Spring was an Italic
institution, but we may legitimately suppose that it existed

---

[1] The German historian Niese thought that the expedition of the Cimbri
was the source of the legend of the first Celtic migration (**CCCXXIV**, vii, p. 613).
Cf. *Z. f. d. Alt.*, 1898, 133 ff.

[2] See *Rise*, p. 141.

[3] e.g. the Helvetii. See above, p. 116.

[4] See below, pp. 122–3.

[5] Just., xxiv, 4, 1–3.

also among the Celts, some of whose prehistoric customs may have had the same effects.[1]

Moreover, the Celtic migrations and their causes varied greatly. From the trek of a whole people to the emigration, often temporary, of a single band of mercenaries, the wandering of the Celts took many forms ; the emigrants might be a social unit or part of one, a people making an exodus *en masse* like the Cimbri and Teutones, or a composite host made up from various groups of tribes.[2]

Those units which were not broken up on the way appear at their journey's end as homogeneous groups, whatever they may have been when they started ; in a word, they were colonies. Those which were broken up re-formed in new units. So each new wave altered not only the racial structure of the widening Celtic world, but its political geography ; frontiers shifted and new dominions were acquired. Each wave left a separate deposit. In Ireland, where the various elements were most mixed of all, the tribes of Goidels, Picts, Gauls, and Belgæ kept their own status well into the Middle Ages. As for the masses, properly so called, they fell into large political and racial divisions, the most conspicuous of which were Belgica, Lugdunensis, and Aquitania, each corresponding to a new migration of the Celts. So the map of the Celtic world presents areas which reflect the original divisions of the Celts.

[1] See above, p. 11.
[2] See above, pp. 103 ff.

CHAPTER V

Celtic Gaul

I

THE FORMATION OF THE GALLIC PEOPLES

IN the last years of life which were left to it, the Celtic world shows the most complete picture of itself within the frontiers of Gaul. Its curiously shifting peoples are condemned, at least in the great mass, to an almost definitely fixed abode. It is now time to inquire into the positions held by the chief peoples and the date at which their frontiers were permanently fixed.

Positive information about the settlement of the peoples of Gaul is almost entirely lacking. The evidence of archæology is also too uncertain. The exploration of what was once Gaul is deplorably incomplete, and we are still very far from having recovered the traces of every Gallic settlement. Their history is almost always impossible to follow. Moreover, the civilization of the Celtic countries in the Hallstatt and La Tène periods is in the main highly homogeneous, so that it is difficult to study local variations. Only at a few points are the finds continuous down to the time of Cæsar ; we may conclude that these areas of uninterrupted occupation correspond to settled peoples. Elsewhere finds are discontinuous, and it is very likely that the population itself changed greatly. Archæology by itself cannot furnish a picture of Gaul at the time of the conquest, and it is to the names of places and men and to the map of Roman Gaul that we must turn for the information which we need in order to study the population.

In a document presented to the Roman Senate after the death of Augustus, 305 Gallic peoples are mentioned.[1] But the historians do not tell us the date of their settlement in the country except in the case of a few—the Aduatuci about 105,

[1] Joseph, ii, 16, 4. In Cæsar's time there were said to be about 330 peoples in Gaul (Plut., *Cæs.*, 15). Cf. Bloch, in Lavisse, **CCCCLXVII**, i, 2, p. 191.

but they were Germans ; part of the Helvetii about 103 ; the Menapii in 54. At the time of Hannibal's expedition, about 218, the Volcae Tectosages and Arecomici were already in the country in which they remained. Hasdrubal passed through the territory of the Arverni. We must come down to about 125 before we know for certain that the Ædui are in their place. At the time of the Cimbric invasion, the Sequani and Nitiobriges appear. The rest of the political map of Gaul is a large blank.

The 305 Gallic peoples officially recorded at the death of Augustus were very different in size and rank. Many were or had been subdivisions of larger groups. In reality, there were about sixty peoples in Gaul, some small and others large, which could call themselves independent. In the centre and in south-eastern Belgica there were large nations whose territory corresponded to that of several modern French departments ; the political map was divided into smaller districts on the shores of the Channel and in the Pyrenees and Alps.

The relationship of the sub-group to the group, either at the time of which we are speaking or at the beginning, is in some useful cases marked by a double name. The Tectosages and Arecomici are Volcae, but they are inserted among the Volcae as independent bodies. The Eburovices, Cenomani, Andecavi, Diablintes, and Brannovices are Aulerci. The first four still compose the people of the Aulerci, while the last have broken away. We find Bituriges Cubi and Bituriges Vivisci. These sub-groups are fractions broken off from their parent-group recently or long ago. Sometimes they have become independent, like the Arecomici and Tectosages, the Cubi and Vivisci, and the Cenomani of Cisalpine Gaul ; or they have become attached to other groups, as the Brannovices to the Ædui. But normally the Gallic people is divided into sub-groups.

In the geographical terminology of Roman Gaul, the sub-group is called a *pagus*, whereas the whole people, unless it is the principal people, is called a *civitas*. The group may have been originally formed by conquest, vassalage, the voluntary union of citizens,[1] or kinship. Independent but

---

[1] Cæsar (v, 39) gives a list of the peoples under the sway of the Nervii— Centrones, Grudii, Levaci, Pleumoxii, Geidumni.

neighbouring peoples, such as the Ambarri and Ædui [1] or the Remi and Suessiones,[2] are related by blood. Have we in these various cases peoples which have gone on organizing their internal divisions to a point at which they have split up, or which have amalgamated ? We find the Gallic nations arranged in composite groups which are perpetually in process of formation and dissolution. However, as within other Celtic societies, we may reasonably suppose that political association at first took the form of kinship.

An examination of the names of peoples shows that Celtic colonization was the work of a fairly few nations which split up and sent out swarms. Some of these names are unintelligible, but the meaning of the rest is plain enough. Some come from the geography of the country occupied— Taurisci from Tauern ; Scordisci from the Shar-Dagh ; Ambiani, people of the river Amb ; Nantuates, people of the valley. The unintelligible names are obviously ancient ; the others are new, adopted names. With this second class is allied a whole series of geographical names which no longer correspond to the last habitat of their bearers (Raurici, people of the Ruhr ; Sequani, people of the Seine), names referring to numbers (Remi, the First [3]; Vocontii, the Twenty Clans),[4] and nicknames or warnames (Ruteni, the Fair-haired [5]; Leuci, the Lightners ; Medulli, the Mead-drinkers).

It is obvious that there are several strata of names of different dates. Some are assuredly very old, such as Bituriges, Kings of the World, Ædui, Burning,[6] and Medio-matrici, the people between the Matrona and the Matra. The antiquity of some others is proved by their corruption, such as that of the Osismii of Finistère, which is explained by the name Uxisama, the Furthest Island.[7] A good number are not perfectly clear, but this very fact is certain proof of their great age. Of these there is a small series grouped in a most interesting way—the names of the Boii, Volcae, Helvetii,

---

[1] Cæs., i, 11.
[2] Cæs., ii, 3.
[3] Irish *riam* " before " ; Welsh *rhwyf* " king ". Cf. *primi*, with the *p* dropped.
[4] **CCCXXIV**, 1911, p. 351.
[5] Jullian, **CCCXLVII**, ii, p. 500, n. 5.
[6] *Aedh* " fire ".
[7] *Uchel* " high ".

and perhaps Turoni, the peoples which remained longest
in the original cradle of the Celts. Among the Belgæ we
have the names of the Nervii, Suessiones, and perhaps Remi ;
in the west, the Veneti, Aulerci, Unelli, Pictones, and Centrones ; in the south, the Cadurci, Gabali, and Vellavi.
This is only a provisional list, which may be extended or
cut down. Of these ancient peoples, some remained first-
class nations, while others attached themselves now to one
neighbour and now to another, such as the Parisii, oscillating
between the Suessiones and the Senones.[1]

Having sorted out these few, we need not attempt to
form hypotheses to make the sixty *civitates* of the Gauls
come as full-blown nations from the Celtic cradle or the
west bank of the Rhine. The Volcae, Boii, Helvetii,
Lemovices, Menapii, Turoni, and perhaps Aulerci and
Pictones stayed there and came from there. The other
peoples were formed on the western and southern edge of
the old Celtic domain, and perhaps sprang from these parent
peoples.

So the great nations of the beginning dispersed
themselves over the Celtic world, where many portions
of them are to be found disguised under new names. They
seem to have preserved a definite memory of their origins,
since in some cases they kept their name. The peoples
which formed later proceeded in the same manner. If we
bring together all these names and certain names of towns
and of sections of the population showing fairly close
resemblances, we can complete our picture of that dispersion.
We find Boii in Bohemia, in the basin of Arcachon, in Italy,
and in Galatia ; Tectosages at Toulouse and in Galatia ;
Brigantes in Britain and at Bregenz ; Parisii and Atrebates
in England. From the Aulerci there broke off the
Brannovices [2] between the Loire and Rhone, the Cenomani
in Italy, other Cenomani [3] among the Volcæ Arecomici, and
Andes in Italy. The Senones, who moved about much,
founded little settlements here and there in Gaul—Cenon
near Bordeaux, Senon in Vienne, Sénonnes in Mayenne. They
passed some time in Belgica. In the Pas-de-Calais,

---

[1] D'Arbois, **CCXCIX**, p. 24.
[2] Jullian, op. cit., i, p. 313.
[3] D'Arbois, op. cit., pp. 153 ff. ; Jullian, in **CXXXIV**, 1913, p. 50.

Sainz-lez-Hautecloque was once Senonis, and Senon in the Meuse has the same origin.

The Caturiges,[1] who must originally have been one single people, were scattered in the valleys of the Ornain and Nère and in Italy, in the form of tribes of peoples which had formed more compact groups.

The Medulli [2] of Médoc and Basse-Maurienne may be of the same extraction, and so may the Centrones of the Nervian country. The Carnutes had sent off a colony to Brittany [3]; the Helvetii had colonies on the west bank of the Rhine, where we find three places called Helvetum in Alsace. It is also quite possible that the Helvii of Ardèche were an off-shoot of them.

In Noricum there dwelt a tribe of Alauni [4] who had goddesses called Alounæ. On the west coast of Brittany are a town named Alauna and a river Alaunus, and in south-eastern Gaul there is an Alaunium. These names doubtless survive in the modern Alleaume and Allonnes.

This wide distribution makes it reasonable to associate, as one is tempted to do, names having only slight differences, such as those of the Picts and Pictones. We may suppose that the names and the peoples are the same.

In Calvados we find the Esuvii. Like their neighbours, the Atesuii of the Orne, they worshipped the god Esus and were descended from him. They were portions of the same people, and their proximity corroborates the likeness of name. A whole series of names of peoples and places contains the word *eburos*, the yew, the most sacred of all trees, and all must be connected. There were Eburones between the Main and Rhine, Eburovices at Évreux, an Eburobriga in Yonne (Aurolles), an Eburomagus in Aude (Bram), an Eburodunum in Switzerland (Yverdon), and another in the Hautes-Alpes (Embrun). The Eburovices were Aulerci or Belgæ associated with them, or else Brythons who had remained in the midst of the Belgæ.

Inscriptions from the neighbourhood of Mainz, two of them from the marches of the Belgæ and Brythons, mention

---

[1] Jullian, ibid.
[2] Strabo, iv, 6, 8; i, 11; i, 7; Pliny, iii, 137; Ptol., ii, 10, 7; Vitruv., viii, 3, 20.
[3] Ptol., ii, 13, 2.
[4] D'Arbois, CCC, p. 49.

the Dii Casses. There are a few peoples whose names contain this element—the Tricasses at Troyes, the Veliocasses in Vexin, the Viducasses on the Orne and in Calvados, and the Baiocasses somewhat lower down.

All these facts call for two remarks. The first is that the names are spread in the direction of the advance of the Celtic tribes, and fanwise. They show that the settlements to which they correspond were the result of more than one expedition, carried out in different directions. The second observation is that in the midst of the territories occupied by the great Celtic peoples there were dozens and perhaps hundreds of little colonies of various origin dotted about. The great swarms founded settlements of their own, while the small ones attached themselves as sub-groups to their larger neighbours. So the unity of the latter comprised heterogeneous elements, of which history had preserved the memory. The various regions of the Celtic world were peopled by groups arriving at different dates and mixing. Their amalgamation contributed to the formation of the great peoples.

II

THE CONSTITUTION OF ROMAN GAUL [1]

The map of Gaul in the Roman period almost exactly represents the political condition of the country at the time of the conquest. That condition was largely a result of the manner in which the population had come into the country.

The political units of Gaul were not destroyed ; only two peoples, the Aduatuci and Eburones, were not Celts. These two, or what remained of them, were placed together under the name and in the administrative district of the Tungri, probably forming a sub-group. This exception confirms the rule. The political divisions of Roman Gaul were those of independent Gaul. So, too, the relationships of the various units with one another were almost always maintained. South of the Garonne, where the population was distributed rather differently from elsewhere, some autonomous groups were founded and the number of *civitates* reduced to five,

[1] Bloch, in **CCCCLXVII**, 1, 2, pp. 126 ff.

to be raised later to nine. In the Rhine Valley, the settlements of the Triboci, Nemetes, Vangiones, and Batavians were made into *civitates*. In the rest of Gaul, a certain number of *clientelæ* were abolished ; the Morini were detached from the Atrebates, the Silvanectes and Meldi from the Suessiones, the Abrincatui from the Unelli, the Viducasses from the Lexovii, the Tricasses from the Lingones, the Segusiavi from the Ædui, and the Vellavi and Gabali from the Arverni. This dismembering process was developed throughout the Imperial period.

Conquered Gaul was at first an extension of the Roman Province,[1] but in 49 B.C. it was separated from it. Under Augustus, Gallia Comata became the Tres Galliae, and this distinction, which was maintained after various experiments and with occasional subdivision as long as the Empire lasted, certainly existed before the Roman Government made use of it. This is plain from Cæsar's words,[2] *Gallia est omnis divisa in partes tres*, save that Cæsar's Aquitania was bounded by the Garonne, whereas that of Augustus reached to the Loire, but the eleven peoples of the greater Aquitania, living between the Garonne and Loire, the Pictones, Santones, Bituriges Cubi, Lemovices, Cadurci, Petrucorii, Nitiobriges, Arverni, Vellavi, Gabali, and Ruteni, formed in certain respects a group distinct from the Province as a whole.[3] Evidence of this is provided by the method of recruiting troops, for under the Empire these peoples had a special *dilectator*.[4] The five or nine peoples north of the Garonne formed another unit, and their territories in the third century were a separate district from the Gallic provinces.[5] In these two cases, as in that of the Belgæ, we have pre-existing relationships between the natives taken into consideration by the Roman Government and finally compelling its attention when they had been neglected. They were like those which made Belgica and Aquitania south of the Garonne separate regions from the rest of Gaul ; they were associations which were political in some cases and racial at bottom, and therein different from true political

[1] Jullian, **CCCXLVII**, iv, pp. 28 ff.
[2] i, 1.
[3] **I**, xiii, 1808.
[4] **I**, xiii, 412. Inscription from Hasparren.
[5] Hirschfeld, "Aquitania in röm. Zeit," in **CXLVIII**, 1896, p. 452.

associations created simply by the alliance of two nations
or the subordination of one to another. The same considerations may explain why certain neighbouring *civitates* are
placed together in small groups, for example for the collection
of taxes, and also the subdivisions of the provinces introduced
under Diocletian.

In short, the political map of Roman Gaul shows the
structure of the Gallic colonization, and inversely the history
of that colonization should explain it.

Some historians [1] have gone further, and have held that
the whole political life of the peoples of Gaul was governed
by racial traditions. According to their view, at the time
when Cæsar commenced operations there were two groups
of allies, two factions, namely that of the Ædui and that
of the Arverni and Sequani, and while the former represented
the true Gauls, the latter represented the " Celticans ",
that is to say, men who were originally Goidels. This is a
mistake. It would be equally erroneous to suppose that the
Gallic peoples were disposed on the map in the order of their
coming. The Belgæ, who were the last to take part in the
great Gallic expansion, had main settlements, in relation to
the old Celtic domain in Germany, behind the Brythonic
Gauls. The Gallic peoples of Italy settled, each in front of
that which preceded it, and that is what happened in many
other cases. The Celtic peoples, advancing one after another,
did not necessarily push their predecessors in front of them ;
more often they passed over their heads.

III

THE POSITIONS OF THE GALLIC PEOPLES

In our inquiry, all these dates are interdependent, for
the position of one people affects that of a certain number of
others, and all depend on the time when the Belgæ settled
in the north of Gaul. We may, therefore, suppose two chronological systems, according as we say that they arrived about
300, coming from the east bank of the Rhine and driving
the Gauls before them, or that they settled in Belgica, in
their own country, about 500.

---

[1] Rhys, **CCXXX**, p. 58.

The latter supposition seems to be confirmed by the facts. In the Marne, Aisne, and Seine-Inférieure [1] we find areas of population belonging to the beginning of the La Tène period and corresponding to the settlements of the Remi, Suessiones, and Caleti and their sub-groups, Catuvellauni, Meldi, Veliocasses of Vexin. It is the same in Lorraine and the valley of the Rhine,[2] where districts inhabited since the Hallstatt period can be attributed to the Treviri and the Mediomatrici.[3] One naturally asks, too, where all the mass of Gallic peoples which from the third century onwards poured into the Danube valley and the East, into Italy and France, could have found room in Germany between the Lippe, Rhine, Main, and Upper Weser.

It appears to me that the Belgæ were from the very beginning astride of the Rhine, and occupied from Neolithic times the whole schistous Rhenish *massif*. On the French side, they had a wide frontier zone extending over the Ardennes, the plains of Belgium, and the northern rim of the Paris basin.[4] It was because they had plenty of elbow-room here that they were the last to expend their energies on distant expeditions.

The Treviri [5] and Leuci [6] had been in the same place since the Bronze Age. The Remi and Suessiones, breaking off from the main Belgic body, formed independent settlements in Marne and Aisne at the beginning of the La Tène period, absorbing or driving away the scanty Hallstatt population of the country. At the same time the Caleti probably took shape as a people, having received contingents from Hessen.[7] The Bellovaci must have come later, for their district is a blank on the archæological map of this period. The Morini, Ambiani, and Atrebates form a compact group which may have been undivided. Under the Empire, they compose a small province for fiscal purposes.[8] They, too, arrived comparatively late. The Eburones, Nervii, and other peoples

[1] Jullian, op. cit., ii, p. 471.
[2] Schumacher, **CCCCIX**, pp. 126 ff. ; Jullian, op. cit., p. 477.
[3] Schumacher, op. cit., pp. 130 ff. ; Fuchs, in **CXVIII**, 1915, p. 227.
[4] Jullian, op. cit., ii, pp. 472 ff., 479 ff.
[5] Ibid., p. 477.
[6] Ibid., p. 476.
[7] Peoples whose names contain the element *casse*—Velicasses. Vendryès, in **CXL**, 1923, p. 172.
[8] *Procurator ad census accipiendos trium civitatum Ambianorum, Murinorum, Atrevatum.* Inscription from Ostia. Héron de Villefosse, in **XCIV**, lxxiii, p. 249.

of the Meuse and northern Ardennes existed as peoples and were settled before the invasion of the Cimbri.

If Strabo [1] is correct in saying that the Armorici were Belgæ, the dispersion of the latter must have been still earlier. Pytheas,[2] who knew the Osismii, called them 'Ωστίωνες. It is tempting to compare this form with the name Œstrymnis, which Avienus [3] in the sixth century uses of the western promontories of Europe and the islands lying off them.

Three points may be urged in support of this opinion, though they have no great force. The first is the relations which we find during the Brittany campaign subsisting between the Armorici, Menapii, and Morini.[4] They have the same relations with the inhabitants of the valleys of the Orne and Touques, who are certainly not described as Belgæ. The second is the discovery of objects in a Belgic district, the valleys of the Rhine and Moselle—columns with giants and horsemen, and drums and bases of columns bearing representations of gods, the seasons, etc.[5]—and of similar objects in Brittany.[6] The third point is a passage in Ausonius, in which the Belgian Viridomar, defeated and slain by Marcellus, has the epithet *Armoricus*.[7]

The Armorici form a compact group, quite distinct from the other peoples of Celtic Gaul. The Hallstatt culture in Brittany presents rather a peculiar appearance.[8] One thing is certain : Brittany contributed from the end of the Hallstatt period to the peopling of Britain.[9] If the Belgæ held the coasts of the Channel in the second Iron Age, the Brythons can have entered the island only from the coast west of the mouth of the Seine.

From the occupation of Belgica by the Belgæ at the beginning of La Tène, one must conclude that the Brythonic Gauls were established, then and much earlier, in the districts

---

[1] iv, 1, 4. Cf. Jullian, op. cit., ii, p. 488, n. 1.
[2] Holder, **CCVII**, s.v. " Osismi ".
[3] v, 90–3.
[4] Cæs., iii, 9, 10. Cf. Jullian, op. cit., pp. 113, 227, n. 9.
[5] Espérandieu, **CCCXXV**, vi–viii *passim*.
[6] Monuments at St. Maho, Kerlot, Guelen. Espérandieu, op. cit., 3036, 3038–9.
[7] *Technopaegnion*, 10, 83.
[8] Déchelette, ii, 2, pp. 681–2 ; Bénard le Pontois, **CCCCLXIII**, pp. 148 ff.
[9] Jullian, op. cit., ii, p. 386, n. 2 ; Allen, **CCXCVIII**, pp. 148 ff.

which they still held in Cæsar's time. In the region north
of the Seine, which was a kind of " Debatable Land " of
the Belgæ, the Hallstatt population, which was probably
sparse, received but little of the industries and fashions of
the districts south of that river. The new culture of La Tène
was brought in here, not by great movements of tribes, but
rather by small groups which went about in this vague belt
between the Belgæ and the Celts, passing through peoples
already settled, which sometimes counted as Belgæ and sometimes as Gauls or Britons.[1] There were conflicts, and above
all, conflicts of influence. At the time when this history
ends, the influence of the Belgæ is on the decline.

There were, however, peoples which were driven back
from the frontier zone or forced to emigrate. In the first La
Tène period one big people, the Sequani, changed its abode
in the north of Gaul, and another, the Helvetii, started off
on wanderings which were not to end for a long time.

In Franche-Comté, which had been thickly populated at
the end of Hallstatt, we have already followed the
imperceptible change from the civilization of the first Iron
Age to that of the second.[2] For some time there was no change
in settlements or funeral rites. The La Tène graves were dug
in the tumuli. One notes, however, that the latest are really
charnel-houses, and that means a radical change of race.
Moreover, all these tombs are earlier than 375, and later
cemeteries are almost unknown. What had happened was
that the population had moved. The old settlements on the
plateau were abandoned, given back to the forest, and the
people descended into the valley-bottoms and the plains of
northern Bresse, which they cultivated. These newcomers
hailed from the country on the banks of the Seine between
the domains of the Lingones and Senones, and they were
Sequani. This was doubtless not the first time that such
a thing had happened in Franche-Comté since there had been
Celts there. The invaders of the end of the Hallstatt period
formed two groups, which were distinguished by their fashions
and also by their way of building tumuli[3] ; both advanced

---

[1] Cæsar (ii, 4, 9 ; v, 5, 2 ; viii, 7, 4) assigns the Veliocasses, Caleti, and
Meldi to Belgica. Afterwards they are in Lugdunensis. Cf. the Parisii, above,
p. 124.
[2] See above, p. 8.
[3] The groups at Moidons and that at Alaise. See *Rise*, pp. 253 ff.

beyond the line of the Saône.[1] The valleys of the Doubs and the longitudinal corridors of the Jura were the way into central and southern Gaul for wandering tribes from beyond the Gap of Belfort.[2]

We see a similar change in Switzerland, but the problem is different. A sparse, comparatively nomadic Hallstatt population is succeeded by a fairly dense, concentrated, settled population.[3] Opinions differ about the origin of the newcomers, and many will not call them Helvetii before the third La Tène period.[4] But this is a mistake.[5] Strabo,[6] in other words Poseidonios, mentions three tribes among the Helvetii, and Cæsar [7] four, excluding the Raurici and other peoples already named. Now, whenever the Helvetii of the east bank of the Rhine are mentioned, we only hear of the Tigurini and Tugeni. So before the invasion of the Cimbri there was at least one Helvetian tribe, that which Cæsar [8] calls the *pagus Verbigenus*, and perhaps there was another. The Tigurini must have had one foot on the left bank of the Rhine north of Zurich, and that explains their return to Switzerland after their adventures in company with the Cimbri.[9] The Raurici must have been in their place near Basle by La Tène II.[10] We must accept this as fairly certain if we regard the station of La Tène itself as a toll-post.[11] A line of similar posts, or at any rate military posts, at Port-sur-la-Thiele near the lake of Bienne, at Tiefenau on the Aar, and at Wipfingen on the Limmatt marks a frontier, in all probability that of the Raurici.[12] It is hard to believe that that people, which barred the important crossing of the Rhine and the way along the Aar, was settled there before the Helvetii.

Nor do the finds of the second Iron Age give any grounds

---

[1] The Ædui and Sequani fought each other for the line of the Saône. Strabo, iv, 3, 2.
[2] Jullian, op. cit., i, p. 315, n. 5.
[3] Viollier, **CCCCXCI**.
[4] Déchelette, ii, 3, p. 941 ; Jullian (ii, pp. 520 ff.) is disinclined to place them in Switzerland before the expedition of the Cimbri.
[5] Schumacher, in **CXVIII**, 1914, pp. 230 ff.
[6] iv, 2, 3 ; vii, 2, 2.
[7] i, 12, 4, 6 ; 27, 4.
[8] i, 27, 4.
[9] See above, p. 106.
[10] Viollier, op. cit., p. 92.
[11] See *Rise*, pp. 85–6.
[12] Viollier, loc. cit.

for making a distinction between the populations of the two Helvetic areas. At the very most, we see in the northern part some influence of their northerly neighbours.

It should be remembered that the Helvetii did not occupy the whole of Switzerland, but only the plateau north of the Bernese Oberland. In the upper valley of the Rhine there were other Celtic peoples, the Nantuates round Saint-Maurice, the Veragri round Martigny, the Seduni round Sion, the Uberi in Haut-Valais.[1] Throughout the Iron Age, the civilization of this valley was quite different from that of the plateau. We have, therefore, very distinct peoples, but we cannot say that any of them were the Gaesati. There is nothing specifically Belgic about the crafts of the Alpine valleys. They developed among peoples in which the native element was doubtless still considerable and the Celtic admixture was reduced to small isolated groups, whose civilizing influence, however, continually increased.

Can we conclude from these movements that there were similar migrations on the part of the Ædui, Senones, Carnutes, and Aulerci ?[2] The fact that the Sequani and Helvetii seem to have formed a separate body among the other Celtic peoples is against this view. None of the reasons given[3] is sufficient to make one regard them as Belgæ, among whom Cæsar did not include them. The settlement of the Sequani and Helvetii coincided with very large movements of population on the fringes of the Celtic world. It happened at the time of the great invasion of Italy. But their predecessors did not appear among those who took part in that expedition.[4] The invaders of Italy buried their dead in cemeteries similar to those of the Marne, whereas the inhabitants of the Sequanian and Helvetian regions at the beginning of La Tène buried them in tumuli. It is on the other side of the Rhine, perhaps among the Allobroges, that we should look for their remnants, if they can still be identified.

There does not seem to have been any great movement among the peoples which had occupied Aquitania north of

[1] Jullian, op. cit., ii, p. 463, n. 5.
[2] Ibid., p. 463.
[3] Pliny (iv, 106) includes them among the Belgæ. They were detached from Lugdunensis to enter the organization of the German border, where, in the fourth century, they formed a special province, the Maxima Sequanorum. See above for the explanation of their partiality for the Germans.
[4] Jullian, op. cit., i, p. 315.

the Garonne. For one thing, this group comprised the
Pictones, whose very name and position on the coast are
sufficient evidence that their settlement was very old, being
contemporaneous with the Pictish migrations.[1] Secondly,
archæological exploration has brought to light certain nuclei
of Hallstatt population which did not disappear. The groups
of tumuli in Indre and Cher correspond to the main mass of
the Bituriges Cubi,[2] a third belongs to the Cadurci, and in
Cantal a fourth is evidence of the settlement of the Arverni.
Tumuli have also been found among the Gabali and in the
north of the country of the Ruteni (Lozère and Aveyron).[3]
These are good evidence of population, which, unfortunately,
is lacking for the greater part of the country of the Arverni
and for that of the Lemovices [4] and Santones.[5] Nor do we
know more about the cemeteries of the people who occupied
these districts in the La Tène period. It was, then, in the two
first Hallstatt periods that this part of Aquitania must have
received the bulk of its population.

Some of the elements which had taken part in the descent
of the northern peoples on the Pyrenean region and Spain
at the end of the first Iron Age [6] likewise contributed to the
making of the population of Aquitania. A very large group
on the plateaus south of Albi and another about Agen correspond to the Ruteni and Nitiobriges. Later on, some Senones
and Lingones took up their abode on the Garonne, not to
mention the Bituriges Vivisci. So the occupation of the
country was finally made complete by bodies which passed
through it at the end of the Hallstatt period and during La
Tène, entering the existing political formations or setting
up new ones.

Between the Loire and Seine the country was held by the
Ædui and their kinsfolk, Ambarri of Lugdunensis and Sequani
of Forez, Lingones, Senones, Aulerci, and the peoples of
Normandy ; to these we must add the Carnutes and Turoni,
whose position astride of the Loire well shows that the constitution given by the Roman Government was not made

---

[1] See *Rise*, pp. 202 ff.
[2] The groups at St.-Aoustrille and Prunay. Déchelette, ii, 2, p. 679.
[3] Ibid., p. 671.
[4] Jullian, op. cit., ii, p. 495.
[5] Ibid., p. 490.
[6] See *Rise*, chap. v.

by geographers, with their eye on natural frontiers, but was inspired by the wish to conform to a pre-existing grouping of the peoples.[1]

Some of these were among the oldest in the Celtic world. But it is very difficult to establish their original position, for too often archæology tells us nothing about them. Even here, however, we find some centres of Hallstatt habitation. The bronze swords discovered in the bed of the Seine bear witness to the passage of armed men [2]—the Parisii ? In the Côte-d'Or the great iron sword remained in use far longer [3] than in Franche-Comté and, what is more, when the sword with antennæ was adopted its length was immediately increased. We have, therefore, a very different population, and one which remained in its place in the La Tène period, using the same tumuli. These may then be regarded as the tombs of a portion of the Ædui. Unfortunately neither Nièvre nor Saône-et-Loire furnishes any equivalent.

In the north, in Yonne, Aube, and Haute-Marne, there appears at the end of the second Iron Age a fashion which barely touched the Æduan country. The women wore hollow, gadrooned, turban-shaped anklets or thigh-rings of thin bronze. It was not a local fashion. Such objects have been found in Germany, in Vendée (introduced by traders or roving bands among the Caturiges, who, however, passed by the Meuse and Haute-Marne), in the environs of Paris, and on the borders of the country of the Senones.[4] The great number of these finds perhaps indicates that there were already groups, distinct from the Ædui, on the territory of the Lingones and Sequani.

Apart from the Boii, it was in this group of peoples that the bands were levied which invaded Italy—Insubres (that is, Ædui), Cenomani and Andes, Lingones and Senones. With the Bituriges and Arverni, they formed the kingdom of Ambicatus, King of Bourges.

The route which Livy [5] describes the Insubres as taking on their march into Italy, though it may have been the shortest way for a people massed between Dijon and Nevers,

---

[1] Déchelette, ii, 2, pp. 680, 725, 728.
[2] Ibid., list of swords, app. iv, Villeneuve-St.-Georges and Paris.
[3] Piroutet, in **XV**, xxix, p. 425.
[4] Déchelette, ii, 2, p. 835.
[5] v, 35. See above, pp. 14 ff.

does not correspond to the position of the Gallic settlements
at the exit from the mountains. Their position indicates
that their founders had entered the plain of Lombardy
by the eastern shore of Lake Maggiore.

We must not credit the Gauls of the fourth century with
too great powers of organization. It would be more reasonable
to explain such a concentration of forces from Anjou to
Bohemia by a deep-seated intimacy between the Boii and
their allies the Lingones, Senones, and Ædui, which had
survived all separations. Grouped at the foot of the Gap
of Belfort, these last could easily have reached the valley
of the Reuss. We can also, if necessary, suppose that the
Insubres, who organized the expedition and were the first
to march, had remained detached from the body of the Ædui
in Germany, like the Cenomani and Andes. The main body
of the Aulerci in its move to the west left a few fragments
in Germany, which joined in the expeditions of the Volcæ
and Boii.

In brief, between the Loire and the Saône the Celtic
peoples were less ancient than between the Loire and the
Garonne. They date at earliest from the second Hallstatt
period. They were reinforced during the third period, and
at the beginning of the second Iron Age, just when the
Suessiones and Remi were settling in Aisne and Marne, they
received a large new admixture, in which there may have
been some Belgæ.[1]

When the colonies composed of these various peoples
were established east of the Ticino, other Gauls descended
into Italy over the French Alps, working up the tributaries
of the Rhine to their sources. On the other side of the Alps
the corresponding valleys were presently occupied by tribes
with Gallic names, which, although they mixed with the
Ligurians of Piedmont, kept some trace of their old selves.

At the beginning of the Hallstatt period Gauls had begun
to travel down the Rhone. Between Valence and Avignon,
on both banks, tumuli have yielded large bronze swords [2]
or somewhat later Hallstatt objects, which are dated by
Greek objects.[3] These tombs represent a fairly large Celtic

---

[1] A place near Orleans is called Belia in the *Antonine Itinerary*.
[2] Déchelette, ii, 2, pp. 660 ff.
[3] Ibid., p. 661, fig. 252, a proto-Corinthian vase from the tumulus of
Trois-Quartiers, at Le Perthuis, Vaucluse.

population in the country of the Vocontii and Cavares, who perhaps already existed as peoples.[1] The area over which these weapons are discovered is a continuation of Franche-Comté and Dombes, and so enables us to connect the Celtic settlements of the Rhone with the old Hallstatt groups between the Saône and the Jura.

The furniture of the tumuli of the Alpine valleys [2] in Late Hallstatt contains, side by side with objects peculiar to the region, types copied from Franche-Comté and beyond. The Celtic infiltration, which was complete in the fourth century, made itself felt among the Ligurians even at this early date. It is the same with the contemporary tumuli of Chablis and Faucigny, which are probably Gallic.

The retreat of the Iberians in Languedoc in the fifth century shows that a new military power was predominant there. It can only have been the Volcae. A hundred years later everything was Gallic or Celticized, except on the coast east of Marseilles.

Of these Gauls, some came from very far or fairly far, like the Volcae, their allies the Cenomani, the Caturiges, the Medulli, and the Centrones. Others had come down from the Cevennes, such as the Sigovellauni of Valentinois, who were a sub-group of the Cavares, or else from the west bank of the Rhone, such as the Allobroges. But the Allobroges, Vocontii, Tricastini, Tritolli, Tricorii, and Cavares are groups of peoples whose names give no indication as to their origin. We may suspect that there were Belgic contingents among them, for the Cavares seem to have taken part in the expeditions of the third century.

The peoples of the Alps were a body apart. Under the Empire they formed three small provinces, the Maritime, Cottian, and Pennine Alps, the last comprising Tarentaise and Valais. The Cottian Alps corresponded in part to the kingdom of Cottiris, the last ruler of the country, Susa being the capital. The peoples of the mountains seem never to have shared the fortunes of those of the plains and the wider valleys, but remained independent between Cisalpine Gaul and the Province. Celtic civilization reached them, changing somewhat as it did so, and it is possible that the Gallic tribes

---

[1] Jullian, **CCCXLVII**, ii, pp. 517, 514.
[2] Déchelette, ii, 2, p. 658.

which entered the higher valleys were absorbed by them.
The racial mixture here cannot have been quite like that of
Dauphiné or Provence. Political relations, types of culture,
and racial character lie at the bottom of this distinction of
the Alpine provinces.

IV

THE GENERAL ASPECT OF CELTIC GAUL

The political face of Gaul, which was still undergoing
variations in Cæsar's time, had been almost fixed since 400 ;
it had taken ten centuries to make it. Of the first Celtic
settlements of the Bronze Age, hardly anything survived.
The Picts were probably the sole representatives of those
heroic days. The Hallstatt period had left definite traces,
and some of the settlements created at that time still existed.
During the first period of La Tène Gaul received a considerable
number of new colonists, who established themselves in the
deserted or little-populated border zones, squeezed their
way into spaces between older settlements, and sometimes
even took the land of the earlier Gallic occupants. The
successive waves—whole peoples or sub-groups associated
with groups already settled—went all over Gaul in search
of a home, intermingling, but to different degrees. Later,
with a few exceptions, all the room was taken up.

It has been supposed that the Celts formed a kind of
military aristocracy, small in numbers compared with the
rest of the population. This view rests on a serious sociological
error about the nature of the Celtic family.

Down to the fifth century the Gallic occupation looks
like a fairly loose network. Gaul had been occupied by
Ligurians and invaded in the south by the Iberians, who
remained where they were in the extreme south-east and
south-west, mingled with the Celts to various extents. The
place-names which can be connected with these two peoples
with certainty are extremely few.[1] The great majority of
place-names which are not Latin or Germanic in origin are
Gaulish. The names of peoples are Gaulish, and they have
endured. That means that between the Garonne, the Durance,

[1] Longnon, **CCXII** ; Jullian, op. cit., i, p. 247.

and the Rhine not only the mass of the population was Celtic but the whole social structure was Celtic. The Celts were the creators of the immense majority of markets, meeting-places, villages, and towns. They took possession of the country, but they altered it. It is very possible that many Ligurians remained among them, but, with a few exceptions, they formed no distinct organized groups. As slaves, isolated farmers, *coloni*, they adopted Celtic customs and speech wholesale. Only in Provence and in the Alps could native tribes find a place within Celtic groups, like the Salyes of Marseilles. Certainly there were foreigners in the Celtic communities. The blood in these was not very pure, and the ancient writers have no illusions on the point. They noted the racial differences between the Gauls of the Continent and those of Britain.[1] But in Gaul itself only the blood was mixed ; society was purely Gallic.

Attempts have been made to reckon the size of the Gallic population,[2] based chiefly on the figures of effectives given by Cæsar for the levy of 52.[3] Since this was not a levy *en masse*, some historians have placed the total number of the population too low. But we have other data. Thus, the Bellovaci were able to put 100,000 men into the line, so that the total population must have been at least 400,000 souls, that is, the present population of their country.

To get a correct idea of the population of Gaul, it is to modern statistics that we must turn, taking into account the number of units of all sizes and multiplying the average ones. According to Poseidonios,[4] the biggest nations of Gaul could raise 200,000 men and the smallest 50,000. That gives an average of 100,000 inhabitants to a people, or thirty million altogether. This figure is still too low, for it seems to allow for too large a proportion of combatants. If we start from the strength of the *pagi*, we must count about 500 of them, and we get the same population. It certainly seems that Gaul must have had, including slaves, at least as many inhabitants as France under Louis XIV. At a time when Greece and Italy were suffering from depopulation, we can well understand that it gave the ancients an impression of

[1] Strabo, iv, 5, 2. Cf. Lucan, *Phars.*, ii, 77.
[2] Jullian, op. cit., ii, pp. 4 ff.
[3] For the censuses taken by the Gauls, see above, p. 117, n. 1.
[4] In Diodoros, v, 25, 1.

inexhaustible fruitfulness and seemed like a brimming reservoir of men who poured out to terrorize the whole world.

Thus constituted, Gaul turned towards poles of attraction outside the country. For some little time Germany, in which new powers were arising, educated by Gaul, attracted chiefly the Belgæ, Sequani, and Helvetii, who were in immediate touch with it. For centuries Greece had exercised its civilizing influence on Gaul and the Gauls had looked to Greece by preference. As early as the fourth century they had been regarded as phil-Hellenes, but this reputation had occasionally been clouded. In the third century they were considered very wild, and perhaps they were better known. But the phil-Hellenism was real enough. While continuing to be themselves, the Gauls who settled in Greek lands borrowed much from their teachers, and the others were influenced by Hellenism in inverse ratio to their distance from its centre. Their coins, copied from Greek types, and their decorative art both show this, and there are still remnants of the Greek articles which were in demand among the Gauls—vessels of bronze and earthenware for holding oil and wine.

Greek influence was followed by that of Rome. Negotiations, intrigues, and wars all contributed to it, but it was particularly the prestige of a higher organization and culture that appealed to these peoples who were so eager for everything that was not Celtic. This trait of the racial character explains their sudden metamorphosis and the continuity of their rôle as civilizers in Europe.

The stranger from the Mediterranean always had a special charm for them.[1] The civilization of La Tène III, which was contemporaneous with the conquest, reveals the growing influence of the arts and industries of the south. Bronze statuettes appear, enamel-working is developed, the technique of pottery is changed, Celtic characteristics disappear from the decoration of vases and jewel-work. New ways of life come in. At Mont Beuvray square houses of the Roman type with a heating-system arise in the midst of the Gallic huts. City life begins and develops under the influence of Rome and Greece. The forts reoccupied or built during the Cimbric War gradually turn into towns. These, it should be noted, grow less frequent as one leaves the coasts of the

[1] Cæs., vi, 24, 5.

Mediterranean. They are dense in the valley of the Rhone. There were some among the Ædui and the Remi, but the Bellovaci had no longer anything but temporary refuges. These towns, such as Bibracte or Gergovia, perched on stony plateaus, with rough, narrow little lanes running up and down, cramped, badly built, full of mud and dung, were certainly not marvels of town-planning.[1] But the Gauls were proud of them, or of some of them, such as Avaricum, the finest city in Gaul,[2] the jewel of the Bituriges. We already find that municipal patriotism was one of the most deep-seated characteristics of Roman Gaul.

But as time went on, Gaul modelled itself on its patterns more and more diligently. The magnificence of Luernius and Bituitus is still mere barbaric splendour. Cæsar shows us nothing of that kind in the Druid Diviciacus, who lived a long time in Rome and talked philosophy with Cicero, or in Orgetorix the Helvetian, or in Ambiorix the Eburonian, the wildest and most picturesque of guerrilla leaders, or in Vercingetorix. These men are very different from those whom Diodoros and Poseidonios met about 100 B.C., uneducated, bragging, noisy, and quarrelsome.[3] The great nobles of whom Cæsar has left many very lively portraits display the fine, gracious manners which the Welsh chieftains may have had later. They were men of taste, too, fond of beautiful things, which they ordered from great distances and even kept in their baggage when at war.[4] That is how the leaders of the war of independence are portrayed by their conqueror.

---

[1] Cic., *De Prov. Cos.*, 12, 29. Cf. Jullian, op. cit., ii, pp. 240 ff.
[2] Cæs., vii, 15, 4.
[3] Jullian, op. cit., ii, pp. 420 ff.
[4] The silver bowl found in the trenches of Alesia bears a Gallic inscription, perhaps the name of the owner. S. Reinach, **CCCLXXII**, ii, p. 283.

PART TWO

THE END OF THE CELTIC WORLD

CHAPTER I

THE ROMANS IN ITALY, SPAIN, AND GAUL

I

THE COMPLETION OF THE ROMAN CONQUEST OF ITALY AND SPAIN

THE independence of the Celtic world was nearing its end. In addition to the Germanic danger, one yet more urgent appeared. The Roman Republic was preparing to complete its domination of the Gallic countries. In Italy [1] something still remained to be done. The four great Gallic peoples had been crushed, and what remained of them had been reduced to the status of *civitates fœderatœ*. But the condition of the Celtic or Ligurian peoples on the outskirts was very uncertain, and remained so for a long time.

In the first century the peasant culture of the Cisalpine country was still entirely Gallic and no change seems to have occurred there when the Cimbri came in. After the end of the Cimbric invasion the policy of founding colonies was at once resumed. In 100 one was erected at Eporedia (Ivrea), to keep watch on the country of the Salassi. As a result of the Social War, the towns of the Insubres and Cenomani obtained Latin rights by the Lex Pompeia of 80. This privilege, which was of certain advantage to the towns, which were incorporated in the Italian municipal system, but of doubtful benefit to people living in the country, completed the breaking-up of the old nations. A few years later Sulla made the Cisalpine region a province, Gallia Cisalpina, which was attached to Italy in 42 and broken up. Colonization was carried on after the Civil War by expropriations and the distribution of land to veterans. The Gallic peasant was the sufferer.

[1] Chapot, **CCCXI**, English pp. 122 ff.

In Spain [1] the fall of Numantia marks the end of the country's independence. The Celtiberians, though exhausted, had found the strength to oppose the Cimbri successfully. But soon afterwards revolts against Rome began again. In 90 the Arevaci rose, and from 81 to 73 Sertorius had all Spain behind him. But the people concerned were Celtiberians, not Celts. And these spurts of independence are no more than episodes in the political history of Rome.

II

THE CONQUEST OF GAUL [2]

The establishment of the Romans in Cisalpine Gaul and Spain after the first Punic War was bound to lead them to take heed to their communications with these provinces by the Provençal coast and Languedoc. In spite of its determination to limit its ambitions by the Alps and the Pyrenees, the Senate was compelled to intervene in Gaul. Its ancient ally Marseilles needed help. Besides, at the end of the second century Rome had discovered new ways of solving her social problems. The thing to do was to distribute lands, to found cities, to colonize.

In 154 and 125, the Salyes having attacked Marseilles, two expeditions were sent against them, the second commanded by the Consul M. Fulvius Flaccus, the friend of the Gracchi. The Romans established themselves in the country and the district was made into a province. The Proconsul C. Sextius Calvinus founded the city of Aquæ Sextiae on the Rhone, if not as a colony, at least as a garrison.

The chiefs of the Salyes took refuge among the Allobroges, who were allied with the king of the Arverni, Bituitus, son of Luernius. This was probably enough to make the Ædui seek an alliance with Rome.

Going on from the Salyes to the Allobroges, Cn. Domitius Ahenobarbus, one of the Consuls of 122, led a small army up the Rhone, treating all the way. At Vindalum, at the confluence of the Sorgue, he fell on the Allobroges. But Bituitus had raised 20,000 men. He crossed the Rhone by a bridge and pontoons and descended the river in pursuit

[1] Ibid., English, p. 154.
[2] Jullian, **CCCXLVII**, iii ; Chapot, op. cit., English pp. 12 ff., 293 ff.

of the Romans, who were joined by C. Fabius Maximus
with new troops. Bituitus was defeated and Fabius carried
the war into the country of the Allobroges. Domitius doubtless succeeded in excluding the influence of the Arverni
from the country of the Cavares, Helvii, and Arecomici
and part of Albigeois, which were reunited to the Province.
The Volcae Tectosages of Toulouse were included,˜under the
euphemistic name of " allies ". Toulouse had a Roman
garrison when the Helvetii appeared in the neighbourhood.

Bituitus desired to treat in person in the name of the
Arverni and Allobroges. Domitius sent him to the Senate,
which interned him at Alba, where he was joined by his son,
Congentiatus or Comm. The Tour Magne at Nîmes represents
the trophy set up by Domitius after his victory. But its most
lasting monument was the Province itself, transformed.
The Domitii and Fabii were its patrons and the Allobroges
were the guests and friends of Domitius. Great public works,
such as the Via Domitia, were carried out.

Shortly afterwards the Cimbri arrived and central Gaul,
after the destruction of the empire of the Arverni, was power-
less to stop them. Small risings procured further easy
triumphs, and then the story of the Province becomes part
of that of the Roman Republic.

In 75 Pompey passed through the country on his way to
fighting Sertorius in Spain. He was followed by M. Fonteius,
who restored order among the Vocontii and Volcae. Literature
has made Fonteius the type of the oppressive, unscrupulous
governor. But did he act differently from Claudius in 64
and Murena in 63 ? However that may be, the Allobroges,
who in this case seem to have had the most life left in them,
brought an action against him before the Senate in 63. In
Rome their envoys became mixed up in the conspiracy of
Catiline, whom they betrayed in return for his failure to
keep his golden promises. Then the Allobroges rose and fell
on Vienne. C. Pomptinus put down the revolt so effectively
that they did not move during Cæsar's campaigns.

The case of Fonteius is a very familiar story.[1] First of
all there were expropriations. Colonies and garrisons were
planted at Vienne and at Toulouse in the Gallic town. Then
the things happened which always happen when two economic

[1] Cic., *Pro Font.*, i, 2.

systems and two political organizations come into contact, the stronger of which is based on money. The financier comes on the scene. The Gauls had money, but not enough for the Roman fiscal system to be anything but a burden. They borrowed, and got into debt. The worst of it was that the governors became involved. Money was to be made quickly in Gaul. But the Province was not really impoverished. It was one of those agricultural countries in which a good harvest at once restores the financial situation. Profitable crops, vine and olive, were being introduced just now. The Romans forbade them, so they must have been prosperous. Besides, Rome, which seems to have been so oppressive in some things, was easy in others. It allowed the Gauls to keep their political organization and their usages. This was the time when the envoys of the Allobroges in their trousers and smocks filled the Forum with their exuberance. For fifty years Gallia Narbonensis was distinguished from Gallia Braccata ; it wore the toga and talked Latin. In 83 the Helvii were admitted to Roman citizenship. The Roman leaders found among these provincials agents, and also friends, such as the Helvetian C. Valerius Pocillus, to whom Cæsar pays an interesting tribute of friendship. Finally, Narbonensis furnished troops and remained loyal.

Outside the Province the Romans had friends among the Ædui and Nitiobriges. From all over Gaul exiled sons of good families came flocking to Rome. There were even treaties with some Gallic nations in which it was provided that the Republic should not receive exiles.[1]

Of what went on in the interior at that time we know nothing save a few names, such as those of Celtillus, father of Vercingetorix, who was put to death for aiming at tyranny, and of Diviciacus, King of the Suessiones, who invaded Britain at least once and seems to have ruled over a kind of Belgic confederation.

The adventure of Celtillus is in itself characteristic of the political crisis in which Cæsar found Gaul involved when he arrived in the country. The old Celtic kingships were breaking up, and doubtless the influence of the Roman Senate had something to do with it. At the same time other kingships were on the point of reviving in virtue of the same

[1] Id., *Pro Balbo*, 14.

rights, though inevitably different in essence. The political conflict was violent. Moreover, after the destruction of the kingdom of the Arverni, Gaul had entered on a period of political dissolution which was not yet ended. One group formed round the Arverni, another round the Ædui, reforming later round the Sequani ; but everything was fluid and chaotic. The great peoples pursued a policy of prestige. Cæsar profited by the weaknesses resulting from that policy and, indeed, it was one of his favourite instruments, of which he made as much use as of military operations. If he succeeded, with 60,000 men, in carrying through the difficult task of conquering a large country, rich in men and owning a glorious past, it was because he had in Gaul allies, friends, spies, who were also traitors, like the Æduan Dumnorix. He always had sources of information among the enemy, an intelligence service which rarely failed him ; but he also had friends like the Pictones, the Lingones, and, above all, the Remi.

All these political weaknesses, all these defects, shine out from the pages of the *Commentaries*. But we see something else there as well. Gallic society had latent powers of co-ordination which came into play with great vigour, but too late, and with some success, but too brief. The assembling of the army of relief during the siege of Alesia, with all the deliberations, sending of messages, and movement of troops entailed, was a remarkably well-conducted operation, which pre-supposes a habit and rules.[1] Vercingetorix used these institutions in a masterly fashion, and Cæsar the historian has given him full credit. He has set him up at the beginning of the history of France and at the end of the history of the Gauls as a wonderful symbol of patriotism—young, good-looking, eloquent, modest, able to learn, expressing himself like an old soldier, interested, no doubt, in everything about the new civilization, but conscious of his own country and jealous of it to the point of sacrifice. Cæsar very nearly failed, and he does not disguise the fact. As the greater Celtic world had, in the time of Hannibal, missed its chance of becoming a kind of great, loose confederation in the world of its day, so the smaller Celtic world of Gaul missed, in Vercingetorix, the opportunity of becoming, side by side with

---

[1] Jullian, **CCCXLVII**, iii, pp. 415 ff.

the Roman Republic, the prototype of the modern great nation.

The conquest took eight years. After the first year,[1] which was taken up with containing the Helvetii and driving Ariovistus across the Rhine, there were four years of partial affairs—unconnected risings and attacks on the part of the Gauls and attempts to conquer territory and military promenades on that of the Romans. At the end of 54 the first concerted rising broke out, and from 53 to 51, the hardest years of the war, the Gauls waged a real national war with great successes in 52. The fall of Alesia brought this series of operations to a close, but it was not the end. The campaign of 51 consisted of scattered but constantly renewed attempts on the part of the Gauls, and at the end of the year the country was subjugated.

It is a commonplace of history to marvel at the rapidity of the conquest. But Gaul had at that time not acquired the rudiments of a state structure, without which a nation cannot be made. Neither their few common institutions nor their more or less connected attempts at collaboration could give the Gallic people a sense that they must regard themselves as one and that they owed duties of love and sacrifice towards the fatherland of which we now speak, but of which they assuredly knew nothing. Gaul had not had time to make the long, painful experiments in common which are necessary to develop the patriotism of a nation.

· For Vercingetorix and his friends there probably was a Gaul, a Gallic fatherland. They also had a great love of political freedom, supported by faith in their country. It was the glory of Gaul to have produced such men. The rest were content to try to reconcile the interests of their small nation, their own small fatherland, with foreign rule. The great mass of the Gauls had not the faith which makes nations ; they had no faith in the language which they gave up, or in the religion which they disguised, or in the institutions which they hastened to Romanize. But they had faith in civilization, which meant that of Rome, and in the prestige of their conqueror. The Roman Empire did more to make Gaul a fatherland than the Republic and Cæsar did to destroy it.

[1] Ibid., iv, p. 21.

For about a hundred years, however, the submission of Gaul might seem uncertain, and minor incidents arose from time to time. It is true that the most serious of these was the work of a Roman army and was connected with the Imperial succession, but none the less the word of " freedom " was spoken.

Even before the death of Cæsar, in the year 46, the Bellovaci revolted ; in 44, the Allobroges ; in 33 and 30, the Aquitani and Morini. Little is known of these affairs—a few dates and a few allusions, no certain history at all. Between 25 and 7 B.C. a series of small campaigns achieved the reduction of the Alpine tribes.[1] Then incidents are fewer and further between, and when they occur they are more serious and of a different character.

The Roman administration, particularly in fiscal matters, did not continue to be so easy as in the early years. The survey operations, commenced in 27, while laying down the rights of ownership in detail, did injury to many. It happened in the new province just as it had happened in Narbonensis over the collection of taxes ; there were outbursts of rage, plots, and risings, even military risings. In A.D. 21, under Tiberius, there was a revolt. Among those involved in it were found two Roman citizens, both Julii, one a Treviran named Florus, and the other an Æduan named Sacrovir, and both officers of cohorts of the regular army.[2]

Graver incidents occurred at the end of Nero's reign in 68. At that time the governor of Lugdunensis was C. Julius Vindex, an Aquitanian of royal descent, recently made a citizen. He declared himself for Galba, the Legate of Spain, and against Nero. Was he acting as the Roman he had become or as the Gaul he still was ? In any case, he had the Gauls with him. He was defeated at Besançon by the troops of Germany, which remained loyal to Nero, and killed himself. During the military anarchy which followed Nero's death, there were Gauls in all the different parties. When Vitellius was holding his court at Lugdunum a rising of a new kind broke out in the Boian country. The leader was a peasant named Mariccus, who assumed the manner of a prophet and proclaimed himself the champion of the Gauls and a god.

[1] Ibid., pp. 69 ff.
[2] For all the following, see Jullian, op. cit., iv, pp. 153–200.

Is this a first specimen of those upheavals from the depths which recur in the history of France—Crusades of the Poor, *Jacqueries* ?   In Gaul, as in the Cisalpine country, the poor had grievances enough ; they were slow to be Romanized, and it is possible, things being so, that the national spirit took shape in that social stratum.   The movement failed deplorably.

It was only the second act.   In Rome the Capitol was burned down.   The news was exploited as an omen by the Druids, who formed a religious opposition and now proceeded to preach a Holy War.   All that remained to be done was to get the malcontents together.   There followed the revolt of Civilis, the Treviri Tutor and Classicus, and the Lugdunensian Sabinus.   Civilis had at his side a prophetess named Velleda, who lived among the Bructeri.   She must have been a German, but her name seems quite Celtic— curious evidence of the intercrossing of Celticism and Germanism.   These four associates were all regular officers commanding cohorts, soldiers by profession.   Classicus donned the purple and had himself proclaimed *Imperator Galliarum*.   Sabinus declared himself a descendant of Cæsar.

But then something happened of far greater importance than the foundation of the Gallic Empire.   The *civitas* of the Remi seems to have taken upon itself to convoke, as in old days, an assembly of the *civitates* of Gaul.   It met as a completely autonomous body, apparently, and discussed the question of independence, which was urged by Tullius Valentinus, a Treviran, as against peace and submission, defended by Julius Auspex of the Remi. If Gaul now, through the mouths of its delegates, declared itself content with the condition to which Cæsar had brought it, it was because it did not yet exist.   The assembly sent to the Treviri, in the name of the Gauls, orders to lay down arms and offers of intercession.   The wisdom of Cerealis did the rest.   Classicus and Tutor vanished.   Sabinus hid with his wife Eponina in an underground place of refuge, but they were eventually taken and both put to death.

This time, the old independent Gaul was really finished. Something new was beginning.

III

THE ROMANIZATION OF GAUL [1]

At the time when the assembly organized by the Remi met, Gaul was already three-quarters Romanized. Dress, utensils, furniture, and jewellery were Roman in style. Latin was spoken. Henceforth the culture of the country was Latin.

No doubt, many Italians came to Gaul, settling chiefly in Narbonensis, on the Rhine, and at Lugdunum, and there must have been a few merchants from Greece and Syria. But all these would not be sufficient to account for the rapidity with which the country was assimilated, and we must suppose that Gaul was spontaneously eager to become Romanized. The sudden development of city life favoured the transformation. All through the first century there was an expenditure on building which may be compared to what went on in France from the twelfth century to the seventeenth. The Gallic peoples became *civitates*, and identified them-selves with them. The cities took the names of the peoples whose capitals they were. And there was no model of city life and municipal organization available but the Roman model.

The general extension of the citizenship had the same effects as in Narbonensis on a larger scale. Under Claudius Gallic senators, already Roman citizens, were admitted to the Roman Senate. Later, the Edict of Caracalla made the assimilation complete by extending the citizenship to the lower classes of the population.

Now, at this time when the whole world contained nothing but Roman citizens, jurisprudence shows by repeated declarations that provincial customs based on ancient rights were respected.[2] Yet we have only three evidences of any kind of survival of a Gallic legal custom. This is very little, for the Gauls had a law of their own.

The national religion was never abolished or persecuted. Indeed, the Gallic gods continued to be worshipped under the ægis of the worship of the Emperor. But they gradually

---

[1] Ibid., iv–vi ; Chapot, op. cit., English pp. 314 ff.
[2] Ulpian, in the *Digest* ; Jullian, op. cit., iv, p. 278.

assumed a Roman disguise ; even the household gods, those
of the hearth and the flame, took the names of Roman gods,
and often their figures, except for some native effigies. Of all
the vast mass of Gallic tradition of which Cæsar speaks,
what remained ?   Nothing was done like the endeavour
of the Irish to collect and catalogue their old poems.   Of
Gallic history and theology we know nothing but what the
Greeks and Latins happen to tell us—what survives of Trogus
Pompeius and a few culinary and magical recipes picked up
by Pliny and Marcellus of Bordeaux. That is all. It is true
that the Empire persecuted the Druids. They were attacked
(partly, doubtless, for political reasons) under the laws
regarding human sacrifice, murder, and magic (Lex Cornelia
de Sicariis) by Tiberius and Claudius.   At that time, if we
are to take a passage in Pomponius Mela literally,[1] they
continued to teach the young in secret.   They too must have
come round, for there is no question of their giving trouble
in the second century, and in the time of Ausonius we find
their descendants among the teachers at the school of
Bordeaux.   In the only cases in which the Romans struck,
they evidently struck rightly, for the Druids alone were in
a position to try to stem the general rush of Gaul to Latinism.

To sum up, all the upper parts of Gallic civilization,
those which make a people other than an amorphous mass
of peasants, fell. All that remained was the lower parts and,
in addition to a good many habits and some handicrafts
of importance, the superstitions and magic of the people.
Higher activities were monopolized by the civilization of
the upper classes. This tradition was reinforced by teaching
in the great schools which succeeded those of the Druids
but were quite different, the first of which we have seen at
work at Autun under Tiberius. The Gaulish language survived
only in the dialect of the peasant, which steadily declined
and did not make much resistance to the Roman domination.

The Gaul which was taking shape under the wing of
Roman institutions was very different from the Gaul which
had gone down with Vercingetorix. It no longer had the
same popular soul. It went on changing very fast. It has
a quite different appearance from what it had worn at the
time of the assembly of the Remi, when it suddenly finds

[1] *Pomp. Mela*, iii, 2, 19,

itself, in the later third century, mistress of its destinies for sixteen years.

The episode is worth telling.

After the death of Alexander Severus the Roman Empire relapsed into the dynastic chaos which it had already experienced more than once. Between 253 and 255 bands of Alemanni and Franks broke through the frontier and perhaps penetrated, even at this early date, into Auvergne. These inroads of barbarians, even in small numbers, destroyed for a long time the peace in which Gaul throve. Measures of protection had to be taken. The towns drew themselves in and girt themselves with fortifications within a few years as in the days of the Cimbri. In 258 the Emperor Gallienus had sent his son Valerian to Germany, but the real command of the frontier lay with the Gaul Marcus Cassianus Latinius Postumus. The legions of the Rhine did what they had done before—wanted an emperor of their own and chose Postumus. Young Valerian was made prisoner at Cologne. Gallienus attempted two or three attacks, but in vain. Postumus systematically made Gaul his object. He does not seem to have had any aspiration to the Empire as a whole ; he does not even seem to have tried to break away from the rest of the Roman world. Gaul was apparently quite unchanged ; above all, there was no question of independence. Postumus set up a fortuitous combination similar to the division of the Empire which was afterwards effected under Diocletian. This combination proved good and salutary. Order and security were restored. There are innumerable coins of this period, and they are of better weight. That is a sign of good, honest government and economic healthiness.

But Postumus's legions grew tired of him and murdered him. His successors, Lælianus and Victorinus, disappeared in their turn. The Germans crossed the frontier. The wife of Victorinus, named Victoria, escaped the slaughter. She was probably a Gallo-Roman of good family. In the little that we know of these events, she makes rather a good impression. She was compared to her contemporary, Zenobia. She was popular with the troops. It is said that she might have been Empress, but she gave the throne to a relation, C. Pius Esuvius Tetricus, who kept it from 268 to 274. He had been governor of Aquitania ; he was not a soldier, but must have been a first-rate administrator. After a disgraceful affair in the army of the Rhine, all was restored to order. Victoria died, and Tetricus continued to reign in peace until Aurelian was free to attend to the West. Tetricus did nothing to defend himself. When his army was defeated, he entered the Imperial army. His career gives a very clear idea of what that Roman Empire of Gaul was like—an essentially transitory regime, which was not destined to survive the circumstances in which it had its birth.

It may be asked, however, whether something of it did not survive—a memory—in the insurrections of the Bagaudæ,[1] which began ten years later, in 283. Bagaudæ is a Gallic name, the first part of which is similar to Irish *baga*, meaning " battle ". They were peasants. Their movements were local and disconnected ; they did not form an army. They belonged to the lower strata of the population, those which had remained most Celtic and in which even the language was still used, as we know from contemporaries. We can imagine what the countryside of Gaul had become like in those successive years of invasion and pillage. The tax-collector took turns with the barbarian. We can understand why they revolted. In 283 they even elected emperors, Ælianus and Amandus. They held out until 285. It should be noted that, when defeated by Maximian, Ælianus and Amandus became martyrs and a kind of saints (in the *Life of St. Babolinus*). This throws a faint gleam of light on the size and popular nature of the movement, which, moreover, went on. Brigandage continued, and the name of Bagaudæ remained attached to it. Reinforced by all the discontented (and these were many), they even came to form small states, like those which the Germans were beginning to set up in Gaul.

But what emerges in clear and convincing fashion, not from the chronicle of events as they occur but from the institutions and opinions of the Gaul of the time, is that,
- over the municipal life and the habits which it had created, the Roman organization had given Gaul provincial formations and habits of normal life based on large units. The three, or

[1] Bagaudæ is a Gallic name, with a termination like *auda* in Alauda, following a first element which is similar to Irish *baga*. Cf. Jullian, in **CXXXIV**, 1920, pp. 107 ff.

the four, provinces were divisions of Gallia. There were fixed frontiers with custom-houses on them and an army to defend the most exposed of them. There was a system of roads. Above all, there were an order of rank, capitals, subordination, stability, and agreement. This was everything that the Gauls had lacked. The country took on what it could not have had in old days—the air of an individual. In the fourth century Gaul begins to present this aspect, with its new features, in literature, in Rutilius Numatianus, in Ausonius, in Avitus. Sidonius Apollinaris even speaks of *patria nostra*, and after that it is always so, down to the day when *France dulce* in the popular tongue takes the place of *Gallia* in Latin.[1] Perhaps those very misfortunes of the third century began to complete the political education of the people by the sufferings of their country. They gave it the venerable wrinkles which men have always loved to see on the face of their motherland.

IV

THE CELTS OF THE DANUBE

So much for Gaul proper. There was another Gaul, that of the Danube, which was connected with the province of Illyricum as Gaul proper with Narbonensis. Cæsar had got Illyricum in his province just as he had got Gaul, and had kept an eye on the country. He had, for example, been in Dalmatia for part of the winter of 57–56. Things might happen on this side as in Gaul. Troops might pass through on the way to Macedonia as they could through Gaul on the way to Spain. Roman policy had sources of intelligence in Noricum, and Roman influence was active there ; the consular coinages were imitated, a sign that Latin traders were travelling and doing business in the country.[2]

Augustus inherited the programme which Cæsar had not carried out completely. The death of Bœrebistas, the break-up of the sort of empire which he had set up, and a series of campaigns conducted by the best generals of Augustus,

---

[1] **CCCLVII**, *Poetæ Latini Ævi Karolini*, pp. 367–8, hymns *de martyribus Agennensibus*.

[2] Roman denarii and copies of consular coins. Forrer, **DXLIII**, pp. 120, 124, 127.

Agrippa, Drusus, and Tiberius, from 35 to 9 B.C. carried
the frontiers of the Empire to the Danube,[1] thus placing
a broad buffer-zone between Italy and Germany and securing
for the Empire a good line of communication. Just at this
time the Germans were arriving among the Gauls who were
still settled on the northern bank of the Danube. It was now,
in my opinion, that the Marcomanni moved into Bohemia
in the place of the Boii.[2] The information which we have
about the campaigns of Augustus's generals between the
Danube and the Elbe confirms this view. Drusus came
upon the Marcomanni on the upper Main and defeated them
in 10 B.C. In 8 B.C. L. Domitius Ahenobarbus[3] marched
out from the Danube in order to reach the Elbe, and
established in their country, at that time unoccupied, a body
of Hermunduri, come from no one knows where and perhaps
themselves dislodged by the migrating Marcomanni.

The Marcomanni must have moved in 9, and settled
after that date in Bohemia, under a famous leader, Marbod
(Maroboduus). The Boii who remained gradually depleted
themselves by migrations and vanished, the remnant being
perhaps absorbed by the Marcomanni, leaving only a name,
which is that of the country at this day. Thus the Celts
were completing the movement which brought them to
a position along the Danube, as on the Rhine, at the time
when the Danubian colonies were finally submitting to
Rome. In the north they left only lost elements. On both
sides the Roman Empire defended the frontier.

On both sides the generals of Augustus crossed it. We
find Marbod again, in A.D. 6, opposing Tiberius, who is
trying to attack Bohemia from the south. But Illyricum
was uncertain. When it was cleared of troops a revolt broke
out, and Tiberius judged it wise to make terms with Marbod.
Marbod suffered for this, and was driven out by the

---

[1] Jullian, CCCXLVII, iv, pp. 100 ff.

[2] The question of this date is important from an archæological standpoint,
for it makes it possible to date the finds of the Hradischt of Stradonitz and
the La Tène III civilization which is there represented as brilliantly as at
Mont Beuvray. It is very clear from Cæsar's words (i, 5) that the Boii of
Noricum who joined forces with the Helvetii and ended up in Gaul were
only a fraction of the people, the greater part of which had remained in
Bohemia and did not emigrate till about the year 8. Almgren, in LXXXV,
1913, p. 265 ff.; d'Arbois, CCXCIX, ii, p. 11.

[3] Müllenhoff, CCCLXII, iv, p. 44.

Marcomanni. He took refuge with the Romans, who established him at Forum Julii.

Strabo,[1] who wrote shortly after, speaks of Pannonia as a ruined country. It had not yet repaired the damages of the conquest when Gaul had long obliterated them. It did recover later, and the Roman ruins of the Danube valley do not give an impression of poverty.

In any case, there was nothing in the way of social organization in this region comparable to what we have seen in Gaul. The reason may be that the native society of the Danube was so much Romanized that it could not become aware of its unity.

[1] vii, 3, 5, 11.

CHAPTER II

THE ROMANS IN BRITAIN

I

BRITAIN BEFORE ITS ROMANIZATION

THE historians tell us that Comm, the chieftain of the Atrebates already mentioned, who was one of the most remarkable figures of the Gallic War, after serving Cæsar became a deadly enemy of Rome in consequence of a quarrel with an officer of the Roman army, who had betrayed him. In 51 he withdrew into Britain with some of his people, continuing the work of colonization done by the Belgæ in the south of the island. He struck coins with Latin characters. He had three sons, who reigned in Britain.[1]

Britain had not yet been conquered by Rome. Celtic civilization held its own there; Celtic art prevailed[2]; ornament developed with taste, particularly enamel-work, with its combinations of colours. This art, indeed, quickly travelled far from the classic models of Celtic art; decorative fancy had free rein, while the workmanship continued to be admirable. The centre of this art, and of all the civilization of Britain, was in the south of England, in a region bounded on the north by a line drawn from the Bristol Channel to the Wash. Only here do we find Celtic coins.

There were a few towns in Britain, open towns or *oppida*, such as Londinium (London), the port of the Cantii, Camulodunum (Colchester), the stronghold of the Trinovantes, Eboracum (York), the capital of the Brigantes. Ptolemy mentions only about sixty, and many of these were doubtless only refuges or markets. Britain does not seem to have been so advanced as Gaul in the organization of city life.

There is never any mention of British shipping. Cæsar's

---

[1] MacNeill, **CCCCXLI**, p. 168; Jullian, **CCCXLVII**, ii, p. 470.
[2] Parkyn, **CCCCXLVI**, p. 101; Reginald A. Smith, " On Late Celtic Antiquities discovered at Welwyn," in **CXXII**; S. Reinach, in **CXXXIX**, 1925, 172. Cf. Collingwood, **CCCCXX**; Bushe Fox, *Excavation of the Late-Celtic Urn-field at Swarling, Kent*, **CXXVI**, 1925. .

two expeditions would have been at the mercy of any such fleet. But the monopoly of the Veneti probably extended to Britain.[1]

II

THE ROMAN CONQUEST

Britain lived in peace until the time of Caligula, when the Romans made an expedition. The resistance was headed, as in Cæsar's time, by the King of the Trinovantes and by Cassivelaunus's successor Cunobelinus, Shakespeare's Cymbeline.[2] The Romans returned under Claudius in 43, for the first time with the fixed intention of remaining. Gradually they had learned to know Britain better. Aulus Plautius, the commander-in-chief of the expedition, was remarkably well informed. The pretext of the expedition was a refusal to deliver up deserters.[3] Cunobelinus's two sons, Togidumnus and Caratacus (Caractacus) led the opponents of the Romans. Camulodunum was taken, and the south of the island reduced to a province. In this campaign the future Vespasian conquered the Isle of Wight (Vectis).[4] The first successors of Plautius, in a series of campaigns of which Tacitus gives a mere summary, tried to extend the new province northwards in the direction of the Brigantes, and westwards in that of the Irish Sea and the Silures. Caratacus took refuge with the Queen of the Brigantes, who gave him up. He was taken to Rome, where he defended his conduct so eloquently that he was restored to liberty.

The Romans established a colony at Camulodunum and a system of small forts in the west facing Cornwall and the Silures, on the last spurs of the chalky uplands.

A serious set-back led to the appointment in 57 of a capable general, Suetonius Paulinus. He organized an expedition against the Druid sanctuary on Anglesey, which is described as a refuge of deserters. The Druids had been

---

[1] Lloyd, **CCCCXXXVIII**, 41.
[2] Ibid., 47.
[3] Windisch, *Das keltische Britannien bis zu Kaiser Arthur*, p. 14 ; Tac., *Agr.*, 14.
[4] Dion Cass., ix, 210 ; Suet., *Vesp.*, 4 ; Eutrop., vii, 19. Cf. Bruton, **CCCCXVI**, 208–210 ; Windisch, p. 15.

an element of opposition in Britain.[1] Suetonius Paulinus
was recalled by a general rising; the Trinovantes had
retaken Camulodunum and massacred the colony, and
a legion had been wiped out. The general, after evacuating
London and Verulamium (near St. Albans), gained a decisive
victory which saved the Roman settlements.[2]

After some years of uncertainty, Vespasian, who knew
the country, revived the attempt to conquer it. The Brigantes
and the Silures were defeated in turn.[3] Then the famous
Agricola arrived, who governed Britain from 78 to 86. Thanks
to him and to his son-in-law Tacitus, the story of the conquest
of the island has become classic, almost as much so as that
of Gaul. He had served under Suetonius Paulinus, and made
Anglesey his objective. Then he advanced north, gaining
ground every year. In his third year in the field he reached
the Firth of Tay, *œstuarium Tanaum*. Subsequently, he
erected a first edition of the *vallum* of Antoninus between
the Clyde and the Firth of Forth. In his sixth and seventh
campaigns he went beyond his *vallum* either with his
fleet or with his land-forces, but did not establish himself
permanently.[4]

After that, Hadrian and Antoninus built each a *vallum*.
Under Commodus the future Emperor Pertinax put down
a rebellion. Later, Septimius Severus made an expedition
into Caledonia, of which we know nothing.[5]

Britain was conquered, except that mysterious Caledonia
and the central portion of Wales, occupied by the Ordovices
and Demetæ, who were to be reinforced by Irish colonies.

The Roman government carried on the same policy of
assimilation in Britain as in Gaul, but with some differences
and less success. Tacitus gives the credit of this policy to
Agricola, who won over the people with the conveniences of
Roman civilization and city life. He advanced money for
building, set up schools, and instituted fashions. The
archæological finds show us a Britain living partly in buildings
of Roman type. Towns sprang up (the remains of about
thirty are known), but less spontaneously than in Gaul,

[1] Tac., *Ann.*, xiv, 29–30 ; cf. Windisch, p. 17.
[2] Tac., *Ann.*, xiv, 32 ; Windisch, pp. 18–19.
[3] Windisch, pp. 19–20.
[4] Tac., **CCCCXXVII**. Cf. Macdonald, **CCCCXL**, pp. 111–138.
[5] Windisch, pp. 42–3. Cf. Paus., vii, 31.

since the legionary camps constituted towns in Britain. The IInd Legion was quartered at Isca Silurum, or Cærleon, " Camp of the Legion " ; the VIth at Eboracum, or York ; the XIVth at Uriconium (Shrewsbury) ; the XXth at Deva (Chester). In the seventh century the *Historia Brittonum* of Nennius gives a list of twenty-six towns whose names begin with *Caer*, derived from *castrum*. These are garrison towns, in which the soldiers seem to have been more intermingled with the population than in Gaul.[1]

In these towns Latin was spoken. It was the official language, that in which the inscriptions are written. But whereas in Gaul it outlasted the Roman rule, in Britain it vanished with it ; much of it lingers in the Welsh vocabulary, but it was British that survived. We may consider the reasons for this.[2]

The chief reason was that in Britain Romanization was far less general and less deep than in Gaul. It is true that the remains of a large number of very luxurious Roman villas have been found, which confirm what Tacitus tells us of the Romanization of the British nobility. In fact it is to this nobility that we must ascribe the permanent buildings rather than to the Roman officials, whose stay was transitory, or to the men planted in the colonies, who must have been chiefly small folk. But the evidences of Roman culture are very definitely confined to certain districts—the neighbourhood of the northern garrisons, the south coast (Kent, Sussex, the Isle of Wight), and the agricultural areas of Gloucestershire and Lincolnshire, which seem to have been supplycentres of the Roman army.[3]

About the towns, one point is to be noted—the absence of municipal inscriptions of any importance. The fact is that the country continued to be military and the administration was purely military until the time of Diocletian. The names of peoples disappeared ; the small nations were not, as in Gaul, made the basis of the political and territorial

---

[1] Windisch, pp. 46–8 ; Sagot, **CCCCLIV**. Cf. Loth, in **CXL**, 1914, p. 109 ; Drexel, " Denkmäler der Brittonen am Limes," in **LXVII**, 1922, p. 31 ; Haverfield and Macdonald, **CCCCXXXI** ; Lethaby, **CCCCXXXVIII** ; Collinge, **CCCCXIX** ; Fabricius, " Neuere Arbeiten über die britannischen Limites," in **LXVIII**, 1923, p. 79.

[2] Budinsky, **CXCII**.

[3] Collingwood, **CCCCXX** ; Taylor, **CCCCLX** ; Macdonald, " The Building of the Antonine Wall," in **LXXVIII**, 1921 ; Miller, **CCCCXLII**.

organization of the country. At any rate each was not centred on a town, as in Gaul, and held together by its town. In Diocletian's time each province corresponds to a group of little nations ; for example Flavia Cæsarensis consists of the Iceni, Trinovantes, Cantii, Regni, and Atrebates.

III

THE ARMY OF BRITAIN. ARTHUR

At the end of the second century, in the *Notitia Dignitatum*, we find in Britain four chief officials, two of whom are military. One commands the fleet, and is called Count of the Saxon Shore (*comes littoris Saxonici*). This proves that the Saxon invasions started nearly two hundred years before Hengist and Horsa. He had the IInd Legion under his orders. The other military official is called Duke of the Britains (*dux Britanniarum*), with the VIth Legion under him. It was his duty to resist the repeated attacks of the northerners, who were no longer held back by the ramparts of Hadrian and Antoninus—Caledonians, Picts or Scots, and also people from the west. The military forces of Britain were caught between these two groups of enemies, and faced now one, now the other, and sometimes both.[1]

These officials, stranded on the very edge of the Empire, beyond the Channel, and left to their own resources, gradually became independent in practice. They also tried to obtain complete independence, and there were revolts. Some sought the Imperial throne, and crossed the sea. The story becomes mixed with legend. The attitude of chroniclers like the pseudo-Nennius and Geoffrey of Monmouth after him is very interesting. The usurper and the rebel are to them the heroes of the story, and in their eyes they are not Romans, but Britons. In the curious work of Gildas entitled *De excidio et conquestu Britanniae* [2] we already find signs of

---

[1] Lloyd, **CCCCXXXVIII**, 59 ; Windisch, *Das keltische Britannien*, pp. 43 ff., 57. Cf. Ridgeway, " Nial of the Nine Hostages," in Phil. Soc. Cambridge, 1924, p. 14 ; R. G. Collingwood, " The Roman Evacuation of Britain," in **LXXIX**, xii, 1922, pp. 74–98.

[2] Published by Mommsen in **CCCLVIII**, xiii, *Chronica Minora*, iii, pp. 1 ff. See Faral, **CCCCXXVI**, i, p. 39. For the sources for the life of Gildas, see Lot, *Mélanges d'histoire bretonne : études et documents*, Paris, 1907. Gildas died in 569 or 570.

the same state of mind, and the *Historia Brittonum* of Nennius, in repeating a passage from Gildas, alters and further amplifies its character in this respect.[1]

In the time of Diocletian, in 286, the Count of the Saxon Shore, Carausius, revolted and assumed the purple, and was killed by one of his lieutenants.[2] A little later Constantius Chlorus took the field in Britain against the Picts and died at York in 306. The attacks of the Picts were repeated ; they came down as far as London ; and Ammianus Marcellinus, the great historian of this period, shows us Theodosius the Great fighting them from 364 to 366. Some years later Britain produced another pretender, Maximus, who must have been the Duke of the Britains. In 387 he left Britain with his army, which was scattered and annihilated by Theodosius. This Maximus is doubtless the hero of the legend which tells of an Emperor of Rome of that name who was attracted to Britain by a wonderful beauty whom he had seen in a dream ; he there forgot his duties. Rome revolted, he reconquered it, and his British troops returned to their country no more. It is the subject of a Mabinogi, the *Dream of Macsen Wledig*.[3]

A line of Claudian suggests that Stilicho defended Britain against the Picts and Saxons. In any case, there were still troops in the country under Honorius,[4] and they there set up three emperors in succession—Marcus, Gratian, and Constantine III. This last, like Maximus, left the island and

---

[1] The question of the composition of the compilation known as the *Historia Britonnum*, ascribed to Nennius, and of the identity of its supposed author, has given rise to a series of important controversial works. The latest is that of M. Faral, op. cit., ii, pp. 56–224 ; in his third volume he has attempted a critical restoration of the text. Mommsen published the text, op. cit., xiii, *Chronica Minora*, iii, pp. iii, 59. Mgr. Duchesne had, in **CXL**, xvii, p. 15, made a preliminary classification of versions which is still a very remarkable piece of work. Zimmer has devoted an important work to Nennius, in which he says that he really existed and ascribes the whole of the original version of the history to him. According to M. Faral, this text is later than 687 and earlier than 801. In any case it contains traditions of older origin, which probably refer to the south of Britain.

For Geoffrey of Monmouth, who wrote about the second quarter of the twelfth century, see Faral, op. cit., ii, and the critical restoration of his *Historia Britanniæ* in the third volume of that work. At the same time as M. Faral's work, Messrs. Griscom and Jones brought out an edition of Geoffrey's text, with a translation and an essay on the author (London, 1929). Cf., too, the important work of Bruce, *The Evolution of Arthurian Romance*, Göttingen, 1923, two vols. Cf. below, p. 266.

[2] Eutr., ix, 22 ; Oros., vii, 25 ; Windisch, op. cit., p. 43.

[3] Windisch, op. cit., p. 44 ; cf. Loth, **CCLXX**, i, p. 219.

[4] Windisch, op. cit., p. 45.

fought Stilicho in Gaul. He had a detachment in Spain, commanded by his son Constans. During this time, the towns of Britain seem to have succeeded in running the affairs of Britain independently. The historian Zosimus quotes a curious circular letter written to them by Honorius, asking them to provide for their own defence.[1] But the loosening bonds were not yet broken, and it appears that in 446 the Britons came into Gaul to help Aëtius. Britain was still theoretically part of the Empire in 537, when Belisarius ceded it to the Goths who had been driven out of Aquitania by Clovis.

During the period of the first Saxon invasions, the office of Duke of the Britains does not seem to have lapsed. We know of two historical Dukes, and there are two others who are chiefly legendary. In Nennius these officials are called *reges*. In Welsh they bear the same title as Maxen Wledig.

The two historical Dukes are Guortigernus or Vortigern, who was certainly a Briton, and Aurelius Ambrosius, who came of a Roman or very much Romanized family and whose father is said to have been a Consul. He is the hero of the story for Gildas and the Latin and Welsh chroniclers.[2]

The two legendary Dukes are Uther Pendragon, the father of Arthur, and Arthur himself. The Triads of the *Red Book of Hergest* make Uther Pendragon the brother of Emreis, that is Ambrosius, and the son of Kustennin Vychan, that is Constantine the Small, the usurper Constantine III. The conquest of Rome is one of the main episodes in the legend of Arthur, which symbolizes and depicts not only the fight of Britain against the northerners and Saxons but also the revolt of Britain against Rome and its defeat of the Roman power.[3]

---

[1] Zosim., vi, 10, 2.
[2] Windisch, op. cit., p. 38 ; cf. Gildas, xiv.
[3] Windisch, op. cit., p. 52. Cf. Faral and Bruce, opp. citt.

CHAPTER III

The End of Celtic Britain and Ireland. Saxons, Scots, and Norsemen

I

THE GERMANIC INVASIONS

THE historians lay the blame of bringing the Saxons into Britain on Vortigern,[1] who is said to have called them in to help him against the Picts in 449. Once again we see the Celts playing the weak man's game of putting yourself in the hands of one enemy to save yourself from another. According to the story, Vortigern married a daughter of Hengist and gave him the isle of Thanet and the Kentish coast in exchange, and the alliance between Vortigern and the Saxons came to an end when the latter treacherously massacred a number of Britons at a banquet.

Vortigern fled to Wales, to the Ordovices, whose country was then called Venedotia (Gwynedd). They were ruled by a line of warlike princes who had their capital at Aberffraw in Anglesey. These kings of Gwynedd, trained by uninterrupted fighting against the Irish and the Picts, seem to have taken on the work of the Dukes of the Britains after Ambrosius or Arthur, and to have been regarded as kings in Britain as a whole.[2]

It was apparently at this time that the name of Cymry, which became the national name of the Britons, came to prevail. The Cymry are the tribes who fight side by side, under the command of a chief called the *Gwledig*, against the Irish, Picts, or Saxons. The country of these Cymry is called Combrog in the British of that day, or Cambria.[3]

A hundred years after this first settlement in Kent, the

---

[1] Lloyd, **CCCCXXXVIII**, 79. Cf. A. W. W. Evans, " Les Saxons dans *l'Excidium Britanniæ* ", in **LVI**, 1916, p. 322. Cf. *R.C.*, 1917–1919, p. 283 ; F.Lot, " Hangist, Horsa, Vortigern, et la conquête de la Gde.-Bretagne par les Saxons," in **CLXXIX**.

[2] Lloyd, op. cit., p. 102.

[3] Ibid., pp. 79, 84.

Saxons advanced rapidly. In 577 they reached the Severn, and cut off Wales from Cornwall for good. About 600 the foundation of a kingdom of Mercia shut the Britons up in the mountains of Wales, where they held their ground.[1] Other kingdoms were founded in the north, which, united in the kingdom of Northumberland, reached the Irish Sea and from 613 onwards separated Wales from a group of Britons who hung on in the north on the borders of the Pictish country. These latter continued to form a kingdom, that of Strathclyde or Cumbria, and its citadel of Dumbarton on the Clyde was not destroyed until the attack of the Norsemen of Ireland in later years.[2]

The introduction of Christianity contributed greatly to the denationalizing of the Celts in Britain. It is true that the Saxons were not Christians when they settled in the island, and in Bede's time the Britons found it difficult to regard them as Christians. But the reforming mission of Augustine, sent to Britain in 596 by St. Gregory, had already shocked British opinion by the sympathetic impartiality which it showed to the newly converted Saxons. In Britain, on account of the rapid conversion of the Saxons and the way in which they were welcomed by the Church, the Celtic resistance could hope for nothing from Christianity.[3]

By the end of the sixth century the game was lost. Celtic Britain had fallen to pieces and only a few fragments remained.

II

THE OCCUPATION OF BRITTANY

The emigration to Brittany or Armorica had begun very early. According to Gildas, who was one of the emigrants and ended his days on the shores of Morbihan, it occurred immediately after the settlement of the first Saxon invaders. Indeed, a bishop of the Britons, Mansuetus, appears at the Council of Tours of 461, and one may wonder whether the Britons who fought on the Loire against the Visigoths in 468 and 472, for Aëtius under a leader named Riotimus,

[1] Ibid., p. 93. Cf. Windisch, p. 62.
[2] Ibid., p. 103.
[3] Ibid., pp. 86, 96.

belonged to Britain or Brittany. The latter was, according to Procopius, one of the most deserted parts of Gaul, and there was plenty of room there for occupation.[1]

The Britons were not contented to fit themselves into a country left empty for them. They really colonized it and founded states, into which they remained divided. One part of Armorica was called Domnonea, and was occupied by Dumnonii of Cornwall ; another was called Cornavia, being settled by Cornavii from Lancashire. They had kings. The story of Cædwalla, the last King of Gwynedd, who was still of some consequence at the beginning of the seventh century, is blended with that of one Salomo, *Rex Armoricanorum Brittonum*, a contemporary of Dagobert (who died in 638).[2]

There were probably more than one emigration. Geoffrey of Monmouth places one in 664. After years of defeat, famine, and plague, Cadwaladr, son of Cædwalla, flees to Armorica, and history adds that his flight marks the end of the British kings and the triumph of the English.

The history of Celtic Brittany is even vaguer than that of the emigration. Legend tells more about it than history, for it is inexhaustible on the subject of the kinships and common endeavours of the heroes and knights of Britain and Brittany. Tristram is a Briton ; Lancelot has come from France to Arthur's court ; Arthur has destroyed the demon of Mont St. Michel ; Merlin flits to and fro between the two countries. This tradition is not without significance. Brittany never ceased to look towards Britain, bound to it by its resuscitated shipping, until the day when it found itself in contact with the very body of France, a France which was no longer Germanic or Celtic but was France, and absorbed Brittany naturally and without a struggle.

III

THE INDEPENDENT CELTS OF SCOTLAND AND IRELAND

The unceasing inroads of the Picts which disturbed Britain in the fourth and fifth centuries seem to point to

---

[1] Loth, **CCCCLXXX**. Cf. Loth, " La Vie la plus ancienne de St.-Samson," in **CXL**, 1923, pp. 1, 8. Cf. Windisch, p. 57.

[2] Loth, op. cit. For Celtic Armorica see Loth, *Mélanges d'histoire bretonne*, Paris, 1907.

a renewal of vitality. But, though we know the dates of their expeditions, we have no information about the Picts themselves or the Caledonians of Scotland. We only know that the Picts had been founding settlements in Ulster since the fourth century, and that they were formidable fighters.[1]

In Ireland, on the other hand, a series of political events occurred which gave a kind of organization, still very patchy, to the racial medley of natives, Goidels, Picts, Britons, and Belgæ,[2] of which I have given some idea in the previous volume. About the time of St. Patrick this organization culminated in the institution of the High Kingship of Ireland, the Kingship of Tara. The strength and health which it gave to Ireland were utilized in expeditions abroad and expressed in civilization at home. All that is historical in the epic Cycles of Ulster and Leinster lies in this period of history.

For these events we have no direct evidence, and contemporary Greek and Latin writers say almost nothing of Ireland. We must be content with two useful pieces of information which we owe to them. One-half of the sixteen peoples of the coast named by Ptolemy are identified anew, and a passage in the polygrapher Solinus, stating that there are no snakes in Ireland, is based on an authentic Irish tradition. For the Irish give to St. Patrick or to Finn mac Coul, as the case may be, the glory of having rid the island of snakes.[3] There were Irish exiles who kept the Roman commanders or governors with whom they happened to come into contact well supplied with information. We have only fragments of what they may have told.

On the other hand, we have a considerable mass of indirect information, furnished by the epics, local legends, laws, and, lastly, the Annals. These last can only be used in the most cautious and critical spirit. The older parts of the dynastic lists and pedigrees are composite, and we should note in general that the Annals hardly mention anything but exceptional occurrences, outside the normal course of life, and so give a false impression of the course of events. All these data have been utilized with great skill by Mr. Eoin MacNeill in the last chapters of his *Phases of Irish History*.[4]

---

[1] MacNeill, **CCCCXLI**, p. 141. [2] Ibid., p. 109.
[3] Joyce, **CCCCXXXIV**, ii, p. 514. [4] MacNeill, op. cit., pp. 178, 190.

Although the Romans did not know Ireland, they were known there and their influence was felt there. Ireland had more or less continuous commercial dealings with Britain and with Gaul, which sent it wine. One curious witness to this influence is the alphabet. The Irish invented an alphabet of their own, in which the letters are represented by strokes drawn above or below or across a chief line, or obliquely to it. It has twenty letters—A, B, C, D, E, F, G, H, I, L, M, N, O, QU, R, S, T, U, V, NG. There was no sign for X or for Y. It has only one letter, NG, which the Latin alphabet lacks. If the Irish had evolved their alphabet entirely out of their own heads, they would obviously have invented signs for the aspirated forms of their dentals, labials, and gutturals. But they did not even adopt those of Greek. It was, therefore, the Latin alphabet which they used when analysing sounds, though they did so in an original fashion—distinction of vowel u from consonant u, classification of sounds. The ogham inscriptions cover the same area as the Irish language of the time just before the earliest Christian phases of Ireland and the earliest manuscripts. Moreover, some ogham inscriptions are Christian. The use of oghams must be placed between an end, somewhere about the sixth century, and a beginning, doubtless about the second or third century.[1]

Yet another feature presented by Ireland in the first centuries of our era may, according to Mr. MacNeill, be due to imitation of the Romans. That is the troops of Fianna, the standing force of professional soldiers, who have their epic in the Leinster Cycle or the Cycle of Finn and failed Ireland so badly in after years. These troops have nothing to do with the early military organization of the Celts, and must have been levied in imitation of Roman military institutions.[2] In any case, it was they who supplied the source of the power which we shall see at work.

The political development of Ireland lies between two terms—the existence of five equal, independent kingdoms in the time of Conchobar mac Nessa, King of Ulster, the king in the epic of Ulster whom the Annals with more or less truth make a contemporary of Christ, and the foundation of the kingdom of Meath as the realm of a High King, with

[1] Ibid., pp. 171 ff. [2] Ibid., p. 150.

his capital at Tara, in 483. An intermediate date emerges
from the Annals, namely that of the reign of Cormac mac
Airt, King of Connacht about 275, who conquers Tara. With
the conquest of Tara by Cormac is connected the idea of
the foundation of a High Kingship held by the Kings of
Connacht.

The time of Conchobar is called *Aimser na Cóicedach*,
the Time of the Five Fifths. Ireland was divided between
the kingdoms of Ulster, Connacht, North Leinster, South
Leinster, and Munster. Tara belonged to North Leinster,
and Ulster stretched a long way westwards. The frontiers
of Munster towards Connacht and Leinster varied a little,
but it is not in that direction that one must look for great
changes, but in the frontiers of Ulster and Leinster towards
Connacht.[1]

The epic of Ulster shows us all Ireland united against
that luckless region, under the leadership of the Kings of
Connacht. Gradually Connacht gains ground to the east
at the expense of Ulster, which it reduces to Counties Down
and Antrim, and of North Leinster, which in the end it
absorbs entirely. These enlargements are the foundations
of its hegemony ; eventually it embraces half Ireland.[2]

For, about 150, the people of Connacht occupy Uisnech.
The Kingdom of Conchobar is by this time unrecognizable ;
moreover, it is almost entirely Pictish. A second stage is
marked by the occupation of Tara by King Cormac ; a third,
by the destruction of the Kingdom of Ulster by exiles from
Connacht, whose dramatic history is known to us. The
single kingdom of Ulster is divided in two—the kingdom
of Airgialla and Ulster properly so called. About 400, at the
time of Niall of the Nine Hostages, Ulster is still further
reduced in the south-west, and the sons of Niall take all that
is still left to it in the north-west in County Donegal. The
year 483 is marked by the battle of Ocha, which leads to
the separation of the kingship of Connacht from the High
Kingship, which is attached to the possession of the kingship
of Meath with Tara.

There are now not five but seven kingdoms in Ireland,[3]
namely Meath, Connacht, Ailech, Airgialla or Oriel, Ulster,

---

[1] Ibid., pp. 100 ff.   [2] Ibid., p. 129.
[3] Ibid., pp. 113–117.

Leinster, and Munster. The last six are subordinate to Meath.
This is the organization which St. Patrick finds in Ireland
some years later. The kingship of Tara was still not firmly
established, and the Saint took up his abode not there,
but at Armagh.[1] Leinster was not yet, after hundreds
of years, resigned to its fallen estate, for it still occasionally
attacked Connacht and the kingdom of Meath. But unity
was practically an accomplished fact. The Irish represented
Ireland or its kingship as a sublime princess, the mythical
or metaphysical bride of the King of Tara, and this conception was expressed in poems which are sometimes
wonderfully beautiful. Moreover, the distinction between
the Goidels and the Aithech-thuatha, the rent-paying
clans of which I have spoken, in which all non-Goidelic
groups were lumped together, was gradually obliterated;
in fact, an Ivernian, Eterscél, appears in the list of the
great pre-historic kings. Yet it was at the end of the first
century that the famous, if ephemeral, revolt of the Rent-
payers took place, which drove the Connacht line out of
the country to Britain, perhaps shortly after the time
of Agricola. But the banished house returned with Tuathal
Teachtmar, more powerful than ever.

A tendency towards unity, the sense of which became
ever deeper, and a fusion of races—these were the results
of the political development of Ireland which we have just
surveyed.

IV

THE INROADS OF THE SCOTS

The Irish had been fighting for four hundred years, and
so were well trained to warfare and daring. Also, some of
them had been defeated. Groups had been driven out
of their homes. The Desi, who lived about Tara, were
reduced to vagabondage by the conquerors of Connacht.
So Ireland seems to have had surplus men and energy to
spend abroad.[2]

From the third century, the Romans in Britain had to

---

[1] Ibid., p. 160.   [2] Ibid., p. 188.

be on their guard against Irish incursions. The invaders
are designated by the historians of the Later Empire under
the names of Hiberni, Attecotti, Scotti. *Scotti* became
one of the usual names of the Goidels of Ireland. *Attecotti*
does not appear outside the documents of that time. Scottus
is a Gaulish name, and seems to mean " skirmisher ",
" runner ".[1]

The Irish did not halt in Britain, but went on to the
Continent. St. Jerome[2] speaks of inroads of the Attecotti,
barbarous men with cruel habits and abominable morals.
They cut off the breasts of women and ate them, he says,
and they lived in promiscuity. They landed at the mouth
of the Loire and engaged in brigandage in the country.
Sometimes they came in large numbers, and Stilicho had
to meet a real invasion of Irish. Sometimes they took
service under Rome ; the *Notitia Dignitatum* gives Attecotti
Juniores and Seniores. Ammianus Marcellinus speaks of
a body of scouts or spies called Areani.[3] These were
Irish *vigiles* (in Irish, *aire* means ." guard ", " watcher ").
The Scots settled down in colonies ; the village of Écuisses
in Saône-et-Loire was originally Scotiæ.[4]

The Irish Annals and other documents show us the
other side of these adventures. We are told, not of bands
of pillagers, but of military expeditions led by kings. The
earliest of these expeditions is ascribed to King Crimthann
Nia Nair, who is said to have reigned over the whole of
Ireland between 74 and 90. The conquests attributed to
Crimthann the Great, who is supposed to have reigned
from 366 to 379, coincide in a curious way with the command
and victories of Theodosius, the father of Theodosius the
Great.[5] The campaigns of Stilicho in Britain and Gaul
have a counterpart in the expeditions of the famous King
Niall of the Nine Hostages. He ravaged the north of Britain,
unpeopled the country, and took thousands of captives,
among whom may have been St. Patrick, who, as we know
was a slave in Ireland. In 405 Niall was killed by a king

---

[1] Haverfield, "Ancient Rome and Ireland," in **LXII**, xxviii, 1913, p. 8.
Cf. Zimmer, in **CXLVIII**, 1891, p. 280 ; Lloyd, **CCCCXXXVIII**, 51 ; MacNeill,
op. cit., p. 148.
[2] Jerome, *In Jovin.*, ii. Cf. Müllenhoff, **CCCLXII**, ii, p. 183.
[3] Amm. Marc., xxviii, 3, 8 ; MacNeill, op. cit., p. 151.
[4] For these settlements, cf. MacNeill, op. cit., p. 144.
[5] Joyce, op. cit., i, 73–4.

of Leinster while fighting in Gaul, and his successor is likewise said to have warred in that country.[1]

At the same time the Irish were establishing themselves
in Britain and on all the projecting parts of the west coast.
Between 250 and 300 the Desi occupied the country of
Dyfed.[2] Then the Ui Liatháin, one of the chief branches of
the Eoganachta of Munster, settled in Cornwall.[3] In the
north, the Dal Riada of Ulster took possession of Argyll
and the neighbouring islands.[4] In Wales, the Goidels also
occupied Anglesey and almost the whole of Gwynedd. The
district held by them is dotted with ogham inscriptions and
such names as Cerrig y Gwyddell (Rocks of the Goidels).[5]
They installed themselves and came to terms with the
natives who remained. There were intermarriages and
associations. This common life is perpetuated in the complete
intermingling of Irish and British traditions, of which the
Mabinogion and the legend of Tristram afford striking
evidence.

Moreover, the Britons occasionally paid back the Irish
in their own coin.[6] In 250 we see an army of Britons led into
Ireland by a claimant of the High Kingship, Lugaidh mac
Conn. St. Patrick speaks of one Coroticus, who raided
Ireland for captives. Now, Coroticus is the same as Ceredig
ap Cunedda, the son and successor of the Cunedda who reconquered Gwynedd from the Irish about 400. A descendant
of Cunedda, Maelgwyn, who died in 547, recovered Dyfed. At
all events, by the middle of the fifth century the Irish kings
seem to have given up expeditions on a big scale. The Britons
had recovered ground in Wales and Cornwall.

V

THE SCOTS IN SCOTLAND

Of their conquests of those days, the Goidels kept the
Isle of Man and Scotland. In Man they left their Goidelic

---

[1] MacNeill, op. cit., p. 157 ; Joyce, op. cit., i, p. 77.

[2] Joyce, op. cit., i, p. 79 ; MacNeill, op. cit., p. 155. Cf. Windisch, *Das
keltische Britannien*, p. 27 ; " Les Irlandais (Desi) en Dyfed," in **CXL**, 1917–1919,
p. 315 ; Kuno Meyer, " Early Relations between Gaels and Brythons," in
CLIV, 1897, pp. 59–195.

[3] MacNeill, op. cit., p. 156.   [4] Ibid.

[5] Joyce, op. cit., i, p. 78. Cf. J. Rhys, " Three Ancient Inscriptions from
Wales," in **CCCLVI**, p. 227. Cf. Windisch, p. 27.

[6] Joyce, loc. cit. ; Loth, in **CXL**, xviii, p. 304.

dialect, which was kept up by constant intercourse with the Irish coast. In Scotland they founded a state which grew steadily, and finally absorbed the Picts and Caledonians (if, indeed, these last two were distinct).

The first landing seems to have been in the first half of the third century. Conaire II, who was a king of Munster but appears in the list of High Kings of Ireland from 212 to 220, had a son Cairbre Riada, who, on a famine breaking out in Munster, set off with his men to settle in the north of Ireland, in Ulster. Some of the Dal Riada remained there, in County Antrim. Another body crossed the sea and settled in Argyll. That, according to tradition, is the origin of the double kingdom of Dal Riada. In 470 Fergus mac Eirc, King of the Ulster Dal Riada and a descendent of Cairbre Riada, crossed into Scotland with his brothers. It was doubtless an attempt to reunite the two halves of the tribe. This is the official date of the foundation of the kingdom of the Scots and its royal line. The attempt succeeded, and a double kingdom was thus founded, the Isle of Man being attached to it.

This double kingdom furnished an interesting case for Irish public law, and the question was not settled until the famous Assembly of Druim Ceata, under the presidency of St. Columba, disposed of this and other like problems in 575. The King of the Scots in Britain was made independent of the authority of the High King of Ireland, and a mixed solution was adopted for the Irish kingdom of the Dal Riada, which had to serve the High King with its land forces and the King of the Scots with its sea forces.[1]

For a long time the Scottish colony of the Dal Riada was inconsiderable. At the end of the seventh century it was still confined to Argyll and the adjoining isles. On the east, the Picts extended southwards to the Firth of Forth. To the south, the Britons held the west coast to beyond Dumbarton, leaving a small group of Picts cut off from the rest in Galloway. But at this date the Scottish kingdom began to grow. By the time of Bede, the Scots had supplanted the Picts in the neighbourhood of the Firth of Forth.

---

[1] MacNeill, op. cit., pp. 194, 599. Cf. **CXL**, xxxix, 388 ; Ore, **CCCCXIII** ; Joyce, op. cit., i, p. 79.

Ireland identified itself with Christianity to such an extent and so successfully that it set it up in the place of its own heroes to express its national soul. St. Patrick became the true national hero of Ireland.[1]

Christianity had certainly reached the country before his time. If we are to believe St. Jerome, Pelagius, who flourished in the fourth century, was an Irishman, swollen with Irish porridge. The Chronicle of Prosper of Aquitaine says that in 431 Pope Celestinus I sent a certain Palladius to the Scots who believed in God. St. Patrick arrived in Ireland in 432 at the earliest.[2] Zimmer, in a work of which I have spoken in connection with the relations of Gaul and Ireland, ingeniously suggests that from 419 to 507, between the date of the settlement of the Visigoths in·northern Aquitania and the time when Clovis restored a little order in Gaul after the troublous years of the fifth century, the educated men of Gaul, and especially of Aquitania, found a refuge in Ireland. It is possible, but not proved.[3]   As a fact, neither the Latin of St. Patrick nor that of St. Columba, who adorned the Irish Church in the following century, shows any sign that they were disciples of the learned men of Aquitania and their preciosity.[4]   In any case, while it is almost certain that St. Patrick was not the first apostle of the Irish, it is beyond all doubt that Christianity was triumphant after his time.

Certain important things are to be observed immediately afterwards. There is no longer the least question of racial diversity in Ireland except in the legendary past. All are Gædhil, whether they be Ivernians, Picts, Gauls, or Belgæ by origin. Mr. MacNeill, who rightly lays stress on the question of the subject tribes, *Aithech-thuatha*, thinks that at this date the distinction expressed by the opposition of the words *soer*, free, and *doer*, unfree, corresponds chiefly to the difference of status between the skilled craftsman, who is likewise called *soer*, and the peasant—a distinction similar to that maintained on the Continent between burgher and villain. These are social, not racial, differences.[5]

---

[1] MacNeill, op. cit., p. 159.   Cf. Czarnowski, **CCCCXXXIII** ; White, **CCCCXLII**.
[2] MacNeill, op. cit., p. 162.   [3] Ibid., p. 165.
[4] Ibid., p. 166.   [5] Ibid., p. 229.

Secondly, St. Patrick seems to have made a special fight against slavery, and particularly against the enslavement of prisoners of war and against war itself. He preached, for example, in favour of Christian brotherhood. He had been a slave in Ireland, and had been summoned back to the country by voices. The success of his preaching is attested by the stoppage of the slave-trade. There were no more expeditions, and, therefore, no more standing armies, and the institution of the Fianna became obsolete. Two hundred years later, the Venerable Bede, in telling of a raid made in Ireland by the Northumbrians in 684, describes them as falling on an inoffensive people.[1]

Lastly, the superabundant energy of which I have spoken found a new outlet—the preaching of the Gospel. St. Columba and the monks of Iona went to the Continent, where they founded monasteries—Luxeuil and St. Gall—in which valuable Irish MSS. are preserved.[2]

From the sixth century onwards Ireland became a centre of Christian culture, a school of theology and morals. The substance of the earliest Penitentials is Irish. Bede tells us that a crowd of young Englishmen followed the teaching of St. Colman. Later, Alcuin corresponded with the monastery of Clonmacnoise.[3]

But the Christian culture of Ireland was now as it were the flower of the national civilization. St. Patrick had attracted one of the intellectual classes to his side—the poets. Christianity gave them a better script than the oghams. In St. Patrick's time they already began to make written collections of the ancient epics. We shall see later that the honour of ordering these collections to be made is ascribed to Loegaire, King of Ireland in St. Patrick's time. It is a fact in the history of the Celts to be compared to the putting of the Homeric poems into writing in the history of the Greeks. In the seventh century, too, the Irish grammarians began to extol and cultivate their language. All this movement likewise was originally started by St. Patrick.[4]

[1] Ibid., p. 159.
[2] See Gougaud, CCCCXXVIII; Lloyd, op. cit., p. 109.
[3] MacNeill, op. cit., p. 242.
[4] Ibid., p. 167.

VI

CHRISTIAN IRELAND TO THE SCANDINAVIAN INVASIONS

It was truly the Golden Age of Ireland that commenced with Christianity and lasted about three hundred years ; three hundred years of continuity, peace, prosperity, and unity, things which no other Celtic people had ever had. The result was that Ireland had time to complete herself and to-day there is an Irish nationality, or rather an Irish nation, which, alone of the Celtic nationalities, has survived persecutions and disasters.

Not that all was golden in that Age of Gold. Ireland suffered by the disappearance of the mercenary militia which gave her a kind of army for defence and attack. She suffered also by her laws of succession. She suffered, lastly, by the rivalry of the ecclesiastical power and the state. There were internal wars, competitions between Leinstermen and men of Connacht and between the families descended from the Kings of Connacht, for the High Kingship. But these conflicts were not more than small incidents. Moreover, there is no history for this period but mere anecdotes.

One anecdote tells of the abandonment of Tara, the seat of the High Kingship, in the reign of Diarmait mac Cearbhail, a great-grandson of Niall, in circumstances which seem to be quite legendary, the city being cursed and abandoned in 545. In reality Tara was not destroyed at all, and probably not cursed, for a council was held there in 780. But it was really a gathering-place for festivals and a military camp rather than a city, and times were changed. Cruachain in Connacht and Ailinn in Leinster, which were likewise great camps, were likewise abandoned. The military organization was disappearing. Besides, although Irish Christianity was of such a national character, it could not do otherwise than change the old system of festivals and secularize the places in which they were held, unless it consecrated them. Now, St. Patrick had not established himself at Tara, but at Armagh. It seems, too, that the High Kingship was no longer absolutely bound up with the possession of Tara.[1]

[1] Ibid.

VII

THE SCANDINAVIAN INVASIONS

The development of Ireland and its civilization in an evangelical and monastic peace along the lines laid down by St. Patrick was cut short at the end of the eighth century by a new movement of peoples. It was at this time that the peoples of the Scandinavian peninsula, followed soon after by those of Denmark, began to migrate. In reality the operations of the Norseman were more systematic and better organized than is usually imagined. They were expeditions of conquest and colonization, in the course of which true states were founded, and these states formed federations with each other and united with the mother-country. Magnificent plans of vast sea-empires for a moment came very near realization.

The Norsemen appeared about 790 in the northern archipelagos of the British Isles and on the coasts of Ireland. Some time after their first piratical raids, they occupied islands and peninsulas, establishing a fortified post at Dublin in 841 and another at Annagassan in County Louth about the same time. At Dublin they were between Leinster and Meath, and took advantage of the enmity of the two districts. Having thus succeeded in interfering in the internal affairs of Ireland, they got a foothold in the country, and in the tenth century a number of agreements and inter-marriages established their position permanently. From time to time they received reinforcements or new leaders, or a Norwegian fleet would come and establish or restore the authority of some distant king. From 863 Harold Fairhair was able, in the course of a long reign lasting three-quarters of a century, to form and consolidate his empire.[1]

The enterprise of the Scandinavians was destroyed by the rivalry of the Norwegians and the Danes. The latter first appear in Ireland in 851, being described in the Annals as black heathen. Ireland, which had been taken by surprise by the Scandinavian invaders when it was without any military organization, had great difficulty in making a recovery. But by 870 the whole north of the country seems to have rid itself of the Norsemen. From that date, the

[1] Ibid., pp. 248–253.

struggle is mainly concentrated in the southern provinces, the Kings of Cashel playing an important part with varying success.

It seems that the Irish never mixed up their civil wars with these national conflicts. Leinster is at war with Munster, and Cormac, the good King-Bishop of Cashel, is slain in 908. In Munster, the rival families of the Eoganachta and the Dal Cais contend for the kingship. About 1000 the Dal Cais are in power, under Brian Bóramha (Brian Boru). He is one of the outstanding figures of Irish history. A shrewd politician and a temporizer, he aimed at the High Kingship, but was content with exercising a real hegemony. It was the whole of Ireland that followed him in 1014 to the victorious battle of Clontarf. Sigtrygg, King of Dublin, had called in Sigurd, Count of Orkney. The battle was decisive ; Brian won the day but was killed. The prestige of the Norsemen was destroyed. An attempt on the part of Magnus, King of Norway, to restore it in 1103 was a failure.[1]

In Scotland, the Scandinavian inroads benefited the small kingdom of the Dal Riada, which successfully opposed them, while they weakened the Picts in the north and the Angles in the south. The Scots, having now a good foothold in the interior, concentrated there, fortified their positions, and made ready to step into the shoes of their neighbours. In the middle of the ninth century the kingdom of the Picts came to an end and was absorbed by that of the Dal Riada. In 870 Olaf and Ivar, the Scandinavian Kings of Dublin, took Dumbarton. But at the end of that century the Scottish kingdom was extending at the expense of the Angles in the old domain of the Britons in the south of the present Scotland. The colonization which followed the conquest is attested by the diffusion of Gaelic place-names all over Scotland. Gaelic also gained ground in the Scandinavian settlements of the west coast and the Isles. Here small states had grown up— the earldom of Orkney, the kingdom of the Isles (the Hebrides), the kingdom of Man—all subject to the King of Norway in varying degrees.[2] The Danes who came after the Norwegians had set up in 980 a Danish kingdom of the Hebrides, which seems to have come to an end in 1005.

[1] Ibid., pp. 253–280. Cf. Vendryès, in **CXL**, 1920–1, p. 348.
[2] MacNeill, op. cit., pp. 211, 216.

Some of these small kingdoms remained in the allegiance of the Kings of Norway, such as that founded by Sumarlidi in Argyll and the Isles, which did not break off from that allegiance until 1269. Orkney was Norwegian until 1470, when James III of Scotland acquired it by marriage. It was still long before the Hebrides and Orkney became Scottish for good.

Wales, too, was touched by the Scandinavians, but they made no settlements there. The Welsh did not take advantage of this comparative tranquillity, nor of the stronger pressure to which the Scandinavians were subjecting the Anglo-Saxons, to reconquer the ground which they had lost. Sometimes, notably in the reign of Alfred the Great, they fought against the Danes by the side of the Anglo-Saxons. A certain amount of assimilation had eventually taken place. The Kings of Wales entered into the allegiance of the Anglo-Saxon Kings. In the tenth century, in time of peace, they appeared at their councils ; Howel the Good called one of his sons Edwin. So Wales did not succeed in forming a strong and really lasting state, in spite of occasional attempts like that of Howel the Good to unify the country.[1]

We must, however, recognize that they were the Celts who best resisted the Scandinavian assault on the Western world, and that their resistance did more than that of any other people to break it. That was a great achievement.

VIII

THE WARS OF INDEPENDENCE

1. *Wales*

The Norman followers of William the Conqueror who took the place of the Anglo-Saxons in 1066 showed themselves more capable than they of reducing and absorbing the Celtic states of the British Isles. The fact was, they had become French in two generations. Their undertaking bears no resemblance to the movements of the Scandinavians described above. It was an act of policy, served by the self-interest

[1] Lloyd, op. cit., pp. 112–129.

of a crowd of adventurers. The object was to enlarge possessions, to obtain feudal lands. The island Celts were the dissenters of the West, and they had against them the Pope, that is the head of the society which was created by the amalgamation of Germanic elements in the now Christian Roman Empire. The Normans conquered the country permanently, and very soon transformed it. The change was not at all unlike that which so surprised us in Roman Gaul. The Normans were great builders, in an age of lavish building. Wherever they set foot, they built churches, castles, and towns, and everywhere they were imitated, until the face of the country was utterly changed.

The Welsh, having committed themselves to resistance, brought the Conqueror down on them. He operated along the Marches in 1070, and left it to the Earls of Chester and Shrewsbury to subjugate them gradually. At the beginning of the twelfth century the Welsh still held the mountains, while the Normans were on the coasts and in the valleys. On the death of Henry I, the Welsh took sides with Matilda, the late King's daughter, against Stephen of Blois. They took sides against King John, and in 1258 with Simon de Montfort against Henry III. Really, the Welsh kings and princes of the twelfth and thirteenth centuries recognized the overlordship of the Norman kings ; but they revolted often. In 1282 Edward III, having put down one of these revolts, reserved the title of Prince of Wales for the heir to the English crown.[1]

The historical development is rather well symbolized by the figure of Giraldus Cambrensis, Gerald of Wales. He was the son of a Norman baron and a Welsh mother, studied in France, and became an official of Henry II. He has left a series of books, including the *Itinerary of Cambria* and the *Conquest of Ireland*, which show a real knowledge of Celtic matters and an interest in them not always friendly.

It was in the days of the Plantagenet kings, perhaps at the court of Henry II, in the circle of Giraldus and Walter Map, that the Arthurian legend developed,[2] based partly on a Welsh narrative which, according to Giraldus, was composed by one Bledri, *famosus ille fabulator Bledhericus*, and partly on the traditions of Glastonbury Abbey.

[1] Ibid., pp. 150–199.   [2] Cf. Faral, Bruce, opp. citt.

The Britons submitted quickly, the Normans and they seem to have taken to each other fairly easily.

2. *Scotland*

The Gaelic kingdoms of Scotland and Ireland did not fall into the arms of the Normans so quickly.   In Scotland, King Malcolm had received and taken under his protection the Anglo-Saxon royal family, and married Margaret, grand-daughter of King Edmund, in 1067.   She, who afterwards became St. Margaret of Scotland, exercised great influence, and it was not in favour of Celticism.   Thanks to her and to most of Malcolm's successors, the Anglo-Saxon element gained in Scotland, in language and in institutions.   But neither William the Conqueror nor his successors made any progress in Scotland.   In spite of the extinction of the royal line and the rivalries of claimants to the succession, neither Edward I nor Edward II managed to conquer the country, and Robert Bruce made a victorious resistance at Bannockburn.   But Scotland was increasingly won over by contact, growing less and less Celtic, until the process culminated when the Stewart line ascended the throne of England in the person of James VI and I.[1]

This does not mean that the spirit of independence disappeared wholly in Wales and Scotland.   The peoples kept their native character.   But the capacity and the desire to form an independent national body had gone.

3. *Ireland* [2]

The case of Ireland was quite different.[3]   It was free of the Scandinavians, but was in a condition of moral and material distress of which we hear from St. Bernard, the friend of the Irish St. Malachy.   There was a movement of Cistercian reform at the beginning of the twelfth century, but it came into conflict with an independent movement of reform in the Irish monasteries, which went with a revival of the schools.   The Cistercian circle of Henry II took offence, and the King suggested to Pope Adrian IV that he should

---

[1] MacNeill, op. cit., pp. 203 ff.   [2] Ibid., pp. 300–322.
[3] Ibid., p. 309.

conquer and reform Ireland. The Pope claimed rights over Ireland in virtue of the famous but apocryphal Donation of Constantine. He gave the King of England *carte blanche*. Once again Norman conquest was to bring the Western dissenters into the fold.

An army of Normans, Flemings, and Welsh landed in Ireland in 1169. Henry II arrived in person in 1171. There was still a High King in Ireland, Rory O'Connor. He was the last of the High Kings, for he was compelled to acknowledge the overlordship of the King of England. But only the edge of Ireland had as yet been touched. The invaders had made hardly any real conquest outside Counties Dublin, Meath, Kildare, and Louth. Henry II left the task of completing the conquest to a few great feudal magnates, the FitzGeralds, the De Courcis, the De Burghs, who had to secure real possession of their fiefs. They took advantage of dynastic rivalries and civil wars, always had Irish supporters on their side, and succeeded in concluding agreements and matrimonial alliances with the families of Irish chiefs. They built castles, and sometimes, as at Downpatrick, transformed fortified monasteries into castles.

After 1255 comes a series of setbacks for the conquerors. A national reaction arises and lasts until Tudor times. The de Burghs, having tried to secure a real hold on the districts in Ulster and Connacht which had been assigned to them, found themselves confronted by an Irish coalition, formed by the Kings of Thomond and Connacht and Brian O'Neill, King of Tir Eoghain (Tyrone), who led the resistance. The Gall-Ghaedhil of the Hebrides supplied a nucleus of permanent troops. The Irish then started looking for allies and leaders abroad ; in 1263 they applied to Hakon, King of Norway, then in the Hebrides, and in 1314 to Robert Bruce, who sent them his brother Edward.[1]

At the beginning of the fourteenth century the son of Brian O'Neill wrote to a successor of Adrian IV, repudiating the Plantagenet overlordship of Ireland and claiming the right of the country to choose its own sovereign. At the same time, the feudal lords established in Ireland sometimes became Irish. The conquerors conformed to the Irish practice of sending children away from home to be brought up by

[1] Ibid., pp. 323 ff.

foster-parents, placing them with Irish people, and so real bonds were created, which were reinforced by matrimonial alliances. The old Irish families restored the kingdoms. Truly national feasts were held—in 1351 by O'Kelly, to celebrate the restoration of his kingdom, and in 1433 by Margaret, daughter of O'Carroll, King of Eile, and wife of O'Connor, King of Offaly.[1]

This state of things went on to the end of the sixteenth century, to the time of Elizabeth and James VI and I, or rather to that of Cromwell and William of Orange. Ireland took up the Stewart cause; it was conquered, but not absorbed, and was always ready to revive. Then began the endless succession of brutalities and extensive expropriations under the ignorant and unskilful direction of legislators, which led to the revival of Ireland at this day.

IX

CONCLUSION OF THIS HISTORY

Such was the history of the Celts, those groups of Aryan tribes which had become aware of their native character and covered half Europe in their migrations. There they were conquered and merged in new nations. In the islands, they resisted. Then they retired. They were turned back on themselves; they were partly absorbed by the Roman Empire. What survived the fall of the Celtic states in Britain was absorbed by the Normans, the last Germanic people to emigrate. There remains nothing but one small, indomitable nation, full of vigour, on the outermost edge of their earliest conquests, and, behind that front, in Scotland, in Wales, in Brittany, Celtic-speaking communities which are no longer nations.

[1] Ibid., p. 344.

PART THREE

THE CIVILIZATION OF THE CELTS

CHAPTER I

THE OBJECTS AND METHOD OF A SOCIOLOGICAL STUDY OF THE CELTS

WE have tried to set forth the main features of the history of the Celts. But another question arises regarding the Celtic peoples; we must inquire what were the bonds which held men together in social organization, how families and clans were constituted, how land was owned (in whole or in part, in precarious possession or in permanent, absolute ownership, in common or individually, in fairly distributed lots or in aristocratic tenures), what was their law, what were their gods, and their priests, how they traded, and travelled, and built. The structure of society ; private law ; public law and political institutions ; religion ; economic life ; craftsmanship ; morphology ; art and literature—these are the headings for a description of Celtic society.

I

THE BASES OF A COMPARATIVE STUDY OF CELTIC CIVILIZATION

We shall, of course, deal with the Celts of antiquity, but not only with those of Gaul. We shall look at Gauls, Irish, and British all together, comparing them.

Before starting on an inquiry of this kind, we must first of all reply to an objection which naturally occurs to the mind. In order to make a description such as we are going to attempt, we must look to literary documents, the Irish and Welsh epics, or summaries of epics, which have come down to us and the Welsh and Irish laws, for light on the little which the classical writers tell us about the institutions and life of Gaul. It will then be objected (such was the opinion of Fustel de Coulanges) that these two sets of information come from very different dates. The Irish documents cannot materially have been put down in writing before the conversion of Ireland in the fifth century. A preface to the *Senchus Mor*, the most important of the Irish legal treatises, states that it was composed by a commission called by King Loegaire on which St. Patrick sat. The anonymous author of the *Book of Acaill*, which comes next in importance, says that it is of the third century, but it was certainly not written down then ; besides, the ancient text is so concise that it cannot be understood without the glossary, which must have been written in the ninth or tenth century at earliest, since it implies the use of the penny, which was not introduced into Ireland before then. Nor can the oldest of the Irish epics have been put together any earlier. It is much the same with the Welsh texts. The compilation of the laws is ascribed in the prefaces to King Howel the Good, who reigned in the first half of the tenth century. The Mabinogion were not compiled later than the first half of the twelfth century, but certainly after the Norman Conquest.[1] Roughly, then, there is an interval of about a thousand years between the information given us about the Continental Celts and that which the island Celts have themselves furnished.

But what was the nature of these documents ? For the mythology and hero-tales of Ireland, there was a tradition preserved orally, like the poems of the Druids of Gaul, which was put into writing because it was beginning to be forgotten, just at the time when the introduction of a new tradition, that of Christianity, threatened to hasten its disappearance. It was said that for the most important of these epics, the *Táin Bó Chuailgné*, the *Cattle-lifting of Cooley*, the ghosts of the dead had to be called in to assist the editor ; Fergus, one of the actors in the story, arose from his grave to relate it.[2] The Welsh Mabinogion consist of mythological material which had long lost its original character, being transformed to a greater or less extent into tales and romances. But in each case the substance of the stories is several centuries older than the literary version.

The same is true of the laws. Neither in Ireland nor in

---

[1] Loth, **CCLXX**, i, p. 44.
[2] Windisch, **CCXCV** ; *Táin*, introd., p. liii. Cf. d'Arbois, in **XXXII**, xl, p. 152 ; Zimmer, in **LXXXIII**, xxviii, pp. 426 ff.

Wales are they legislative texts. They are customs. Now, a custom necessarily has no date in itself. The date is that of the state of society to which it corresponds.

That is why there is no reason for refraining from using the Irish and Welsh documents because they were written late. With their aid, we can make up a picture of much earlier times. We only need to keep our critical faculty awake in dealing with them, as, indeed, we must do with the classical authors, who did not understand the institutions which they described.

II

THE SOLIDARITY OF THE CELTIC SOCIETIES. THE ACTION OF THE DRUIDS

On the other hand, there are good reasons for studying all parts of the Celtic world together. They were in communication, they were inter-connected, they must have had resemblances. Here is one fact which gives food for thought. It was at the time of the first Roman campaigns in Asia Minor after the Punic Wars. In 197-196 the city of Lampsacos sent envoys to Rome. They landed at Marseilles, which was allied to the Romans, doubtless expecting to receive recommendations and information there. The Senate of Marseilles gave them, among other things for their return journey, a public letter of recommendation to the Galatian Tolistoagii, who lived west of the Tectosages in the valley of the Sangarios, separated from Lampsacos by the kingdom of Pergamon, with which, as we know, they were on friendly terms. The people of Marseilles had relations with the Gauls of Gaul, and they probably made the most of the fact in writing to the Tolistoagii, whose good offices the Lampsacenians must have desired, with a view either to recruiting mercenaries or to persuading them not to supply any to Antiochos III. These facts are related in an inscription in honour of the envoys, which M. Holleaux has recently edited. They show that the Greeks of Marseilles and of Lampsacos knew that they would find among Celtic peoples living very far apart a sense of oneness of which the Romans had been aware some years earlier when they had sent ambassadors to ask the Volcae to be neutral when Hannibal passed through the country.[1]

This solidarity of the Celtic peoples, even when distant from one another, is sufficiently explained by the sense of kinship, of common origin, acting in a fairly restricted world, all the parts of which were in communication. But the Celts had at least one institution which could effectively bind them together, namely the Druids, a priestly class expressly entrusted with the preservation of traditions. The Druids were not an institution of the small Celtic peoples, of the tribes, of the *civitates* ; they were a kind of international institution within the Celtic world, with provinces corresponding to the great racial or territorial groups constituted by Ireland, Britain, and Gaul. Cæsar tells us that the Druids of Gaul were in touch with those of Britain, and Irish tradition gives evidence of the relations of the Druids of Britain and Ireland. It is certain that this priesthood, provided, as we shall see later,[2] with a legal doctrine, a moral doctrine, a doctrine of the immortality of the soul, and an authority recognized by all, covered the greater part of the Celtic world, and it is almost unthinkable that it did not cover it all. The bonds which united the Celtic peoples were made secure by the spread of Druidism, and we can be sure that those peoples owed to those professional teachers moral ideas, conceptions about the future life, mythological traditions, ritual practices, and legal solutions which they all had in common—that is, that similar principles everywhere governed or reformed the structure and working of society.

III

CELTIC   SOCIETIES   AND   INDO-EUROPEAN   SOCIETIES.   THE
CELTS AND THE INDO-EUROPEAN WORLD

In the course of this account we shall have occasion to compare the various Celtic peoples in respect of their institutions, not only with one another, but with various Mediterranean and Germanic peoples with which they had relations, which gave them something or received something

---

[1] Holleaux, **CCCXL**, ii, " Lampsaque et les Galates en 197/6."
[2] Cf. below, ch. iii.

from them. I have already spoken twice of the influence
exercised by the Celts, and particularly the Gauls, in Germany.
Germanic took from Celtic important terms in the language
of politics, law, and economics—the words for king, office,
hostage, value.

The peoples of Italy, which once formed with the Celts
a single group which, in its undivided state, I made the
starting-point of this history, developed rapidly. They took
a host of words from their Mediterranean neighbours, and
they became city-dwellers like the Greeks and Etruscans.
On the whole, they were to the Celts in respect of institutions
much what the Gauls of Gaul were to the Irish. For example,
they invented the State ; they had a clear notion of the
respublica, of which the most progressive of the Celts certainly
had no more than a rather vague idea. Their institutions
give the impression of a term of social development at which
the Celts would have arrived if only they had remained
independent. But there are many things in the civilization
of the Celts and the Italici which recall the times when the
two peoples were one. The Latin word for a king, *rex*, is the
same as the Celtic *rix*, but the Romans confined it to the
religious side of the office. The name of the Latin tribe,
tribus, another institution becoming fossilized, is probably
the same as Welsh *tref* (Irish *treb*), which appears in the
name Atrebates.

There is another Indo-European group with which the
Celtic group is connected by verbal relations and analogies
of a particular type—the Indo-Iranian group. The analogies
appear especially in the religous and political vocabulary,
as M. Vendryès has pointed out.[1]

There are, moreover, religious scruples and practices
which are identical in the two groups, though not designated
by the same names. At Kildare, for example, the nuns of
St. Brigid (who took the place of a previous goddess) were
as careful as the Persian Magi not to soil with their breath
the flame of the sacred fire which they kept alight.[2]

So, too, in Irish law the pursuer cannot demand the
seizure of the goods of a person who is superior to him, who
is *nemed* in regard to him, that is sacred (a noble, a *filè*,

[1] **XCIII**, 1918, xxi, pp. 265–285.
[2] *R.E.G.*, 1915, p. 189.

a clerk). He sits down before his door and patiently proceeds to fast. The person against whom he fasts must, under pain of disqualification, give the pledge desired. This process of coercion by mystical methods is simply the Hindu *dhârṇa*, which was regularly practised all over India as late as the end of the eighteenth century. *Dhârṇa* seems to mean the same as Latin *capio*, " taking possession." In *dhârṇa* the Brahmin sits and fasts at the defender's door until the pursuer has obtained satisfaction, and he has poison, a dagger, or some other means of suicide by him in case violence should be attempted against him. A man who allowed the faster to die would bring down a capital crime on his head for all eternity. *Dhârṇa* seems to have been used like the old *pignoris capio* of Roman law. One may reasonably suppose that it is very ancient, even if the written formulas regarding it are comparatively recent.[1]

A still more striking resemblance is furnished by the very existence of the Druids. Nothing could be liker to the Druids than the Brahmins of India and the Magi of Iran, except perhaps the College of Pontifices at Rome and the Flamens attached to it. The Flamen has the same name as the Brahmin, and M. Vendryès has shown the similarity between the terms relating to priests and sacrifices. The priesthoods are not merely very similar, but exactly the same, and they are preserved nowhere so completely as at the two opposite ends of the Indo-European world. Between the two, the remnants of similar priesthoods once survived, as in Thrace and among the Getae.

All these similarities prove that institutions mentioned even in late texts are of very great antiquity. This will be confirmed by our further analysis.

IV

CELTIC SOCIETIES AND MORE PRIMITIVE SOCIETIES. PRACTICES
DATING FROM BEFORE THE FORMATION OF THE INDO-EUROPEAN
GROUP

In addition to these survivals from a past common to all the different branches of the Indo-European stock,

[1] Maine, **CCCLII**, pp. 40, 291, 297. Cf. **CCXLVII**, *Senchus Mor*, 113 ; d'Arbois **CCXLVII** (Droit), i, 269 ; ii, 46 ; Joyce, **CCCCXXXIV**, i, p. 205.

Celtic institutions present some strangely preserved relics of a past lying in the depths of prehistory. The Indo-European societies, so far as one can attempt to imagine them in the remote time when the members of the race were beginning to part company, were already societies of a high type. They had chiefs, priests, and a formal law, and their organization of the family implies development through a long past. But these societies had evidently gone through the stage at which men are grouped in clans, which are politico-domestic groups of kinsmen, in which kinship is constituted by the notion of a common origin and often by participation in the nature of a living species or some inanimate thing. That stage is known as totemism. The species or thing is regarded as akin to the men, and provides them with their mythical ancestors, their name, and their heraldic device. In this condition of society, the whole of social life is concentrated, as it were, without political, religious, or even economic differentiation, in the life of the clan and the ceremonies which it entails.[1] As a fact, European societies had long advanced beyond this stage.

Yet we can see, among the Celts, in a state of remarkable preservation, three systems of institutions or rites which correspond to certain forms of early life—head-hunting, the blood-covenant, and the gift.

1. *Head-hunting*

What is head-hunting ? The Gauls [2] cut off the heads of their slain enemies. Poseidonios, who travelled in Gaul, says that horsemen hung them at the necks of their horses, or nailed them to the timbers of their houses like trophies of the chase,[3] or dressed and embalmed them. He adds that his hosts showed him these trophies with pleasure and boasted of the great sums offered by the families of the victims to buy them back. In the Celtiberian *oppidum* of Puig-Castelar, near Barcelona, human skulls have been found, pierced by a nail,[4] and cut-off heads are depicted on Gallic

---

[1] See **CCCLX**.
[2] **CXL**, 1919, p. 274. Cf. A. Reinach, in **CXL**. Cf. Amm. Marc., xxvii, 4, on the Scordisci using skulls as drinking-cups ; Livy, xxiii, 24, on the Boii.
[3] Diod., v, 29, 4 ; Strabo, iv, 4, 5.
[4] Déchelette, ii, 3, p. 946.

coins and monuments (for example, at Entremont in Bouches-du-Rhône). The Irish had the same custom [1] ; a battle was a " head-harvest " (*árcenn*). The Annals of the Four Masters relate that Aed Finnliath, King of Ireland, having defeated the Danes in 864, caused the heads of the slain to be piled in a heap. When the famous Bishop-King Cormac was killed in 908, somebody cut off his head and presented it to the victorious King Flann Sina, who, as a matter of fact, restored it with honour to Cormac's party. This collecting of trophies might be an obligatory ritual matter connected with the period when a youth arrived at man's age and left his school of military training. When a young Ulsterman went to war for the first time, he had to cross the border into Connacht and try to kill a man there. This was what the hero Cuchulainn did.[2]

We find an exact parallel to this custom in one which is quite general all over the Austro-Asiatic world, from Assam to Papuasia. Among the Dyaks of Borneo, for instance, head-hunting is the consecration of the initiation of the young men, who are grouped in classes according to age like *hetairiai* of *epheboi* and live in the Men's House. They go off hunting, and when they have brought back their trophies they have proved their worth and can enter on the life of grown men and marry, just as Cuchulainn, having proved his worth, could marry Emer.

2. *Blood-covenant*

Another institution which survived among the Celts was the blood-covenant. Giraldus Cambrensis says that the Irish sealed their leagues by a rite of this kind, each party drinking some drops of blood of the other. In spite of assertions to the contrary, that this custom really existed is attested by other documents. St. Cairnech, having succeeded in bringing the Hy Neill and the Cian Nachta to form an alliance, caused blood of the two tribes to be mixed in a vessel, that the treaty might be written with it and so be inviolable.[3] Similar incidents are told of the Scottish islesmen, but we have no evidence about the Gauls.

[1] Joyce, op. cit., i, p. 150. Cf. Hull, **CCLXII**, 75.
[2] Joyce, i, p. 99. Cf. *Coir Anmann*, in **CCXCV**, iii, p. 405.
[3] Giraldus Cambrensis, *De Conquestu*, iii, xxii. Cf. *Silva Gadelica*, 413 ; R.C., xiii, 73 ; Joyce, **CCLXVI**, ii, 463 ; Martin, **CCLXXI**, p. 109.

Now, the blood-covenant is a well-known institution. It was one of the first things to be studied and interpreted by science dealing with the materials furnished by ethnography. Robertson Smith [1] was calling attention to it fifty years ago. The object is, however small the quantity of blood used, to make the same blood run in the veins of the parties concerned and so to create or confirm kinship between them. In Ireland the rite serves to confirm a contract, making it more solemn and giving it a mystical sense. But it is a relic of an earlier condition, the segmentary condition of society, in which there was no express contract and legal relationships were not distinguishable from those of kinship.

3. Potlatch.

A third system of facts and rites preserved in Celtic institutions was what we call the system of the gift. It belongs to an order of facts to which attention has only recently been drawn, by M. Mauss [2] in *Mémoires de l'Année sociologique* and in a certain number of articles. These are designated by the name of *potlatch*.

In the Romances of the Round Table, we find that a number of episodes begin in this way. A knight or damsel appears at Arthur's court, goes to the King, and asks for a boon, without saying what, and the King promises it and has to keep his word. What is usually requested is some adventurous or dangerous service on the part of the King or of a knight. Arthur is liberal and anxious to maintain his repute ; his table is free to all, and he heaps those about him with munificent gifts.

Similar episodes are found in Irish and Welsh literature, for example the *Tochmarc Etaine* [3] (the *Wooing of Etain*), one of the finest Irish stories. Etain is a goddess, the wife of the god Mider, and has become mortal and married King

---

[1] **CCCLXXXIV** ; **CCCLXXXIV**a.

[2] See Mauss, " Le Don," in **XIII**, N.S., ii ; id., " Une forme ancienne de contrats chez les Thraces," in **CXXXV**, 1921, p. 988. Cf. also Davy, in **CCCXVI**. All these practices are collected under the name of *potlatch*, taken from the Chinook vocabulary of north-western America, where these phenomena are especially developed. Cf. H. Hubert, " Le Système des prestations totales dans les littératures celtiques," in **CXL**, xliii, 1925, pp. 330–5 ; Hubert and Mauss, in **CXL**, 1926.

[3] Windisch, **CCXCV**, i, p. 127. Cf. d'Arbois, **CCL**, pp. 218 ff.

Eochaid Airem. One day Mider appears, and challenges the King to a game of chess. The King accepts. They speak of stakes ; Mider offers fifty horses, and the King offers whatever his opponent wishes. He loses, and the god asks for Etain. The King claims a revenge game, which is arranged for a year later. Mider returns punctually and, having won again, takes away his stake at the end of a month.

In the Mabinogion the story of Pwyll turns on a similar episode. Pwyll, the god of the Underworld, is about to marry the goddess Rhiannon. In the midst of the banquet, Gwawl, a god of light, stands up and asks for a boon. Pwyll grants it, and Gwawl demands Rhiannon herself. Here again a future date is fixed, but this time, after a year, Pwyll appears at his rival's wedding and demands a gift. He only asks to be allowed to fill a small bag which he has in his hand, but everything goes into it, including Gwawl, who gets a beating.[1]

The fact is that the gift implies a return. The gift is compulsory, but it places an obligation on the asker, and the whole fairy world which revolves round Arthur—knights of the Round Table, squires, ladies, even demons—is involved in an extraordinary round of gifts and services in which all vie in generosity or malice, often by arms. The tourney certainly forms part of this vast system of competition and outbidding, which we also find in the Irish stories grouped round the person of Finn and in what has been called the Leinster or Ossianic Cycle.[2]

But, if the boon depends on the person of whom it is asked, it cannot be just anything ; it must be proportionate to his condition, and a little above it. The donor is challenged to be generous or to be able to be so, and he takes up the challenge. A third feature to note is the sanction of obligations which are granted ; a man who does not fulfil his undertaking loses countenance and falls in rank. Rhiannon says as much to Pwyll when he hesitates to keep his promise. The injured or disappointed party has a hold on the other, on his liberty and his life.

For these subjects of romances and myths there were actual practices, of which something survived in all Celtic

---

[1] Loth, **CCLXX**, i, pp. 26–63.
[2] Cf. below, ch. v.

countries. In Ireland homage is expressed by an exchange of gifts between superior and inferior.[1] The superior chief gives a present called *tuarastal*, to accept which is a sign of allegiance, and the inferior chief gives a present of cattle. Moreover, there is usually some outbidding in the exchange of gifts which constitutes these ties in Gaul, Britain, and Ireland. The whole of Ireland is involved in an unending cycle of obligatory loans and borrowings of cattle at a high rate of interest, which affect the condition of individuals in causing their social position to change.

These practises are explained if they are taken in connection with the state of society in which they first arose. Societies on a clan basis are divided into opposing groups which are, however, united because they exchange wives. This division is as fundamental as the law of exogamy. Often the clans are distributed in two groups, doubtless the two old original clans, which are usually called phratries. The phratries, already united one with the other by the constant exchange of gifts constituted by each supplying the other with wives, are still further united by many other means, but always in the form of gifts, service, both in secular, daily life and in mystical, social, and religious life. In this system of exchanges, the presenting of objects develops, but without prejudice to the furnishing of services. The ceremonial exchange of gifts is so important in these societies that it comes to be performed for its own sake, and by itself to give occasion for feasting, outbidding, challenge, ostentation, and competition on the part of individuals and of groups. We must picture these societies as coming together in winter and concentrating their liturgy on that period, spending a large part of the bad season in the exchange of ostentatious entertainments, prepared beforehand, and in a series of operations as speculative as those of a stock exchange, in which gains and losses are paid in social advantages—consideration, rank, the possession of heraldic insignia.

Of this institution of potlatch we find indisputable traces in two Celtic tales, one Irish and the other Welsh. The *Feast of Briccriu* relates how that individual invited King Conchobar and his people to a feast (*fled*).[2] The feast was

---

[1] Cf. Joyce, **CCCCXXXIV**.

[2] D'Arbois, **CCXLVIII**, v, pp. 80–147 ; Windisch, op. cit., i, pp. 235–311.

passed in competitions, mingled with challenges, for the place of honour and the " hero's share " among the heroes and their wives. At the end, the place of honour fell to Cuchulainn and the men of Emain Macha. In the Mabinogion we have the story of Kulhwch and Olwen, the daughter of the giant Yspaddaden. Kulhwch learns that his foredestined bride is Olwen. He goes to Arthur's court and asks for a boon, which is granted, namely assistance in making his suit. Accompanied by the comrades of Arthur, Kulhwch goes to Yspaddaden, who states his terms : a certain number of things must be brought to him for the bride-feast. The things are brought, and Kulhwch kills Yspaddaden and marries Olwen.[1]

So it is evident that our sources, the literature and law of the Celts, even though they were compiled very late, contain distinct and quite authentic traces of the law and institutions of a state of society far earlier than the Celtic societies themselves. There is, therefore, no reason for doubting the quality and authority of the Welsh and Irish sources, and we can use them to make up a picture, composite no doubt, but fairly accurate, of the social system of the Celts.

[1] Loth, op. cit., i, pp. 175–283.

CHAPTER II

THE STRUCTURE OF SOCIETY. LEGAL AND POLITICAL INSTITUTIONS

I

THE SEGMENTARY CHARACTER OF CELTIC SOCIETY AND THE POLITICO-DOMESTIC CHARACTER OF ITS INSTITUTIONS

IN a Celtic society, the state usually remains rudimentary and almost undifferentiated. The King was never more than the direct head of a small unit, with definite powers, limited and personal, over the other elements in his kingdom. When the kings disappeared in Gaul, their place was taken by aristocratic bodies of magistrates which did not constitute republics.

The cells of the Celtic societies are of the politico-domestic order ; their political functions are of the same nature as those of the family. There is no state to interfere in their administration or in their dealings with one another ; there is no public ministry to punish offences.[1] The Celtic societies are at the tribal stage, and have only a private law. Disputes can lead only to arbitration. It is for the injured party to compel the injurer to accept arbitration. Wrongs can be corrected only by private vengeance or compensation. Celtic law is based on arbitration, compensation, and seizure. The system of compensation was to a great extent codified and developed by the establishment of a scale of fines, fixed and co-ordinated according to the quality of the person entitled to damages and the nature of the offence. This scale of compensation-fines as it were stereotyped the inequalities of Celtic society.[2]

Inequalities were introduced from above by the action of the chiefs and the families of chiefs, who embodied all the public power of which these societies were capable. Other

---

[1] Cf. Sophie Bryant, *Liberty, Order, and Law under Native Irish Rule : a study in the Book of the Ancient Laws of Ireland.* London, 1923.
[2] D'Arbois, **CCXLVIII**, viii, ch. i, pp. 1 ff. ; Joyce **CCCCXXXIV**.

inequalities came from below, partly as a result of the round game of private vengeance and the ruinous rates of compensation. So a class of men outside the law grew up. Outlaws established themselves somewhere in the service and under the protection of wealthy and powerful chiefs. Debtors were dependent on their creditors. In the institutions of the Celtic world there were internal causes of evolution which led it, after creating aristocracies, to create plebeian classes which tended to become democracies.

II

THE DIVISIONS OF SOCIETY

1. *The Tribe*

In a Celtic society, the tribe is the group of cells which constitutes the first self-sufficing social unit. For neither clans nor families are self-sufficing ; one clan needs another to supply it with wives and do other indispensable services, and the same is true of the family. In Ireland, the unit is called *tuath*, plural *tuatha*.[1] Its equivalent existed in Gaul ; this is attested by the name of the god Teutates, who is probably the *genius* of the *tuath* ; by the word *toutio* in an inscription from Briona, apparently meaning " citizen " ; and by the word *toutiorix*, apparently meaning " king of the *tuath* ". The word also exists in Oscan and Umbrian, and evidently belongs to the Western Indo-European vocabulary.[2]

The members of the *tuath* are putatively kinsmen, united, fed on the same milk, living on the same soil. They are descended from the same ancestor, and that descent is indicated by the name, which is a gentile, collective, or composite name, indicating the ancestry. If the ancestor, as is more frequently the case, is a historical personage, the history to which he belongs borders on legend.

Mr. MacNeill [3] disagrees with this conception of the *tuath*. He holds that all we have is an onomastic method,

---

[1] Joyce, op. cit., i, p. 39. Cf. Czarnowski, **CCCCXXIII.**
[2] Czarnowski, op. cit., p. 231, n. 1.
[3] MacNeill, **CCCCXLI,** pp. 350, 353. Cf. ibid., pp. 293, 297.

designating by the name of the ruling family a whole territory and the people living on it.   He shows that, for example, the Ui Maine comprised people of different race and unequal condition, grouped under the rule of kings descended from Maine Mor.   But he fails to see that if, even in the case of a highly developed *tuath* like the Ui Maine, territories with the groups of men on them are still designated by gentile names, it is because they have in theory been populated by groups of kinsmen which were once true tribes.

The equivalent of the *tuath* in Gaul is probably the *pagus* of the *Commentaries* and Roman Gaul.   The Greek writers call these *pagi* φῦλα or φυλαί, in contrast to the *civitates*, which they call ἔθνη.   The *pagi* are still managing their own affairs under the Roman Empire.   In independent Gaul, the citizens may pursue the policy of the *civitas*, but they remain grouped by *pagi*.   The army of the Helvetii marches in *pagi*, like the army of Queen Medb in Ireland.[1]   The corresponding unit in Wales is called *cantref*, that is the hundred *trefs* or units of agriculture and economic activity in general. The notion of a tribe, in the sociological sense, implies a limitation ; the members of the tribe must not be too many, nor its territory too large, for them to be able to live together to some extent and to meet periodically.   The Welsh word *cantref* likewise implies a limitation on the territory and the proximity of other *cantrefs*.   Irish seems to have, in addition to *tuath*, an equivalent to *cantref*, namely *tricha ced*, thirty hundreds, thirty groups of a hundred hearths.[2]

In general, we may reasonably suppose that the settlement of a population in a district and its accumulation must have tightened up the rather loose organization of the tribe and favoured the territorial aspects of the term at the expense of the aspect of kinship.

2.   *The Clan*

By some chance, ethnographers and sociologists have taken from the Celtic vocabulary the word *clan* ; it is a Goidelic word which does not designate a type of unit of a definable shape or size.   It means " descendant "

---

[1] Czarnowski, op. cit., p. 232, nn. 3–4.
[2] Ibid., p. 232.

or " descent ". In the plural, for instance, in Irish, *clanna Morna* means the descendants of Morann, but the *clanna Morna* may equally well constitute what sociologists would call a tribe, a family, or perhaps a clan. So, too, in Welsh, the equivalent word *cenedl* means a nation, tribe, or family.

Now, it so happens that the clan, in the sense in which the word is used by modern sociology,[1] does not exist—or does so no longer—as an institution in Celtic countries. A somewhat vague term taken from the Celtic vocabulary has been used to designate an institution which had already almost entirely vanished in the Celtic civilizations. The result is that there has been some confusion in the accounts of the societies which we are considering.[2]

So the clan, in the Celtic sense of the word, is something very different from the normal clan, and in particular the totemic clan. A fair number of Irish *tuatha* were formed round historical families which were collateral branches of royal lines. This is the case with the whole series of the Ui Neill, where one family, perpetuated and growing greater, formed the nucleus of the tribe. The Celtic clans are families, or tribes regarded as families or from the point of view of families, and therefore not at all the same thing as the totemic clan.

Nevertheless, certain facts seem to suggest that it was not always so. The *tuath* or tribe of Erainn comprised twenty-four *forslointe* or denominations, grouped in pairs in twelve *aicme* or stocks.[3] The Soghan tribe, in the territory of the Ui Maine, comprised six clans.[4] There must, therefore, have been clans within the tribe, but it must be admitted that in Celtic society no clan-law survives outside tribal law and family law.

Yet there are some relics of the totemic clan in Celtic institutions. M. Salomon Reinach[5] has endeavoured to trace remains of early totemism in the food-taboos and animal worships still in force among the Celts. Thus a Connacht tribe, Clanna Coneely, might not eat seals (*coneely*

---

[1] See Davy and Moret, **CCCLX**.
[2] As in Vinogradoff's, **CCCXC**.
[3] Windisch, **CCXCVI**, p. 832, n. 3.
[4] O'Donovan, *Hy Many*, p. 70. Cf. Czarnowski, op. cit., p. 248 ; Joyce, **CCCCXXXIV**, i, p. 167.
[5] In his article on survivals of totemism among the Celts, in **CXL**, xxi, repr. in **CCCLXXIV**, i.

meaning " seal "), and it was said that the forbears of the tribe had been turned into seals.[1]

But, above all, there survived in the Celtic societies (and this argument is far more important) remnants of the normal organization of the clan. In the history of Munster two royal houses appear, Clanna Deirgthene and Clanna Dairenne, which hold the power generation about, intermarry, and put their children out to board with each other. These two lines stand in the relation of two exogamous clans belonging to different phratries, especially if we suppose that descent went by the distaff side.[2] This method of reckoning descent, moreover, presented a difficult problem in regard to the education of the children and their preparation for initiation. For the child belonged to his mother's clan, but she lived in the clan of his father ; he was sent to his mother's clan, at least for some considerable time. The children of a clan were also often placed together under qualified persons in a large house, the Men's House. This institution had another object too : to keep these growing youths under supervision and away from women whom they should not marry.

This institution, which is usually called by the Anglo-Norman name of " fosterage ", was kept up in Celtic countries. We find children entrusted to foster-parents, with whom they form real bonds of kinship, as is shown by the fact that some individuals mention their foster-father in declaring their descent, and that mutual legal obligations, comparable to those of kinship, bind the foster-father to his ward. In Ireland the institution is called *altram*.[3] It takes different forms, according to the choice of the *aite* or foster-father. Men were selected for this trust from the members of the mother's family, or else from the intellectual classes, Druids or *fili*.[4] There are many instances of children brought up by the mother's family. King Muirchertach mac Erca spent his childhood in Scotland with his maternal grandfather, and I have already spoken of the two royal families of Munster. There are still more examples of children educated by Druids or *fili*—Cuchulainn, and the two daughters of King Loegaire

[1] Joyce, op. cit., ii, p. 129. Cf. Conrady, **CCCCXXI**.
[2] Czarnowski, op. cit., p. 255.
[3] D'Arbois, **CCXLVIII** (Droit), i, pp. 112, 187 ; ii, p. 36. Cf. Czarnowski, op. cit., p. 257 ; Maine, **CCCLIII**, p. 242.
[4] Joyce, op. cit., ii, p. 18.

who were converted by St. Patrick. In this case the institution tended to take on the form of a school; the Druid Cathbad teaches a hundred pupils besides Cuchulainn. Conn of the Hundred Fights, King of Ireland, has a guard of fifty foster-brothers, who are evidently the companions of his childhood and school-days. So, too, Cæsar and Pomponius Mela remark on the way young men flock round the Druids. Now, the Druidical priesthood, whose civilizing and educative influence was so great, was, as we shall see presently, a clan or group of clans transformed into a secret society.[1]

It can, therefore, be proved that Celtic institutions contained many relics of organization in clans. The mentality which has elsewhere manifested itself in totemism still survived among the Celts; it contributed to giving to the tribe on the one hand and to the family on the other features so like those of the old clans as to be hard to distinguish from them, and it gave them that love of emblems, colours, and heraldic devices for which the Celtic clans have always been conspicuous.

3. *The Family*

A family is a group of men having certain forbears, known or remembered, but usually fairly recent, from whom they are descended direct. In Irish the family is called *fine*. The proper name Venicarius shows that a corresponding word existed in Gaulish. It was replaced in Welsh by *teulu*, which properly means " the occupants of the house " (*ty* " house "; *llu* " guest "). The word belongs to the Western Indo-European group; in Germanic *Wini* means " friend ". In Ireland *fine* designates both the big family of several households and the small family or household; it contains the idea of legal solidarity which constitutes the essence of these kinship-groups. This family, while presenting the general characteristics of the agnatic, undivided family and the patriarchal Indo-European family, also presents in some points interesting relics of the uterine family.[2]

[1] Cf. below, ch. iii.
[2] See d'Arbois, op. cit. (Droit), i, p. 185 ; Joyce, op. cit., i.

4. Marriage and Descent

The ancient writers went to the Gauls for heroes embodying the virtues, particularly in respect of the family and marriage.[1] They have left us a fine conception of marital fidelity and dignity among the Gauls. But the passages in which they speak of the island Celts and their matrimonial ways give a very different picture. The literature of Ireland and Wales leaves one with rather mixed impressions. There is a magnificent song of love and married faithfulness in the Irish *Exile of the Sons of Usnach*.[2] But on the whole sexual morals seem to have been fairly lax. The true explanation, as we shall see, lies in the survival of old institutions which had lost their meaning and often conflicted one with another.

Strabo [3] tells us that the Irish boasted of their licence and that they recognized neither mothers nor sisters, and for Northern Europe Strabo copies Pytheas, whose information often comes from good sources. But Pytheas may very well have heard some story related like that of Conchobar and his sister Dechtiré, or that of Clothru.[4] Clothru, who was the sister of Medb, Queen of Connacht, had three brothers, who fought their father for the kingship of Ireland, and before the battle she bore to the three of them a son, whom she married.[5]

Cæsar [6] gives us more detailed information. According to his account, among the Celts of Britain one wife was owned by ten or twelve men, the husbands being each other's brothers, fathers, and sons and the children belonging to a nominal father who had contracted the marriage and taken the woman into his house. One might at first sight suppose that we have here a group of clan kinsmen, sharing wives as the women share husbands. But probably it is really a form of polyandry suited to a fairly large group, living together in one large house, not deriving enough from its common

---

[1] Ibid., i, pp. 219–229. Cf. A. Bayet, *La Morale des Gaulois*, Paris, 1930.
[2] D'Arbois, op. cit., i, pp. 217–319.
[3] Strabo, iv, 5, 4. Cf. Jerome, *Adv. Jovinian.*, ii, 7 ; Dion. Cass., lxii, 6, 3 ; lxxvi, 12, 2.
[4] These events are placed nearer our own time by the Irish annalists. Really they go back to a very ancient foundation.
[5] CCL, English pp. 206, 212. Cf. Vendryès, in *IFA.*, 21st June, 1923.
[6] Cæs., *Gall. War*, v, 14.

labour to support many wives and perhaps not needing female labour because it does little agriculture. Similar phenomena are reported in Northern India and among the Southern Slavs. Cæsar's description, which is quite credible, does not reveal the survival of a very ancient phase of marriage, but a rather peculiar manner of applying the rules of the Celtic family.

But the epics, history, and law of the Celts contain memories or important remnants of the uterine family.

The descent of heroes like Cuchulainn and Conchobar is indicated by their mother's name. Moreover, they were of irregular birth, and Irish law assigned children born out of wedlock to the mother's family. When, too, the husband was a foreigner, having no family in Ireland, the small family which he founded was attached to that of his wife, being called the " blue family ", *glasfine*, because the man was supposed to have come over the sea.[1] In that case the " marriage " was said to be " of the man " and the " property " " of the woman ". We have instances of succession in the female line and even of matriarchy in the legendary ruling houses of Ireland [2] and the historical ruling houses of Britain.[3] Celtic law implied that women had some political competence. Plutarch, in his essay *On the Virtues of Women*, describes them smoothing over quarrels, taking part in the discussions of assemblies, and being appointed arbiters by a treaty between Hannibal and the Volcæ.[4] Strabo, following Poseidonios, says that the Armorican priestesses were very independent of their husbands.[5]

It has been observed that the Celtic women wore trousers. Those of Gaul certainly did, witness a statue in the British Museum.[6] The Gallic women accompanied their husbands in war, and those of Ireland had military duties proportionate to their rights to landed property. They were only relieved of them by Christianity, and stage by stage. One stage was the purchase of exemption from service by giving up half

---

[1] D'Arbois, op. cit. (Droit), i, 187.
[2] Ibid., i, 237.
[3] Joyce, op. cit., i, 41, cites the instance of Macha Mongruad, the legendary foundress of Emain.
[4] Plut., *De Mul. Virtut.*, 24, 66.
[5] Strabo, iv, 4, 6.
[6] A. J. Reinach, in **CVII**, xviii.

one's property to the family.[1] This was one episode in the process of depriving woman of her powers which everywhere accompanied her loss of the privilege of conveying descent.

Apart from these exceptional cases and relics of the past, the normal Celtic family was an almost entirely agnatic family. The woman was the instrument of natural parentage but not of legal parentage. The son of a daughter did not belong to his grandfather's line save in one single case : a man without male issue might give his daughter in marriage, reserving to himself any child which should be born, and that child became legally, not his grandson, but his son.[2]

This family was gathered round a hearth, which was the centre of its worship and never ceased to hold a central place in the representation of its essence and unity. It worshipped its dead and its ancestors, like the Latin family, but no trace of that worship survives. The father of the family was master in his own house, master of the house and of his folk.[3] Cæsar and the jurist Gaius [4] observed that *patria potestas* of the Roman kind was exercised in Gaul. The father had, according to Cæsar, the right of life and death over his children. The laws of Ireland and Wales bear witness to the same powers. They differ on the age of emancipation. In Ireland, *patria potestas* could be terminated only by the death or incapacity of the father. In Northern Welsh law emancipation came at the age of military service, namely fourteen. But we should note that in this case the youth escaped from the tutelage of his father only to enter into dependence on the chief to whom he had been presented.[5]

According to Cæsar the Gaul had the same power over his wife as over his children. In the noble families, on the death of the paterfamilias, the women fell into the power of his relations, who could, if the death was suspicious, have them tortured or slain.[6] It could be a method of settling the inheritance of the childless widow. But in fact the situation was not so simple. Married women might have property ; accounts had to be rendered to them. Cæsar himself in the

---

[1] Joyce, op. cit., ii, N.
[2] Czarnowski, op. cit., p. 239.
[3] **CCXLVI**, vii, pp. 244–7. Cf. Havet, " Les Institutions et le droit spéciaux aux Italo-Celtes," in **CXL**, xxviii, pp. 113 ff.
[4] Cæs., *Gall. War*, vi, 19 ; Gaius, *Instit. Comm.* i, 51–2, 55.
[5] D'Arbois, op. cit., i, pp. 242, 245, 247.
[6] Cæs., vi, 19.

same passage indicates that the wife was far from being completely in the *manus* of her husband.   She brought a dowry, in the form of property, *pecunia*; the amount of it was reckoned and the husband doubled it, and this constituted a stock ; accounts of it were kept and the *fructus*, the profits, were retained. The survivor became the owner of both halves and of the sum total of previous profits. Whatever may have been the nature of the property to which Cæsar here refers, the passage proves that it was possible for these common goods to be managed jointly or in some other equitable fashion.[1]

Now this account agrees with the Irish and Welsh laws, in which we again find the dowry and the wife's jointure. The woman whose marriage is the occasion of these patrimonial arrangements is of the same rank as her husband.[2] On general principle, a woman is incapable, under Irish law, of making a contract without her husband's consent, except where their properties are exactly equal. The *Táin* begins with a long discussion between Queen Medb and her husband Ailill about the amount of their wealth and therefore of their rights.[3] The Celtic family, then, included the position of matron, *cet muinter*, the chief woman of the family. Her position was, however, more independent than that of the matron who had married again. In this respect the Celtic family is at an earlier stage in the development of the paternal family than the Roman.

The Celtic societies were evidently moving towards monogamy, but polygamy was allowed.[4] Normally there was only one matron in a family, but there were other women, slaves or wives. The marriage of the matron involved purchase, but the rites of purchase were simpler for women of lower condition. Concubines (in Irish *ben urnadma*) were bought at the great annual fairs for the term of a year. By this time-limit the woman was saved from coming under the *manus* of the man. But in practice this marriage often lasted more than one year.[5]

---

[1] Cf. Jullian, **CCCXLVII**, ii, p. 407.
[2] D'Arbois, op. cit. (Droit), i, p. 231 ; Joyce, ii, p. 8.
[3] Ibid., i, p. 229.
[4] D'Arbois, op. cit. (Droit), i, p. 216. Cf. Stokes, **CCLXXXVIII**, pp. 52–6 ; **CCLXIX**, pp. 35–6 ; Joyce, ii, 7.
[5] D'Arbois, op. cit. (Droit), i, p. 227 ; **CCXLVI**, ii, p. 380, 390.

As in Rome, the purely civil forms of marriage had superseded the ancient religious forms among the Celts. Giraldus Cambrensis declares that a similar kind of marriage was in force among the Welsh, where the purchase was no more than a lease, and it was really a trial marriage, since it did not become permanent until children were born.[1] This type of marriage was practised in the families of Scottish chiefs down to the end of the Middle Ages. Divorce was allowed even by mutual consent, and Canon Law itself had to accept it. In Ireland, under the ancient law, a woman leaving her husband kept even the products of her domestic labour.[2]

For the children, *altram* made up for the weakness of the marriage tie. The mother's rank did not affect that of the children ; the consequences of descent by the father were absolute.

5. *Extension of the Family*

Among the Celts, the family is a large family, tracing kinship fairly far back in the ancestral line and forming a considerable group of agnates. This is true of Ireland, Wales, and Gaul. The Irish family, in particular, comprises four groups of relations named *gelfine*, the family of the hand (*geil*), *derbfine*, the certain family, *iarfine*, the distant family, and *indfine*, the final family.[3] The *gelfine* includes the man himself with his father, son, grandson, great-grandson, and great-great-grandson. The *derbfine* adds the grandfather in the direct line and, in the collateral line, the uncle, first cousin, and first cousin's son. The *iarfine* takes in, in the direct line, the great-grandfather and, in the collateral line, the great-uncle and two degrees of cousinship, namely his sons and grandsons. The *indfine* includes, in the direct line, the great-great-grandfather and, in the collateral, the great-great-uncle and two degrees of cousinship, namely his sons and grandsons. All these kinsmen are agnates, but of these concentric circles of kinship only the *gelfine* and *derbfine* constitute the family in the strict sense.[4]

[1] Girald. Cambr., *Descriptio Kambriæ*, ii, 6. Cf. Vinogradoff, **CCCXC**, i, p. 246.

[2] D'Arbois, op. cit.. (Droit), i, p. 228.

[3] Ibid., i, pp. 185 ff.

[4] Ibid. (Droit), i, 188. Cf. Maine, **CCCLII**, p. 216 ; Vinogradoff, op. cit., i, p. 305.

In the Gaelic clans of Scotland kinship is still wider, being traced further up in the ancestral line and down into the collateral branches.[1] It is extremely probable that the Gaulish family was organized in some similar fashion.

The family tie is expressed or revealed in the sense which all members of the family have that they are one and have certain rights and duties in respect of each other.[2] The whole family is responsible for the crimes committed by one member, and shares according to the positions of its members in the payment of fines.[3] But the tie is strongest within the *derbfine*. Murder is forbidden inside that smaller family ; the murderer in such a case loses the advantages of kinship while remaining subject to some of its burdens. In fact, the *gelfine* and *derbfine* constitute the normal family.[4]

6. *Inheritance*

The manner in which the succession was conferred and property was inherited is explained by this organization of the family. This is true, in particular, in the case of something which could not be divided—the kingship. As a rule, a king was not succeeded by his son. The reason is that the son was not designated by the system of descent of the *derbfine* to be his heir. He may have been his natural next-of-kin, but not his civil next-of-kin. That civil next-of-kin was his younger brother or some representative of his own or an earlier generation in the *derbfine*. Moreover, while the kingship was hereditary, the heir was chosen from among a number of kinsmen presumed equal, comprising the living agnates of the late king, that is, his uncles and cousins.[5] Irish history contains many tragedies which show how the royal families tried to evade these rules.

To secure a regular succession, pains were taken in Ireland to name the heir beforehand—from among the agnates, of course. He was called the *tanaiste* or tanist—a title difficult to explain—and acted as lieutenant to his predecessor. There were tanists for every degree of royalty, from the

---

[1] Meitzen, **CCCLIII**, p. 205.
[2] D'Arbois, op. cit. (Droit), i, p. 181. Cf. *Domesday Book*, i, 179.
[3] D'Arbois, ibid., p. 66.
[4] Ibid., p. 67. Cf. *Senchus Mor*, i, 182, 260 ; **CCXLVII**, iv, p. 284.
[5] See, e.g., the order of succession in the royal family of Eochaid between 398 and 533. Cf. MacNeill, **CCCCXLI**, pp. 230, 294.

chieftainship of a tribe to the High Kingship, and even in
certain noble families ; in short, wherever a succession was
indivisible. This system is called tanistry.[1]

Divisible goods were apportioned so as to take the agnates
into account on a system designated by the English word
gavelkind [2] ; they were divided into gavels, or portions,
which were based on a count of the heirs by heads (*per
capita*) or by lines (*per stirpes*).   The right to make a will
existed in Celtic law ; but it seems to have been brought in
chiefly by Christianity and under the influence of Roman
law.[3] In this respect the power of the Irish or Welsh father
seems to be far less than that of the Roman paterfamilias.
He only enjoys the usufruct of the family property ; he must
render account of the latter to the family and in theory he
cannot dispose of it. But this last right he gradually obtained.

The head of a family makes a line of nobles.[4] The head
of the Irish *fine* is a noble ; it is not so certain that the head
of a Welsh family is. The head of the *fine* has political,
judicial, and military functions ; he represents the family,
speaks for it, leads it in war. In Gaul the head of a family,
to judge from the Æduan Dumnorix, seems to have had the
guardianship of such women of the family as were not in
the power of husbands.[5] But in Ireland and Wales he was
chosen from among all eligible members of the family, his
wealth, popularity, and strength being taken into account.
Perhaps he suffered by the lack of that mystical predestina-
tion which a stricter succession would have given him.

To sum up, the Celtic family is in essence a fairly
undivided group of agnates, much more clearly defined as
such than the Roman group of agnates, since in it the
succession devolves on the agnates and not on the sons, and,
apart from the constitution of property, the agnates are
ranked in it by generation and age-class. This explains,
but does not justify, the confusion sometimes made between
the Celtic clan and the totemic clan.

But this family was evolving, and natural kinship was

---

[1] Maine, op. cit., 201. Cf. Spencer, **CCCCLVIII**.
[2] Mackay, " Notes on the Custom of Gavelkind in Kent, Ireland, Wales,
and Scotland," in **CXXIV**, xxxii, 1898, pp. 133 ff. Cf. **CCXLVII**, iv, pp. 284–
295 ; i, p. 250 ; iii, p. 331.
[3] Vinogradoff, op. cit., i, 289.
[4] **CCXLVII**, iv, pp. 346, 348. Cf. Czarnowski, p. 246.
[5] Jullian, **CCCXLVII**, ii, 407. Cf. Cæs., i, 18, 6, 7.

becoming more important. Even in the case of the royal families of Ireland, we see kings working for the future of their sons or grandsons, and gradually becoming more successful, and more frequently so, in securing for them the direct succession to the crown.[1] The same change was taking place in Gaul, where, for example, Comm of the Atrebates was succeeded by his own sons.[2]

7. Floating Elements

There is no society without floating elements. By the side of the Celts there were native populations—few in Gaul outside Aquitania and the Provençal coast, very few in Wales, regarding which our texts are very precise on the conquest of the Cymry in the sixth century, and not many in Ireland. There were slaves, also few, for the Gauls did not take many prisoners. Above all, there were the outcasts, men who had left their family, and then their tribe, after committing a crime, or to avoid responsibility for a debt, or for some other reason. Cæsar indicates that they were numerous in Gaul, and they played an important part in Ireland.[3] Lastly, there were the intellectual men—Druids, poets, bards.

Some of these elements, slaves and freedmen, had become absorbed in the organization of the families, which, besides, could legally adopt members.[4] Some of them had succeeded in forming families of the same type as the Irish or Welsh families, and enjoyed a legal status after passing a certain stage. Some constituted tribes living in dependence on free tribes. But most gathered round the chiefs and nobles ; these *hetairiai*, these bodies of companions, impressed the first Greek writers who came into contact with the Gauls.[5] The Gallic chief was surrounded by shield-bearers and spear-bearers, and Cæsar speaks of the devotion of the *soldurii*. The chiefs with whom he had dealings had hosts

---

[1] MacNeill, op. cit., pp. 114, 238, 290.
[2] D'Arbois, op. cit. (Droit), i, 97.
[3] Maine, op. cit., p. 173.
[4] Joyce, **CCCCXXXIV**, i, 166. Cf. Maine, op. cit., p. 231 ; and, for emancipation, Cæs., v, 45.
[5] Polyb., ii, xviii ; Diod., v, 29, 2. Cf. d'Arbois, op. cit., p. 62.

of dependents, forming small armies.[1] So, too, in Ireland the nobles were surrounded by dependents.[2]

All these floating elements had their place in the plebs of which Cæsar speaks in connection with the Celtic societies. He distinguishes between three orders—Druids, *equites*, and plebs—but in that plebs he confuses the free families (except their chiefs and the families founded by them) with another stratum of families. This second stratum had formed in consequence of an evolution which took place through contact with the soil.

III

THE LAND AND OWNERSHIP

The Celts had always been very mobile, and therefore not very strongly rooted in the places where they stopped.[3] But the soil had its place in their social conceptions. I have already pointed out a word common to the Italo-Celtic languages, represented by Latin *tribus*, Welsh *tref* " portion of the tribe ", and Irish *treb* " house ". This word stands in essence for a group of men who clear and work a certain tract of ground, and also designates the ground which they occupy. In Old Slavonic, *trèbiti* means " he clears " (ground). The tribe lives in a clearing and is surrounded by a line of boundary-marks. At an early date the Celts on the whole, and particularly in Britain and Ireland, were at pains to mark their frontiers by ditches, hedges, and walls.[4] In Gaul the frontier was marked by custom-posts, watch-houses, and boundary-lines.[5] The Roman government took over these limits, which continued to bound bishoprics and bailiwicks until recent times.

We can now see how the elements of which the tribe was composed, namely the families, established themselves on the land, how the soil was appropriated by men, as

---

[1] Fustel de Coulanges, **CCCXXXIV**, pp. 27, 195 ; Cæs., vi, 15 ; cf. Cæs., vii, 40 ; iii, 22 ; i, 18 ; Diod., v, 29.

[2] Maine, op. cit., p. 273.

[3] See the account of the migration of the Helvetii in Cæsar.

[4] Joyce, op. cit., ii, p. 266. Cf. MacNeill, op. cit., p. 131 ; **CXL**, xxxvii, p. 367.

[5] **I**, xiii, 6127. Cf. Jullian, op. cit., ii, p. 53, n. 2.

individuals or in families.   There was a long controversy once between Fustel de Coulanges and d'Arbois de Jubainville,[1] who, interpreting Cæsar's remarks and working down to the Middle Ages, discussed whether there was individual appropriation or collective ownership.   The fact is that both types existed, as they do to-day.   It is also true that the land was divided into the estates of large families, which were afterwards grabbed by individual chiefs of those families.   Among the island Celts and in Gaul before Cæsar's time most property was collective.   An Irish law-treatise declares that the observance of common rules in agriculture is one of the fundamental institutions of Ireland.[2]   It is also plain from the laws of Ireland and Wales that ploughing with the large eight-ox plough required the co-operation of several persons interested.[3]   But as a rule among the Celts the village is not the effective owner of the land on which it stands.

In Ireland it is the tribe which has the eminent owner-ship of the land.   It was only later, it seems, that the country became covered with hedges.   We can imagine a tribe of stock-raisers, on finding itself in possession of a vast territory, grouping the flocks and herds of its families, and the families installing themselves as they pleased on ground which no other claimed.   That is how the ancient writers depict the Gauls of Italy, and all the Celts must have been the same at first.[4]

But this condition of undivided property implies an unlimited extent of available ground and an almost entirely pastoral life Now, the Celts were great husbandmen.   After saying that the Cisalpine Gauls lived solely on meat, Polybios [5] describes a country abounding in corn, which

---

[1] D'Arbois, op. cit. (Propr.), p. 104.
[2] Maine, op. cit., p. 101.
[3] Cf. Dottin, **CCCXXII**, p. 185.
[4] Polyb., ii, 17. Cf. d'Arbois, op. cit., pp. 61, 69, 100 ; Joyce, op. cit., i, p. 184 ; Lloyd, **CCCCXXXVIII**, p. 138. See MacNiell, op. cit., p. 351 ; the annalists place the first erection of the hedges dividing estates in the reign of Aodh Sláine, about A.D. 600. A passage in the story of Cuchulainn indicates that in ancient times horsemen could ride about freely without being held up by hedges. See the text entitled *Compert Conculaind*, in Windisch, **CCXCV**, i, p. 136.
[5] See above, p. 23.

was what he had seen ; the rest was tradition. Gaul was
a corn-country. The army at Alesia starved for lack of
corn. Ireland must always have eaten as much barley as
meat. A developed agriculture means some fixity. Besides,
stock-raisers in all ages must have known that a cow needs
a certain amount of fodder daily, summer and winter, and
this must have led them to make the area of the ground
proportionate to the number of beasts and, therefore, to
distribute it. As a fact, we find the land of the Celts divided
into the estates of families. Let us see what these families
were like.

Family property in Irish is called *baile*.[1] It is an old
word of the common Celtic, which, through Gaulish, has
left a descendant in French *bailliage*. There were 30 *baile*
in a tribe, and a *baile* normally corresponded to 300 cows
and between 2,500 and 3,500 acres. It was divided into
four quarters, which were subdivided into four households
each.[2] While the *baile* tends to become an administrative
unit, the quarter keeps its character as landed property.
Ireland is a chess-board, on which the squares are quarters,
measuring from 160 to 320 acres. They have been subdivided
and amalgamated, but they are fixed.

The *Senchus Mor* tells us that the members of the *fine*
have one house and one bed.[3] Strabo [4] says that the Britons
lived in enclosures like round kraals, in which the cattle
also were kept. The topographical accounts of Ireland
show circles inside the quarters, which may have been the
common dwelling of the people of the *baile* or of the quarter.
Often the great families had *duns* and *raths*, fortified houses
or collections of houses with a stone wall round them.[5] The
roof of the house was borne on two rows of three columns (Irish
gabhal, Welsh *gafl* " fork " or " branch "). The centre was a
common hall, with the hearth. The two sides formed four
divisions, which were again subdivided into four ; here the
beds were. The house sheltered sixteen *ménages* ; it was a
replica of the family. The Welsh, indeed, took from the house

---

[1] **CXL**, xxxix, p. 57. Cf. Joyce, op. cit., ii, p. 372.
[2] Meitzen, **CCCLIII**, i, p. 175.
[3] Czarnowski, **CCCCXXXIII**, p. 246. Cf. *Senchus Mor*, i, pp. 122, 130,
132 ; **CCXLVII**, iv, p. 374.
[4] Strabo, iv, 5.
[5] D'Arbois, op. cit. (Droit), ii, 71.

the various terms designating the divisions of territorial property.[1]   These family estates were the collective properties of the large family. On the extinction of each generation, the land was redistributed. The free Welshman seems to have had an inviolable right to a share of the tribal land in the portion of the family, and it seems that there was a legal obligation that each member of the family should receive a *trev* of land (about five acres) on reaching manhood.

This system seems to have gone on working, fairly successfully, in Wales until the fourteenth century. The chief inconvenience was the practice of a father of a family giving part of his land to the Church on condition that it reserved the working of it for his own descendants.[2]   There was plenty of available land in the Welsh mountains ; it was not so in Ireland, where the system of dividing landed property proved less elastic, and it was the large family that altered until it was no more than a kind of territorial division of the *tuath*.[3]

The family broke up. In some cases, to fill gaps, it had to call in strangers [4] ; or else it had to multiply shares so that they became too small. The number of *bailes* increased. The result was much emigration and transplanting of groups, which contributed to transforming the character of the *tuath*.[5]

1. *Causes of the Formation of a Landed Aristocracy*

The working of the institutions described above might have produced a society of equally poor persons. But there developed in the Celtic societies an aristocracy, a plutocracy, while the freeman was reduced to the position of tenant farmer and even servile tenant.[6]   There were four reasons for this : (i) the custom of giving appanages to kings, heads of families, and tanists of the various classes [7] ; (ii) the

[1] Ibid. (Propr.), xxv ; Joyce, op. cit., i, pp. 39, 196 ; Meitzen, op. cit., i, p. 184 ; Vinogradoff, CCCXC, i, p. 309.
[2] Meitzen, op. cit., i, p. 196.
[3] Czarnowski, op. cit., p 248.
[4] Meitzen, op. cit., pp. 187, 202.
[5] Ibid., p. 196.
[6] *Senchus Mor*, iii, p. 52 ; cf. ii, p. 282 ; iii, p. 303 ; Czarnowski, op. cit., p. 242 ; Joyce, op. cit., i, p. 186 ; d'Arbois, op. cit. (Droit), ii, 78 (cf. ibid., p. 2) ; CCXLVII, iv, pp. 68, 159.
[7] *Senchus Mor*, in CCCXLVIII, ii, p. 280 ; cf. Czarnowski, p. 235, n. 5 ; Joyce, op. cit., i, p. 147.

grabbing of unappropriated land by chiefs ; (iii) the development of movable wealth ; (iv) the substitution of contractual
relations of feudal type for the statutory relations of men
within groups. The tribe's eminent right to the land was
seized by individuals. In consequence, landed property
ceased to be collective and became individual, but
aristocratic.

1. The territory of a tribe comprised the chief's mensal
land, the portions appropriated by families and divided
into *bailes*, a proportion of available pasturage, and, lastly,
moorland, swamps, and rocky tracts. The freemen had the
limited enjoyment of part of these commons. Now, not
only kings but nobles carved out private estates from the
tribal territory and added them to their share of the family
property. The tenants who established themselves there
for a limited period were really tenants of the king and
nobles.

2. Inequality in movable fortune also contributed
to the creation of an aristocracy. Wealth was wealth in
cattle, which the rich man grazed on the commons, which
he tended to appropriate.[1] But as his stock increased he
lent cattle, and his debtors became a *clientela*. You could
lend *free* cattle, that is without change in the condition of
the borrower, or *serf* cattle, which entailed a change in his
condition. Debtors preferred serf cattle, at the cost of their
freedom, for in that case the loan was economically more
advantageous. So there grew up in Ireland a class of persons
known as *bo-aire*, cattle-nobles.[2] At the same time the
practice of compensation, with its heavy fines, in a society
involved in a maze of interconnected feuds and the contract-
ing of debts to pay blood-prices created further inequalities.
The whole of society gradually became arranged in a scale
of vassalage and clientship.[3] In Cæsar's time the heads of
families must have had their large family among their debtors
and clients, and they alone formed the knightly class of the
equites.[4] As in Gaul, so in Wales, the head of the family

---

[1] Cæs., vi, 22, 3 ; 11, 4 ; i, 4, 2. Cf. Maine, p. 159 ; d'Arbois, op. cit.
(Droit), i, p. 119 ; **CCXLVII**, ii, pp. 126, 206, 222 ; Joyce, op. cit., i, p. 188.
[2] Joyce, op. cit., i, p. 158.
[3] D'Arbois, op. cit. (Droit), i, p. 105. Cf. Joyce, op. cit., i, p. 157 ; Maine,
CCCLVIII, pp. 131, 136.
[4] Cæs., vi, 15. Cf. d'Arbois, op. cit. (Propr.), p. 52 ; Jullian, **CCCXLVII**,
ii, p. 69.

alone fought on horseback. His kinsmen, dispossessed of their collective rights by mortgage of otherwise, usually remained on the family estate. A number of the villages of France were once the estates of Celtic nobles, the Gallo-Roman *fundi*.

So the tribal system of the Celts gradually became an aristocratic feudal system. But the aristocracy sprang from the Celts themselves.

2. *The System of Agriculture*

Irish and Welsh family properties and their subdivisions were surrounded by hedges, ditches, or earth banks. There were only the rudiments of villages where roads crossed.[1] This is still the case in Brittany and Vendée, and in varying degrees in Central France. In the north and east of France, on the other hand, we find large villages, few isolated farms, and few hedges, and the fields run down the slopes in parallel bands. This disposition comes from a past age in which the village had common land, with alternate fields which were not appropriated but merely allotted. The same arrangement of the fields is found in Ireland and Wales around the towns and large villages; in Scotland it is called *runrig*, division into elongated fields. These towns and villages are later creations, as we have seen.

Both methods of occupation are of Celtic origin, and both correspond to a distribution of the tribal soil into family estates. But the park system corresponds to a pastoral life and the field system to an agricultural.

IV

PENAL LAW

As I said at the beginning of this chapter, the Celtic state had no magistrates, but only arbiters—originally Druids, *fili*, *prud'hommes*, or Brehons. These did not intervene unless called in by both parties, or at least one. Normally, the man who had suffered by the infraction of the law had a right to exact justice himself.[2]

[1] Meitzen, op. cit., i, p. 214. Cf. Joyce, ii, p. 264.
[2] S. Bryant, *Liberty, Order, and Law under Native Irish Rule*, London, 1923, p. 259.

The payment of compensation was at the very foundation of Celtic penal law. It was also a method of avoiding bloodshed. The amount was determined by the victim's rank, whether the crime was murder, wounding, or injustice. If he was a free man of superior class, there was added to the price of the body the price of honour, proportionate to his dignity.[1] As late as the sixteenth century, when a man was murdered in Ireland, the brehon made the murderer and the kinsfolk of the victim effect a transaction whereby, on payment of an indemnity (*eric*, meaning compensation-fine), the crime was extinguished.[2] In Gaul, in Cæsar's time, the Druids fixed the *poenas*, that is, apparently, the fine paid by the defender, if he lost the case and was solvent, or by his family in his default, if it was itself solvent. At the same time they laid down the punishment which he should receive if insolvent. The Druids also fixed what the Latins called the *prœmia*, the sum to be shared by the family of a murdered man or to be received by one wounded or treated with injustice. The fine not only repaired the damage done, but paid for the outrage on honour and enriched the injured individual or family.[3] To escape the payment of it, which fell on all members of the family, as has been said already, the guilty man or even part or the whole of the family would go into exile. We have already seen the importance of the exile in Celtic society.[4]

For the murder of a free man the body-price (Irish *dire*) was seven female slaves.[5] To this was added the price of honour (*enechlann* or *log eneich*), which was graded according to the rank of the victim. That of the king of a *tuath* in Ireland was fixed at seven female slaves, or twenty-one cows, or thirty-five horned cattle of medium value.[6] In legend this figure appears among the teachings of the famous King Cormac mac Airt. According to the *Senchus Mor* the price of the honour of the king of a province is twenty-one slave-women or sixty-three cows or a hundred and five horned cattle of medium value. Lastly, the price of the honour of the High King rises to twenty-eight slave-women or eighty-three cows or a hundred and forty horned cattle

[1] D'Arbois, i, pp. 76, 199.   [2] *R.C.*, ix, p. 143.
[3] D'Arbois, pp. 82 ff.   [4] Ibid., p. 83.
[5] In *Ancient Laws of Ireland*, iii, p. 70.
[6] Ibid., iv, p. 346.

of medium value.[1] Tariffs of compensation are laid down for the price of the honour of the various categories of *aire* or free men.

Similar conceptions are found in Wales, where the *gwyneb garth* or "price of the face" seems to correspond fairly exactly to the Irish *enechlann*.[2]

From the date of summons before the arbiter to the date of appearing there are forty days. When that time has passed, the pursuer can proceed to seize the immovable property after fulfilling certain formalities.

The fine is fixed by the arbiters. We shall see how this function was performed by the Druids, and by the *fili*, who were attached to the Druids as subordinates, became their rivals, and finally superseded them in their capacity of arbiters and judges.

The payment of the fine fell on the family in the strict sense, the *gelfine*, and if it could not meet it by itself, the responsibility was extended to the wider family, the *derbfine*, and so on to the *iarfine*,

By the side of the private penal law based on compensation and dispensed by arbitration, there were some rudiments of a public penal law, marked by the increasing intervention of the great assemblies, which tended to form a kind of supreme court of conciliation, and to judge offences against the state or what took the place of a state.

V

POLITICAL INSTITUTIONS

1. *The King and the Evolution of Kingship*

To designate chiefs of a certain dignity, the Celts had inherited from their Indo-European past the word *rix*, corresponding to the Latin *rex* and the *râja* of the Hindus. They had, therefore, had kings before they had been long parted from their Indo-European kinsfolk.[3] In Ireland there was a whole scale of kings, ranging from the king of

---

[1] Ibid., ii, pp. 224, 226. Cf. i, p. 230 ; iv, p. 236 ; iii, p. 42.
[2] J. Loth, *Les Mabinogion du Livre Rouge de Hergest*, Paris, 1913, i, p. 127, n. 2. Cf. d'Arbois, *Études sur le droit celtique* i, pp. 134–5, 153.
[3] D'Arbois, op. cit., i, p. 192.

the *tuath* to the High King of Ireland.[1] Among the Gauls of the Continent the Latin writers mention *reges* and *reguli*. These latter were doubtless the petty kings of the *pagi*, in other words of the *tuatha*, or tribes.[2]

The Irish kings [3] have all the appearance of sacred kings, endowed with mystical powers far exceeding their real political power. In the reign of Cormac mac Airt, says an Irish poem, the world was happy and pleasant ; there were nine nuts on every branch and nine branches on every bough. The king is a chief, embodying the mystical powers of the clans. A good king makes the land fruitful and is a guarantee of plenty, prosperity, and security.[4] He is in relations with the order of nature ; his movements are connected with the movement of the sun.[5] His mystical virtues are protected by taboos, *geasa*. He must not do any work, any slavish labour ; he must not rear pigs, although the domestication of that animal is one of the gifts of the heroes ; he must not till the soil, although he is the great creator of fertility.[6] His physical perfection is the guarantee of his virtues ; when Cormac mac Airt lost an eye he was deposed.[7] He answers on his head for the victories expected of him.

It was the same among the Continental Gauls. The suicide of Brennus after Delphi corresponds to that of Ailill Inbanna, King of Connacht, after his defeat.[8] Deiotarus, the soothsayer king of the Galatians, is a king of the same type.[9]

The relationship of these kings to their subjects was certainly originally conceived on the model of that of the head of a family or clan to his family or clan. In Ireland, the king appears in his capacity of father of a family when he collects a tax, called the maiden's ring, for the marriage of the girls of the tribe.[10] In Irish law the chief acts as family to those who have none.[11]

---

[1] Joyce, op. cit., i, pp. 41, 599. Cf. d'Arbois, **CCXLVIII** (Droit), i, p. 105
[2] Polyb., iii, 50 ; Jullian, **CCCXLVII**, ii, p. 39.
[3] MacNeill, **CCCCXLI**, p. 26. Cf. **CXL**, xxix, p. 5.
[4] **CXL**, xxxix, p. 21. Cf. Joyce, op. cit., i, pp. 55–6.
[5] **CXXXIV**, 1917, p. 37.
[6] Joyce, op. cit., i, p. 60 ; cf. p. 55.
[7] Maine, **CCCLII**, p. 37.   [8] Joyce, op. cit., ii, p. 532.
[9] Jullian, op. cit., ii, p. 44. Cf. **XI**, vi, p. 168.
[10] Joyce, op. cit., ii, p. 7.   [11] D'Arbois, op. cit., i, p. 63.

The king is the head of a royal line in a society composed of lines. In Ireland and Wales at least he seems to have ruled his kingdom in the manner of the father of a family. He is elected by the *aire*, the nobles. In Ireland and Gaul the election did not always go off peacefully. The kingship was conferred, then, both by right divine and by election.[1]

The existence of several royal houses, of the same origin or rivals, complicated the problem of the succession. Sometimes, particularly in the case of the High Kings of Ireland, the kingship went to the paternal and the maternal family alternately. At other times (there are five instances in the list of High Kings from 565 to 664), rival ambitions were satisfied by the association of both kings in the sovereignty.[2] The election was attended by ceremonies of divination which gave the gods a part in the proceedings, and was complicated by ceremonies of inauguration. There was a stone of inauguration—a stone seat or a stone with an impression on which the king set his feet. The new king, unarmed and holding a white rod, turned round several times, listened to the royal *file* reading the laws, and took the oath.[3]

Once appointed, the king possessed all power, religious, judicial, and military ; he had certain subsidies in addition to the revenues of the royal land,[4] and lived at his subjects' expense on his official tours. He had a regular retinue, a court [5]; he was hospitable by tradition and kept open table.[6] He travelled often and was the guest of his vassals.

Ireland had a very high ideal of kingship,[7] an ideal of loyalty, fairness, fidelity to the laws, knowledge, and judgment. The legendary instructions of King Cormac mac Airt to his son Cairbre are an exposition of this ideal.[8]

At the time when Cæsar conquered Gaul, royalty was passing through the same crisis in that country as it had undergone centuries before in Italy and Greece. There

---

[1] Jullian, op. cit., ii, p. 44. Cf. Joyce, op. cit., i, p. 44 ; MacNeill, op. cit., p. 353.

[2] Ibid., i, p. 45.

[3] Ibid., i, p. 46.

[4] Ibid., i, p. 50. See Cæs., vi, 15.

[5] Ibid., i, p. 61.

[6] Ibid., i, p. 48.

[7] CCXLVII, iv, p. 51.

[8] Cf. Maine, op. cit., p. 184 ; Joyce, op. cit., i, p. 57. See, in Kuno Meyer's ed. and trans., *Tecosca Cormaic*, CCXCI, ser. xv (1909) (the *Instructions of Cormac*). Cf. MacNeill, op. cit., p. 320.

were no kings left except among the Nitiobriges and the
Senones.[1] In Britain, on the other hand, the institution was
still untouched.[2] The men who destroyed the kingships of
Gaul were the heads of the great families, the patricians, as
is plain in the case of the Arverni and Ædui. The royal
families took part in the government with the other aristocratic houses. About Cæsar's time attempts were made to
create monarchies of a new type. Among the Arverni,
Vercingetorix succeeded where his father Celtillus had failed ;
he relied on the numerous outcasts, who formed the body of
companions enlisted by a rich and powerful chief. These
might be called democratic kingships.[3] At first Cæsar favoured
the re-establishment of monarchies, until the success of
Vercingetorix revealed the latent power of the masses, to
which a king could give unity.[4]

The royal authority seems to have remained stronger
among the island Celts than in Gaul, where many states,
such as the republic of the Ædui, presented a spectacle
of anarchy. The Gauls made an effort to set up constitutions [5]
and magistrates, who bore the title of *vergobret* [6] (*vergo*,
effective ; *breto*, judgment) and exercised the executive
power among the Ædui, Santones, and Lexovii. Among
some peoples there was a military leader besides.[7] Among
the Ædui, the *vergobret* became military leader when his
office expired.

2. *Public Bodies and Assemblies*

The assembly of free men still took some share in the
sovereignty in the Gaul which Cæsar knew.[8] He speaks of
the *publicum concilium*, which in some cases becomes the
armatum concilium when the leader in war has to be appointed.
The Irish texts are less definite, and speak chiefly of
assemblies for feasting.

---

[1] Jullian, in **XXXIV**, 1919, p. 104. See the passages on the Gallic kings
in Just., xliii, 3, 8, and Cæs., v, 24, 26 ; iii, 22.
[2] Diod., v, 21 (following Pytheas).
[3] Fustel de Coulanges, **CCCCLXV**, p. 42.
[4] For Vercingetorix, see Jullian, **CCCXLVII**, iii, 45, 197 ; Cæs., vii, 4, 1.
Cf. Jullian, op. cit., iii, pp. 138, 315.
[5] Cæs., vii, 32–3.
[6] Cæs., vii, 20 ; i, 16. Cf. Jullian, ii, p. 46.
[7] Cæs., vii, 4 ; 6 ; 57, 3 ; iv, 17, 2. Cf. Jullian, ii, p. 203.
[8] Dottin, **CCCXXII**, pp. 173 ff. ; Cæs., v, 27, 3. Cf. Jullian, ii, p. 57.

In Gaul there were restricted councils which the Romans likened to their own Senate.[1] Were these assemblies of the chiefs of tribes or of former magistrates ? In any case, they were administrative councils of the patricians, which saw to it that the Gallic republics maintained a continuous policy. For anarchic as they may appear, they had given up none of their national ambitions. They had a policy of expansion and prestige or one of security, and they had a diplomacy. Cæsar gives us a detailed account of the ups and downs of that policy, and introduces us to men who were not lacking in talent, ideas, or character.

3. *The Nation*

The elements which made up the nation, whether individuals or secondary groups, were held together by very loose ties. An Irish law says, " He is no king who has no hostages in his chains." There was a House of the Hostages at Tara. These hostages were a pledge for the loyalty of the groups associated and united under the High King.[2] Their loyalty must have been a precarious thing. The Celts had nothing like our notion of the definite, permanent character of the union of men in a state or nation. The hero Fergus leaves Ulster and settles in Connacht without becoming discredited. The state does not embrace men from their birth to their death.

Cæsar represents all the peoples as devoured by political activity and divided by factions.[3] Ireland shows nothing of that kind. The reason is that Gaul had advanced much further in the direction of aristocracy. Tribes and clans had disappeared in *pagi* and *fundi* ; *civitates* arose over the *pagi* ; the body of companions and territorial situation were the principles of the new organizations. A veritable revolution, social and political, had levelled all the lower ranks of the communities living together on the same territory and created a wide gap between them and the higher stages of the social scale.[4] In Ireland and Wales groups of foreigners survived unassimilated, subject tribes or clans, vassals, who

---

[1] D'Arbois, **CCXLVIII** (Propr.), p. 57.   Cf. Dottin, op. cit., p. 172 ; Jullian, ii, p. 48.

[2] Joyce, **CCCCXXXIV**, i, 53.

[3] Cæs., vi, 11.

[4] Ibid., i, 4, 18.   Cf. Jullian, iii, p. 120 ; Dottin, op. cit., p. 175.

remained outside the political society formed by the true
Celts and Welsh.

4. *The Army*

There was no standing army in Gaul. A levy was made in
time of war, in virtue of the statutory obligations of certain
members of society. The cavalry was an aristocratic body.
The noble who serves does so on horseback, and fights with
his servants attending him on foot.[1] By his side we find paid
horsemen, enlisting individually.[2] The rest of the army
marches in *pagi* under the leadership of its natural chiefs.[3]
Among the Welsh and Irish, on the other hand, the chiefs
fight on chariots or horseback, but among their own men ;
they do not form a separate body of cavalry. So the Celts
of the islands march in tribes or clans with their signs and
emblems.[4]   In tribes, too, march the permanent mercenary
troops of Ireland, the Fianna.[5]

5. *The Nation. Relations of the Celtic Peoples. The Celtic Empire*

The grouping or subdivision of social units does not
take place haphazard, but according to a sort of rhythm or
numerical law.   Hence comes the wholly ideal conception
of the five kingdoms of Ireland, that is the four kingdoms of
Ulster, Connacht, Leinster, and Munster, with the central
kingdom of Meath, containing the *omphalos*, or navel, the
central country, the point of divergence of the great roads.[6]
Ireland dreamed of a quadripartite organization of the state
and the nation corresponding to the similar organization of
the family.   In Wales this organization was brought about
by the grouping of the people in four tribes—Gwynedd,
Powys, Deheubarth, and Morganwy.[7]   In Gaul it is revealed
by the name of the Petrucorii.[8]   This division, which the Celts
seem to have regarded as the ideal form of society (four is
the perfect number), seems to come from a more distant

---

[1] Jullian, iii, p. 352.
[2] Cæs., i, 18, 5.
[3] Cæs., ii, 28, 2. Cf. Jullian, ii, p. 50.
[4] Joyce, op. cit., i, p. 91.
[5] Ibid., i, pp. 87 ff.
[6] Loth, in **CXXXIV**, xvii, pp. 193–206. Cf. **CXL**, xxvii, 1917, p. 142.
[7] Lloyd, **CCCCXXXVIII**, p. 131. This division corresponded to that of
the four bishoprics.
[8] Loth, in **CXXXIV**, 1916, p. 280.

age. For it is the theoretical division of a society composed of two phratries containing two clans each, inter-connected by marriage and the exchange of gifts or services.

The political societies of the Celts were composed of autonomous elements standing in juxtaposition ; in practice these heterogeneous elements often amalgamated. In Cæsar we see the peoples of Gaul, which are themselves agglomerations of *pagi*, agglomerating into compact groups. For example in the relief-army at Alesia we find the Cadurci, Gabali, and Vellavi combining their contingents with those of the Arverni,[1] and the Segusiavi, Ambivareti, and Aulerci Brannovices with those of the Ædui. This combination was not merely made to meet the occasion, but was the result of long-standing, deep-rooted associations. Cæsar describes these associations of Gallic peoples as kinships or *clientelæ*. The notion of *clientela* is defined in a certain number of cases by that of *imperium*[2] ; the client peoples were the subjects of the patron peoples, and *clientela* was a natural relationship and one of blood.[3] In this way there was a perfect network of ties among the peoples of Gaul. In addition, there were hierarchies, hegemonies,[4] assemblies.[5] So, too, in Ireland the four great kingdoms were subordinate to the High King, though rather loosely so. But their union was always conceived of on the same principle of kinship and *clientela*. The northern and western kingdoms were called Milesian, that is, kin ; Leinster was tributary,[6] and so a client kingdom.

The Celts seem to have risen to the notion of empire. When they first come into Roman history, Livy depicts a sort of great kingdom, the sovereign of which was a Biturix, that is, a King of the World, namely Ambicatus. He sent his two nephews on two great imperial expeditions, one to Germany and the other to Italy. It is idle to ask whether the empire of Ambicatus ever existed.[7] It is certain that the

---

[1] Bloch, **CCCCLXVII,** p. 79. Cf. Rhys, **CCXXX,** p. 60.
[2] Fustel de Coulanges, op. cit., p. 69. See Cæs., vii, 75, 2.
[3] Jullian, op. cit., ii, p. 442 ; Cæs., ii, 14, 2 ; vii, 5, 2 ; vi, 4, 2 ; vii, 75, 2.
[4] Jullian, op. cit., ii, p. 543 ; Cæs., v, 3, 1 ; vii, 64, 8 ; iii, 8, 1.
[5] Livy, xxi, 20, 3 ; Jullian, op. cit., iii, p. 223. The first general assembly of Gaul was held at Bibracte in 58 B.C., after the departure of the Helvetii.
[6] MacNeill, **CCCCXLI,** p. 238.
[7] D'Arbois, " L'Empire celtique au IVe siècle avant notre ère," in **CXLI,** xxx (1886), pp. 35–41, maintains that Ambicatus was a real person. M. Jullian has shown that this tradition is unlikely (op. cit., ii, p. 544).

idea of it was conceived by the Celts, for Livy's account comes from a Celtic tradition. Of that tradition Ireland presents an equivalent. It regards itself as a microcosm, an image of the greater universe. It enthusiastically adopts the idea of the King of the World, introduced by a St. Jerome or an Orosius.[1] But the Celts, while they failed to create an empire themselves, readily rallied to the imperial idea.

[1] MacNeill, op. cit., p. 270.

CHAPTER III

THE STRUCTURE OF SOCIETY (*continued*)

THE RELIGION OF THE CELTS AND THE DRUIDIC PRIESTHOOD

I

THE DRUIDIC PRIESTHOOD A PAN-CELTIC INSTITUTION

RELIGION is yet another element of social organization. Celtic religion in particular has the appearance of being such, for its most interesting and striking aspect was the constitution of the priesthood of the Druids, the organization of a religious society which made the whole series of Celtic peoples into one cohesive people.

First of all, this priesthood is a pan-Celtic institution, cementing Celtic society. There were Druids in Ireland. The modern Welsh Druids are only an archæological revival, but there were Druids in Britain, of whose power Cæsar gives evidence.[1] Gaul, too, had them. If we hear nothing of Druids in the Celtic settlements in Spain, Italy, the Danube valley, and Galatia, that seems to be no reason for denying that they existed among those branches of the race. If, moreover, it is true that the Latin word *vates* is borrowed from Celtic, the Gauls of Italy had among them persons described as *vates*, who were like the Druids, and organized like them.

Cæsar tells us that Druidism first started in Britain, and that the Druids of Gaul used to go to Britain to visit famous schools and sanctuaries. British Druidism had an equally high reputation in Ireland, and the Irish Druids went to Britain to complete their education. Does this mean that Druidism was unknown to the Celts as a whole and took shape among the Britons of Britain ? [2] We have no ground for saying that.

Some students, starting from this idea that Druidism had its origin in the west of the Celtic counties, have said that

---

[1] Cæs., vi, 13. Cf. d'Arbois, **CCXLVIII**, i, and Dottin, **CCCXXIII**, p. 38.
[2] Desjardins, in **CCCCLXXIV**, ii, p. 519, notes the absence of references to the Druids in Aquitania, Narbonensis, and the country near the Rhine.

it was not Celtic at all.[1] They have tried to attach it to the peoples which the Celts found established in the west of Europe, the builders of the megalithic monuments. But an analytical, comparative study of the institution shows that it is an essential part of the organization of the Celtic societies. History, moreover, shows clearly enough that it was an element of resistance to the Romans in Gaul and Britain and to Christianity in Ireland, and that it was attacked as such by persecution in Gaul, by the campaigns of the Roman generals against the sanctuaries in Britain, and by a kind of degradation in Ireland.[2] It was an element of resistance because it was an element of cohesion. The travels and meetings of the Druids cemented the union of the Celtic peoples and encouraged that sense of kinship which might have given birth to unity.

II

THE CHARACTER AND WORKING OF THE DRUIDIC PRIESTHOOD

The Druids are known to us by long passages in the Greek and Latin historians and polygraphers—Cæsar,[3] Diodoros,[4] Strabo,[5] Ammianus Marcellinus[6]—who all owe their information to Poseidonios and Timagenes. These writers enumerated the functions and powers of the Druids.

For Ireland, a great number of epic texts speak of the Druids. There are also many legal texts regarding the functions and powers of the *fili* (the poets and men of letters), who formed a corporation parallel and to some extent rival to that of the Druids and were spared by Christianity, whereas it wrought havoc with the Druids.[7] But the two bodies lived side by side and were complementary to each other, and in earlier times had been associated in their

---

[1] Rhys, **CCCCLI,** fourth ed., 1908, p. 9. Cf. id., **CCLXXXII,** p. 216. A similar theory is maintained by Pokorny, " Der Ursprung des Druidenthums," in **C,** 38, 1 (Vortrag), translated in **CXXIX,** 1910, pp. 589 ff.

[2] Tac., *Ann.,* xiv, 30, account of the expedition of Suetonius Paulinus against Anglesey. But Fustel, **CCCCLV,** p. 103, denies that the Druids were persecuted in Gaul. D'Arbois has proved the contrary, **CCXLVIII** (Droit), i, pp. 172 ff.

[3] vi, 13–14.

[4] vii, 31.

[5] iv, 197.

[6] xv, 9, 8 (following Timagenes).

[7] See a discussion of the question in Joyce, **CCCCXXXIV,** i, 222.

organizations and privileges. The literature and laws of Ireland were not written down until after the introduction of Christianity, and the work was done by *fili*, who therefore appear in a more favourable light than the Druids. But if we boldly fill in the gaps in our knowledge of the Druids from what we know about the *fili*, we get a picture of the Druids of Ireland which corresponds at every point to that of the Druids of Gaul. So we obtain a check on the accuracy of both portraits and a strong presumption that we are dealing with a common institution dating from the most distant past of the two peoples. The Latin variants of the name take one back to a declension identical with that of the Irish name of the Druids (*drui*, *druad*). The ancients connected this name with that of the oak,[1] regarding the Druids as dryads, priests of the oak (δρύς). In Wales, the late name of the Druids, *derwydd*, is a restoration based on the name of the oak, *derw*. But now, following Thurneysen and d'Arbois, Celticists prefer to connect *drúi* with *súi* " wise ", on the ground that these words are composed of a qualifing element, *su* " well " or *dru* " strong," and a verb-root, *uid* " know," which also comes into priestly names in Germanic, Slavonic, and the Baltic languages. So the Druids would be the very wise men, soothsayers.[2]

However that may be, it is certain that in Gaul the Druids were connected with the oak, plucking the mistletoe and eating the acorns to acquire their prophetic powers. In Ireland, the walnut and rowan are their trees, and certain nuts reveal the future. The Irish Druids have wands cut from their favourite tree, with the aid of which they exercise their powers, or silver branches representing the boughs of a sacred tree or of a Tree of Life in the next world. They are attached to these trees as totemic clans are to their totems.[3]

There are certain priests, called *gutuatri*, attached to a sanctuary.[4] But these may very well have been Druids, for Ausonius, in speaking of one of them, says that he was of a Druid family—*stirpe Druidarum satus*. The Druids

---

[1] A. W. Bird, "A Note on Druidism," in **XIX**, 1922, p. 152, 4. Cf. ibid., p. 155.

[2] MacBain, p. 141. Cf. Pedersen, i, 175 ; d'Arbois, **CCC**, p. 1.

[3] Luc., *Phars.*, i, 53 ; Tac., *Ann.*, xiv, 30 ; Pliny, xvi, xliii, 249.

[4] Loth, in **CXL**, xxviii, 118 Cf. Holder, i, col. 2046 ; d'Arbois, **CCXCIX**, p. 32.

formed a large clergy, which could have many special functions.[1]

In most Indo-European peoples functions were divided between the king and specialists. In Rome the *rex* and the *flamen* had each his own duties. The Irish King had his Druid, who probably received his powers from him in delegation.[2] M. Jullian has, I think wrongly, described the Druids of Gaul as priest-kings and the Assembly of Druids as a convention of kings of the *pagi*.[3]

In Gaul the Druids took part in sacrifices, public and private ; they ordered the ceremony and perhaps acted as sacrificers or ministers, at least in certain exceptional cases, where human beings were sacrificed, or white bulls at the plucking of the mistletoe.[4]

But their chief religious function was divination. The Druids were diviners, seers. Cicero in his *De Divinatione* introduces Diviciacus (although he was, rather, a statesman), on the ground of his augural science, served by his knowledge of man.[5] Some of the human sacrifices in Gaul and those sacrifices in Ireland in which the sacrificing was done by Druids were of a mantic character. The Irish texts show us the Druids at work, prophesying, interpreting omens, using the divining-wheel. The Druids are men of science, but they are also men of God, enjoying direct intercourse with the deities and able to speak in their name. They can also influence fate by making those who consult them observe positive rules or ritual taboos (the *geasa* which figure so largely in the Irish epics) or by determining the days to be chosen or avoided for an action which is contemplated.[6]

Between these religious functions and magic the distinction is vague. The Druids of Gaul certainly slipped into magic, and those of Ireland always practised it, with methods which are very obscurely described.[7]

[1] Livy, xxiii, 24.
[2] See Joyce, op. cit., i, p. 238.
[3] Cf. Jullian, **CCCLXVII**, ii ; Cæs., vi, 16, 5 ; iv, 4, 4.
[4] Cæs., vi, 16 ; Strabo, iv, 4, 5 ; Diod., v, 31, 4 ; 32, 6 ; Poseid., in *F.H.G.*, i, 261. Cf. d'Arbois, **CCXLVIII**, i, p. 151 ; Frazer, **CCCXXXII**, p. 234.
[5] Cic., *De Div.*, i, 41, 90 ; Cæs., vi, 13 ; Tac., *Hist.*, iv, 54 ; cf. Dion. Chrys., *Or.*, 49 ; Mela, iii, 19.
[6] Diod., v, xxxi, 4 ; Strabo, iv, 198. Cf. Joyce, op. cit., i, p. 229 ; d'Arbois, **CCCI**, p. 99 ; Windisch, **CCXCV**, pp. 69–70 ; Czarnowski, **CCCCXIII**, p. 95 ; *Táin*, i, 10, 70.
[7] Pliny, xvi, 249 ; xxiv, 62–3 ; xvi, 95 ; xxix, 12 and 52 ; Joyce, op. cit., i, pp. 245, 227, 247. Cf. *Silva Gadelica*, ii, pp. 85, 516.

The Druids also had judicial powers, for Cæsar tells us that they had to give judgment on almost all suits, public and private. In private law they dealt with matters of murder and inheritance and disputes about property. In international law (which is probably what Cæsar means by public suits) they acted as arbiters in disputes between political groups. In Ireland the same judicial powers, those of the Brehons, were exercised by *fili*, and we may fairly suppose that these took them over from the Druids. We find the Brehons at their work in the law-books which they compiled. They are jurisconsults, arbiters, and advocates rather than judges. They give consultations, based on precedents interpreted in the light of equity. They act as arbiters in matters of private law ; for instance, they lay down compensation to settle suits arising from injuries which call for private vengeance. In the evolution of Celtic law, the public powers of the state eventually exceeded those of the Druids and the Brehons. The king and the assembly give judgment ; the Brehon proposes the sentence, gives an opinion. But the Druids and Brehons seem, both in Gaul and in Ireland, to have been able to pronounce some kind of ban against those who did not accept their decision, and to this the *fili* added a magical enforcement.[1]

The Druids also had privileges and an authority of a political nature. Cæsar tells us that they were exempt from military service and taxation. We find Druids, such as Diviciacus and Cathbad, the Druid of King Conchobar, fighting ; but they do so of their free will and not by obligation.

In Ireland, moreover, the *fili* had a sort of permanent safe-conduct pass, even during the intestine wars which ravaged the country ; and this gave them an inter-tribal function. Every king in Ireland, great or small, had a Druid who was his political adviser. Cæsar gives evidence of the authority and social position of the Druids, whom he places in the same rank as the *equites*. Many sprang from royal or aristocratic families. In the order of precedence observed

---

[1] Cæs., vi, 13 ; Diod., v, 31 ; Strabo, iv, 4, 4 ; *Senchus Mor*, **CCXLVII,** i, pp. 22, 80, 86. Cf. O'Curry, **CCCCXXXII,** ii, p. 20 ; d'Arbois, **CCXLVIII** (Droit), i, pp. 271, 279, 294, 315 ; id., **CCC,** Druides, p. 103 ; Maine, **CCCLII,** i, pp. 4, 21, 25 ; id., **CCCLIII,** pp. 51 ff. ; **CCXLVII,** i, pp. 788, 250.

at Tara, the *fili*, who took the place of the Druids, appear
in the same ranks as the nobles.[1]

I have said above that the Druids acted as teachers
of the young. Cæsar shows that they sometimes raised their
pupils to power. Education was one of their essential functions
and perhaps it was the only one of a constitutional kind
in the organization of the Celtic society. The Druids lingered
on in Gaul as the teachers of higher schools ; in Ireland the
fili, who succeeded them as educators, founded schools
which, handed over to Christianity, survived all through
the Middle Ages. So the Druids and their successors were
a permanent element of civilization in Celtic societies.[2]
But before they taught classical learning, they diffused
ideas which must be defined.

Their teaching was purely oral, both in Ireland down to
Christian times and in Gaul, and seems to have consisted
in the setting forth of a tradition, recorded in innumerable
poems which were learned by heart. These doubtless included
epico-historical accounts of the origin of the race, as
a specimen of which we may take the *Leabhar Gabhála* ;
perhaps some cosmological digressions, such as are found
in the *Senchus Mor* ; certainly travels into the next world,
like the literature of the *Imrama* (Voyages).[3] And in all this
a doctrine was expounded. The ancient writers, who on the
whole were fairly well informed by good observers, have
given us an idea of this doctrine in a few brief words which
are full of sense. They placed the Druids among the mystic
philosophers associated with the ancient Greek philosophers
who evolved the doctrine of the immortality of the soul.

The Druids had a complete doctrine of that immortality,
with a moral system, general view of the world, mythology,
ritual, and funerary practice to match.[4] They taught that
death is only a changing of place and that life goes on with

---

[1] Cæs., vi, 14 ; d'Arbois, **CCCCXLVIII**, i, pp. 126, 342. Cf. *Book of Leinster*,
p. 29 ; *Táin*, i, 47, 23 ; ibid., 93 ; Dion. Chrys., *Or.*, 49 ; Joyce, op. cit.,
i, p. 237.

[2] Cæs., vi, 14, 2–3 ; Mela, iii, 18 ; Tac., *Ann.*, iii, 43 ; *Táin ; L. na
hUidhre*, p. 61, 1, 21, 23 ; ib., 64, 2, 10, 13 ; K. Meyer, in **CXL**, xi, pp. 442–453.
Cf. d'Arbois, **CCC**, Druides, p. 115 ; **CCXLVIII** (Droit), i, p. 339 ; **CCXLVII**,
ii, pp. 150–5 ; Czarnowski, **CCCCXXIII**, pp. 291, 294.

[3] Diod., iv, 56. See above, ch. vi.

[4] Cæs., vi, 14, 5–6 ; 16 ; Strabo, iv, 4, 4 ; Amm. Marc., xv, 9, 8 ; Diog.
Laërt., *Prooem.*, 5 ; Diod., vi, 27, 6 ; Luc., i, 450 ; Mela, iii, 19 ; iii, 2, 19 ;
Val. Max., ii, 6, 10.

its forms and its goods in another world, the world of the dead, which rules the dead and gives up living men. It is a world of life, forming a reservoir of available souls. A constant, floating capital of souls is distributed between the two counterpart worlds, and exchanges take place between them, life for life and soul for soul. But, what is more, this stock of souls is apparently not confined to the human species ; souls pass from one species to another. The Druids seem to have held a belief in metempsychosis, traces of which are found in the myths and stories.[1] With some notions of physics and astronomy, applied in the construction of calendars, some knowledge of plants and their properties (which was passed on to the physicians), and a few magical prescriptions, this stock of philosophical ideas seems to have formed the bulk of the wisdom of the Druids, which contributed in no small degree to the spiritual education of the Celts.[2]

The Druids formed an *order* in Celtic society, but that order was a brotherhood (*sodaliciis adstricti consortiis*), a society of individuals collectively exercising a social function. Their organization cut across the divisions of tribes and states ; the Druids of Ireland were one single body, those of Britain turned their eyes to the sanctuary of Mona (Anglesey), and those of Gaul turned to the shrine among the Carnutes.[3] All these groups communicated with one another. The Druidical colleges obtained new members by training and co-option, but there were also Druid families. There must have been initiations, a preparation, and stages, of which we find traces among the *fili*. There seem to have been Druidesses in Gaul and Ireland, but we cannot be sure whether they really belonged to the college of Druids, or merely got the name by analogy, on account of their gifts in magic. In any case, the Druids formed a widespread college, the members of which, distributed about the political framework of the nation, performed the most varied functions. The college asserted its unity in its sanctuaries, its schools,

---

[1] Czarnowski, op. cit., pp. 156 ff. Cf. Windisch, **CCXCV**, i, p. 117 ; Nutt, in **CCLXXIV**, ii, p. 96.

[2] Pomp. Mela, ii, 2 ; Strabo, iv, 197 ; 4, 4 ; **CCXLVII**, i, p. 22 ; Pliny, xvi, p. 250 ; Cæs., vi, 18 ; Windisch, op. cit., i, p. 215 ; d'Arbois, **CCXLVIII**, i, p. 141. Cf. Maine, **CCCLII**, p. 34 ; Joyce, op. cit., i, 230.

[3] Joyce, op. cit., i, p. 223 ; O. Curry, **CCCCXXXII**, ii, 182 ; Jullian, *R.E.A.*, 1919, p. 109.

and its assemblies, like the assembly of the country of the
Carnutes, held in Gaul, which was at once a council and
a guild-congress of the Druids.

By the side of the Druids, the ancient authors, following
Poseidonios and Timagenes, mention the bards, who were
popular poets with less refined methods, and the *vates*, who
were seer-poets and ἱεροποίοι.[1] In Ireland we hear of bards
and singers (*cainte*), *fili*, and Druids. The *fili* and their Welsh
equivalents are much the same as the *vates* of Gaul. Several
corporations were lumped together under this title.[2] They
were at first subordinate to the Druids, but eclipsed them
when Christianity came in.

III

THE DRUIDS AND OTHER INDO-EUROPEAN BROTHERHOODS

This account of the college of Druids naturally brings
to mind the similar colleges of the ancient world, and first
of all those of the Romans [3]—Flamens, Augurs, Vestals,
Arval Brothers, Luperci. But the Roman priesthood had
a larger number of brotherhoods, with fewer members in
each. Moreover, the ancients were struck by the resemblance
of the doctrine of the Druids to that of the Pythagorean
syssitiai which had developed among the Dorians of Southern
Italy.[4] It is highly probable that the Dorians, before moving
down into Greece and then over to Italy, had been quite
near the Celts in Central Europe. What is more, the country
extending from the Middle Danube to the Ægean, from
which the Dorians came, had been a nursery of institutions
like the Pythagorean communities. It was there that
Orphicism, which the ancients likened to Pythagoreanism,

---

[1] Cæs., vi, 13 ; Amm. Marc., xv, 9 ; ii, 8 ; Stokes, *Tripartite Life*, pp. 235,
326.   Cf. Dottin, **CCCXXII**, p. 54 ; Czarnowski, op. cit., pp. 287, 278 ;
d'Arbois, **CCXLVIII**, i, p. 234.

[2] Diod., v, 31 ; Strabo, iv, 4, 4 ; Cæs., vi, 13 ; Amm. Marc., xv, 98 ;
Ath., iv, 37 ; vi, 49 ; Luc., i, 44, 7 ; Joyce, op. cit., i, pp. 223, 230 ;
Czarnowski, op. cit., pp. 227, 278 ; d'Arbois, **CCXLVIII**, i, p. 196.

[3] D'Arbois, **CCC**, p. 9 ; Schrader, "Aryan Religion," in **CCCXXXVI**, ii,
p. 43.

[4] Pliny, xxx, 5 ; Clem., *Strom.*, i, 15, in *F.H.G.* (following Alexander
Polyhistor, a historian of the first century), iii, 233 ; Amm. Marc., xv, 9, 8 ;
Val. Maz., vi, 6, 10. Cf. Delatte, "Études sur la littérature pythagoricienne,"
in *Bibl. de l'Éc. des Htes. Études*, 1915, p. 217.

came into being.[1] Orphicism comprised the worship of the
Getic god or hero Zalmoxis, a brotherhood of priests, a doctrine
of immortality, a myth of the descent into the underworld,
and, like the ritual of the Druids, human sacrifice.[2] In
Thrace, among the Satrae, there was a brotherhood of priests
called Bessi, who ran an oracle of Dionysos, a Thracian
god.[3] Here we have one same family of cults, in which the
societies in which they were observed were merely onlookers
and the active part was played by brotherhoods of initiates.

Moreover, in the east of the Indo-European region we
find societies of priests very like the Druids in the credit
which they enjoy and the area over which they are spread—
the Iranian Magi and the Brahmins of India. The Druids
seem to differ from the latter only in that they do not form
a closed caste. We have previously seen the analogies in
religious vocabulary between the two most widely separated
branches of the Indo-European family, the Italo-Celts
and the Indo-Iranians.[4] This series of similarities proves
that Druidism was an Indo-European institution, and that
its origins went back to the most distant past of the Indo-
European societies. But we can go back yet further.

Sir James Frazer and M. Jullian after him have supposed
that Druidism was derived from the kind of sacrifice described
in the *Golden Bough*, the sacrifice of god-priest-kings like the
Priest of Nemi whom Sir James makes the central example
in his great work.[5] Really, Druidism is something quite
different. In the various types of priestly society which we
have been considering, the collective exercise of spiritual
functions is essential to the nature of the institution. We
must, therefore, go back to a type of collective body, not
to one of individuals. The god-priest-kings are individuals.

But the forms of these collective bodies, these brotherhoods, which we have been surveying are as different from
one another as the societies in which they appear. Some
are mere colleges, others are colleges of initiates, others
are societies on a basis of kinship (castes or priestly families).

---

[1] Diod., iii, 65, 6. Cf. d'Arbois, CCCI, i, p. 296.
[2] Hdt., iv, 94 ; Strabo, vii, 35. Cf. Dottin, CCCXXII, p. 58.
[3] Hdt., vii, iii ; Strabo, vii, 3, 3 ; Dion Cass., 51, 25 ; 54, 34 ; Apollod.,
iii, 5, 1–2 ; Macrob., i, 18, 11 ; *F.H.G.*, iii, 641, 20. Cf. d'Arbois, CCCI, i,
pp. 292–6 ; Farnell, v, p. 102.
[4] See above, pt. iii, ch. i ; Vendryès, in XCIII, xx, 6, 265.
[5] Frazer, CCCXXII, pp. 82, 129, 218, 225–6 ; Jullian, in CXXXIV.

Now, comparison with non-Indo-European phenomena will give us the key to these institutions, showing us collective bodies which are just like those of the Druids and Brahmins and have a perfectly clear place in the evolution of totemism. These are the so-called secret societies of British Columbia and Melanesia, which are really brotherhoods.[1]   These brotherhoods are constituted alongside of totemic clans, and are copied from them. Each secret society has originated in a revelation which is represented in myths similar to those of Zalmoxis or Pythagoras. They are recruited by co-option, and members, belonging to successive generations, qualify themselves by initiations. Their activity centres on the periods of feasts in which the members of the brotherhood are the actors. Thus they assume functions which fall to them by escheat in communities where totemism is breaking up. It is brotherhoods of this kind that lie at the source of Brahminism and Druidism.

The influence of the Druids was always meeting opposition, in Gaul from the jealousy of the *equites*, which partly explains the rapid decline of Druidism, and in Ireland from the hostility of certain kings. Thus, some of the texts tell us of the incredulity of Cormac mac Airt. The elevation of the *fili* at the expense of the Druids was doubtless favoured by such opposition. It was only through the intervention of St. Columba at the Assembly of Druim Ceata in 574 that the *fili* themselves were allowed to maintain some of their prerogatives, which they had inherited from Druidism.[2]

IV

WHAT CELTIC RELIGION OWED TO DRUIDISM

One thing strikes us at the very first in the religion of the Celts, and that is the supreme importance of agrarian rites, which, with their myths, play the chief part in religious life. Fruitfulness, fertility, and life have always been the chief concern of these orgiastic brotherhoods, and they have always

---

[1] Hutton Webster, *Primitive Secret Societies* ; Boas, *Social Organization and Secret Societies of the Kwakiutl* (for North American practices).   Cf. Frazer, op. cit., iii, pp. 449, 459, 490. For interpretation, see Durkheim, in **XIII**, iii, p. 336 ; Davy, **CCCXVI**, pp. 201, 328 ; **CCCLX**, English, p. 102.

[2] Joyce, op. cit, i, p. 456.

stretched out their hand, over the head of the state religion, to the herdsman and the husbandman. Secondly, we see a metaphysical and moral system developed in religion. Interest in the soul, its origin and destiny, the world of souls and the dead, and the myth of the Beyond stand in the forefront of representations, as agrarian rites stand in the forefront of ritual.

V

THE UNITY OF THE CELTIC RELIGIONS

The existence of a pan-Celtic priesthood, dating from the origin of the race, must have ensured a certain unity for the religions of the various Celtic peoples. It is true that such unity is far from obvious. The reason is that the various Celtic religions are not known to us from documents of the same kind, and the different branches of the Celts did not develop equally and at one time everywhere. In Cæsar's time Gaul was ahead of Ireland. Moreover, for Gaul, about which our evidence comes from the Greek geographers, we know a good deal about ritual, but nothing at all of mythology, whereas for Ireland, where our sources are epic and lyric poems collected after the Celtic religion was dead, we have a body of tales and legends and know nothing definite about ritual. As for Welsh literature, it is a miracle that it contains any traces of British religion at all, for it was created in a Christian country, first Romanized and then colonized by Irishmen.

In spite of these difficulties, we find signs of a deep-lying identity. The Brythonic Celts of Gaul, Britain, and the Danube, being of the same family and united by a thousand different bonds, had the same gods, or gods of the same name, and they were many. But the Goidels and Brythons of the island and the Continent shared them too. They may not have been so many, but they were important gods. There was Lugh, the great sun-god, who gave Lugdunun its name and was represented in Spain by the Lugoves.[1] There was Taranis, the god of lightning,[2] represented in

---

[1] Loth, *Le Dieu Lug, la Terre Mère et les Lugoves*, in **CXXXIX**, ii, 1914, pp. 205–210. Cf. **XL**, xii, p. 52.
[2] Luc, *Phars.*, i, 444. See MacCulloch, **CCCXIV**, pp. 20–48.

Ireland by a little-known hero, Tornà. Esus, a Gallic god, appears in the Irish name Eogan (= Esugenos). Goibniu, the smith-god of the Goidels, had a Brythonic counterpart whose name appears in that of Gobannitio, the uncle of Vercingetorix. Corresponding to the name of the Gallic and British god Camulos we have that of the Irish hero Cumhal, father of Finn. For the Goidelic goddess Brigid there was a Brythonic Brigantia.[1] It is better not to look for homonyms of the Irish deities among the characters of the Welsh Mabinogion, since the Welsh may have borrowed from Irish tradition. Manawyddan is the same as the sea-god Manannán. All these facts taken together enable one to picture an ancient stock of common cults and myths, preserved better in one place than another.

VI

STAGES OF THE CELTIC RELIGIONS

Attempts have often been made to distinguish in the Celtic religions the elements of Aryan origin and those belonging to the earlier inhabitants of Ireland. Mr. Cook holds that the Aryan gods were the gods of the sky, light, the sun, the stormy sky (like Tanaris) or the sunny sky (like Lugh), and that the worship of the oak and mistletoe were likewise Aryan.[2] The non-Aryan gods, he believes, were the dark gods (and, more especially, goddesses) and those of vegetation. That would explain why the gods of the underworld and those of light are engaged in furious strife in the mythology of Ireland and Wales. But such theories fail to observe that these mythological conflicts are imposed on the gods by the dramatic parts which they play in the seasonal festivals. These cults are not the memory of historical wars, but the mythological version of a ritual. One might say that the conflicts of the gods are syntheses of various functions which are antithetic or successive. The racial ingredients of the Celtic peoples were fused together at an early date, and the differences presented

[1] Caes, vi, 17 ; Cormac, 23 ; Holder, **CCVII**, s.v. ; d'Arbois, **CCXLVIII**, ii, p. 273.
[2] A. B. Cook, in **LXIV**, xvii, p. 30. Cf. id. *Zeus : a study in ancient religion*, London, 3 vol., 1914–1925 ; Rhys, in **CCCLXXXII**.

by the lists of gods drawn up for the various parts of Ireland
have told us nothing so far. It must, too, be remembered
that the study of these local pantheons is still in its infancy.

Certainly the Celts owed much to their predecessors.
They made use of the megalithic monuments. The great
tumuli or funerary chambers of New Grange in Ireland (Brugh-
na-Boyne) were regarded as the dwelling-place of gods and
revered as sanctuaries. The twelve stones which formed the
satellites of the Irish idol Cromm Crúaich were the pillars
of a cromlech. In Britain, and doubtless in Gaul, the Celts
likewise took over the megalithic monuments, but we do
not know what they really borrowed from the predecessors
of their civilizations.[1]

The most interesting trace of the old stock is, as we have
seen, Druidism itself. Can one go still further back, to
totemism ? The Gauls had beast-gods, such as the horse
of Neuvy-en-Sullias, Rudiobos, the mule of Nuits,[2] and
Segomo, the ram-headed serpent represented on monuments
at Mavilly, Paris, and Rheims ; anthropomorphic gods
with some touch of a beast-god, such as Cernunnos with
his antlers and March (Mark) of the Britons with his horse's
ears [3] ; and sacred animals attached to certain gods, like
the horse of Epona,[4] the dog of the hammer-god,[5] the bear
of the goddess Artio,[6] and the boar of Diana Arduinna.[7] But
a beast-god is not necessarily a totem. Often the animals
portrayed on the monuments represent the popular elements
of the myths, and though these may be derived from totemism
we cannot say by what road. In Irish literature there are
several heroes with animal affinities, including the most
famous of all, Cuchulainn, the Dog of Culann, who was
forbidden to eat dog, and Oisin, whose mother was changed
into a doe and who was himself a fawn. We find traces of
animal emblems of clans, food-taboos. But in any case these
are only survivals of a long-superseded past. In the course

[1] Squire, **CCCCLIX**, p. 38 ; cf. K. Meyer, **CCLXXIV**, app. B. to *The Voyage of Bran.*

[2] Loth, *Le Dieu gaulois Rudiobos, Rudianos,* in **CXXXIX**, p. 195, 2, 210.

[3] Squire, op. cit., p. 327.

[4] Espérandieu, **CCCXXV**. Cf., for Epona, H. Hubert, in **XV**, xxxii, 1922, pp. 291–2 ; id. *Le Mythe d'Epona* in **CLXXXIV**, 1925, pp. 187–191, repr. in **CCXLIV**.

[5] Id., in **CXXXIX**, 1915.

[6] Reinach, **CCCLXXIII**.

[7] Kruger, *Diana Arduinna,* in **LXXXI**, i, 1917, p. 4.

of the evolution which took place, heroes took shape, civilizers
or founders of social groups, some of whom may have once
been totems while others may have been provided with totemic
emblems. One thing is certain—in Celtic societies, in the
place of the totem of the clan we find the hero of the clan,
of the tribe, of the nation.

VII

POLITICO-DOMESTIC ORGANIZATION AND HERO-WORSHIP

This worship of hero-gods corresponds very closely to
the extremely loose organization of political and family
life in Ireland. We know that Gaul at the time of the Roman
conquest was moving towards a different state of things,
but in Ireland society was far less centralized, and religion
was of the same character. The great seasonal feasts of
agricultural life marked a momentary concentration.[1]

Not only does Irish mythology take the form of a history
in which several generations of invaders [2] (the chief being
the Fomorians [3] and the Tuatha Dé Danann) [4] disappear
one after the other, but these Fomorians and Tuatha Dé
Danann are always represented as men who have lived on earth
and retired into death. Now, these spirits include the gods,
and indeed the great gods—Ler,[5] Nuadu,[6] Manannán,[7]
Dagda,[8] Brigid,[9] and Ogma [10] among the Tuatha Dé Danann
and others among the Fomorians,[11] Lugh belonging to both
sides. They dwell in tombs, which are actual megalithic
tombs.[12] So the gods are superhuman beings, not super-
natural, and this is true of them all, especially the local
gods attached to a district or a natural feature ; they are

---

[1] See Hubert, **CCCXLIII**, and *Le Culte des héros et ses conditions sociales*,
introd. to Czarnowski, **CCCCXXIII**, *Rev. de l'hist. des religions*, lxx, pp. 1–20,
and lxxi, pp. 195–247.
[2] See Squire, op. cit. ; d'Arbois, **CCXLVIII** and **CCC**. Cf. above, ch. iv.
[3] Squire, op. cit., pp. 48 ff.
[4] Ibid., pp. 70, 140, etc. ; cf. d'Arbois, **CCXLVIII**, ii, p. 155.
[5] Ibid., p. 136.
[6] D'Arbois, ii, p. 155. Cf. Rhys, **CCLXXXI**, p. 122.
[7] Squire, op. cit., pp. 60–1.
[8] Ibid., pp. 54, 78.
[9] D'Arbois, op. cit., ii, p. 373.
[10] Squire, op. cit., p. 122.
[11] Ibid., p. 140.
[12] Ibid.

bound to it by their tomb, by the memory of their death. The Celts liked this funereal aspect of their gods ; their pantheon might be described as a cemetery.[1]

These gods and their myths were subjected to a general process of rejuvenation which placed their date later and later and brought them closer to existing human communities. This rejuvenation of myths is very characteristic. A famous Irish story tells how the god Mider, one of the Tuatha Dé Danann, dwelling in the tomb of Bri Leith, tried to recover his wife Etain from the King of Ireland, Eochaid Airem, who is contemporaneous with Cæsar in the *Annals*. The name Etain is found again in the south of Ulster.[2] The god Nuadu is brought into recent times by the legend which makes him a grandfather of Finn.[3] Gods produce sons and grandsons ; Cuchulainn is descended from Lugh[4] and Mongan from Manannán. Others are reincarnated ; according to one tradition Mongan was reincarnated in Finn. The mythico-heroic literature of Ireland is full of gods returning to human life and men visiting the world of gods and the dead, and both are merged in the form of heroes.

The gods appear in the genealogies. The whole race claims descent from the great god Bile, father of Mile, the ancestor of the latest conquerors, who was a kind of god of the dead.[5] Similarly the Gauls, according to Cæsar, claimed descent from Dispater.[6] The forts, the rallying-places of tribes and families, were built on heights which were tombs. The residence of the Kings of Leinster stood on the tumulus of Slanga the Fir Bolg.[7]

The religion of Ireland was that of the politico-domestic groups of which society was composed. These centred on their ancestors, who were heroes and gods ; their cults were ancestor-worships and their feasts were commemorations. The type of the hero absorbs the whole of mythology, and is succeeded by that of the saint. M. Czarnowski has demonstrated that the immense popularity of St. Patrick, who is

[1] Joyce, **CCCCXXXIV**.
[2] Squire, op. cit., p. 332.
[3] K. Meyer, **CCCXXIV**, ii.   Cf. E. McNeill, *Duanaire Finn*, vol. vii of **CCLXV**, introd., pp xliii ff.
[4] Windisch, op. cit.
[5] Squire, op. cit., pp. 121–2, 153.
[6] Rhys, **CCLXXXII**, pp. 90–1 ; cf. Caes, vi, 17, 18.
[7] Joyce, op. cit.

a national hero in Ireland, completed the evolution of the
ancient religion of the nation.

VIII

FESTIVALS

The Irish tribes normally lived in a dispersed manner,
and the sanctuaries were also fair-grounds, without anything
implying permanent worship.   The population met at the
political and religious centre of the tribes, which was the
place where the tombs of its ancestors stood, and it did this
on feast-days.[1]

There were four chief feasts.   Samhain [2] (1st November)
marked the end of summer (*samos*) and probably the
beginning of the year.   Six months later, on the 1st May, at
the beginning of summer (*cèt-saman*), came Beltane, the
feast of the fire (*tein*) of Bel or Bile.[3]   Between these two,
at intervals of three months, there were the feasts of
Lugnassad,[4] the marriage of Lugh, which is the best described
of all, on the 1st August, and Oimelc or Imbolc, on the
1st February, which survived in the feast of St. Brigid.
Samhain was held chiefly at Tara,[5] Beltane at Uisnech,[6] and
Lugnassad at Tailtiu (these three towns were in the central
kingdom of Meath).   But Lugnassad was also celebrated at
Emain Macha in Ulster and at Carman in Leinster.[7]   These
four festivals divided the year into four seasons of three
months or eighty-five days, which seem to have been
subdivided by other feasts each into two periods of forty-
five days.   There is no record of these other feasts save in
those of certain great Irish saints, which sometimes fall
on the same dates—St. Finnian's in December and, above
all, St. Patrick's on the 15th, 16th, and 17th March.

These feasts stood in the very forefront of the life and
thoughts of the Irish.   We are always coming upon them

[1] Ibid., ii, pp. 389, 447–9.
[2] D'Arbois, op. cit. (Droit), i, p. 317.
[3] Ibid., p. 297 ; cf. Henderson, **CCCCXXXIII**, p. 187.
[4] Joyce, op. cit., ii, p. 441 ; Rhys, **VIII**.
[5] Joyce, ii, p. 436.
[6] D'Arbois, op. cit. (Droit), i, 302. Cf. Loth, " L'Omphalos chez les Celtes,"
in **CXXXIV**, 1915, p. 192.
[7] Rhys, **CCLXXXII**, p. 414 ; Loth, in *R.A.*, ii, 1914, p. 216 ;   *Metrical
Dindsenchas*, iii, 57 ; Joyce, op. cit., ii, p. 439 ; Rhys, **VIII**, pp. 17, 27, 55, 57.

in their tradition, which is very historical, and in their epic literature. Moreover, all legend or mythology revolves round the dates of festivals and a large number of the myths are festival-myths. These feasts were fairs, political or judicial assemblies, and also an occasion for amusement and games, some of which, such as the races, were of religious origin (the horse-races at Tailtiu and Emain Macha, the races of women at Carman). Above all, they were religious assemblies.

They were conducted in an atmosphere of myth and legend. The day of Beltane commemorated the landing of the first invaders of Ireland, the sons of Partholon ; the first fire, that of Uisnech, was lit by their latest successors. Later on, about the middle of the sixth century, in the plain of Uisnech, King Diarmait mac Cearbhail laid siege to the house of one Flann, who drowned himself in a vat while his house was burning ; the feast was a commemoration and expiation of his death.[1] At Lugnassad the wives of Lugh or his foster-mother Tailtiu died. Carman the sorceress, who came from Greece like the Fomorians, the people of the other world, also perished on this day, a captive of the Goidels, and in Conchobar's time the goddess Macha, who had beaten the King's horses at the races, died in giving birth to two children.[2] At Samhain the great battle of the gods was fought at Moytura, between the Fomorians and the Tuatha Dé Danann. On this day, too, King Muirchertach mac Erca, having broken the prohibitions laid on him by a fairy whom he had married, was attacked by the ghosts and while the fairy set fire to his palace drowned himself in a barrel like Flann.[3] Cuchulainn himself died on the first day of autumn. The times of the feasts were times when spirits were let loose and wonders were expected and normally happened.

In Wales the year was divided in the same way as in Ireland, at the Calends of May and of November. It was the same in Gaul ; in the Coligny Calendar we can distinguish

[1] D'Arbois, op. cit. (Droit), pp. 299 ff. Cf. Joyce, op. cit.
[2] Loth, in CXXXIX, ii, 1914, pp. 217, 220 ; Rhys, VIII, pp. 19, 55 ; CCLXXXII, p. 414.
[3] Rhys, CCLXXXII, p. 396. Cf. d'Arbois, op. cit. (Droit), i, p. 317 ; at the end of the feast these temporary sanctuaries were doubtless set on fire. This rite is recalled in the stories of Flann and Muirchertach.

the two great seasons Samonos and Giamonos.[1] The great solitary sanctuaries in the mountains, those of the Donon and the Puy-de-Dôme, show that similar festivals were held in Gaul at one period in its history. For a long time there were no permanent shrines in Gaul.

IX

HOW RELIGION DEVELOPED

Gaul had already advanced a long way, starting from the common Celtic stock.

Doubtless it already had temples, and many of them. In any case, Roman civilization covered it with religious buildings [2] But the native character of the Gallic temple is proved by the fact that among these temples of the Roman period some are of such a peculiar type that they can be explained only by the assumption of a Gallic inheritance. The Temple of Vesona at Périgueux and that of Janus at Autun have nothing in common with classical architecture. They have been compared to the little square *fana* surrounded by a peristyle which have been found in the Rhine valley and Normandy. We must picture two-storied buildings, with a roofed peristyle below (that is, the side-aisles) and a central roofed portion (or nave) rising above it.

Ancient writers who treat of the religion of the Celts always begin by giving the names of their gods. Lucan mentions a triad of Gallic gods, Teutates, Esus, and Taranis.[3] We know that the literatures of Ireland and Wales give the gods and heroes in threes. Cæsar gives us a valuable piece of information when he enumerates the gods of Gaul not under their Celtic names but under Roman names, Mercury, Apollo, Mars, Jupiter, and Minerva, to whom we must add Dispater, whom he mentions elsewhere. These are the very gods whom we find represented in the archæology of Roman Gaul by monuments of every sort, inscriptions, bronze statuettes, sculptures in stone. It appears to me that Cæsar set the seal on a process of identification which had

---

[1] Rhys, **VIII.**

[2] De Vesly, **CCCCLXXXIX** ; Wheeler, " A Romano-Celtic Temple near Harlow, and a note on the type," in **XVI,** 1928, p. 301.

[3] *Phars.*, i, 444.

already taken place to some extent in the mind of the Gauls. Moreover, the names of the Gallic gods survived in the form of epithets attached to their Latin names,[1] Mercurius Cissonius, Mars Camulus, Mars Caturix, etc. In any case, after the conquest there was a kind of classification of the deities in types, which were furnished by the Roman pantheon. Sometimes there has been doubt about the label; one same god may have become Mercury, Mars, and Dispater in turn. Also, the gods became vulgarized. Who would recognize the noble Lugh, the victor of Moytura, in the little Mercury with the heavy purse, or the god of the dead, the brewer of mystic beer, in the hammer-god, the genial, homely patron of the coopers, married to a peaceable, colourless Fortuna ? [2] These are commonplace, harmless figures, like modern village saints. In Gaul the hero was supplanted by the household genius, who assumed a classical appearance for which Rome supplied the type and the means of reproduction. The breaking-up of the politico-domestic groups and the formation of territorial groups in their place did away with the reason for the existence of the god-hero.

X

RITUAL

The Celtic religions were sacrificial religions, of the ritual of which we unfortunately know very little. There were blood-sacrifices and others, which were offerings of first-fruits. The ancient authors speak of human sacrifices among the Gauls, and massacres of prisoners which had a sacrificial character.[3] In Ireland there are very few allusions to human sacrifice ; one might mention the sacrifice of newborn infants to the idol Cromm Crúaich.[4] The ritual of Celtic sacrifice allowed the substitute-victim, as we see in the story of the goddess Becuma. She was married to a king of Ireland, and her ill-luck brought sterility upon the country. Expiation had to be made by the sacrifice of the young son of a virgin, but the sacrifice of a cow was accepted

---

[1] Toutain, in *Rev. hist. des. relig.*, lxxiv, 1916, p. 373.
[2] H. Hubert, " Une Nouvelle Figure de dieu au maillet," in **CXXXIX**, 1915, i, pp. 26–39.
[3] **CXXXIV**, 1913, p. 432 ; *R.P.*, 1908, p. 343 ; d'Arbois, i, 154 ; Joyce, op. cit., i, 239. Cf. Eriu, ii, 86 ; iii, 155.
[4] Squire, **CCCCLIX**, p. 38.

instead, and was effective.[1] There is reason for believing
that the blood-sacrifices for which the Celts have been
blamed were not so very bloody ; the victim was a divine
victim, who died transcendentally. When one reads the
long series of deaths of heroes commemorated by the festivals,
one cannot help thinking that these legends are derived
from myths of divine sacrifices renewed in the form of human,
animal, and vegetable victims. The stories of houses burnt
down and heroes burnt in their houses on feast-days belong to
the same order of facts. These sacrifices at feasts, which
appear also in other forms, such as games and races in which
the victor perishes and is the victim, were agrarian sacrifices,
the sole object of which was to maintain the life of nature
and to secure the fertility of the land.

Sacrifice was the foremost thing in Celtic religion. But
the power of the formula, the spell, even a mere poem
uttered by a man of power, a Druid or *file*, grew as time
went on. The wizard plays a particularly large part in the
religions of the Celts of the British Isles. Among the Britons,
Merlin and Taliesin are famous heroes. With them, religious
power becomes magic.

XI

REPRESENTATIONS OF THE GODS

Very few purely Celtic portraits of gods survive. A few
bronzes, some coins, and the Gundestrup cauldron in the
Copenhagen Museum give us some divine types—the horned
god, the god with the wheel, the god with the hammer, the
three-headed god, the ram-headed serpent, the matron
Epona, etc.

On the other hand, there are a good many sculptures
of the Gallo-Roman period representing the same gods and
some others, which have been identified with varying
success.

XII

MYTHOLOGY

The Celts had a rich and colourful mythology, much
better preserved among the Gaels and Welsh than in Gaul.

[1] Czarnowski, **CCCCXXIII**, p. 123.

It has come down to us in the form of epics built up out of materials which were the common stock of the professional reciters, local traditions of a more special interest which in Ireland make up the literature of the *Dinnshenchas*,[1] and the allusions made in the Welsh triads, which enumerate and classify gods or heroes. Almost all these elements are incorporated in cycles—the mythological cycle, the Cycle of Ulster, and the Cycle of Finn or the heroes of Leinster in Ireland and the mythological and Arthurian cycles in Wales. In these various cycles the story of divine families is unfolded—Fomorians and Tuatha Dé Danann in Ireland and the families of Pwyll, Don, and Beli in Wales. Many of these traditions relate the origin of the great festivals, and the number of variants shows that they were still living. A whole series of myths of origin are connected with holy places and feasts.[2]

One large group consists of stories of a voyage to the country of the blest or the dead. A hero—Bran, son of Febal, or Cuchulainn, or Connla, or Oisin—is drawn by a mysterious beauty. He puts out on a magic boat, often made of bronze. He meets Manannán, god of the sea and the dead, either on the way or on his arrival in a wonderful country, where he is welcomed with open arms. After staying there a while, he grows weary and wants to return. In the end he does so, only to die.[3] This type of story reappears in the Christian stories of the voyages of Maeldune [4] and St. Brendan [5] to marvellous islands.

A second type of story describes the descent of heroes underground ; for example, Conn goes into a *sidh* or mound at Tara and visits the god Lugh, in the *Champion's Prophecy*.[6] A similar adventure at Cruachain is related in a prologue to the *Táin* entitled the *Journey of Nera to the Other World*.[7]

A third series of stories is preserved in St. Patrick's accounts of Purgatory.[8]   The hero goes down into a cave,

---

[1] Gwynn, **CCLXI**.
[2] See below, ch. v.
[3] See, in particular, the admirable *Voyage of Bran*, **CCLXXIV**, edited and translated by Kuno Meyer, with commentaries by Nutt.
[4] D'Arbois and Loth, in **CCXLVIII**, vol. v, " L'Épopée celtique en Irlande," i, pp. 449–500.
[5] Ibid., Cf. Schirmer, **CCLXXXVI**, pp. 17–26.
[6] Squire, op. cit., p. 201. Cf. O. Curry, **CCLXXVIII**, app. cxxviii.
[7] Thurneysen, **CCLXXXIX**, pp. 311–17.
[8] De Felice, **CCCXXVII**.

which is a holy place, he falls asleep, and the pains of Purgatory are revealed to him. An initiation-myth probably underlies these legends.

Lastly, a fourth series tells of attacks on the other world, forays with the object of capturing wonderful things like the inexhaustible cauldron which Cuchulainn took twice. A similar cauldron is captured by Pwyll and Arthur in the Welsh legends[1]; Pwyll at the same time brings back the art of pig-breeding, and another family of gods, that of Gwyn fights him for his herd. Here we have myths of civilizing heroes who are at the same time agrarian gods and kings of the dead.

All these stories form part of a larger cycle which might be called that of myths of death, in which the very origin of the race is connected with the world of the dead by a perpetual process of exchanges between that world and the world of the living.

All this Celtic mythology is a heroic mythology. The Celts made their gods into heroes and the typical ancestors of their clans and families. In the lives of these heroes they represented the state of their people and the essence of their religious traditions. Whatever certain modern scholars who have applied their analytical methods to the Arthurian cycle may think,[2] that cycle has its roots in the same circumstances and tradition as the other heroic cycles of the Celtic world. Arthur has the same adventures and his companions perform the same feats and carry out the same quests as Finn and his Fianna and the other Celtic heroes. So through the heroes the tradition of the Celtic gods has been kept alive and handed down.

[1] For Pwyll, see Loth, **CCLXX**, i, pp. 81–117. Cf. ibid., p. 307, and for the magic cauldron, Squire, op. cit., p. 273. I am of opinion that these legends may contain the Celtic prototype of the stories of the quest of the Grail.

[2] Particularly Bruce, Faral, and Wilmotte, in the works quoted. Cf. below, p. 266.

CHAPTER IV

The Setting of Social Life

CELTIC societies lived in a setting which they had in part made themselves—time, space, and number.

I

SPACE : FIELDS, DWELLINGS, AND DISTRIBUTION OF THE POPULATION

We can get an idea of the space, the landscape in which our Celtic societies moved, if we interpret the features presented by the same regions to-day. Gaul had none of the long curtains of poplars which give such unity to the aspect of modern France. But the look of a cultivated country—and the Celtic lands were cultivated—is chiefly due to the shape of the fields, which in its turn is due to the conception of the ownership of land. The law is written down on the soil. The Celts of both Ireland and Gaul had a system of land-measurement.[1] The French still have the Gallic *arpent* (*arepennum*) and the Gallic league (*leuga*) [2] ; the servants of the Roman Fiscus who made the survey took over the Gaulish names. In France there are still two types of field, the closed field and the long, open field. The first type makes a landscape of hedges, the second a landscape of plains or hillsides whose unbroken surface is patched with variously coloured strips of crop. As we have already seen, the first type is found in Ireland, Wales, England, Brittany, Vendée, Western France, and part of North-Western Germany ; the second predominates north of the Seine to the Rhine. The first corresponds to family groups settled in isolation and to family property, the second to village communities working common property under common rules, particularly as regards fallow, with possible partitions. Both systems existed among the Celts. The

---

[1] Jullian, **CCCXLVII**, ii, 394 ; iv, 283.
[2] **CXXXIX**, 1914, ii, p. 137, on the Gallic league.

first covers a region corresponding to their earliest settlements in Gaul and the British Isles, the second to their later settlements in Gaul and their settlements on the Rhine.

Traces of prehistoric cultivation have been found in the forests round the Hallstatt settlements. These consist of parallel depressions, which were once fields with raised edges like garden beds, probably worked with the mattock or hoe. German archæologists call them *Hochäcker*, " high fields." [1] In general cultivation moved downwards towards the plains, encroaching on the swamp and swampy forest. Clearing extended in the valleys, and the forest gained ground on the heights. But the general aspect has changed little since Cæsar's time. The Gallic population, as described by Polybios,[2] lived dispersed about the cultivated land, being particularly scattered in districts where the park system obtained and everywhere in the grazing season. Some French villages, which get their names from estates (*fundi*), have their origin in Gallo-Roman villas ; and so we must imagine the Gallic village as a small collection of huts in which the remoter relations or servants of a great man lived round his house ; that was what a villa was.[3] There were quite large rural communities in Gaul, to judge from the size of their cemeteries.[4]

As well as these open settlements, the Celts had fortified settlements. Ireland bristled with little forts built on hills, called raths or duns, to which the names of the heroic families of the epics were attached. As we have seen, these were private strongholds, and they were also refuges.[5] In the plains in which the assemblies of Ireland were held the raths were occupied only temporarily. But in Gaul, a more highly developed country, they tended to be used as permanent abodes. At Gergovia the Arvernian nobility had their residences just as the later French provincial nobles had their mansions in the towns in which their interests lay.[6] In Gaul the town grew up round the *oppidum*, and even

---

[1] Weber, "Neue Beobachtungen zur Alterfrage der Hochäcker," in **LXXXIII**, xxix, 1908, p. 17. Cf. id., " Das Verhalten der Hochäcker," in **XX**, 1906 ; **CXXXI**, xxvii ; *Pr. Z.*, 1911, p. 189.

[2] See above, p. 210.

[3] **LXXX**, 1911, p. 118.

[4] D'Arbois, **CCXCIX**, p. 96.

[5] **LXXX**, loc. cit.

[6] Jullian, **CCCXLVII**, ii, p. 62.

had its suburbs. In theory, the Gallic *oppidum* was the capital of a *civitas* or a *pagus*[1]; but some *oppida* continued to be strongholds. An *oppidum* usually stood on an isolated height with a distant view, and sometimes (e.g. Lutetia and Melun) on an easily-defended island. In their demand for security, at the end of the La Tène period the Celts revived the tradition of building palafittes ; an example is the lake-village of Glastonbury, where much excavation has been done.[2] These were sometimes built on piles and sometimes on an artificial island consisting of a timber framework filled with stones.

Apart from some stone houses of Roman type excavated at Mont Beuvray, town and country buildings were usually made of wood and roofed with thatch.[3] There were round huts and rectangular houses. In the first century B.C. the timbers were nailed together and the walls of woven branches were coated with clay. A farm was a group of huts rather than one big house. The Celts stored their provisions in silos, which developed into cellars of masonry. At the same time they erected drystone buildings, of which there are many specimens in Ireland and Scotland ; they had walls composed of two faces filled with rubble, and roofs consisting of false vaults. In this way they built small round huts like bee-hives, rectangular chapels, galleries, and guardrooms in the Irish duns, and in Scotland they erected brochs. These brochs were round towers with a central court, with stairs and vaulted galleries and chambers in the thickness of the wall.[4]

The sites of these settlements were determined by the crossings of roads. Peoples established themselves along a river, and when they had done so they made arrangements together for free transit or the collection of tolls, as the Senones did with the Parisii and Ædui.[5] Forts were placed

---

[1] D'Arbois, **CCCXLVII** (Propr.). Cf. **CIX**, 1910, p. 723 ; **CXXIV**, 1912, p. 205 ; and, for the excavation of Sos, an *oppidum* in Lot-et-Garonne, **CXXXIV**, 1913. Cf. Thompson, **CCCCLXI** ; **CCCLXXXIV**, p. 122 ; Philipon, " Le Gaulois Duros," in **CXL**, 1909, p. 73 ; Dottin, **CCCXXII**, p. 332.

[2] **CXXXIV**, 1912. Cf. " The Glastonbury Lake-village ", in *Gl. Antiquarian Society*, 1911 ; Déchelette, iii, pp. 974–7.

[3] Joyce, **CCCCXXXIV**, ii, p. 65 ; Caes, v, 43, and viii, 5. Cf. Macleod, " Further Notes on the Antiquities of Skye," in **CXXIV**, xlvi, 1911–12, p. 202.

[4] E. Sloat, " Some Shetland Brochs," ibid., p. 94.

[5] Strabo, iv, 3, 5, ; 1, 14. Cf. Jullian, **CCCXLVII**, ii, p. 223.

on peninsulas. Natural roads, some of which were international routes, like the tin route, received very little
engineering.[1] There were fords, bridges, and ports to which
tracks ran, and these tracks were raised on causeways in
swampy parts.[2] So life developed in the Celtic communities
on the chess-board of the land-survey, along ways of communication which formed the veins and nerves of the settlements.[3]

II

TIME AND NUMBER

The movements of this life were set in the year, divided
up by seasonal occupations, assembly-days, and the cycle
of the months. The Coligny Calendar shows that on the top
of the calendar of the seasons, which seems to have been
the popular calendar of Northern Europe, the Celts had
superposed a calendar which was at first purely lunar and
was afterwards brought into agreement with the course of
the sun by means of intercalations. The months continued
to be lunations, but not of a strict kind. The interior of the
month seems to have been arranged on another principle,
that by which the year is divided into half-years and the
season into half-seasons. The Celts adopted the fortnight,
and it has survived in the British Isles and in France. They
divided the month into two halves, originally marked
roughly by the full moon. In the Coligny Calendar the
second half is called *atenoux* (perhaps cf. Irish *athnugud*,
renewal). The Irish expression " the three fortnights "
shows for one thing that the fortnight is a unit and
for another that the system of half-seasons of forty-five
days was maintained side by side with the system of
months.

The Celts reckoned time by moons and nights. It seems,
too, that the Irish year began with its dark half, at the feast
of Samhain (1st November). The Coligny Calendar would
seem to indicate that the year began between May and June.
But it is known that all over Northern Europe the beginning

[1] Jullian, op. cit., iii, p. 17. Cf. Caes., ii, 5, 6.
[2] **CIX**, 1911, pp. 55–6.
[3] Polyb., iii, 42, 2 ; Strabo, iv, 1, 11. Cf. Jullian, op. cit., ii, p. 228 ;
Joyce, op. cit., ii, pp. 393, 399.

of the year wavered between the spring festival and that of harvest.

In general, all reckoning in social life, all repetition and division, was governed by a numerical law and favourite numbers—periods of three and of nine nights, cycles of three and of seven years, and divisions into two, three, twelve and, above all, four.

CHAPTER V

SOCIAL ACTIVITIES

THIS is not the place to reproduce the picture of the social life of the Celts which has already been drawn for two Celtic peoples by M. Jullian in the third volume of his *Histoire des Gaules* and by Mr. Joyce in his admirable *Social History of Ancient Ireland*. We have not to describe, but to bring out, the essential features which give Celtic societies their pecular character, to show how far they had progressed when their independent evolution was arrested, and in particular to determine the native characteristics of their economic and industrial activity.

Some of these activities, namely law and religion, I have described in speaking of the structure of society. Another, warfare, we have considered in dealing with the history of the Celts. The Celts were fond of fighting, and war held a very great place in their social life. Peace was precarious, and was disturbed by feuds and rivalries, between families and inside them. Here we have to speak of economic and industrial activity.

I

ECONOMIC LIFE

The Coins of Gaul [1]

Before making regular use of coin struck in the Greek fashion the Celtic peoples tried various kinds of money. In Cæsar's time [2] the Britons still used bars or rings of copper or silver of a determined weight. A good deal of iron currency has been found, in hoards or scattered about, in the shape of bars weighing multiples of a pound of 309 grammes (11 oz.) with an average weight of a mina of 618 grammes (22 oz.).[3]

---

[1] For Gallic coinage in general, see Blanchet, **CCCVI** ; Forrer, **DXLIII** ; Déchelette, ii, 3, pp. 1557 ff.

[2] Caes., v, 12 ; iii, 21.

[3] Déchelette, ii, 3, p. 1558, fig. 720.

Déchelette held that he had proved that the Gauls used a currency of spits,[1] as the Greeks did at one time.

Coined money did not come into use among the Celts before the third century B.C. From then onwards they were amply furnished with coins of Greek origin, and they copied them extensively for their own use. The Celts of the Danube and the East copied the tetradrachms and silver staters of Tarsos, Thasos, Byzantion, the Pæonian ruling houses, and, above all, the Kings of Macedonia. Those of the West imitated the drachmæ of Marseilles, Rhoda, and Emporion. A gold coinage also appeared, based chiefly on the famous " Philips ", which came through Marseilles and were copied as far as Britain, while staters of Alexander reached Celtic lands by way of Raetia. Roman models furnished new types, and gold and silver were supplemented at an early date, but always on the same models, by a very abundant and plentiful coinage of bronze or tin.

The Celts copied not only the types but also the sizes and weights of their models. In general, silver coins were based on the tetradrachm in the East and on the drachma in the West, and gold coins on the gold stater. So Gallic coinage is an extension of Greek coinage. It is indeed a counterfeit of it in every respect. Execution, weight, and quality of the metal deteriorated, and depreciation took place so fast that it is obvious that there was no regular control of issues. It is very possible that the right of striking coin was not reserved by the state ; yet peoples certainly seem to have exercised this right. Certain late coins of the Meldi, Mediomatrici, and Lexovii bear the word *Arcantodan*, which must designate some mint official.[2]

Meanwhile, either because coin was still rare or because its bad quality made it unpopular, the old way of reckoning values did not go out completely. We find the connection between *pecunia* and *pecus* reappearing in Low Breton, where *saout* " cow " comes from *soldus*,[3] although the relationship is here reversed and it is the coin which has given its name to the animal used as a standard of value. The trade which we may suppose to have taken place between Gaul and Ireland did not bring coinage into the latter country.

---

[1] Id., in **CXLIII**, 1911, pp. 1 ff.   [2] Loth, in **CXXXIV**, 1919, p. 263.
[3] Id., in **CXXXIV**, 1916, p. 281.

No stamped coins are found there before the seventh century, and the name by which they are called, *pinginn*, is of Anglo-Saxon origin.[1] For money there were " standard values "— gold pins weighing an ounce (*briar*), gold rings or necklaces, open rings (now often called *fibulæ*), also having a determined weight and being used as ingots. But in the practice of law and probably of trade, prices were reckoned in cattle or slaves.

It must have been the same in Gaul, although there was coin in the country. For coin ceases to exist in trade as soon as the standard and weight have to be checked every time, and it is evident that the Gallic financier must often have had his scales in his hand.[2] Yet money circulated actively. The spread of types in Gallic copies is a proof of this ; but the composition of treasures, in which four-fifths are local types, shows that they were used only to a limited extent in payments between one district and another.[3] It is also unlikely that the bad coinage of the Celts was ever used for settling commercial accounts between Celtic and foreign countries.[4] But the only exchanges of money between Celts and non-Celts of which we hear are the payment of mercenaries and political subsidies ; and certain Gallic issues known to us, coins of Vercingetorix, of the league against Ariovistus or the Helvetii, were definitely struck for political purposes.

Even though confined to these services, money had, and from the very beginning, a place in general economic life, by the mere fact of its accumulation. It certainly did not constitute capital, though it was the best measure of it, but it was the instrument of the formation of the movable capital which is in part made of credit, of belief in a power. In all phases of its history, money has been a sign of power, of which its purchasing capacity is only one manifestation. If Gaul fairly quickly became a country of movable capital after the conquest, it was because the development which

[1] Joyce, **CCCCXXXIV**, ii, p. 381. Cf. Ridgeway, *The Origin of Metallic Currency and Weight Standards*, 1892.

[2] Scales from Beuvray and Gergovia. Déchelette, ii, 3, p. 1573, n. 2.

[3] Forrer, op. cit. (list giving provenance of Celtic coins). This list indicates that some of the purchases made by Mediterranean merchants among the Celts were paid for in Greek coin, and that the native middlemen paid gold for the goods which they were commissioned to buy from those merchants.

[4] Blanchet, op. cit., ii, p. 517.

at once took form under the Roman Empire had begun in the days of independence.

One must not picture the Celtic societies as groups of specialized warriors leaving their wives to look after the cattle and the crops with the aid of captives. In Ireland the king was forbidden to touch the plough or oversee his byres ; but that was only because he was the king. All other men took their share in the work of their farms ; only the king had to stand aloof. So the economic life of the Celts was chiefly rural [1]—mainly pastoral in Ireland, part of Britain, and Spain, and mainly agricultural among the Gauls and Belgæ. It is probable that agriculture began to gain ground in the Hallstatt period. The Celts practised fallow and invented the great two-wheeled plough, drawn by several span of oxen (Pliny calls it *ploum*), which made it possible to work heavy land.[2]

Rural activities aimed at the market [3] and were not confined to production. Exchange and sale were the object as well as exploitation of the soil. Gallic bacon filled the pickle-tubs of Italy in the time of Cato, and in the days of Cæsar and Varro Gaul was famous for its hams. The rapid development of the culture of the vine and olive in Provence shows that Gallic agriculture could adapt itself to the requirements of an international market.[4] Once wine-growing was introduced in Gaul, Gallic wine travelled to Britain and Ireland. The organs of rural trade were the markets and fairs.[5]

This development of marketing introduced into Celtic society specialists in trade and in industry [6] ; it was the development in trade which gave birth to industry. The Celts of the Bronze Age had already advanced beyond the stage of household economy. A Celtic household made part of its material and repaired its tools, but it bought them outside. And Celtic artisans had spread in foreign countries, like the smith Elico, who was established in Rome and summoned Brennus.[7] With the rise of town life, professional crafts increased at the expense of household

---

[1] See the evidence of Pytheas in Diod., v, 21.
[2] Pliny, 18, p. 172, Roth's ed., p. 288.
[3] Jullian, **CCCXLVII**, ii, p. 239.
[4] Pliny, x, 53 ; xix, 8 ; xi, 240.   [5] Caes, iv, 2, 1.
[6] Jullian, op. cit., ii, p. 237.   Cf. Strabo, iv, 2, 1.   [7] Pliny, xii, 5.

industry, and the town population was formed of the waste material of the tribal organization. Among this material there were slaves, who were a large part of the industrial labouring class. But there were also free workers who hired themselves out. Strabo, following Poseidonios, tells us of a man at Marseilles who hired out men and women for navvy work.[1] In Gaul the crafts were chiefly pursued by free workers, masters and men. In Ireland the craftsmen formed groups [2] which aspired to imitate the college of *fili*. A large part of society, perhaps the greater part of that amorphous plebs of which Cæsar speaks, became reconstituted on the basis of the crafts. Economic life had become an organizing principle for Celtic society.

The state then stepped into the organization of trade and industry, by means of taxes and tolls and by creating markets and policing them. The holding of the great fairs necessitated truces. Here we see the outlines of a market-law which must have been fairly complex.

We know little about the internal trade of the Celtic world before the Middle Ages,[3] when we have definite evidence of the commercial relations connecting Ireland with a no longer Celtic Gaul. On the other hand, the trade of Gaul with the Mediterranean countries is attested by many discoveries of Greek or Italian objects in Celtic tombs or settlements.[4] Déchelette gives a list of these objects, gold wreaths, mirrors, bronze hydriæ, and cups of painted ware. The Greek, Italian, or Gallic traders went up the Rhone and its tributaries, bringing, in particular, amphoræ of wine and other requisites of the drinker to the fairs of Franche-Comté, Burgundy, and the Rhineland. The Celts appreciated wine.[5] They paid for their purchases with a great variety of articles, such as textiles, particularly woollen garments. We know, too, of the trade and traffic in British tin, which was landed at the mouth of the Loire and taken by a portage to the valley of the Rhone.[6] Slaves, too, were doubtless offered by the Celts in payment for goods.[7]

[1] Strabo, iii, 4, 7.
[2] MacNeill, **CCCCXLI**, pp. 75, 82.
[3] Zimmer, in **CXLVIII**, 1909, pp. 363–400. Cf. Tac., *Agr.*, 24.
[4] See *Rise*, pp. 162–4.
[5] Müllenhoff, ii, p. 137 ; Jullian, op. cit., ii, p. 225 ; Caes, xi, 22, 3.
[6] Lloyd, **CCCCXXXVIII**, p. 41.
[7] Diod., v, 26.

The Celtic countries were also rich in gold [1] ; the Helvetii had an established reputation in this respect.[2] The gold which the Celts gave in exchange was not money, but it did the work of money.

II

CRAFTS

The literatures of the Celts give a lively picture of their industrial activity. The Mabinogi of Manawyddan, son of Llyr,[3] is particularly rich in information about the trades plied in towns and villages. Manawyddan, a sea-god, and Pryderi, son of Pwyll, the sole survivors of a massacre of gods, fled into Dyfed, but one day the country was turned by enchantment into a wilderness, and they were compelled to leave it. They then settled at Hereford, where they opened a saddlery and did so well that they took all the custom from the saddlers of the town. The latter plotted to kill them, and the two heroes went off to seek their fortune elsewhere. They established themselves as shield-makers and the same thing happened again. In a third town they started as cordwainers and joined a goldsmith, whose trade Manawyddan learned, but once again they had to fly. The Celtic mythologies tell of other working gods,[4] and people who own or make marvellous tools.[5] In religion these great artisans are the protectors of the crafts, which are grouped in guilds like those of the Middle Ages, equally exclusive and unfriendly to outsiders.[6]

Manawyddan learned the trades of goldsmith and cordwainer in the course of his wanderings, Now, enamelling and leather-work were just the arts in which the Celts excelled, and the former is perhaps the best-known of all the industries

---

[1] Déchelette, ii, 3, p. 1207.

[2] Strabo, iv, 3, 3 ; vii, 2, 2.

[3] Loth, **CCLXX**, i, pp. 151, 599.

[4] Thus Goibniu, the smith or cooper, became one of the most popular figures in Irish folklore, the Gobhan Saer, the all-round craftsman.

[5] Cf. the Welsh romance *Kulhwch and Olwen*. Loth, op. cit., i, pp. 243, 599.

[6] In the *Mabinogion* these heroes live in the midst of craftsmen. But the state of society described in this work is not that of the Middle Ages ; it takes us back to the time of the Roman conquest of Britain. For instance, Manawyddan adorns the metal parts of the saddles which he makes with blue enamel (Loth, op. cit., p. 46) which is the Celtic enamel of Britain rather than French enamel of the twelfth century.

of Gaul.[1] At Mont Beuvray [2] enamellers and blacksmiths
had their workshops in humble buildings of drystone with
thatched roofs. But if their premises were wretched, their
stock of tools was quite good. They seem to have specialized
in the manufacture of buttons of enamelled bronze,[3] which
must have had a respectable market and been sold largely
at the fairs of Bibracte.

In the mining areas we find industrial establishments
of another kind, isolated but grouped in districts. These
were the ironworks, which were fortified workshops, with
their heaps of slag.[4]

The manufacture and decoration of metal articles seem
to have been practised industrially. The story of Elico the
Helvetian [5] shows that at an early date they had a reputation
as past-masters. They exported pigs of raw iron to
Germany.[6] For the treatment of ore [7] and the preparation
of the various qualities of the metal they seem to have had
processes as scientific and highly developed as those of the
other metal-workers of antiquity. Irish literature contains
magnificent descriptions of the arms of its warriors,[8] and
excavations have yielded specimens which reveal extraordinary
skill and taste—the helmets of Amfreville, La Gorge-Meillet,
and Berru, and the Battersea and Thames shields.[9] Every
technical method which can be used for the decoration of
metal—gilding, enamelling, engraving with the point and with
acid [10]—was employed by the Celts. These processes, which
a god like Manawyddan could learn in no time, imply professional
training and trade traditions in mere mortals.

Leather-work seems to have been another craft which
appealed to the Celtic imagination, since the gods excelled
in it. The Gallic shoemakers who made the *caliga* or Celtic

---

[1] Déchelette, ii, 3, pp. 1547 ff.   [2] Bulliot, **CCCLXIX**.
[3] Buttons were a part of Gallic costume. One type of blouse in use was
buttoned down the front from top to bottom ; and, since the sleeves are
represented as open, these too were probably buttoned. Cf. a relief from
Dijon ; Espérandieu, **CCCXV**, 3473, 3475.
[4] These settlements have not yet been studied except in the valleys
running into the lower Loire (L. Maitre, in **CXXXIX**, i, 1919, pp. 234 ff. ; cf.
id. in *B.A.C.*, 1905, p. xliv).
[5] Pliny, xii, 11.   [6] Kossinna, in **LXXXV**, 1915, p. 117.
[7] Refining-furnace.   Bushe-Fox, **CCCVIII**, p. 72.   Déchelette, ii, 3,
pp. 1539 ff.
[8] *Táin*, ed. Windisch, p. 17.
[9] See *Rise*, p. 95, fig. 4 ; p. 125, fig. 31.
[10] Déchelette, ii, 3, p. 1148.

boot fashionable in the Roman world [1] were doubtless better than others. The goods produced by the weavers were equally in demand, but we do not yet know what was the nature of the woollens and linens which the Gauls sold to Italy.[2]

By the side of these industries of metal, leather, wool, and linen, we must allow a large place to the manufacture of metal vessels and coopering in estimating the position of the Celtic crafts in ancient industry as a whole. The Gauls were not only expert horsemen, keenly interested in the harness and trappings of their mounts [3]; they contributed more than any other people in Europe to the use of the horse as a draught-animal. They invented a war-chariot, the *essedum*,[4] and their various types of vehicle, the *carpentum* or heavy travelling-waggon, the *rheda*, and the *cissum* or two-wheeled gig were adopted, name and all, by the Latins. Of all these vehicles nothing remains but some representations [5] and great quantities of ironwork,[6] the complexity of which bears witness to great inventiveness.

The Gallic coopers, of whom we have some complete barrels, and the makers of wooden utensils, who have left only a few fragments, plied trades which had thriven from the earliest times in the countries of Northern Europe, where men had abundant raw material at their disposal and could study it and choose it according to its qualities. The share of the Celts in the progress of these industries is attested by the name of the *tun*, which seems to have been taken from the Celtic languages.[7]

Inventors in coopering, coach-building, and enamel-work, the Celts were also inventors in the manufacture of various tools, the more complicated of which are unknown to us.[8] They introduced some new agricultural implements—

---

[1] Jullian, op. cit., ii.

[2] Textiles of the Cadurci ; Jullian, op. cit., ii, pp. 272, 525, n. 5.

[3] Bits peculiar to the Celts ; Arr., *Ind.*, 16, 10 ; Hor., *Odes*, i, 8, 6. Cf. Déchelette, ii, 3, pp. 1199–202.

[4] Jullian, op. cit., ii, pp. 187, 234.

[5] Expérandieu, op. cit.

[6] Déchelette, ii, 3, pp. 1197–9.

[7] *Tunna* (Low Lat.).   MacBain, **CLXXXIX**, p. 382.   Barrels of the Roman period found in Holland (**CXXXIX**, 1918, p. 249).

[8] E.g. the *terebra Gallica*, an auger with a spiral bit (Pliny, xvii, 15). The great quantity of tools found in tombs and *oppida* bears witness to the skill of the Gallic metal-worker (cf. Déchelette, ii, 3, pp. 1352 ff.).

the large hay-sickle, types of harrow, the great plough, and even a reaper.[1] We must not forget the riddle in cooperage nor the coat of mail in metal-work.[2] So the Celts not only practised most of the industrial arts of the ancients with skill but brought to them an originality and inventiveness which can be explained only by the great place held by industry in social life, whether through the needs which it had to meet or through the quality of the men engaged in it.

III

ART

On the whole the art of the Celts is entirely decorative.[3] The kind of decoration which the Celtic artist put on his works usually has no meaning, except in some objects used for religious purposes. We find neither representations nor symbols. Ornament generally consists of geometrical patterns without ritual significance, stylized foliage, scrolls, and the like. Except in a few religious objects like the Gundestrup cauldron and the gods of Bouray and Stuttgart, art has added nothing but beauty. The Celts made works of art in almost every class of manufactured article, even the humblest brooch, for example. The plainest sword had a handsome chape ; shields, helmets, and vases were decorated. The Celtic craftsman liked beauty, and he had taste. He was particularly drawn to curvilinear decoration, the elements of which he took from the Greek palmette.

In their decoration the Celts broke up the model selected and conventionalized it. The artists of Gaul and Ireland were not given to realism.[4] On the stela of Entremont, on which, of all the monuments of independent Gaul, human and animal forms are treated with the most freedom (and that under Greek influence), the horsemen are framed in a decorative scroll. The outer figures of the Gundestrup cauldron are treated as pure decoration. Celtic art went in for broad planes in relief, maintaining a right balance between broad and delicate features in decoration and a right

---

[1] Four-wheeled plough (Pliny, xviii, 48) ; reaper (ibid., 72) ; harrow (Jullian, op. cit., ii, p. 276).
[2] Sieve (Jullian, op. cit., p. 277) ; coat of mail (Déchelette, ii, 3, p. 1155).
[3] Cf. Allen, **CCXCVIII** ; Verworn, **CCCLXXXIX**.
[4] **CXL**, 1911, p. 245.

balance between the field and the ornament standing against
it. In Roman Gaul, human figures of the Roman type were
cast in bronze or carved in stone ; it was an art full of homely
geniality and facility. The Celts were always addicted to
fine weapons, beautiful jewellery, and rich, brightly-coloured
garments. The decorative art of the Celts is art of good
quality, but not a strong art. The Celtic genius was to
expand more in another form of æsthetic activity—literature.

IV

LITERATURE

It is very difficult to obtain an idea of Celtic literature
as a whole, for what remains of it comes entirely from the
British Isles. Literature so much depends on changing tastes
and fashions that it would be very rash to try to picture
one literature from what one knows of another some hundreds
of years later, even though it belongs to a people of the same
stock.

First, we are faced with a complete absence of any
definite information about the literature of the Continental
Gauls. They were great talkers, and interested in things
of the mind.[1] Men like Deiotarus and Diviciacus impressed
Roman intellectuals by their culture. The Druids had a
reputation as philosophers. Gauls like Vercingetorix displayed
a broad and elevated intelligence in the political domain.
Lastly, when Gaul was Romanized it at once produced such
a crop of teachers, great advocates, and distinguished
administrators that we must suppose that the people was
already prepared. It had had the literature of its *vates*, epic
traditions such as the story of Ambicatus which Livy has
transmitted to us ; this fragment of a history of the begin-
nings of the race must have been something corresponding
to the histories of origins incorporated in the *Leabhar Gabhála*.[2]
But these were the traditions of a society, and, as we have
seen, that society was disappearing when the Roman conquest intervened. Gallic society was already divided into
two parts, a nobility which was above tradition and a popular

[1] Diod., v, 31, 1. Cf. Jullian, op. cit., ii, p. 360.
[2] See d'Arbois, **CCL.**

class which was beneath it. This revolution hastened the neglect and loss of the national tradition.

Ireland, too, underwent a rather similar development. By the seventh century its ancient literature was becoming forgotten, being perhaps discredited or superseded by Christianity. The great ecclesiastical histories and, above all, the stories of the saints offered the newly converted Irish novel and attractive matter. But an effort was made to save tradition. This was done chiefly by the corporation of *fili*, who were interested in the preservation of the old tales. Their chief, Senchan Torpeist, who lived in the time of Guaire Aidne, King of Connacht (died 659), endeavoured to collect the fragments of the *Táin*.[1] The difficulty of the undertaking is shown by the legend that his son Muirgen had to call up the soul of the hero Fergus from the dead.[2] But tradition, once revived, was not lost again, and Christianity, which had made an alliance with the *fili*, kept it up.

The Britons had thrown all their literary traditions overboard and become Romanized. Only scraps of the Mabinogion, which form the oldest part of Welsh tradition, can be older than the Irish conquest of the west coast of Britain, and they contain a mass of Irish traditions. The rest of the tradition, which centres on Arthur, dates from the Saxon conquest, if it is true that Arthur was a historical personage who developed into a national hero. It is true that this new cycle of traditions contains some remains of an older tradition in the form of allusions, isolated names, and mythical subjects. But here Celtic tradition was saved by the conquerors, especially the Normans, who by adopting the history of the hero of the conquered in this way caused it to pass into literature.[3] The Welsh reconstructed their literature, the Irish rediscovered theirs, but that of the Gauls is lost. We lack the essential portion, and the most ancient.

We meet a second blank in regard to what may be called dramatic literature. Festivals in Gaul must have included dramatic performances, as is shown by the erection of a great number of theatres and arenas in the country in the very first years of the Empire. Some stood at places which

---

[1] Thurneysen, **CCLXXXIX**.   [2] See above, pt. iii, ch. i.
[3] Cf. Rhys, **CCLXXXI**.

were the scene of great pilgrimages, such as Saint Cybard of Aixe and Champlieu ; others were too large for the towns by which they stood and can only have been filled by crowds drawn from outside by the games.

It is certain, too, that the Irish feasts comprised dramatic representations, since they comprised games which are a kind of drama. Legends of heroes were attached to them and commemorated. But of these performances we have not the barest scenario. It is a whole side of the creative activity of the Celts of which we know nothing.

Let us, then, be content with what we have, namely, the written literature of Ireland and Wales. This literature, particularly that of Ireland, although it cannot have assumed its written form earlier than the seventh century, contains ancient elements which are often hard to understand. It may be able to give us an idea of its own past.[1]

It is composed mainly of *chansons de geste* in prose mixed with verse on epic and mythological subjects. In Ireland they are classified and catalogued under titles which describe them by class. There were Takings of Cities or Houses, Feasts (like that of Briccriu), and series of Battles (*Cath Muighe Tured*), Wooings (*Tochmarc Emire, Tochmarc Etaine*), Forays (*Táin*), Rapes (such as the story of Grainne), and Journeys to the Other World (like the *Journey of Bran*). These stories were arranged in three cycles, a Mythological Cycle and the two heroic cycles of Ulster and Leinster.[2]

The Mythological Cycle is the history of the successive gods and invasions of Ireland. The versions which have come down to us have undergone many transformations. One of them is the *Leabhar Gabhála*, the Book of Invasions, in which a great many narratives are linked together ; it was recast by O'Clery as late as 1631.[3]

The Ulster Cycle is that which has Cuchulainn and King Conchobar for its principal heroes. The chief epic in the cycle is the *Táin Bó Chuailgné*, which is over six thousand lines

---

[1] See. O'Curry, **CCLXXVIII** ; d'Arbois, **CCXLVIII**, and esp. **CCXLIX** ; Best, **CCLII** ; K. Meyer, " Addenda to the *Essai d'un catalogue de la littérature épique de l'Irlande*," in **CXL** ; D. Hyde, *Story of Early Gaelic Literature*, Dublin, 1920.

[2] Squire, **CCCCLIX** ; Hyde, **CCLXIV**. Cf. K. Meyer, " The Death-tales of the Ulster Heroes," in **CXXII**, xiv ; d'Arbois, op. cit.

[3] Squire, op. cit., pp. 61–135 ; d'Arbois, op. cit., ii, p. 155 ; Rhys, **CCLXXXII**, p. 146.

long. It tells of a great war waged upon the heroes of Ulster by the rest of Ireland, led by Queen Medb, for the sake of a wonderful bull. Many famous passages which have come down to us separately are connected with this central theme, such as the stories of the birth of Conchobar, the conception of Cuchulainn, his sickness, his love of the goddess Fand, and the intoxication of the Ultonians, which compelled Cuchulainn to defend Ulster single-handed for several days. That is the most ancient part of this epic literature. But the whole cycle was modernized by the men who recast it, just as the annalists place King Conchobar about the beginning of the Christian era.[1]

The Leinster Cycle is known as the Fenian or Ossianic Cycle. It tells of Finn, his son Oisin or Ossian, and their kinsmen and comrades, the Fianna. It is represented in the ancient manuscripts by a not very large number of complete stories, and there are allusions and lists of subjects for recitation which show that its main elements were in existence about the seventh century. The annalists place Finn in 200 B.C. These datings, done long afterwards, are of no great importance, but the cycle in its original form seems to correspond to a state of civilization and society obtaining about that time. It developed later than the Ulster Cycle, but lived on in the folklore of Ireland and Gælic Scotland. Its origins are very ancient. Finn is probably a hunter-god, particularly a hunter of the boar, like the typical Celtic hero. He is designated by the epithet Fair-haired, springs from the family of the gods of death, and is the same as the Welsh Gwyn. This cycle never attained the cohesion of the Ulster cycle,[2] although it was

---

[1] The chief texts regarding Ulster are collected in Windisch, **CCXCV**. A translation of the more important ones will be found in d'Arbois, **CCXLVIII**, v, " L'Épopée celtique en Irlande." For the Ulster cycle, see Hull, **CCLXIII** ; Thurneysen, **CCXC** ; Nutt, **CCLXXVI** ; Lady Gregory, **CCLIX** ; Faraday, **CCLVIII** ; Windisch, **CCXCVI** ; E. MacNeill, " Relation of the Ulster Epics to History," in **CXI**, Feb., 1907 ; Joseph Dunn, *The Ancient Irish Epic Tale Tain Bo Cuailnge*, London, 1914 ; and above all Thurneysen's admirable work **CCLXXXIX**, which deals with the constitution, text, and interpretation of the whole cycle.

[2] The chief ancient texts of this cycle will be found dated and in part translated in K. Meyer's excellent *Fianaigecht*, in **CXII**, xvi, 1910. Many texts, usually later, are collected and translated by O'Grady in **CCLXXIX**. Lastly, a large number of valuable texts have been published, often somewhat hastily and from late versions, in the six volumes of **CCXCII**. Mr. MacNeill has edited, with an important introduction, a collection of poems related to this cycle in his *Duanaire Finn*, in **CCCXV**, vii. A great many

the cycle of the Fianna or mercenary troops of Ireland and was taken up by the poets and popular story-tellers.

The principal and most valuable portion of Welsh literature consists of the collection of plots of epic narratives called the Mabinogion, the plural of *Mabinogi*, meaning " literary apprentice ".[1] Four of these stories intended for " literary apprenticeship " deserve the name more particularly ; the Red Book of Hergest calls them the Four Branches of Mabinogi. They are mythology heroicized, based on legends of South Wales. The first tells the story of Pwyll, Prince of Dyfed and god of the dead ; the second, of the marriage of Bronwen, the daughter of the sea-god Llyr, to a King of Ireland ; the third, the hero of which is Manawyddan, son of Llyr, is a continuation of the first two ; the fourth is about Math, son of Mathonwy. Five other stories belong to the Arthurian cycle, but behind three of these lie the earliest French poems of the Round Table.[2] Another, entitled *Kulhwch and Olwen*, is of genuine Welsh inspiration. Two others are closely associated with them, namely the *Dream of Macsen Wledig* and a mythological story called *Lludd and Llevelys*, a doublet of the story of Manawyddan.

The great Welsh manuscripts also contain poems, many

stories linked with this cycle have been collected in the chief collections of tales of the Gaelic countries, particularly in three volumes published under the name *Waifs and Strays of Celtic Tradition, Argyllshire Series* (**CCXCIII**) : MacInnes and Nutt, *Folk and Hero Tales* ; Macdougall and Nutt, *Folk and Hero Tales* ; J. F. Campbell and Nutt, *The Fians*, all three volumes containing interesting commentaries by Nutt. Consult also Campbell, **CCLIV** ; Curting, **CCLV** ; Croker, **CCLVII**. One should also mention the collections of popular ballads and poems in Gaelic in Campbell, **CCLIII**, and in the *Book of the Dean of Lismore*, a sixteenth century collection edited by Skene (Edin., 1862). For these ballads and the use made of them by Macpherson, see Stern, in **CLXXIII**, vii, pp. 51 ff. Certain texts connected with the Leinster cycle are translated in d'Arbois, *L'Epopée celtique en Irlande*. Some of the finest stories in this cycle are adapted rather than translated, but on the whole delightfully and faithfully, by Joyce in his *Old Celtic Romances*.

For the interpretation of the whole cycle, see Nutt in the appendices to the collection of tales cited above ; Rhys, **CCCXXXII**, pp. 355, 553 ; Squire, pp. 201–216. These writers believe that the cycle is ancient and its origin mythological. MacNeill, in his introduction to the *Duanaire Finn* quoted above and **CCCCXLI**, favours a later date. Zimmer connects the cycle with the time of the Scandinavian invasions, particularly in **CCXLVI**.

[1] **CCLXXXIV** ; Loth, **CCLXX**. Cf. Lady Guest, **CCLX** ; Skene, **CCLXXXVII** ; Rhys, **CCLXXXI–CCLXXXIII**.

[2] Weston, **CCXCIV** ; Nutt, **CCLXXVII**. Cf. Faral, **CCCCXXVI** ; Bruce, *The Evolution of Arthurian Romance*, Göttingen, 1923 ; Wilmotte, *Le Poème du Gral et ses auteurs*, Paris, 1930.

of them very ancient, which are ascribed to four bards, Aneurin, Taliesin, Myrddin (Merlin), and Llywarch Hen. They seem to represent the tradition of the north of British lands.

To all this romantic and poetic literature we must add a literature which might be called gnomic. In Ireland it consists of the *acallamh*, dialogues or colloquies,[1] such as the dialogue of Oisin and St. Patrick, dialogues of old men, and of the two wise men, which are connected with the romantic cycles. In Wales the literature of the Triads gives lists of allusions in gnomic form.

In both countries annals flourished. In Ireland a whole literature of antiquarianism, of dictionaries, of collections of local traditions and etymologies (*Dinnshenchas*) grew up.[2] We need not, of course, touch upon Christian literature.

One thing should be noted. The Cycles of Ulster and Leinster, which have survived, are composed of the traditions of those Irish kingdoms which were least successful politically, at whose expense the others expanded, and which were sometimes regarded by them as being peopled by foreigners. The truth is that what has come down to us is an inter-tribal tradition, which forgets internal conflicts. The subjects are selected on their æsthetic merits. It is the same in Wales, where the traditions of Dyfed, a conquered country, are preserved best. In other words, these literatures are already national literatures.

Starting from these data, we can recover in some measure the common characteristics of the ancient literatures of the Celts and the distinctive features of their intellectual activity.

The literature of the Gauls was an oral literature, and so were those of the Welsh and Irish. Every oral literature is a paraphrase of known themes and centos. Since the most powerful memory has its limitations, these themes are few. Popular literature is poor, although there are so many collections of folklore ; oral literature partakes of the nature of popular literature. It is not very varied. In Ireland the *ollamh*, or chief of the *fili*, had to know three hundred and

---

[1] See esp. **CCLXXIX**, i, ii.
[2] See Squire, **CCCCLIX** ; D. Hyde, op. cit. ; Loth, op. cit. ; Gwynn, **CCLXI**.

fifty stories, two hundred and fifty long and a hundred short. We have catalogues of the resources of the *fili*. The prose parts of the Irish romances seem to have been a foundation on which all kinds of fancies could be built up. The metrical parts were those which had acquired more permanence ; they were usually *bravura* passages. The oral tradition went on long after the form of the story had been fixed by erudition. Some of the most famous and affecting passages in the heroic legends and even in the Mythological Cycle, to which the ancient texts merely allude, were only developed in late poems of the seventeenth or eighteenth century—for example, the story of the sons of Ler being turned into swans by their stepmother. From this point of view we may say that " Ossian " Macpherson remained in the Celtic tradition ; only he took greater liberties than the ordinary arrangers of these themes.

Celtic literature was essentially a poetic literature. The Irish probably invented rhyme cn their own account.[1] The Celtic reciter added music to verse, like the minstrel of the Middle Ages. The harp was the tool of his trade. The literary profession was exercised by clans of specialists, who had their order of rank. We must not think of Celtic poetry as lyrical outpourings, but as elaborately ingenious exercises on the part of rather pedantic literary men. Yet Celtic literature was popular as no other was. The whole nation entered the field, not as specialists, and some of the best modern Celtic poets have been men sprung from the people. Romance literature also became popular. Nowhere else do oral tales contain more memories of heroic literature. In Celtic lands there is constant interchange between literature and folk-tale.

This literature [2] has a remarkably dramatic quality. Not only are the epics extremely interesting, lively, and full if movement, but the actors in them are real characters. Cuchulainn, Emer, King Conchobar, and Cathbad the Druid are living people. The Celts gave to the literature of the world Tristram and Yseult, to say nothing of Arthur and his companions. *Tristram and Yseult* is a Cornish tale, the

---

[1] Joyce, **CCCCXXXIV**, ii, pp. 499–501.
[2] For the general character of Celtic literature, see Arnold, **CCLI** ; Renan, **CCLXXX** ; Magnus MacLean, *The Literature of the Celts*, London, 1902 ; Nutt, **CCLXXV**.

Irish pendant to which is that of Diarmait and Grainne.[1]
These last are passionate lovers who fly to the forest, whither
they are pursued by Finn, Grainne's husband. It is hard
to imagine that the story-tellers of Gaul had less aptitude
for dramatic narrative than their brethren in the British
Isles. And one thinks of the men who were probably carrying on their work in French or Franco-Latin literature, and
more especially of the long succession of chroniclers who,
from Gregory of Tours and the monks of Saint-Denis, have
made the history of France the finest historical narrative
in the world.

Moreover, even if the Celtic literatures are not alone
in presenting heroes who are on the one hand dipped in the
marvellous and on the other bound to a chain of fates and
responsibilites which can never be broken, at least they have
obtained incomparable æsthetic effects from these two
elements. The fantastic is always there. Gods or fairies
are behind the door. You never know whether you are
dealing with a man or a spirit. A man is often a reincarnation
and sometimes he remembers it. The mysterious world
which makes the setting of the story is the world of the dead ;
the idea of death dominates everything, and everything
reveals it. All Celtic literature suggests mystery with a rare
power of evocation. And it is also because that literature
carries a hidden meaning that it turns readily to humour.
There is in Celtic literature a humorous vein we find even in
the finest of its early products, the *Feast of Briccriu* [2] and
Kulhwch and Olwen.[3]

V

A PICTURE OF CELTIC LIFE. THE MORALITY OF HONOUR

Let us end by trying to picture the Celts in peace and
ease, for example at one of the banquets described for Ireland
in the *Feast of Briccriu* and for Gaul in Athenaeos. Luckily

---

[1] Joyce, **CCLXVII**, pp. 274–350. Cf. **CCXCII**, iii.
[2] For editions of this text and its composition, see Thurneysen, **CCLXXXIX**,
pp. 445 ff. It is edited by Windisch in **CCXCV**, i, p. 235. Stern has published
an edition from another manuscript in *Z.C.P.*, iv, 143, there is a complete
edition by Henderson in **CCLXV**, ii, 1899, and it is translated by d'Arbois in
L'Épopée celtique en Irlande, p. 81.
[3] See Loth, **CCLXX**, i, pp. 243–599.

the ancients found the Gauls picturesque enough to be worth describing or portraying.

The Gauls sit in a circle in a round building, with the chief or host in the middle, at an equal distance from all men of equal rank. If they are nobles, the guests have with them, behind them, some seated and some standing, according to their degree and office, their squires or servants. In Ireland the arrangement is different. The building is rectangular and divided into compartments, and every man has his proper place according to his station. The women are apart, but they appear when the time comes. Strangers are welcomed, for we are hospitable.[1]

All are clean and well dressed. The Celt is very particular about his person, and is not afraid of a bath. They are clean-shaven save for the moustache, and their hair, which they wear at half-length, is drawn back from the brow and is sometimes dyed, or rather bleached ; soap (*sapo*) is a Celtic invention, used for this purpose.[2] Tattooing or painting of the body completes the adornment.[3] The men wear trousers or breeches which vary according to the country, smocks, and cloaks fastened with brooches ; their footgear is hose not sandals. The colours of the clothes are bright and varied. The Gaul even had tartan, and the colours may have been governed by tribal rules, as at the present day. The men carry arms.

The furniture is meagre.[4] The party sit on bundles of reeds on the ground.[5] Seats, if not unknown, are rare. The meat and bread are laid out on low tables. Meals consist mainly of butcher-meat and venison ; there is plenty of this latter, for game is abundant, and the Celts are keen and well-equipped hunters, with famous hounds. Fish also appears on the table. Meat is either roasted and taken off the spit on the table or boiled and lifted out of the pot with iron hooks.[6] It is also baked on hot stones in holes dug in the ground. In addition there is porridge made of oats or barley. Poseidonios says that the Celts ate their meat in their fingers, occasionally using a small knife to cut stringy bits and to separate bones. The meal is washed down

---

[1] Diod., v, 28.   [2] Ibid., p. 270 ; Pliny, xxviii.
[3] Déchelette, ii, 3, p. 1206 ; Isid. Sev., 19, 23. Cf. **XIII**, xii, 1913, p. 73.
[4] Pliny, viii, 73 ; xix, 2. Cf. Girald. Cambr., i, 3.
[5] Diod., vi, 28.
[6] Déchelette, ii, 3, p. 1028. Cf. Joyce, **CCCCXXXIV**, ii, p. 123.

with beer or wine.[1] At first wine came from Italy or Greece in amphoræ, and it was drunk in the Greek fashion with all the complicated apparatus of the Greek drinker. Later on the Gauls produced their own wine and exported it. Beer was made with wheat or barley and seems to have been flavoured with herbs. It was drunk when new-brewed. Mead was also made.

Festive parties drank deep and heads grew hot.[2] Drunkenness was a failing of the Celts, and things often ended ill, since all were armed. But causes of strife arose at the very beginning of a meal. Various portions of the food had their order of superiority, corresponding to the order of rank among men, and nobody would have deigned to accept anything but what was his due. An inferior portion offered to the wrong man might be a serious insult. But many might have a claim to the best portions, and it was not easy to satisfy them all. In the *Feast of Briccriu*, Briccriu wants to lead the heroes on to kill one another. He invites them to a banquet. There was a "hero's bit", the best portion. To whom is it to be given ? All rise up, ready to fight. The women join in. They agree to undergo trials, from which Cuchulainn emerges victorious. The Celts were a touchy race, and this sensitiveness was easily exasperated in company. In addition, there were memories of old quarrels, some of which had not been properly settled.

I have chosen this example rather than others because the feasters here afford an illustration of the very principle of social and moral life among the Celts, namely honour. The moral tales which the Greek writers relate of the Celts, that of Chiomara throwing down at her husband's feet the head of the centurion who had violated her, and that of Camma poisoning herself with her persecutor before the altar of Artemis, are all based on this morality of honour. The Celts did not excel as citizens, and that was one great source of their weakness. But in this refinement of the morality of honour there was a principle of civilization which did not cease to develop on the political collapse of the Celtic societies. The Celts bequeathed it to their descendants.

---

[1] Ath., iv, 152 ; Dioscorid., ii, p. 110. Cf. Windisch, **CCXCV**, i, pp. 319–320 ; Vendryès, "Les Vins de Gaule en Irlande," in **CXL**, xxxviii, 1920, p. 19.
[2] D'Arbois, **CCXLVIII**, i, p. 297.

CONCLUSION

The Heritage of the Celts

THE peculiar destiny of the Celts had carried them in a few centuries over the greater part of Europe, of which they had conquered and colonized a good third—the British Isles, France, Spain, the plain of the Po, Illyria, Thrace, Galatia, and the Danube valley, in addition to Germany, almost to the Elbe, which was their cradle. In a still shorter time they had lost all their Continental domain and part of the British Isles, being reduced to subjection in one place, driven out of another, and everywhere deprived of all political power. Then there had been a respite. But from the sixth century onwards the independent states in the British Isles were subjected to unceasing attacks, to which they succumbed. Only one is reviving, Ireland. The political creations of the Celts are among the great failures of the ancient history of Europe. The historical role of the Celtic peoples, except the Irish, for whom the future is opening again, is a thing of the past. I have tried to suggest that that role was once a large one, and that much of it remained. Certainly this was the feeling of their opponents. One has only to try to imagine what the history of the Celts would have been if Cæsar had not described the resistance of Vercingetorix and the Anglo-Normans had not adopted Arthur. But also how little evidence the Celts have left of themselves, compared with what we know of the Egyptians, the Greeks, the Romans, even the Germans! Even now, there may be some who fear, when confronted with this history, which has left so few monuments but which we are none the less tempted to regard as great, that they are the victims of a mirage produced by the imagination of Greek and Latin writers and the fancy of Celtic archæologists. One last check is needed, that of language.

There are still Celtic languages in existence, but they are no longer, as it were, languages working full time, completely sufficient for the social life of a whole society and, what is more, sufficient to themselves. Irish, it is true, has once more become an official language, now that Ireland is once more a political community. But many Irish patriots have had to learn their language anew. The example of Breton is still more striking ; it is the mother-tongue of a dwindling part of the population and a learned or rather a poetic language for a few lovers of the past. In different degrees, all Celtic languages were in this state. The difference which we see in the case of Irish and Welsh is due to the existence in both countries of an older and richer literary tradition. These various languages borrowed largely from all those which brought them into contact with a new life, particularly Latin. The degree of their independence is proportionate to the extent to which the peoples who spoke them resisted those who sought to assimilate them. They did not maintain themselves in their original independence and dignity.

But the Celtic languages are no longer spoken save in a very small part of the regions in which the Celts have left descendants. Great numbers of Britons remained in Britain after the Roman, Anglo-Saxon, and Norman conquests. Celts also remained in Gaul, where they formed the basis of the population. Many certainly remained in Spain and Northern Italy. But it is interesting to note how many remnants of Gaulish were preserved in Low Latin and French.

For Gaulish did not vanish as if by magic, quickly though Latin spread in Gaul.[1] A preacher like St. Irenaeus still had to learn it at the end of the second century,[2] and the Emperor Alexander Severus seems to have understood it.[3] In the time of Ulpian, the beginning of the third century, it was possible to draft certain acts in Celtic.[4] In the fourth century, St. Jerome could compare the speech of Treves and that of the Galatians. Sulpicius Severus in the fifth century perhaps knew a little Celtic,[5] and Ausonius, Gregory of Tours, Fortunatus, and Marcellus of Bordeaux [6] knew a few words each. This evidence is confirmed by inscriptions. Celtic continued in use for a long time, but in circles which grew ever smaller. Still, in abandoning their

---

[1] Loth, in **LVIII**, 1916, p. 169 ; Babut, " Le Celtique en Gaule au début du Ve siècle," in **CXLI**, 1910, pp. 287–292.
[2] Iren., *Contra Haereses*, i, pref.
[3] *Life of Alex. Severus*, p. 60.
[4] Ulp., *Digest*, xxxii, 11.
[5] Sulp. Sev., *Dial.*, i, p. 27, 1–4·
[6] *R.C.*, 1904, p. 351. See **CXXXIV**.

language, the vast majority of Gauls kept their manner of speaking and a great number of words for which Latin gave no equivalent.

Thus, Gaulish had lost *u* ; the Gauls did not take up the Latin *u*, pronouncing it *u*.[1] In the syllable *um* in the genitive plural and accusative singular masculine of stems in *u* or in the nominative and accusative singular neuter of the same stems, they gave it a sound rather like *o*, which assimilated these terminations to Celtic terminations in *om*. They said *dominom*. So, too, they kept certain methods of noun-formation which were peculiar to their language, which formed adjectives in *-acos*. Names of *fundi* and some other words were formed in *-acus*.[2] Certain words passed into the Latin vocabulary, such as *cantus*, the iron felloe of a wheel, from Gaulish *cantos*[3] (Welsh *cant* " circle ").[4] Others survived in the Latin of Gaul, such as *esox* " salmon " (Welsh *ehawk*, Irish *eo*), *cavannus* " owl " (Welsh *cuan*). A large number of these relics remained in the Romance languages and some in French, in addition to the geographical names, proper or common nouns, which remain in languages as fossils. Gaulish left to the Romance languages names of plants like *verveine* (verbena), beasts like *alouette* (lark), and others. *Clock* and *cloche* (bell) are Celtic (Low Latin *clocca*, Old Irish *cloc*) ; bells were worn by animals, but in Ireland only by those of *nemed* or holy men. *Cruche* (jug) is of Celtic origin (Irish *crocan*, Welsh *crochan*). *Bar*, *tringle*, *barque*, *beret*, *chimney*, and *biretta*, and their French equivalents all come from Gaulish, and so do *chemin* and *bief* (mill-race). M. Dottin has made as full a list of these words as possible but it is not yet complete, and research among local *patois* will increase it.

On the whole, a great deal of Gaulish has survived in the Romance tongues. When one people progressively adopts the language of civilization of another people which rules it, it never completely gives up its own ; the two languages become blended. Latin must have been spoken in Gaul in the same way as French in Périgord. First people go over from one language to another ; then a time comes

---

[1] Meillet, in **XLVII**, 1922, 5. Cf. ibid., xxi, i, 1918, p. 40.
[2] MacNeill, **CCCCXLI**, p. 152.
[3] Schoell, " Zur lateinischen Wortforschung," in **LXXI**, xxxi, p. 319.
[4] **CXL**, 1913, p. 240.

when a mixed tongue comes into being. To a certain extent, French stands in the same relation to Gaulish as the English dialect of the Lowlands to Gælic.

So the Celtic languages survive in two ways, in structure (but with the admission of many foreign elements) or in the shape of single elements embedded in languages of other structures. Everywhere there is something left of them, but they were only the remnants of a vanishing life until the revival of Irish, because the Celtic societies had not lasted as Celtic nations and states. The language will be saved by the Irish Free State.

Such, as I said, has been the peculiar fate of the Celts ; they were unable to create lasting states, and their languages have survived only in a partial and diminished condition. But that original, vigorous race, although it failed politically, chiefly through having no sense of the state or an insufficient sense of discipline, made very great contributions to civilization, to industry, art and, above all, literature. The La Tène craftsmen were masters in the arts and industries in general, and particularly in jewellery, and the earliest tellers of the Celtic epics showed a feeling for heroic poetry, a sense of the marvellous, mingled with humour, and a dramatic conception of fatality which truly belong to the Celts alone. Gaston Paris made the profound observation that the romance of Tristram and Yseult has a particular sound, which is hardly found elsewhere in Mediæval literature, and he explained it by the Celtic origin of these poems. It was through Tristram and Arthur that all that was clearest and most valuable in the Celtic genius was incorporated in the mind of Europe. And that tradition has been kept up by the unending line of poets and prose-writers of Ireland, Scotland, Wales, and Brittany who have adorned English and French literature by bringing to it the genius of their race.

I said above that the historians of France, who wrote such a peculiarly fine history, had in them the spirit of the Celtic race. But the very story which they were telling, the history of that undestroyable people of peasants, warriors, and artists, with its glories and tumults, its hopes and enthusiasms, its discords and rebirths, is surely the story of a nation whose blood and bones are mainly composed of Celtic elements.

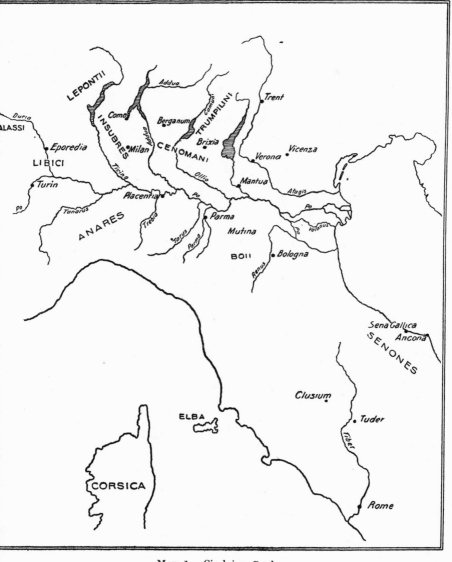

MAP 1. Cisalpine Gaul.

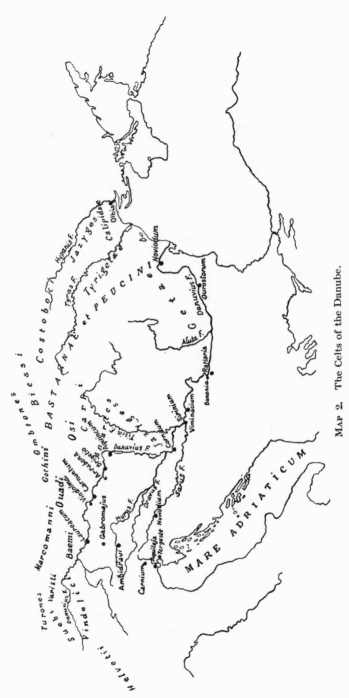

MAP 2. The Celts of the Danube.

MAP 3. Gaul.

[*Page* 279.

BIBLIOGRAPHY

I. SOURCES

Greek and Latin authors are indicated by the usual abbreviations. *F.H.G.* stands for Carolus Müller, *Fragmenta Historicorum Græcorum*, in the Collection Didot.

[Certain English editions have been added in square brackets, but the footnotes do not refer to the pages of these editions unless it is so stated.—Trs.]

II. INSCRIPTIONS

Corpus Inscriptionum Latinarum, consilio et auctoritate Academiæ Regiæ Borussicæ, Berlin, 1863, etc. .   **I**

Ephemeris Epigraphica . . . . . .   **II**

ALLMER (A.), *Inscriptions antiques de Vienne*, Viennc, 1875–8 . . . .   **III**

DITTENBERGER (G.), *Sylloge Inscriptionum Græcarum*, 2nd ed., Leipzig, 1898 ; 3rd ed., 1915–1923 .   **IV**

DURRBACH (F.), *Choix d'inscriptions de Délos*, Paris, 1921 . . . .   **V**

RHYS (Sir John), *The Celtic Inscriptions of Gaul and Italy*, London, 1910 . . . . . .   **VI**

—— *Gleanings in the Italian Field of Celtic Epigraphy*, repr. from **CXXI**, London, 1915 . . . .   **VII**

—— *Notes on the Coligny Calendar*, London, 1910 .   **VIII**

III. PERIODICALS

Abhandlungen der königlichen preussischen Akademie der Wissenschaften, phil. hist. Klasse, Berlin .   **IX**

Abhandlungen der naturhistorischen Gesellschaft zu Nürnberg, Nuremberg . . . . .   **X**

Annales de la Faculté des sciences de Marseille . .   **XI**

Annales de la Société Éduenne, Autun . . .   **XII**

Année sociologique, Paris . . . . .   **XIII**

Anuari de l'Institut d'Estudis catalans, Barcelona .   **XIV**

Anthropologie, Paris . . . . . .   **XV**

Antiquaries' Journal, London . . . . .   **XVI**

Anzeiger für schweizerische Altertumskunde (Indicateur d'antiquités suisses), Zurich . . . .   **XVII**

Archæologia, or miscellaneous tracts relating to antiquity, published by the Society of Antiquaries of London, London . . . . . .   **XVIII**

Archæologia Cambrensis, Cambridge . . . .   **XIX**

Archaeologischer Anzeiger, Berlin . . . .   **XX**

Archaelogiai értesitö, Budapest . . . .   **XXI**

Archeologo portugues, Lisbon . . . . .   **XXII**

Archiv für Anthropologie, Brunswick . . . **XXIII**
Archiv für slavische Philologie, Berlin . . . **XXIV**
Archives suisses d'anthropologie générale, Geneva . **XXV**
Association française pour l'avancement des sciences.
　Comptes rendus des Congrès annuels, Paris . . **XXVI**
Atti della reale Accademia dei Lincei, scienze morali,
　Rome . . . . **XXVII**
Atti della Soc. arch. e B. Arti di Torino, Turin . . **XXVIII**
Bericht der römisch-germanischen Kommission des
　kaiserlichen archäologischen Instituts, afterwards
　deutschen Arch. Instit., Frankfort on Main . . **XXIX**
Berliner philologische Wochenschrift, Berlin . . **XXX**
Berliner Monatschrift, Berlin . . . . . **XXXI**
Bibliothèque de l'École des Chartes, Paris . . . **XXXII**
Biblos . . . . **XXXIII**
Boletín de la Academia de la Historia, Madrid . . **XXXIV**
Boletín de la Sociedad Española de Excursiones,
　Madrid . . . . **XXXV**
Boletín de la Sociedad geográfica, Madrid . . . **XXXVI**
Bonner Jahrbücher, Jahrbücher des Vereins von Alter-
　tumsfreunden im Rheinlande, Bonn . . . **XXXVII**
Bulletin archéologique du Comité des travaux
　historiques, Paris . . . . . **XXXVIII**
Bulletin de correspondance hellénique, Athens . . **XXXIX**
Bulletín de la Commission archéologique de Narbonne **XL**
Bulletin de la Société d'anthropologie, Paris . . **XLI**
Bulletin de la Société anthropologique de Bruxelles . **XLII**
Bulletin de la Société archéologique du Finistère,
　Quimper . . . . **XLIII**
Bulletin de la Société archéologique de Provence,
　Marseilles . . . . **XLIV**
Bulletin de la Société d'émulation du Doubs, Besançon **XLV**
Bulletin de la Société Jersiaise, Jersey . . . **XLVI**
Bulletin de la Société de linguistique, Paris . . **XLVII**
Bulletin de la Société préhistorique française, Paris . **XLVIII**
Bulletin de la Société des sciences historiques et
　naturelles de l'Yonne, Auxerre . . . **XLIX**
Bulletin anthropologique et biologique de Lyon . . **L**
Bulletin hispanique, Bordeaux . . . . . **LI**
Bullettino dell'Instituto di correspondenza archeologica,
　Rome . . . . **LII**
Bullettino di paletnologia italiana, Parma . . **LIII**
Cahiers d'histoire et d'archéologie d'Alsace, Strasburg. **LIV**
Cechiset Revue, Prague . . . . . . **LV**
Celtic Review . . . . **LVI**
Classical Review, London . . . . . **LVII**
Comptes rendus de l'Académie des Inscriptions et
　Belles-Lettres, Paris . . . . . **LVIII**
Congrès international d'anthropologie et d'archéologie
　préhistoriques . . . . **LIX**
Congrès préhistorique de France, C. R. des sessions,
　Paris . . . . **LX**
Congrès archéologique de France . . . . **LXI**
English historical Review, London . . . . **LXII**
Erin, Dublin . . . . **LXIII**

Mitteilungen der Anthropologischen Gesellschaft,
Zurich   CI
Mitteilungen des deutschen archäologischen Instituts,
Athenische Abteilung, Athens   CII
—— —— Römische Abteilung, Rome . . .   CIII
Mitteilungen der prähistorischen Commission der kais.
Akademie der Wissenschaften, Vienna . .   CIV
Mitteilungen (wissenschaftliche) aus Bosnien und
Herzegowina, Vienna   CV
Monumenti antichi pubblicati per cura della R.
Academia dei Lincei, Milan   CVI
Monuments Piot, Paris   CVII
Musée Belge, Liége and Paris   CVIII
Musée Neuchâtelois, Neuchâtel   CIX
Nassauische Annalen   CX
New Ireland Review, Dublin   CXI
Notizie degli scavi di antichità, Rome . . .   CXII
Nouvelles Archives des missions scientifiques, Paris .   CXIII
Orientalische Literaturzeitung, Berlin . . .   CXIV
Památky archœologické, Prague   CXV
Philologica, Journal of Comparative Philology, London   CXVI
Portugalia, Oporto (1899–1908)   CXVII
Prähistorische Zeitschrift, Berlin   CXVIII
Pro Alesia, Paris   CXIX
Pro Nervia, Bavay   CXX
Proceedings of the British Academy, London . .   CXXI
Proceedings of the Royal Irish Academy, Dublin .   CXXII
Proceedings of the Society of Antiquaries of London .   CXXIII
Proceedings of the Society of Antiquaries of Scotland,
Edinburgh   CXXIV
Rassegna delle scienze geologiche, Rome . . .   CXXV
Reports of the Research Committee of the Society of
Antiquaries of London   CXXVI
Report of . . . the British Association, London . .   CXXVII
Rendiconti della R. Accademia dei Lincei, classe di
scienze morali, storiche e filologiche, Rome .   CXXVIII
Reports of the Smithsonian Institute, Washington .   CXXIX
Revue d'anthropologie, Paris   CXXX
Revue de l'Instruction publique en Belgique, Bruges .   CXXXI
Revue de Nîmes   CXXXII
Revue de phonétique, Paris   CXXXIII
Revue des Études anciennes, Bordeaux . . .   CXXXIV
Revue des Études grecques, Paris   CXXXV
Revue des questions scientifiques, Paris . . .   CXXXVI
Revue du Mois, Paris   CXXXVII
Revue anthropologique, Paris   CXXXVIII
Revue archéologique, Paris   CXXXIX
Revue celtique, Paris   CXL
Revue historique, Paris   CXLI
Revue numismatique, Paris   CXLII
Revue préhistorique. Annales de palethnologie, Paris   CXLIII
Rheinisches Museum für Philologie, Frankfort on Main   CXLIV
Rivista archeologica della provincia di Como . .   CXLV
Rhodania, Vienne   CXLVI
Scottish Review, Edinburgh   CXLVII

Sitzungsberichte der koenig. preussischen Akademie der
Wissenschaften, Berlin CXLVIII
Sitzungsberichte der kais. Akademie der Wissenschaften
zu Wien, philos. hist. Klasse, Vienna . . . CXLIX
Société de statistique, d'histoire et d'archéologie de
Marseille et de la Provence. Volume du
Centenaire CL
Sonderhefte des österr. arch. Institut, Vienna . . CLI
Symbolæ Osloenses, Oslo CLII
Syria, Paris CLIII
Transactions of the Honourable Society of
Cymmrodorion CLIV
Travaux de la section numismatique et archéologique
du musée de Koloszvar CLV
Trabalhos da Sociedade portugueza de Antropologia e
Etnologia, Oporto CLVI
Trierer Jahresberichte, Treves CLVII
Verhandlungen der Berliner Gesellschaft für Anthro-
pologie, Ethnologie und Urgeschichte, Berlin . CLVIII
Veröffentlichungen des oberhessischen Museums und der
galischen Sammlungen zu Giessen, Abteilung für
Vorgeschichte CLIX
Westdeutsche Zeitschrift für Geschichte und Kunst,
Bonn CLX
Wiener Studien, Vienna CLXI
Indogermanisches Jahrbuch CLXII
Wochenschrift für klassische Philologie, Berlin . . CLXIII
Wörter und Sachen CLXIV
Würtembergische Vierteljahrsschriften für Landes-
geschichte, Stuttgart CLXV
Zeitschrift der deutsch. Morgenländischen Gesellschaft,
Leipzig CLXVI
Zeitschrift der Savigny-Stiftung für Rechtsgeschichte,
Berlin CLXVII
Zeitschrift für deutsche Altertumskunde . . . CLXVIII
Zeitschrift für Ethnologie, Berlin CLXIX
Zeitschrift für romanische Philologie, Halle . . CLXX
Zeitschrift für celtische Philologie CLXXI
Zeitschrift für Sozialwissenschaft CLXXII
Zeitschrift für vergleichende Literaturgeschichte, Berlin CLXXIII
Zeitschrift für vergleichende Sprachforschung, auf dem
Gebiete der indogermanischen Sprachen, Berlin . CLXXIV

IV. MISCELLANIES

Festgabe für Hugo Blümner, Zurich, 1914 . . . CLXXV
Festschrift W. Stokes, Leipzig, 1900 CLXXVI
Festschrift zur Feier des fünfundsiebzigjährigen
Bestehens des röm.-germ. Centralmuseums zu
Mainz, 1902 CLXXVII
Heilbronner Festschrift CLXXVIII
Mélanges Ch. Bémont, Paris, 1913 CLXXIX
Mélanges R. Cagnat, Paris, 1912 CLXXX
Mélanges L. Havet, Paris, 1909 CLXXXI

Essays and Studies presented to William Ridgeway,
    Cambridge, 1913 CLXXXII
Mélanges de Saussure, Paris, 1908 CLXXXIII
Mélanges Vendryès, Paris, 1925 CLXXXIV
Opuscula archaeologica Oscari Montelio dedicata,
    Stockholm, 1913 CLXXXV
Recueil d'études égyptologiques dédiées à la mémoire
    de J.-F. Champollion, Paris, 1922 . . . CLXXXVI
Recueil Kondakow, Prague, 1926 . . . . CLXXXVII.

V. LANGUAGE

Arbois de Jubainville (H. d'), *Éléments de la
grammaire celtique*, Paris, 1903 CLXXXVIII
MacBain (Alexander), *An Etymological Dictionary of
the Gaelic Language*, 2nd ed., Inverness, 1911 . CLXXXIX, CXC
Berneker (E.), *Slavisches etymologisches Wörterbuch*,
Heidelberg, 1908–1913 CXC
Budinszky (A.), *Die Ausbreitung der lateinischen
Sprache*, Berlin, 1881 CXCII
Clinton (O. H. Fynes), *The Welsh Vocabulary of the
Bangor District*, Oxford, 1913 CXCIII
Corpus Glossariorum Latinorum, Leipzig, 1888–1901 . CXCIV
Cramer, *Rheinische Ortsnamen*, Düsseldorf, 1901 . CXCV
Dottin (Georges), *La Langue gauloise*, Paris, 1920 . CXCVI
—— *Manuel d'irlandais moyen*, vol. i (grammar),
Paris, 1913 CXCVII
Ernault (E.), *Glossaire moyen-breton*, Paris, 1895–6 . CXCVIII
Finck (F. N.), *Die Araner Mundart*, Marburg, 1899 . CXCIX
Fischer (F. T. T. A.), *Die Lehnwörter des Altwest-
nordischen* (Palaestra, lxxxv), Berlin, 1909 . . CC
Fraser (John), *History and Etymology*, Oxford, 1923 . CCI
Giles (Peter), *A Short Manual of Comparative
Philology*, London, 1901 CCII
Gillies (H. C.), *Elements of Gaelic Grammar, based on
the work of the Rev. Alexander Stewart*, London,
1902 CCIII
Ginneken (van), *Principes de linguistique psychologique*,
Paris, etc., 1907 CCIV
Henebry (Richard), *Contribution to the Phonology of
Desi-Irish*, Greifswald, 1901 CCV
Hermet (Abbé F.), *Les Grafittes de la Graufesenque*,
Rodez, 1923 CCVI
Holder (A. T.), *Alt-celtischer Sprachschatz*, 3 vols.,
Leipzig, 1896–1913 CCVII
Jones (Sir John Morris), *A Welsh Grammar, historical
and comparative*, Oxford, 1913 CCVIII
Keil (Heinrich), *Grammatici Latini*, Leipzig, 1857–80 . CCIX
Kluge (F.), *Etymologisches Wörterbuch der deutschen
Sprache*, 6th ed., Strasburg, 1899 [*An Etymological
Dictionary of the German Language*, London, 1891] CCX
—— *Vorgeschichte der altgermanischen Dialekte*, in
H. Paul, *Grundriss der germanischen Philologie*,
vol. i, 1901 CCXI

LONGNON (A.), *Noms de lieux anciens de la France,*
Paris, 1926 CCXII
LOTH (J.), *Chrestomathie bretonne,* Paris, 1890 . . CCXIII
—— *Vocabulaire vieux-breton* (Bibl. É.H.É., vi), Paris,
1884 CCXIV
MACALISTER (Robert A. Stewart), *Studies in Irish
Epigraphy,* 3 vols., London, 1897–1907 . . CCXV
MEILLET (A.), *Les Dialectes indo-européens,* Paris, 1922 CCXVI
—— *Introduction à l'étude comparative des langues
indo-européennes,* 3rd ed., Paris, 1912 . . . CCXVII
—— and COHEN (M.), *Les Langues du monde,* Paris,
1924 CCXVIII
MOLLOY (John H.), *A Grammar of the Irish Language,*
Dublin, 1867 CCXIX
MORRIS (Meredith), *A Glossary of the Demetian Dialect,*
Tonypandy, 1910 CCXX
MOULTON (James H.), *Two Lectures on the Science of
Language,* Cambridge, 1903 CCXXI
MEYER (W.), *Fragmenta Burana,* Berlin, 1901 . . CCXXII
NICHOLSON (Edward W. Byron), *Keltic Researches :
studies in the history and distribution of the ancient
Goidelic language and peoples,* London, 1904 . . CCXXIII
—— *Sequanian : first steps in the investigation of a
newly discovered ancient European language,*
London, 1898 CCXXIV
O'DONOVAN (John), *A Grammar of the Irish Language,*
Dublin, 1845 CCXXV
O'NOLAN (Rev. Gerald), *Studies in Modern Irish,*
Dublin, 1919 CCXXVI
PEDERSEN (Holger), *Vergleichende Grammatik der
keltischen Sprachen,* Göttingen, 1909–13 . . CCXXVII
QUIGGIN (Edmund C.), *A Dialect of Donegal,* Cam-
bridge, 1906 CCXXVIII
REID (Duncan), *A Course of Gaelic Grammar,* Glasgow,
1902 [3rd ed., 1908] CCXXIX
RHYS (Sir John), *Celtæ and Galli,* London, 1905 . CCXXX
ROWLAND (T.), *A Grammar of the Welsh Language*
Wrexham, n.d., 4th ed. CCXXXI
[For **CCXXXII**, see below, STOKES, **CCXXXVI**]
SOMMERFELT (A.), *Dē en Italo-celtique : son rôle dans
l'évolution morphologique des langues italo-celtiques,*
Oslo, 1920 CCXXXIII
—— *The Dialect of Torr, Co. Donegal,* Oslo, 1922 . CCXXXIV
STOKES (Whitley) and STRACHAN (J.), *Thesaurus
Palæohibernicus,* 2 vols., Cambridge, 1901–3 . CCXXXV
—— *Three Irish Glossaries,* London, 1862 . . CCXXXVI
—— *Urkeltischer Sprachschatz,* trans. BEZZENBERGER,
Göttingen, 1894 [pt. iii of A. FICK, *Wörterbuch der
indogermanischen Grundsprache,* 4th ed., 1890–1909) CCXXXVII
Beiträge zur Kunde der indogermanischen Sprachen,
Göttingen, 1877–1900 CCXXXVIII
[For **CCXXXIX**, see above, STOKES, **CCXXXVII**]
THURNEYSEN (Rudolf), *Keltoromanisches,* Halle, 1884 . CCXL
VALLÉE (F.), *La Langue bretonne et le français,* 4th ed.,
Saint-Brieuc, 1916 CCXLI

VENDRYÈS (Joseph), *Grammaire du vieil irlandais*, Paris,
1908 CCXLII
WALDE (A.), *Lateinisches etymologisches Wörterbuch*,
2nd ed., Heidelberg, 1910 CCXLIII
—— *Über älteste sprachliche Beziehungen zwischen
Kelten und Italikern*, Innsbruck, 1917 . CCXLIV
WINDISCH (E.), in GROEBER, *Grundriss der romanischen
Philologie*, 2nd ed., Strasburg, 1905, pp. 390–4 . CCXLV
ZIMMER (H.), *Keltische Beiträge, Studien*, in CLXXIV,
1888 CCXLVI

VI. LITERATURE

Ancient Laws of Ireland, 6 vols., Dublin, 1865–79 . CCXLVII
ARBOIS DE JUBAINVILLE (H. d'), *Cours de littérature
celtique*, 12 vols., Paris, 1883–1902 . . . CCXLVIII
—— *Essai d'un catalogue de la littérature épique de
l'Irlande*, Paris, 1883 CCXLIX
—— *Le cycle mythologique irlandais et la mythologie
celtique*, Paris, 1884 [*The Irish Mythological Cycle
and Celtic Mythology*, Dublin, 1903] . . . CCL
ARNOLD (Matthew), *The Study of Celtic Literature*,
London, 1891 [new ed., 1910] CCLI
BEST (R. I.), *Bibliography of Irish Philology and
Literature*, Dublin, 1913 CCLII
CAMPBELL (John F.), *Leabhar na Feinne*, London, 1872 CCLIII
—— *Popular Tales of the West Highlands*, Edinburgh,
1890 CCLIV
CURTIN (Jeremiah), *Hero-tales of Ireland*, London, 1894 CCLV
Domesday Book CCLVI
CROKER (Thomas Crofton), *Fairy Legends and Traditions
of the South of Ireland*, London, 1882 . . . CCLVII
FARADAY (Winifred), *The Cattle Raid of Cuailnge*,
London, 1901 CCLVIII
GREGORY (Isabella A.), Lady Gregory, *Cuchulain of
Muirthemne*, London, 1902 CCLIX
GUEST (Lady Charlotte), *The Mabinogion* . . . CCLX
GWYNN (Edward), *The Metrical Dindsenchas* (Todd
Lectures, viii, ix, x), 3 vols., Dublin, 1908–13 . CCLXI
HULL (Eleanor), *A Text-book of Irish Literature*, 2 pts.,
Dublin, 1906 CCLXII
—— *The Cuchullin Saga in Irish Literature*, London,
1898 CCLXIII
HYDE (Douglas), *A Literary History of Ireland*, London,
1899 CCLXIV
Irish Texts Society, *Publications*, London, 1899, etc. . CCLXV
JOYCE (P. W.), *The Origin and History of Irish Names
of Places*, 2 ser., Dublin, 1869–75 . . . CCLXVI
—— *Old Celtic Romances*, London, 1879 [2nd ed., 1894] CCLXVII
MACALISTER (Robert A. Stewart) and MACNEILL (John),
ed., *Leabhar Gabhála. The Book of Conquests of
Ireland*, 1917 CCLXVIII
Lives of Saints, from the Book of Lismore, ed. W. STOKES,
Oxford, 1890 CCLXIX

LOTH (J.), *Les Mabinogion*, 2 vols., Paris, 1913 . . **CCLXX**

MARTIN (Martin), *A Description of the Islands of Scotland*, London, 1703 . . . . **CCLXXI**

MEYER (Kuno), *Fianaigecht*, Dublin, 1910 . . **CCLXXII**

—— *Totenklage um König Niall Noigiallach*, in **CLXXVI** **CCLXXIII**

—— and NUTT (Alfred), *The Voyage of Bran*, 2 vols., London, 1895–7 . . . . . . **CCLXXIV**

NUTT (Alfred), *Celtic and Medieval Romance*, London, 1899 . . . . **CCLXXV**

—— *Cuchulain, the Irish Achilles*, London, 1900 . **CCLXXVI**

—— *Legends of the Holy Grail*, London, 1902 . . **CCLXXVII**

O'CURRY (Eugene), *Lectures on the Manuscript Materials of Ancient Irish History*, 8 vols., Dublin, 1861 . **CCLXXVIII**

O'GRADY (Standish), *Silva Gadelica*. 2 vols., London, 1892 . . . . **CCLXXIX**

RENAN (Ernest), *La Poésie des races celtiques*, Paris [*The Poetry of the Celtic Races*, London, 1896] . **CCLXXX**

RHYS (Sir John), *Studies in the Arthurian Legend*, Oxford and New York, 1891 . . . . **CCLXXXI**

—— *Lectures on the Origin and Growth of Religion as illustrated by Celtic Heathendom* (Hibbert Lectures), London, 1888 . . . . **CCLXXXII**

—— *The Mabinogion*, London, 1901 . . . **CCLXXXIII**

—— and EVANS (J. G.), ed., *Mabinogion*, Oxford, 1887 . . . . **CCLXXXIV**

Sanas Cormaic, ed. K. MEYER, Halle, 1912 . . **CCLXXXV**

SCHIRMER (G.), *Zur Brendanus-Legende*, Leipzig, 1888 . **CCLXXXVI**

SKENE (William F.), *Four Ancient Books of Wales*, 2 vols., Edinburgh, 1868 . . . . . **CCLXXXVII**

STOKES (Whitley), *Three Middle Irish Homilies*, Calcutta, 1877 . . . . . . **CCLXXXVIII**

THURNEYSEN (Rudolf), *Die irische Helden- und Königssage bis zum siebzehnten Jahrhundert*, Halle, 1921 . . . . **CCLXXXIX**

—— *Sagen aus dem Alten Irland*, Berlin, 1901 . . **CCXC**

Todd Lectures, Dublin, 1885–1924 . . . . **CCXCI**

Transactions of the Ossianic Society, Dublin, 1855–61 . **CCXCII**

Waifs and Strays of Celtic Tradition, Argyllshire series, 3 vols., London, edited by Lord Archibald CAMPBELL and others . . . . . **CCXCII**

WESTON (Jessie L.), *King Arthur and his Knights*, London, 1899 . . . . . . **CCXCIV**

WINDISCH (E.), *Irische Texte*, Leipzig, 1880 . . **CCXCV**

—— *Die altirischen Heldensage, Táin Bo Cuailnge, nach dem Buch von Leinster*, Leipzig, 1905 . . **CCXCVI**

VII. GENERAL WORKS

ÅBERG (Nils), *Das nordische Kulturgebiet in Mitteleuropa während der jüngeren Steinzeit*, 2 vols., Upsala, 1918 **CCXCVII**

ALLEN (John Romilly), *Celtic Art in Pagan and Christian Times*, 2nd ed., London, 1912 . . . **CCXCVIII**

ARBOIS DE JUBAINVILLE (H. d'), *Les Celtes depuis les temps les plus reculés jusqu'en l'an 100 avant notre ère*, Paris, 1904. . . . . . . **CCXCIX**

ARBOIS DE JUBAINVILLE (H. d'), *Les Druides et les dieux celtiques à forme d'animaux*, Paris, 1906 . . CCC

—— *Les Premiers Habitants de l'Europe*, 2nd ed., 2 vols., Paris, 1889–94 CCCI

ARMSTRONG (E. C. R.), *Guide to the Collection of Irish Antiquities. Catalogue of Irish Gold Ornaments in the Collection of the Royal Irish Academy*, Dublin, 1920 CCCII

BERTRAND (A.), *Archéologie celtique et gauloise*, Paris, 1876 CCCIII

BIENKOWSKI (P.), *Les Celts dans les arts mineurs gréco-romains*, Cracow, 1928 . . . CCCIV

BIENKOWSKI (P. R. von), *Die Darstellungen der Gallier in der hellenischen Kunst*, Vienna, 1908 . . CCCV

BLANCHET (A.), *Traité des monnaies gauloises*, Paris, 1905 CCCVI

BOAS, *The Social Organization and the Secret Societies of the Kwakiutl Indians*, Washington, n.d. . . CCCVII

BUSHE-FOX (J. P.), *Excavations at Hengistbury Head*, in **CXXVI** 1915, ... CCCVIII

CASTILLO YURRITA (A. del), *La Cultura del vaso campaniforme*, Barcelona, 1928 . . . CCCIX

CAVAIGNAC (E.), *Histoire du Monde*, Paris . . . CCCX

CHAPOT (V.), *Le Monde romain*, Paris, 1927 [*The Roman World*, in this series, London and New York, 1928] CCCXI

COOK (A. B.), *The European Sky-god*, repr. from **LXIV**, 1904 CCCXII

Corpus Vasorum Antiquorum CCCXIII

MACCULLOCH (Rev. John A.), *The Religion of the Ancient Celts*, Edinburgh, 1911 CCCXIV

DAREMBERG and SAGLIO, *Dictionnaire des antiquités grecques et romaines*, Paris, 1877–1919 . . CCCXV

DAVY (G.), *La foi jurée*, Paris, 1922 CCCXVI

DÉCHELETTE (J.), *La Collection Millon. Antiquités préhistoriques et gallo-romaines*, Paris, 1913 . . CCCXVII

—— *Manuel d'archéologie préhistorique, celtique, et gallo-romaine*, 4 vols., Paris, 1908–14 . . CCCXVIII

DELATTE (A.), *Études sur la littérature pythagoricienne*, Bibl. É.H.É., Paris, 1915 CCCXIX

DENIKER (J.), *Les Races et les peuples de la terre*, Paris, 1900 [*The Races of Man*, London, 1900] . . CCCXX

DOTTIN (G.), *Les Anciens Peuples de l'Europe*, Paris, 1916 CCCXXI

—— *Manuel pour servir à l'étude de l'antiquité celtique*, 2nd ed., Paris, 1915 CCCXXII

—— *La Religion des Celtes*, Paris, 1904 . . . CCCXXIII

EBERT (M.), *Reallexikon der Vorgeschichte*, 15 vols., Berlin, 1924–32 CCCXXIV

ESPÉRANDIEU (E.), *Recueil général des bas-reliefs de la Gaule*, Paris, 1907–30 CCCXXV

FEIST (S.), *Kultur, Ausbreitung, und Herkunft der Indogermanen*, Berlin, 1913 CCCXXVI

FELICE (P. de), *L'Autre Monde: mythes et légendes. Le purgatoire de Saint Patrice*, Paris 1906 . . CCCXXVII

FLEURE (Herbert J.), *The Races of England and Wales*, London, 1923 CCCXXVIII

FÖHR (Julius von), *Hügelgräber auf der Schwäbischen Alb*, ed. L. MAYER, Stuttgart, 1892 . . . CCCXXIX

FORRER (R.), *Reallexikon der prähistorischen, klassischen, und frühchristlichen Altertümer*, Berlin, 1907 . CCCXXX

FOUGÈRES (G.), GROUSSET (R.), JOUGUET (P.), and LESQUIER (J.), *Les Premières Civilisations*, vol. i of *Peuples et civilisations*, Paris, 1926 . . . CCCXXXI

FRAZER (Sir James G.), *Les Origines magiques de la royauté*, Paris, 1920 [*Lectures on the Early History of the Kingship*, London, 1905] CCCXXXII

—— *Le Totémisme*, Paris, 1898 [*Totemism*, Edinburgh, 1887] CCCXXXIII

FUSTEL DE COULANGES (N.-D.), *Histoire des institutions politiques de l'ancienne France*, 2nd ed., 5 vols., Paris, 1900–7 CCCXXXIV

GÖTZE (Alfred), *Führer auf die Steinsburg bei Römhild*, in **CXVIII**, 1921–2 CCCXXXV

HASTINGS (James), *Encyclopædia of Religion and Ethics*, Edinburgh, 1908–18 CCCXXXVI

HIRSCHFELD (H. O.), *Timagenes und die gallische Wandersage* (*Kleine Schriften*, Berlin, 1913) . . CCCXXXVII

HIRT (H. A.), *Die Indogermanen, ihre Verbreitung, ihre Urheimat, und ihre Kultur*, 2 vols., Strasburg, 1905–7 CCCXXXVIII

HÖRNES (Moriz), Yr., *Urgeschichte der bildenden Kunst*, ed. O. MENGHIN, 3rd ed., Vienna, 1925 . . CCCXXXIX

HOLLEAUX (M.), *Rome, la Grèce et les monarchies hellénistiques au IIIᵉ siècle avant J.-C.*, Paris, 1921 CCCXL

HOMO (Léon), *L'Italie primitive et les débuts de l'impérialisme romain*, Paris, 1925 [*Primitive Italy*, in this series, London and New York, 1927] . . CCCXLI

HOOPS (J.), ed., *Reallexikon der germanischen Altertums-kunde*, Strasburg, 1911–12 CCCXLII

HUBERT (Henri), *Le Culte des héros et ses conditions sociales*, Paris, n.d. CCCXLIII

—— *Divinités gauloises. Sucelus et Nantosuelta, Epona, dieux de l'autre monde*, Mâcon, 1925 . . CCCXLIV

JARDÉ (A.), *La Formation du peuple grec*, Paris, 1923 [*The Formation of the Greek People*, in this series, London and New York, 1926] CCCXLV

JULLIAN (Camille), *De la Gaule à la France*, Paris, 1922 CCCXLVI

—— *Histoire de la Gaule*, 3rd ed., Paris, 1920, etc. . CCCXLVII

KAUFMANN (F.), *Deutsche Altertumskunde*, 2 vols., Munich, 1913–23 CCCXLVIII

KEANE (Augustus H.), *Man, Past and Present*, Cambridge, 1899 [revised ed., 1920] CCCXLIX

KEMBLE (John M.), *Horae Ferales ; or, Studies in the Archæology of the Northern Nations*, London, 1863 CCCL

LEUZE (O.), *Die römische Jahrzahlung*, 1909 . . CCCLI

MAINE (Sir Henry J. Sumner), *Lectures on the Early History of Institutions*, 8 vols., London, 1875 . CCCLII

MEITZEN, *Siedelung und Agrarwesen der Westgermanen und Ostgermanen*, Berlin, 1895 CCCLIII

MEYER (Éduard), *Geschichte des Altertums*, 1st and 3rd eds., Stuttgart, 1893–1913 CCCLIV
—— *Histoire de l'Antiquité*, vol. i, *Introduction à l'étude des Sociétés anciennes*, Paris, 1912 . . . CCCLV
MEYER (Kuno), *Miscellanea Hibernica*, Urbana, 1916 . CCCLVI
MONTELIUS (O.), *Die älteren Kulturperioden in Orient und Europa*. i. *Die Methode*, Stockholm, 1913 . CCCLVII
MOMMSEN (Theodor), *Monumenta Germaniæ historica*, Berlin CCCLVIII
—— *Histoire romaine*, translation, 8 vols., Paris, 1863–72 [English translation, London and New York, 1911] CCCLIX
MORET (A.) and DAVY (G.), *Des clans aux empires*, Paris, 1923 [*From Tribe to Empire*, in this series, London and New York, 1926] CCCLX
MUCH (A.), *Kunsthistorischer Atlas*, Vienna, 1889 . CCCLXI
MÜLLENHOFF (K. V.), *Deutsche Altertumskunde*, 2nd ed., Berlin, 1890, etc. CCCLXII
MUNRO (Robert), *Les Stations lacustres de l'Europe aux âges de la Pierre et du Bronze*, Paris, 1907 [*The Lake Dwellings of Europe*, London, 1890] . . CCCLXIII
NIEDERLÉ (Lubor), *Manuel de l'antiquité slave*, 2 vols., Paris, 1923–6 CCCLXIV
NIESE (B.), *Geschichte der griechischen und makedonischen Staaten*, 2 vols., Gotha, 1893–1908 . . . CCCLXV
PARKYN (E. A.), *An Introduction to the Study of Prehistoric Art*, London, 1915 CCCLXVI
PAUL (H.), *Grundriss der germanischen Philologie*, 3 vols., 2nd ed., Strasburg, 1901, etc. . . . CCCLXVII
PAULY and WISSOWA, *Real-Encyclopädie der klass. Altertumswissenschaft*, Stuttgart, 1894, etc. . . CCCLXVIII
PHILIPON (E.), *Les Peuples primitifs de l'Europe méridionale*, Paris, 1925 CCCLXIX
RANKE (J.), *Der Mensch*, 2 vols., 2nd ed., Leipzig, 1890 CCCLXX
RIDGEWAY (Sir William), *The Origin of Tragedy*, Cambridge, 1910 CCCLXXI
REINACH (Salomon), *Description raisonnée du Musée des Antiquités nationales*. ii. *Bronzes figurés*, Paris, 1895 CCCLXXII
—— *Catalogue illustré du Musée des Antiquités nationales au Château de Saint-Germain-en-Laye*, vol. i, 2nd ed., Paris, 1926 ; vol. ii, 1924 . . CCCLXXIII
—— *Cultes, mythes et religions*, 4 vols., Paris, 1905–12 [*Cults, Myths, and Religions*, London, 1912] . CCCLXXIV
—— *Les Gaulois dans l'art antique et le sarcophage de la vigne Ammendola*, Paris, 1889 . . . CCCLXXV
—— *Répertoire de peintures grecques et romaines*, Paris, 1922 CCCLXXVI
—— *Répertoire de la statuaire grecque et romaine*, 7 vols., Paris, 1897, etc. CCCLXXVII
RIPLEY (William Z.), *The Races of Europe*, London, 1900 CCCLXXVIII
ROGET DE BELLOGUET (D. F. L.), Baron, *Ethnogénie gauloise*, 2nd ed., 4 pts., Paris, 1872 . . . CCCLXXIX
ROSCHER (W. H.), *Ausführliches Lexikon der griechischen und römischen Mythologie*, Leipzig, 1884, etc. . CCCLXXX

SCHRADER, *Die Indogermanen*, 1911 . . . . . **CCCLXXXI**
—— *Reallexikon der indogermanischen Altertumskunde*,
2nd ed., Berlin, 1917–28 . . . . . . **CCCLXXXII**
SCHUCHARDT (C.), *Alt-Europa*, Strasburg and Berlin,
1919 . . . . **CCCLXXXIII**
SMITH (Reginald A.), *Guide to Early Iron Age
Antiquities* (British Museum), 2nd ed., London, 1925 **CCCLXXXIV**
SMITH (William Robertson), *Kinship and Marriage in
Early Arabia*, Cambridge, 1885 [New ed., London,
1903] . . . . **CCCLXXXV**
—— *Lectures on the Religion of the Semites*, Edinburgh,
1889 [3rd ed., London, 1927] . . . . **CCCLXXXVa**
TAYLOR (Isaac), [*The Origin of the Aryans*, London,
1890] *L'Origine des Aryens*, Paris, 1895 . . **CCCLXXXVI**
THIERRY (Amédée), *Histoire des Gaulois*, 10th ed.,
Paris, 1877 . . . . **CCCLXXXVII**
TOUTAIN (J.), *Les Cultes païens dans l'Empire romain*,
3 vols., Paris, 1907–20 . . . . . **CCCLXXXVIII**
VERWORN (M.), *Keltische Kunst*, Berlin, 1919 . . **CCCLXXXIX**
VINOGRADOFF (Sir Paul), *Historical Jurisprudence*,
Oxford, 1920 . . . . **CCCXC**

VIII. GERMANY

BEHRENS (G.), *Bronzezeit Süddeutschlands* (*Katalog d.
röm.-germ. Central-Museums*, 6), Mainz, 1916 . **CCCXCI**
GÖTZE, HÖFER, and ZSCHIESCHE, *Die vor- und früh-
geschichtliche Altertümer Thuringens*, Würzburg,
1909 . . . . **CCCXCII**
GROSS (V.), *La Tène. Un oppidum helvète*, Paris, 1886 **CCCXCIII**
GRUPP (G.), *Kultur der alten Kelten und Germanen*,
Munich, 1905 . . . . **CCCXCIV**
KOSSINNA (G.), *Die deutsche Vorgeschichte* (Mannus-
Bibliothek, 9), 2nd ed., Berlin, 1925 . . . **CCCXCV**
—— *Ursprung und Verbreitung der Germanen in vor-
und frühgeschichtlicher Zeit* (Mannus-Bibliothek, 6),
Leipzig, 1926 . . . . **CCCXCVI**
KRAUSE (W.), *Die keltische Urbevölkerung Deutschlands*,
Leipzig, 1906 . . . . **CCCXCVII**
KROPP (P.), *La-Tènezeitliche Funde an der keltisch-
germanischen Völkergrenze zwischen Saale und
Weisser Elster* (Mannus-Bibliothek, 5), Würzburg,
1911 . . . . **CCCXCVIII**
LINDENSCHMIT (L.), *Die Altertümer unserer heidnischen
Vorzeit*, Mainz, 1858–1911 . . . . . **CCCXCIX**
MONTELIUS (O.), *Chronologie der ältesten Bronzezeit in
Nord-Deutschland und Skandinavien*, Brunswick,
1900 . . . . **CCCC**
Nationalmuseet : Bogspændefund fra de Seneste, Copen-
hagen, 1925 . . . . **CCCCI**
NAUE (J.), *Die Bronzezeit in Oberbayern*, Munich, 1894 **CCCCII**
—— *Die Hügelgräber zwischen Ammer- und Staffelsee*,
Stuttgart, 1887 . . . . . . **CCCCIII**
NORDEN (E.), *Die germanische Urgeschichte in Tacitus
Germania*, Berlin, 1922 . . . . . **CCCCIV**

NORDEN (A.), *Kivike graven och andra fornminnen i Kivikstrakten*, Stockholm, 1926 CCCCV

REINECKE (P.), *Zur Kenntniss der La Tène Denkmäler der Zone nordwärts der Alpen*, in *Festschrift des röm.-germ. Central-museums zu Mainz*, Mainz, 1902 CCCCVI

SCHAEFFER (F. A.), *Les Tertres funéraires préhistoriques dans la forêt de Haguenau*, 2 vols., Hagenau, 1926–30 CCCCVII

SCHUMACHER (N.), *Materialen zur Besiedelungs-Geschichte Deutschlands (Katalog des röm.-germ. Centralmuseums*, 5), Mainz, 1918 . . . CCCCVIII

—— *Siedelungs- und Kulturgeschichte der Rheinlande. i. Die vorrömische Zeit*, Mainz, 1922 . . CCCCIX

—— *Verzeichniss der Abgüsse und wichtigere Photographien mit Gallier Darstellungen*, Mainz, 1911 . CCCCX

WAGNER (E.), *Hügelgräber und Urnenfriedhöfe in Baden*, Carlsruhe, 1895 CCCCXI

IX. BRITISH ISLES

ABERCROMBY (Hon. John), *A Study of the Bronze Age Pottery of Great Britain and Ireland and its Associated Grave-Goods*, Oxford, 1912 . . . CCCCXII

ANDERSON (Alan Orr), *Early Sources of Scottish History*, A.D. 500 *to* 1286, 2 vols., Edinburgh, 1922 . . CCCCXIII

ANDERSON (Joseph), *Scotland in Pagan Times*, 2 vols., Edinburgh, 1886 CCCCXIV

ARMSTRONG (L. A.), *Archæological Notes from Ireland*, 1909–1910 CCCCXV

BRUTON, *The Caratacus Stone on Exmoor* . . CCCCXVI

BULLEID (Arthur) and GRAY (H. St. G.), *The Glastonbury Lake Village*, 2 vols., Taunton, 1911–17 . CCCCXVII

COFFEY (George), *The Bronze Age in Ireland*, Dublin, 1913 CCCCXVIII

COLLINGE, *Roman York*, Oxford, 1927 . . . CCCCXIX

COLLINGWOOD (R.), *Roman Britain*, London, 1923 . CCCCXX

CONRADY (Alexander), *Geschichte der Clanverfassung in dem schottischen Hochlande*, Leipzig, 1898 . . CCCCXXI

O'CURRY (Eugene), *On the Manners and Customs of the Ancient Irish*, 3 vols., London, 1873 . . CCCCXXII

CZARNOWSKI (S.), *Saint Patrick et le culte des héros en Irlande*, Paris, 1919 CCCCXXIII

EVANS (John), *Ancient Stone Implements*, London, 1897 CCCCXXIV

—— *Ancient Bronze Implements*, London, 1898 . . CCCCXXV

FARAL (Edmond), *La Légende arthurienne*, 3 vols., Paris, 1929 CCCCXXVI

FURNEAUX and ANDERSON, ed., TACITUS, *Agricola*, Oxford, 1923 CCCCXXVII

GOUGAUD (L.), *Les Chrétientés celtiques*, Paris, 1911 [*Christianity in Celtic Lands*, London, 1932] . CCCCXXVIII

GREENWELL (William), *British Barrows*, Oxford, 1877 . CCCCXXIX

GUEST (Edwin), *Origines Celticæ*, London, 1883 . CCCCXXX

HAVERFIELD (Francis J.), *The Roman Occupation of Britain*, revised by Sir George MACDONALD, Oxford, 1924 CCCCXXXI

HENDERSON (George), *Survivals in Belief among the Celts*, Glasgow, 1911   CCCCXXXII

HOLMES (T. Rice), *Ancient Britain and the Invasions of Julius Cæsar*, Oxford, 1907   CCCCXXXIII

JOYCE (P. W.), *A Social History of Ancient Ireland*, 2 vols., London, 1903   CCCCXXXIV

KEATING (Geoffrey), *The History of Ireland*, New York, 1866 [London, 1902–14]   CCCCXXXV

KEITH (Sir Arthur), *The Antiquity of Man*, London, 1915 [new ed., 1925]   CCCCXXXVI

LETHABY, *Roman London*, London, 1924 .   CCCCXXXVII

LLOYD (John E.), *A History of Wales*, London, 1911 .   CCCCXXXVIII

MACALISTER (Robert A. S.), *Ireland in Pre-Celtic Times*, Dublin and London, 1921 . . .   CCCCXXXIX

MACDONALD (Sir George), " The Agricolan Occupation of North Britain " in **LXXIX**, ix (1919) . .   CCCCXL

MACNEILL (Eoin), *Phases of Irish History*, Dublin, 1919   CCCCXLI

MILLER (S. N.), *The Roman Fort at Balmuildy on the Antonine Wall*, Glasgow, 1922 . . .   CCCCXLII

WHITE (Newport J. D.), *St. Patrick, his Writings and Life*, London, 1920   CCCCXLIII

MONTGOMERY (William E.), *The History of Land Tenure In Ireland*, Cambridge, 1889 . . .   CCCCXLIV

O'DONOVAN, *The Tribes and Customs of Hy Many*, Dublin, 1843   CCCCXLV

PARKYN (E. A.), *An Introduction to the Study of Pre-historic Art*, London, 1915   CCCCXLVI

PEAKE (Harold), *The Bronze Age and the Celtic World*, London, 1922   CCCCXLVII

POKORNY (J.), *The Origin of Druidism (Ann. Report of Smithsonian Institute*, 1911) . . .   CCCCXLVIII

RHYS (Sir John), *Lectures on Welsh Philology*, 2nd ed., London, 1879   CCCCXLIX

—— *Celtic Folk-Lore*, 2 vols., Oxford, 1901 . .   CCCCL

—— *Early Britain, Celtic Britain*, 3rd ed., London, 1904   CCCCLI

—— and JONES (David Brynnor), *The Welsh People*, 4th ed., London, 1906   CCCCLII

LEROUX (H.), *L'Armée romaine de Bretagne*, Paris, 1911   CCCCLIII

SAGOT (François), *La Bretagne romaine*, Paris, 1911 .   CCCCLIV

SKENE (William F.), *Celtic Scotland*, 3 vols., Edinburgh, 1876–80   CCCCLV

—— *Chronicles of the Picts, Chronicles of the Scots, etc.*, Edinburgh, 1867   CCCCLVI

—— *The Highlanders of Scotland*, 2 vols., Edinburgh, 1836 [new ed., 1902]   CCCCLVII

SPENSER (Edmund), *View of the State of Ireland*, Dublin, 1713   CCCCLVIII

SQUIRE (Charles), *The Mythology of the British Islands*, London, 1905 [new ed., 1910] . . .   CCCCLIX

TAYLOR (M. V.), *The Roman Villa at North Leigh*, Oxford, 1923   CCCCLX

THOMPSON (A. Hamilton), *Military Architecture in England during the Middle Ages*, Oxford, 1913 .   CCCCLXI

X.　GAUL

BEAUPRÉ (J.), *Les Études préhistoriques en Lorraine de 1889 à 1902*, Nancy, 1902　　.　　.　　.　　.　　**CCCCLXII**

BÉNARD LEPONTOIS, *Le Finistère préhistorique*, Paris, 1929　.　.　.　.　.　.　.　.　**CCCCLXIII**

BLANCHET (A.), *Les Enceintes romaines de la Gaule*, Paris, 1907　.　.　.　.　.　.　**CCCCLXIV**
—— *Les Souterrains-refuges de la France*, Paris, 1927　**CCCCLXV**

BLEICHER (G.) and BEAUPRÉ (J.), *Guide pour les recherches archéologiques . . . dans l'Est de la France*, Nancy, 1896　.　.　.　.　**CCCCLXVI**

BLOCH (G.), *La Gaule romaine* (E. LAVISSE, *Histoire de France*, vol. i, 2), Paris, 1901　.　.　.　**CCCCLXVII**

BONSTETTEN (G. de), *Baron, Notice sur des armes et chariots de guerre découverts à Tiefenau, près de Berne, en 1851*, Lausanne, 1852　.　.　.　**CCCCLXVIII**

BULLIOT (J. G.), *Mémoire sur l'émaillerie gauloise à l'oppidum du Mont-Beuvray*, Paris, 1872　.　.　**CCCCLXIX**

CHATELLIER (P. du), *Les Époques préhistorique et gauloise dans le Finistère*, Rennes and Quimper, 2nd ed., 1907　.　.　.　.　.　.　.　.　**CCCCLXX**
—— *La Poterie aux époques préhistorique et gauloise en Armorique*, Paris, 1897　.　.　.　.　**CCCCLXXI**

DÉCHELETTE (J.), *Les Fouilles du Mont-Beuvray de 1897 a 1901*, Paris, 1904　.　.　.　.　**CCCCLXXII**
—— *Les Vases céramiques ornés de la Gaule romaine*, 2 vols., Paris, 1904　.　.　.　.　.　**CCCCLXXIII**

DESJARDINS (E.), *Géographie historique et administrative de la Gaule romaine*, 4 vols., Paris, 1876–93　.　.　**CCCCLXXIV**

FUSTEL DE COULANGES (Numa D.), *La Gaule romaine*, Paris, 1891　.　.　.　.　.　.　.　**CCCCLXXV**

GERIN-RICARD (H. de), *Le Sanctuaire pré-romain de Roquepertune*, Marseilles, 1928　.　.　.　**CCCCLXXVI**

GOURY (G.), *Les Étapes de l'Humanité*, 2 vols., Nancy, 1911　.　.　.　.　.　.　.　.　**CCCCLXXVII**

GRENIER (A.), *Les Gaulois*, Paris, 1924　.　.　**CCCCLXXVIII**

ISCHER (T.), *Die Pfahlbauten des Bielersees*, Biel, 1928　**CCCCLXXIX**

LOTH (J.), *L'Émigration bretonne en Armorique du Ve au VIIe siècle*, Paris, 1883　.　.　.　**CCCCLXXX**

LOT (F.), *Mélanges d'histoire bretonne*, Paris, 1907　.　**CCCCLXXXI**

MARTEAUX and LEROUX, *Les Fins d'Annecy*, Annecy, 1913　.　.　.　.　.　.　.　.　**CCCCLXXXII**

MOREAU (F.), *Collection Caranda aux époques préhistorique, gauloise, romaine, et franque*, St. Quentin, 1877, 1881, 1887　.　.　.　.　.　**CCCCLXXXIII**

MOREL (L.), *La Champagne souterraine*, Rheims, 1898　**CCCCLXXXIV**

NICAISE (A.), *L'Époque gauloise dans le Département de la Marne*, Paris, 1866　.　.　.　.　**CCCCLXXXV**

PEYNAU (B.), *Découvertes archéologiques dans le Pays de Buch*, Bordeaux, 1926　.　.　.　.　**CCCCLXXXVI**

PHILIPPE (Abbé), *Cinq ans de fouilles au Fort-Harrouard*, Rouen, 1927　.　.　.　.　.　**CCCCLXXXVII**

POTHIER (General), *Les Tombes du Plateau de Ger*, Paris, 1900　.　.　.　.　.　.　.　.　**CCCCLXXXVIII**

VESLY (L. de), *Les Fana*, Rouen, 1910 . . . CCCCLXXXIX

VIOLLIER (D.), *Essai sur les fibules de l'âge du fer trouvées en Suisse. Essai de typologie et de chronologie*, Zurich, 1907 CCCCXC

—— *Le Cimetière gallo-helvète d'Andelfingen*, Zurich, 1912 CCCCXCI

—— *Essai sur les rites funéraires en Suisse des origines à la conquête romaine* (*Bibl. de l'Éc. des H.-Études*, sciences relig., vol. xxiv, 1), Paris, 1911 . . CCCCXCII

—— *Les Civilisations primitives de la Suisse. Sépultures du IIe âge du fer sur le plateau suisse*, Geneva, 1916 CCCCXCIII

VOUGA (P.), *La Tène*, Leipzig, 1923 CCCCXCIV

XI. SPAIN AND PORTUGAL

ÅBERG (N.), *La Civilisation énéolithique dans la péninsule ibérique*, Upsala, 1921 CCCCXCV

BONSOR (G.), *Les Colonies agricoles préromaines dans la vallée du Bétis*, Paris, 1899 CCCCXCVI

—— and THOUVENOT, *Nécropole ibérique de Setefilla*, Paris and Bordeaux, 1929 CCCCXCVII

BOSCH-GIMPERA (P.), *La Arqueologia pre-romana hispanica*, Barcelona, 1920 CCCCXCVIII

—— *Los Celtas y la civilización celtica en la peninsula iberica*, Madrid, 1923 CCCCXCIX

—— *Els Celtes y la cultura de la primera edat del ferro a Catalunya*, Barcelona, 1924 . . . . D

—— *La Ceramica iberica*, Madrid, 1915 . . . DI

—— *Ensayo de una reconstruccion de la etnologia prehistorica de la peninsula iberica*, Santander, 1923 DII

—— *El problema etnologico vasco y la arqueologia*, St. Sebastian, 1923 . . . . DIII

—— *La Prehistoria de los Iberos y la etnologia vasca*, Santander, 1926 . . . . DIV

—— *Prehistoria catalana*, Barcelona, 1919 . . DV

BOUDARD (P. A.), *Essai sur la numismatique ibérienne*, Paris, 1859 . . . . DVI

CARTAILHAC (E.), *Les Âges préhistoriques de l'Espagne et du Portugal*, Paris, 1886 . . . . DVII

CERRALBO (Marquis de), *El Alto Jalon*, Madrid, 1909 . DVIII

DÉCHELETTE (J.), *Essai sur la chronologie préhistorique de la péninsule ibérique*, Paris, 1909 . . . DIX

Fontes Hispaniæ antiquæ. Avieni Ora Maritima, ed. A. SCHULTEN and P. BOSCH, Barcelona and Berlin, 1922 . . . . DX

LANTIER (R.), *El Santuario iberico de Castellar de Santisteban*, Madrid, 1917 . . . . DXI

LEITE DE VASCONCELLOS (J.), *Religiões da Lusitania*, 4 vols., Lisbon, 1904, etc. . . . . DXII

MENDEZ-CORREA (A. A.), *Os Povos primitivos da Lusitania*, Oporto, 1924 . . . . . DXIII

PARIS (P.), *Essai sur l'art et l'industrie de l'Espagne primitive*, 2 vols., Paris, 1902–04 . . . DXIV

PERICOT (L.), *La Prehistoria de la peninsula iberica*,
Barcelona, 1923 . . . . . . DXV
PHILIPON (E.), *Les Ibères*, Paris, 1909 . . . DXVI
SCHULTEN (A.), *Hispania*, Barcelona, 1920 . . DXVII
—— *Numantia : eine topographisch-historische Unter-
suchung* (*Abhandl. d. Göttinger Ges. d. Wiss.*, 1905) DXVIII
—— *Numantia*. i. *Die Keltiberer und ihre Kriege mit
Rom*, Munich, 1914 . . . . . DXIX
—— *Tartessos*, Hamburg, 1922 . . . . . DXX
SIRET (H.) and (L.), *Les Premiers Âges du Métal dans le
sud-est de l'Espagne*, Antwerp, 1887 . . . DXXI
SIRET (L.), *Questions de chronologie et d'ethnographie
ibérique*, Paris, 1913 . . . . . DXXII
—— *Villaricos y Herrerias*, Madrid, 1908 . . . DXXIII
VEGA (Estacio da), *Antiguedades monumentaes do
Algarve*, 4 vols., Lisbon, 1886–91 . . . DXXIV

XII. ITALY

BRIZIO (E.), *Il Sepolcreto gallico di Montefortino*, Rome,
1901 . . . . DXXV
CASTELFRANCO (P.), *Cimeli del museo Ponti nell' Isola
Virginia* (*Lago di Varese*), Milan, 1913 . . DXXVI
DUHN (F. von), *Italische Gräberkunde*, Heidelberg, 1924 DXXVII
DUCATI (P.), *Storia di Bologna*. i. *I Tempi antichi*,
Bologna, 1928 . . . . DXXVIII
GRENIER (A.), *Bologne villanovienne et étrusque*, Paris,
1912 . . . . DXXIX
ISSEL (A.), *Liguria preistorica*, Genoa, 1908 . . DXXX
MAGNI (A.), *Le Necropoli ligure-gallice di Pianezzo nel
canton Ticino*, Milan, 1907 . . . . DXXXI
MARCHESETTI (C.), *La Necropoli di S. Lucia presso
Tolmino*, Trieste, 1886 . . . . . DXXXII
MILANI, *Studi e materiali di archeologia e numismatica*. DXXXIII
MONTELIUS (O.), *La Civilisation primitive en Italie
depuis l'introduction des métaux*. i. *Italie sep-
tentrionale*, Stockholm, 1904 . . . . DXXXIV
—— —— ii. *Italie centrale*, 1910 . . . DXXXV
MODESTOW (B.), *Introduction à l'histoire romaine*, Paris,
1907 . . . . DXXXVI
NISSEN (H.), *Italische Landeskunde*, Berlin, 1902 . DXXXVII
PAULY (C.), *Altitalische Forschungen*, 3 vols., Leipzig,
1885–91 . . . . DXXXVIII
PEET (T. E.), *The Stone and Bronze Ages in Italy and
Sicily*, Oxford, 1909 . . . . . DXXXIX
SERGI (G.), *Arii e Italici*, Turin, 1898 . . . DXL
ULRICH, *Graberfeld Bellinzona* . . . . DXLI

XIII. DANUBIAN CELTS

BERTRAND (A.) and REINACH (S.), *Les Celtes dans
les vallées du Pô et du Danube*, Paris, 1894 . . DXLII
FORRER (R.), *Keltische Numismatik der Rhein- und
Donaulande*, Strasburg, 1908 . . . . DXLIII

JOUGUET (P.), *L'Impérialisme macédonien et l'hellénisation de l'Orient*, Paris, 1926, [*Macédonian Imperialism*, in this series, London and New York, 1928] . . . . DXLIV

MEHLIS, *Raetia* . . . . DXLV

ODOBESCO (A.), *Le Trésor de Petrossa*, Paris, 1889 . DXLVI

PARVAN (Vasile), *Dacia*, Cambridge, 1928 . . . DXLVII

—— *Getica*, Bukarest, 1926 . . . . . DXLVIII

PIČ, *Le Hradischt de Stradonitz en Bohême*, Leipzig, 1906 . . . . DXLIX

RADIMSKY (W.), *Nekropola na Jezerinama u Pritoci cid Bisca*, repr. from *Glasnik Zemaljskog museja u Bosni i Hercegovini*, Sarajevo, v, 1893 . . DL

REINACH (T.), *Mithridate Eupator, roi de Pont*, Paris, 1890 . . . . DLI

RICHLY (H.), *Bronzezeit in Böhmen*, Vienna, 1891 . DLII

RIDGEWAY (Sir William), *Early Age of Greece*, Cambridge, 1901 . . . . . . DLIII

STAEHELIN (P.), *Geschichte der kleinasiatischen Galater*, Leipzig, 1907 . . . . DLIV

STOCKY (A.), *La Bohême à l'âge de la pierre*, Prague, 1924 DLV

INDEX

4322